SO-BBD-423

PR
6019
.09
Z935
1991
cop.1

$34.95

R00809 61838

Watt, Stephen.

Joyce, O'Casey, and
the Irish popular
theater.

4-27-92   DATE

CHICAGO PUBLIC LIBRARY
BEVERLY BRANCH
1962 W. 95th STREET
CHICAGO, IL   60643

© THE BAKER & TAYLOR CO.

Joyce, O'Casey, and the Irish Popular Theater

 RICHARD FALLIS, Series Editor

BEVERLY BRANCH
2121 W. 95th STREET
CHICAGO, ILLINOIS 60643

Joyce, O'Casey,
and the Irish Popular Theater

STEPHEN WATT

SYRACUSE UNIVERSITY PRESS

CHICAGO PUBLIC LIBRARY
BEVERLY BRANCH
1962 W. 95th STREET
CHICAGO, IL   60643

PR
6019
.O9
Z935
1991
cop.1

Copyright © 1991 by SYRACUSE UNIVERSITY PRESS
Syracuse, New York 13244-5160

All Rights Reserved

First Edition 1991
91 92 93 94 95 96 97 98 99   6 5 4 3 2 1

The paper used in this publication meets the minimum requirements of American National Standard for Information Sciences–Permanence of Paper for Printed Library Materials, ANSI Z39.48-1984. ∞™

Library of Congress Cataloging-in-Publication Data

Watt, Stephen.
    Joyce, O'Casey, and the Irish popular theater / by Stephen Watt. – 1st ed.
        p. cm. – (Irish studies)
    Includes bibliographical references and index.
    ISBN 0-8156-2527-8 (alk. paper)
    1. Joyce, James, 1882–1941–Knowledge–Performing arts.
2. O'Casey, Sean, 1880–1964–Knowledge–Performing arts. 3. Dublin (Ireland)–Popular culture–History–19th century. 4. English literature–Irish authors–History and criticism. 5. Theater–Ireland–Dublin–History–19th century. 6. Dublin (Ireland) in literature. 7. Performing arts in literature. 8. Theater in literature. I. Title. II. Series: Irish studies (Syracuse, N.Y.)
PR6019.O9Z35   1991
823'.912–dc20   90-24489
                                                           CIP

Manufactured in the United States of America

R0080961838

R07133 00319

For CAITLIN

CHICAGO PUBLIC LIBRARY
BEVERLY BRANCH
1962 W. 95th STREET
CHICAGO, IL   60643

STEPHEN WATT is an Associate Professor of English and Victorian Studies at Indiana University. He is coeditor (with Judith L. Fisher) of *When They Weren't Doing Shakespeare: Essays on Nineteenth-Century British and American Theatre* (1989) and author of numerous articles on Irish Studies and modern drama that have appeared in such journals as *PMLA, Mosaic, Comparative Drama, Éire-Ireland, Critical Texts, Perspectives on Contemporary Literature,* and the *Journal of Irish Literature.*

CONTENTS

ILLUSTRATIONS

x   *Illustrations*

PREFACE

IT IS CONVENTIONAL in prefaces to summarize the motivations that prompted the writing of a book and to explain one's intentions or aims, the big or not so big ideas that reside behind the project. I shall not neglect these responsibilities. My original motive, one common enough in the writing of most academic books, was to learn something. In this case, the something involved cultural forms and their reception: namely, late nineteenth-century English and Irish drama, Dublin audiences' reactions to this drama, and, more specifically, the effect of the theater and other cultural forms on James Joyce and Sean O'Casey. Albeit often alluded to in literary and other studies, this entire cultural moment as far as the theater is concerned has seemed to most scholars unworthy of any concerted attention. Yet, although pre–Abbey Theatre Irish and popular drama has been discountenanced by many, numerous studies of James Joyce and Sean O'Casey strongly imply its importance. Some years ago C. Desmond Greaves, for example, when describing the Dublin of O'Casey's boyhood, said: "Working-class Dublin was as addicted to the theatre as London to the music hall . . . [and besides the Mechanics Theatre] the other theatres were to varying degrees popular as well."[1] I wanted to understand more about the nature of this addiction – to what cultural products Dubliners were addicted and why – and, accepting Greaves's ascription of popular elements to all the theaters of late nineteenth-century Dublin, I needed therefore to consider those theaters that attracted bourgeois audiences as well. Several years ago I undertook to learn what I could, and what follows serves as my report of what I discovered.

I have always intuited a close relationship between Joyce and O'Casey, even though they never met, their backgrounds (educational and religious, for instance) were quite different, and their literary production extremely dissimilar. Once again, Irish scholars have articulated more substantial analogies between the two than my intuition could produce, even if as these same interpreters illuminate one matter, they frequently introduce another of a more contestable nature. John Wilson Foster, for example, explains that perhaps the strongest similarity between Joyce and O'Casey exists in the relatively powerless characters they often create: "Most of Joyce's people cannot pick and choose among the forces that influence them, as could the Anglo-Irish writers, though they feel the enormous weight of them. . . . How much more difficult it is for Joyce's lower and declining middle classes and O'Casey's working class—almost bereft of intellectual heritage—to know and be themselves."[2] As David Cairns and Shaun Richards put it, Joyce's "sympathies," like O'Casey's, were with "'the starving rabblement' on whom 'Caesar' and 'Christ' waxed fat."[3] Foster's emphasis on the intense subjugation of Irish men and women in turn-of-the-century Dublin by various ideological apparatuses is well-placed and taken up in this book, among other places; so too is Foster's implication of the role this subordination plays in constructing the subject. His notion that the working class is "almost bereft of intellectual heritage" is another matter entirely, and assessing the theater's contribution to this heritage, intellectual or otherwise, is also part of my project.

Needless to say, I have been aided in this work by a great number of people to whom I am truly grateful. It is difficult and finally rather silly to order this group in any hierarchical way, but I must reserve my special thanks to James Hurt, Cheryl Herr, and Séamus de Búrca, all of whom have been exceedingly generous of their time and, in Cheryl and Séamus's cases, of materials relating to this study. Cynthia Maude-Gembler of the Syracuse University Press deserves special recognition as well, not just as a terrific editor but as a compassionate and understanding listener at a moment in the history of the academy when compassion and understanding are in desperately short supply. I wish also to thank Bernard Benstock and Richard Fallis for their careful reading of my manuscript and several of my colleagues at Indiana University for performing the same labor: Matei Calinescu, Lewis Miller, and Tim Wiles. Mary Burgan, Patrick Brantlinger, Donald R. Dickson, Kathryn Flannery, Katherine Burkman, Arthur L. Simpson, and Robert Stillman have also encouraged me throughout this and other projects, an encouragement that has meant a great deal to me. I should also acknowledge the assistance of Paula Krebs and Mary Ellen Boyle in the preparation of the typescript, and to Shakir Mustafu for assisting with the index.

A number of librarians and archivists have also assisted me in the location and reproduction of illustrations, the use of which has been made possible in part by the financial support of the Indiana University office of Research and Graduate Development and Dean Roger Farr. Mary Clark of the Irish Theatre Archive has been, over the years, a source of continuing support; it is impossible to enumerate here her many kindnesses to me. Thanks also are due to Richard Mangan of the Raymond Mander–Joe Mitchenson Theatre Collection in Kent, Lori Lewis of the Folger Shakespeare Library, and Paul Camp of the University of South Florida Library for his assistance with the Dion Boucicault Collection housed there. I also thank the several librarians at the National Library of Ireland, the British Library's Manuscript Division, and the British Library's Newspaper Collection at Colindale for their help.

Finally, I wish to acknowledge the support and patience of my parents, Bob and Ginny; my brother and sister, Rob and Sally; and my wife, Nona, who spent many long hours reading Dublin newspapers and other sources with me to compile the Appendix for this book. She has been a cheerful collaborator for a long time now in various projects, the most important being our daughter Caitlin Grace, to whom I dedicate this book.

Bloomington, Indiana
September 1990

STEPHEN WATT

NOTES ON THE TEXT

PART OF CHAPTER 2 was published as "Boucicault and Whitbread: The Dublin Stage at the Turn of the Century," *Éire-Ireland* 18 (Fall 1983): 23–53.

Page references for works cited frequently appear within the text, and their abbreviations appear in the list below. In the case of James Joyce's *Ulysses,* quotations are followed by episode and line numbers.

Autobiographies	Sean O'Casey. *Autobiographies 1 and 2.* London: Pan Books, 1980.
CP	Sean O'Casey. *The Complete Plays of Sean O'Casey.* 5 vols. London: Macmillan, 1984.
CPP	Bernard Shaw. *Collected Plays with Their Prefaces.* 7 vols. Edited by Dan H. Laurence. New York: Dodd Mead, 1971.
CW	James Joyce. *The Critical Writings of James Joyce.* Edited by Ellsworth Mason and Richard Ellmann. New York: Viking, 1959.
D	James Joyce. *Dubliners.* Edited by Robert Scholes. New York: Viking, 1967.
DB	*The Dolmen Boucicault.* Edited by David Krause. Dublin: Dufour Editions, 1963.
FW	James Joyce. *Finnegans Wake.* New York: Viking, 1939.
JJ	Richard Ellmann. *James Joyce.* New and rev. ed. Oxford: Oxford Univ. Press, 1982.
Letters	Sean O'Casey. *The Letters of Sean O'Casey, 1910–1941,* vol. 1. Edited by David Krause. New York: Macmillan, 1975.
MBK	Stanislaus Joyce. *My Brother's Keeper: James Joyce's Early Years.* Edited by Richard Ellmann. New York: Viking, 1958.

P   James Joyce. *A Portrait of the Artist as a Young Man: Text, Criticism, and Notes.* Edited by Chester G. Anderson. New York: Viking, 1968.

SH   James Joyce. *Stephen Hero.* Edited by John J. Slocum and Herbert Cahoon. New York: New Directions, 1944.

Theatres   Bernard Shaw. *Our Theatres in the Nineties.* 3 vols. London: Constable, 1932.

U   James Joyce. *Ulysses: The Corrected Text.* Edited by Hans Walter Gabler with Wolfhard Steppe and Claus Melchior. New York: Vintage Books, 1986.

UP   William Butler Yeats. *Uncollected Prose.* 2 vols. Edited by John P. Frayne and Colton Johnson. New York: Columbia Univ. Press, 1970–76.

Joyce, O'Casey, and the Irish Popular Theater

A Popular Theater
Forgotten and Remembered

> So ignoble has the drama of the nineteenth century been
> considered that only now is it emerging from that arid
> wasteland of indifference and contempt to which opinion
> has consigned it, but its steps are slow and painful.
>
> — MICHAEL BOOTH

FORGOTTEN PLAYWRIGHTS and their forgettable plays, mythical lands of
blarney and blather – turn-of-the-century popular theater in London and
Dublin is often so characterized. As Michael Booth suggests, however, interest in Victorian drama and theater is on the rise, a phenomenon fueled
in part by the increasing prominence within the academy of cultural studies;
and academic presses in particular have responded by publishing a number
of distinguished theater histories, critical anthologies, and new editions of
primary texts. Cambridge University Press's series British and American
Playwrights, 1750–1920, to mention just one example, has rekindled enthusiasm for such seldom-read playwrights as Tom Taylor and H. J. Byron
by making available new editions of their most representative plays. One
of the Victorian stage's greatest actresses, Ellen Terry, has received much-
deserved critical attention of late with the publication of new biographies;[1]
and Richard Foulkes's volume *Shakespeare and the Victorian Stage* (1986) re-
assesses celebrated adaptations of Shakespeare and Victorians' appropriation

1

of Shakespeare to reaffirm their privileged position within the dominant culture. Still, most undergraduate courses in nineteenth-century English literature and all but the most specialized postgraduate seminars in theater history remain unaffected by this development. The steps of scholarly recovery to which Booth alludes, therefore, may not be quite so painful today, but they remain slow indeed.

The reclamation of nineteenth-century Irish drama is even more difficult, in part because of the widespread acceptance of harsh verdicts such as Hugh Hunt's when he says, "J. W. Whitbread, Fred Cooke, John Baldwin Buckstone and others, whose names and plays are best forgotten, presented a mythical land of blarney and blather. . . . Dion Boucicault alone among the hack writers of Irish melodrama can claim a place, if not as a major dramatist, at least as a highly competent one."[2] One need only review chronicles of the Irish theater from Andrew E. Malone's *Irish Drama* (1927) through the work of Peter Kavanagh, Christopher Fitz-simon, and D. E. S. Maxwell to confirm this diagnosis.[3] Nor are popular Irish playwrights and their English counterparts contained in any distinctly literary, as opposed to theatrical, memory. Some exceptions exist, of course. The *Dictionary of Irish Literature* (1979), edited by Robert Hogan, who over the years has contributed substantially to our knowledge of Irish theater, contains an exemplary essay on Dion Boucicault and informative, albeit much shorter, passages on John O'Keeffe (1747–1833) and Séamus de Búrca.[4] These entries, though, constitute the extent of commentary on dramatic authorship before the rise of Bernard Shaw and Oscar Wilde. Similarly, whereas in their *Biographical Dictionary of Irish Writers* (1985) Anne M. Brady and Brian Cleeve include thoughtful introductions to such nineteenth-century novelists as William Carleton, Gerald Griffin, Charles Lever, Samuel Lover, and Charles Kickham, the only Irish dramatists of the century mentioned, excluding Shaw and Wilde, are O'Keeffe (sometimes spelled O'Keefe) and Boucicault. And these entries amount to little more than asides. Happily, however, there exists some reason for optimism about the future of Irish theater studies. In the 1980s two editions of Boucicault (by Peter Thomson and Andrew Parkin) and de Búrca's history of the Queen's Royal Theatre in Dublin were published; and published earlier this year was Cheryl Herr's *For the Land They Loved: Irish Political Melodramas, 1890–1925,* an anthology of four Irish political melodramas (two by J. W. Whitbread, two by P. J. Bourke) based on the historical events of 1798. In a recent essay in *Éire-Ireland,* James Hurt has outlined several ways in which the "canon" of Irish drama might be reconstrued, so one might expect more such labors of historical recovery to follow in the 1990s.[5]

Adopting a view of nineteenth-century drama similar to Hunt's, most artistic directors of major theaters have retrieved few plays from the "arid wasteland of indifference and contempt" to which most such antiques have been banished. Again, exceptions exist, as theater companies in both the United Kingdom and the United States continue to revive Henrik Ibsen, early Shaw, and Wilde, thereby garnering the reputation of "legitimacy" productions of Shakespeare afforded Victorian actor-managers. Occasionally, the Abbey Theatre reprises one of Boucicault's most famous Irish plays— *The Colleen Bawn* (1860), *Arrah-na-Pogue* (1865), and *The Shaughraun* (1874) — and in 1977 staged O'Keeffe's comedy *Wild Oats* (1798). The Royal Shakespeare Company's revivals of Boucicault's *London Assurance* (1841) in 1970 and O'Keeffe's *Wild Oats* in 1976, and the long-running National Theatre production in 1988 of *The Shaughraun*, serve as conspicuous exceptions to the rule of exclusion generally applied to nineteenth-century drama. Once in a great while, an adventuresome company like the Actors Theatre of Louisville redresses this situation by producing French Romantic and Victorian dramas, as it did during the 1987 and 1988 seasons. Still, theatergoers today seldom gain access to the dramatic worlds of Boucicault, W. G. Wills, Sir Arthur Wing Pinero, and others whose plays enjoyed tremendous popularity not only in the rapidly growing number of theaters in nineteenth-century London, New York, and Dublin, but on stages in the inaugural decades of this century as well.[6] Rarer still is entrance into the smaller orbit of such light operas as Michael Balfe's *The Bohemian Girl* (1843) and Edward Fitzball's *Maritana* (1845), both much enjoyed in turn-of-the-century Dublin, or the more distinctly Irish constellation of melodramas of the 1880s and 1890s by J. W. Whitbread, Hubert O'Grady, Fred Jarman, Walter Howard, Chalmers Mackey, and others. Peter Kavanagh generously recommends that it is "interesting to remember" O'Grady and *The Famine* (1886), his most celebrated play, and other similarly successful Irish playwrights.[7] But few scholars have.

The phrase "popular theaters" of James Joyce and Sean O'Casey, on one level, seems fairly straightforward; on another, the level of theoretical discourse on the "popular," such a term is richly fraught with ambiguity. At base, "popular theaters" denotes commercially successful drama of the late Victorian and early modern periods, the theatrical conventions by which it was actualized on stage, and the audiences' tastes it satisfied. The dramatic

fare of Dublin's three principal theaters at the turn of the century–the Theatre Royal, Gaiety Theatre, and Queen's Royal Theatre–is of especial interest here. Because the theatrical calendars of the Theatre Royal and Gaiety
were dominated by plays, musicals, and operas that originated in London,
however, it is impossible to describe the Dublin stage of Joyce's and O'Casey's
adolescent years without considering such transplanted entertainments as
well.[8] Also, Ireland's status as a cultural satellite of London and colonial
property gains added relevance; that is, the manner in which popular drama
is implicated in colonialist discourse and its potential for serving as an
ideological apparatus of the colonizer must also be considered. Still another
connotation of "popular theaters" concerns Joyce's and O'Casey's playgoing
experiences, the effects of these experiences, and the degree of determination the popular exerted on both writers' representations of life in Ireland.
By the later 1890s, Joyce and O'Casey, growing into manhood, were becoming experienced playgoers in Dublin; at the same time, Bernard Shaw had
become London's most irreverent drama critic and William Butler Yeats,
Lady Augusta Gregory, and their confederates in founding the Irish Literary Theatre were articulating, in some cases debating about, the principles
of a "literary" national drama. This book is about the plays and actors Joyce,
many of his characters, and O'Casey saw; it concerns the impressions these
plays and players registered on them. Moreover, my readings of texts and
interrogations of various theories of popular culture rest on one assumption: that by forgetting these theaters we neglect a powerful contributor to
discourses on sexuality and nationalism that partially accomplish what Louis
Althusser terms the "interpellation" of subjects in early modern Dublin.[9]
I hope in what follows both to continue in the project of historical recovery
initiated by de Búrca and Herr and to shape knowledge of the late Victorian
popular theater into an interpretive instrument to illuminate Joyce's and
O'Casey's often conflicted stances toward popular culture, demonstrating
how their deployment of the popular marks their self-location at a critical
distance from the ideological commitments these same cultural forms promoted *and* from Yeats's (and others') returns to the "Celtic hearthstone."

In the contemporary critical climate of "new historicism" and cultural
studies, such a thesis hardly seems surprising, nor does the project of re-
vising long-standing binaristic understandings of the relationship between
popular culture and the more elevated "high" or literary culture to which
it is typically subordinated: to wit, literary/commercial, artistic/popular,
high/low, with the imputation that the right-hand or second term performs

a parasitic or destabilizing function against its more elevated counterpart.[10] In such views, popular texts are discountenanced as inartistic commodities, their consumers denigrated as working class and unsophisticated, semiliterate at best. Regarded as the vulgar opposite of "high" theatrical art, popular drama resembles other cheaply made products that, once manufactured and marketed, can be quickly redesigned and resold. The Irish melodramas of Whitbread, O'Grady, John Baldwin Buckstone, and Edmund Falconer—in Hunt's estimation—are typical of such commodities and thus related to the detractions of the popular adumbrated by Leo Lowenthal: "standardization, stereotype, conservatism, mendacity, manipulated consumer goods." In this view, if "genuine" drama of literary pretension is concerned with the pursuit of truth, popular drama promises both escape and excitement; totally "estranged from values," it offers nothing but "entertainment and distraction."[11] Because of their putative invitations to escapism, their repetitive and inartistic constructions, and their largely emotional trajectories, popular plays are thus, for many scholars, eminently forgettable.

Most historians of Irish theater, however unwittingly, accept these judgments and as a result direct little attention to Irish drama before the founding of the Irish Literary Theatre in 1897 or its inaugural program at the Antient Concert Rooms two years later. This bias against the popular theater of late nineteenth-century Dublin, in particular, typically manifests itself in a fashion less strident than Hugh Hunt's. Rather, it emerges in the misleading absences in numerous theater historians' accounts of the evolution of the Irish stage. In *The Irish Theatre* (1983), a handsomely designed coffee-table history whose few deficiencies should perhaps not be censured too severely, Christopher Fitz-simon replicates a familiar pattern by devoting only ten pages to Irish drama and theater between 1827 and 1890, organizing his synopsis under the heading "The Stage Irishman." In so doing, he merely retraces an already distorted miniature of Irish drama and popular culture before the Irish Literary Renaissance and the plays of Yeats, Lady Gregory, and John Millington Synge. For Fitz-simon, as for so many other commentators on Irish drama, all Irish plays from the time of Richard Brinsley Sheridan to the rise of Shaw center around the exploits of two predictable character types. "Irishmen on the stage prior to the foundation of the Irish Literary Theatre of 1898 tend to fall into one or other of two categories—one, the lazy, crafty, and (in all probability) inebriated buffoon who nonetheless has the gift of good humour and a nimble way with words . . . ; the other the braggart (also partial to a 'dhrop of the besht') who is likely to be a soldier or ex-soldier, boasting of having seen a great deal of the world when he has probably been no further from his own country than some English barracks or camp."[12]

Putting aside for the moment the racial prejudice such repetition of stereotypes furthers (and ultimately justifies), surely common sense militates against the notion that a century of English and Irish playgoers could be satisfied, night in and night out, with endless successions of conniving Irish servants and drunken braggarts modeled after Shakespeare's Falstaff. More crucial, two typical critical elisions underlie Fitz-simon's observation: first, the failure to historicize adequately potential differences between London and Dublin audiences in the way stereotypes were received at various moments throughout the nineteenth century, thus conflating various responses to the same character into an unconvincing unity (Irishmen on one homogeneous "stage," *not* on "stage*s*" at different times and places); second, a common enough tendency to regard stereotyping (and here Fitz-simon *is* describing stereotyping) as fixed and therefore unresponsive to the changing needs of the colonizer in whose service the Stage Irishman labors.[13] In short, critical oversimplification of pre-Abbey drama in Ireland tends not only to distort our understanding of the popular theaters of Joyce and O'Casey but also to impair our ability to read the effects of the popular theater on their most distinguished works and on the culture these works endeavor to represent.

In *A Critical History of Irish Drama, 1891–1980* (1984), D. E. S. Maxwell similarly evinces little interest in pre-Abbey Irish theater, although he significantly revises fallacious conceptions of stereotyping in Irish melodrama. Besides undertaking this correction, Maxwell also commends Boucicault's most famous Irish plays as "lively" and "well crafted," even as he remarks that they "were not the plays to germinate a theatre expressive of lives and sensibilities whose reality had been so far unregarded by the drama."[14] As accurate as this assessment is, Maxwell nevertheless fails to consider that although plays like Boucicault's clearly did not provide a model for *some* modern Irish drama,[15] their popularity persisted well into this century. Indeed, an Irish melodrama by Boucicault, Whitbread, O'Grady, Buckstone— and, in the years before and after World War I, by Ira Allen and P. J. Bourke, to name but two popular dramatists—was successfully produced *at least* once, usually numerous times in the late nineteenth century, in *every* year from 1860 (the date of *The Colleen Bawn*) through the 1920s. What accounts for this widespread success? Further, and as a result of the enduring attractiveness of Irish melodrama, the "reality" of many of the Dubliners of whom Maxwell speaks included experience of the very drama so routinely dismissed as unworthy of critical scrutiny. Any theater expressive of the "real" or of people's everyday lived experience must perforce confront this popular tradition – and so must students of more elevated literature.

For these and other reasons, the history of the condemnation of popular drama merits our reconsideration, especially at that moment in which modern dramatists who competed for audiences with popular playwrights and other entertainments enunciated their antipopulist biases. For Lowenthal's catalog of pejorative denunciations of popular culture – that it relies on formulas of "standardization" and "stereotype" and consists only of intellectually mendacious and politically conservative "consumer goods" – parallels Yeats's and Frank J. Fay's characterizations of the contemporary Irish drama, William Archer's and Shaw's criticism of the spectacular drama produced by Henry Irving at London's Lyceum Theatre, and the academy's long-standing contempt for this entire epoch of English and Irish theater. But are these charges all accurate? And even if they are, does this mean that popular dramas are any less potent in their effect on real theatergoers? In most cases, to answer this latter question, the very conventions of popular drama most modernists revile actually form the provenance of the popular theater's potential to construct representations of history and to inflect human subjectivity. This ideological and modeling power extends into the modern era and into the literature we not only remember but have institutionalized as worthy of our most careful reflection. How thoughtful can this study be, how profound can our understanding of Joyce and O'Casey be, if we ignore the very cultural forms that they and many of their most representative characters could not?

THE CASE AGAINST THE POPULAR THEATRE:
The "Popular" versus the "Real"

It is helpful, I think, to consider in turn the principal claims of the modernist indictment of the popular, exposing in the process the suppositions my study challenges and attempts to overturn. Among the several charges upon which Yeats and Shaw, among others, agreed, foremost was the unintellectual, "nonliterariness" of the popular theater and their resolve to have little to do with it. In this view Shaw and Yeats find a precedent in Shake-speare's unfortunate cultural critics Rosencrantz and Guildenstern, who report to Hamlet that on the stage there has of late been "much throwing about of / brains" (2.2.358–59). But what does it mean to be nonliterary– and can a writer have absolutely nothing to do with popular convention? If such a rupture were possible, then it would seem to follow logically that the work of Shaw and the Irish Literary Theatre playwrights would bear little relationship, indeed *no* relationship, to its predecessors on the popular stage. In this negative or iconoclastic paradigm of literary change, the new must annihilate the old before it can thrive because no point of sympathetic contact exists between the two. Fredric Jameson, in another version of this notion, discusses postmodernism as the social reality and cultural dominant of late capitalism and installs for the generation growing up in the 1960s, representative works of high modernism as the "establishment and the enemy–dead, stifling, canonical, the reified monuments one has to destroy to do anything new."[16] In his "Apology" to *Our Theatres in the Nineties,* the three-volume collection of his drama criticism for the *Saturday Review* between 1895 and 1898, Shaw similarly formulates a model of literary change based primarily on negation by portraying his reviews as a "siege" on the nineteenth-century theater. For Shaw, the most formidable "defender" of this theater, an emblem of its newly won respectability and intellectual banality, was Henry Irving, abetted by reactionary drama critics (and opponents of Ibsen) such as Clement Scott of the *Daily Telegraph.* These were the antagonists of a genuinely literary theater made possible, in many respects, by Ibsen. Shaw, the knight crusading for the causes of literature and social reform, did battle with powerful adversaries both in his criticism and in the prefaces of his plays and remained vociferously loyal to the cause of ridding the theater of popular inducements to the "throwing about of brains."

Shaw, of course, was not a knight–but after 18 July 1895 Irving was. Yet for Shaw, Sir Henry's popularity and royal endorsement could not compensate for his management of a theater devoid of "literary" value, one characteristic of which was the ascendancy of elaborate stage pictures over language. This issue resonates, often clamorously, in Shaw's assaults on Lyceum Theatre productions, as his disdain for Irving's *King Arthur* (January 1895) indicates: "But how am I to praise this deed [the "ready-made success" of the play] when my own art, the art of literature, is left shabby and ashamed amid the triumph of the arts of the painter and the actor? I sometimes wonder where Mr Irving will go when he dies—whether he will dare to claim, as a master artist, to walk where he may any day meet Shakespear[e] whom he has mutilated, Goethe whom he has travestied" (*Theatres* 1:14–15). In Shaw's review, the "art of literature" left "shabby and ashamed" means the subordination of language both to spectacle and to histrionic opportunity for the star actor: hence the triumphs of the painter and the "tragedian." Although Irving retained such accomplished artists as Sir Edward Burne-Jones to design productions, he typically entrusted the composition of original plays to lesser talents, "house playwrights" Shaw called them, including W. G. Wills or J. Comyns Carr. In the case of Irving's production of Lord Tennyson's *Becket* in 1893, "nonliterary" describes Irving's thoughtless paring down of Tennyson's enormous manuscript into an acting version, confirming for Shaw that Irving could not discern "fine literature from penny-a-liner's fustian" (*Theatres* 1:34). Such editorial "blue-penciling" by powerful actor-managers, a practice Shaw also deplored in the "improvement" of Shakespeare's plays for the stage, inevitably meant the sacrifice of refined language and aesthetic beauty. And as Shaw complained nearly twenty years after his stint with the *Saturday Review,* even if Irving *were* possessed of a more discriminating sensibility, contemporary playwrights labored within a cultural institution that provided them little opportunity for experimentation. In his "Apology" to *Great Catherine* (1913) Shaw defined the "evil tradition" of the popular which limited dramatists' creative choices: they could either invent a few "glaringly artificial high horses for the great actors" or compete unsuccessfully with Shakespeare, a bard "who was not of an age but for all time and who had, moreover, the overwhelming attraction for the actor-managers of not charging author's fees" (*CPP* 4:902).

Like Shaw, Yeats did all he could to dissociate himself from what he termed the "commercial theatre" and, also like Shaw, chief among his complaints about the popular theater was its nonliterary quality. During the formative years of the Irish Literary Theatre, which was to become the Abbey Theatre in December 1904, Yeats lectured on the state of drama in Europe, delineating the measures he, Edward Martyn, and Lady Gregory would take to raise the Irish stage from its artistic impoverishment to the comparatively superior achievements of Norway, Spain, and Germany. Yeats's enunciation of such measures was premised on a now firmly entrenched opposition between popular drama and "literary" art. He maintained in May 1899, for example, that the term "'literary' sounded ill in playgoers' ears," stating that, regardless of his own reservations about Ibsen's realistic dramas, only the Norwegian theater was "at once literary and popular" (*UP2* 163). In England and Ireland, Yeats declared in January of the same year, "and there is no difference of opinion on this matter among men of letters, vulgarity and triviality have an almost perfect possession of the theatre" (*UP2* 139). Yeats averred that "people who read books . . . have ceased to go to the theatre"–and maintained that the best of popular dramas merely reflected "the image of a passing fancy." "Common playgoers," Yeats believed, who "do not understand that we offer them plays written in a more sincere spirit than plays which are written to please as many people as possible," may only in the best case not "dislike us very much" (*UP2* 140). Yeats's criticism of both popular drama and its audience is, in several respects, replicated by Hugh Hunt: "popular" means "illiterate" blather and the conveyance of ephemera in which educated audiences can take little interest. Consequently, Adrian Frazier's provocative admonition notwithstanding that Yeats's "politics" insofar as theater is concerned are various and strategic, Yeats advocated in 1899 an elitist theater: a theater "for a few simple people who understand from sheer simplicity what we understand from scholarship and thought."[17] Frazier may be right in correcting those scholars who see only one Yeats who always means what he says–but here and elsewhere his censure of the popular theater seems clear and unequivocal. In short, I think Yeats means precisely what he says.

Yeats stipulates that drama performed in this theater of the few will be "for the most part remote, spiritual, and ideal,"[18] adjectives that recur in his essays and lectures on a literary theater and surface as well in his exchange concerning Irish national drama with John Eglinton (W. K. Magee) published in the *Daily Express* (and collected in May 1899 in the volume *Literary Ideals in Ireland*). In part, Yeats privileges the spiritual over the material, the ideal over the real, because like Shaw he despised the primacies of the visual over the verbal, the material over the spiritual, in the commercial theater. Entering into a dispute between William Archer and George Moore over the former's review in January 1899 of Martyn's *Heather Field*, Yeats echoes Shaw's denunciations of Irving's lavish productions at the Lyceum Theatre in commentary critical of the visual emphasis of popular production. "I have noticed at a rehearsal how the modern coats and the litter on the stage draw one's attention, and baffle the evocation, which needs all one's thought that it may fall before one's eyes lovers escaping through a forest, or men in armour upon a mountain side. I have noticed, too, how

elaborate costumes and scenery silence the evocation completely, and substitute the cheap effects of a dressmaker and of a meretricious painter for
an imaginative glory. . . . I want to be able to forget everything in the real
world, in watching an imaginative glory."[19] Rather differently, then, from
the motives underlying Shaw's early attempts at realistic social drama, Yeats
conceived of an "aristocratic esoteric Irish Literature" that would allow the
reader-audience to "forget the real world." "We have," he insisted in an 1897
letter to John O'Leary, "a literature for the people but nothing yet for the
few."[20] The project of a spiritual and poetic drama mounted without the
distractions created by realistic staging practices led Yeats, as is well known,
to the "New Stagecraft" of Edward Gordon Craig.

Thus, regardless of the many points of agreement between popular
drama's many detractors, realism of the Ibsenite vein created a schism between those who endorsed a modern drama of contemporary life and several of the founders of the Irish Literary Theatre who advocated a poetic
return to Ireland's Celtic past or a dramatic treatment of Irish peasant life.
For Shaw, as for Archer and the young Joyce, Ibsen's plays were the embodiment of the "literary drama." Ibsen was, as Yeats posited in a moment
of generosity, that rare playwright who collapsed the opposition between
the literary and the popular, although as is well-known Ibsen was not embraced by orthodox London theater critics between 1889–the year of the
Novelty Theatre production of *A Doll's House*–and the beginning of this
century. Ibsen's ill-treatment by these critics prompted lengthy defenses by
both Shaw and Archer, who in their skirmishes with Ibsen's detractors ex-
patiated upon the literary qualities the commercial theater lacked. Archer
deplored the "distorted simulacrum" of Ibsen that hostile reviews had created and countered that the "real" Ibsen was summed up in one phrase:
"master-poet." His abilities included a gift of "intense insight" into the "foundations of things" based on a pluralistic conception of truth, *not,* as was
commonly and mistakenly alleged, on an obsession with preaching either
a socialistic or a pessimistic gospel; a style in which characters talk "natu-
rally" and at times eloquently, though not by way of the "antitheses, word-
play, and conceits" in the comedies of manners which critics were used to
hearing; and a sense of dramatic action in which "human nature throws off
its conventional integuments and expresses itself at its highest potency," not
a morbid proclivity to expose human evil which is better left concealed.[21]
Archer, it should be added, regretted that Ibsen reached the largest audience through the mischaracterizations of his works by drama reviewers, who,

after years of exposure to popular theater, were incapable of recognizing theatrical artistry.

"Literary," then, for Shaw, Archer, and, in many respects, the young Joyce connotes several things: a commitment to a search for truth without a descent into didacticism; a sense of "real language" unadorned by hackneyed tropes or witticisms; a subordination of spectacle, histrionics, and other conventional stage gestures (false "indicated" movements, as the American acting teacher Lee Strasberg would later term them); a dramatic craftsmanship leading to the economical construction of plot, which, as Archer observes, may not consistently be subsumed under the traditional genres of tragedy or comedy. "Literary" refers to form and content, style and substance, mode of representation and thing(s) represented. Most significantly, in a mood of optimism that predates poststructuralist dismantlings of essentiality and the bourgeois or liberal-humanist subject, modern concepts of the literary depended upon an aggregation of unexamined suppositions: truth resides in *things,* not in relationships or recombinations of codes; there is a *real* language that governs and characterizes the utterances of *real* people; there exists something describable as *meaning* which literature conveys and popular cultural forms do not. Literary texts, in this sense, deal with matters of human import. Unlike his classical predecessors, though, Ibsen achieves greatness, at least in Joyce's view in his early essay "Ibsen's New Drama" (1900), by drawing moving dramas of "average lives in their uncompromising truth" (*CW* 63). The search for a truth which is by definition plural, the use of appropriate if not poetical language, the development of meaningful issues from the lives of ordinary people–these are the attributes of a literary theater that the popular turn-of-the-century theater lacked.

Yeats and George Russell (AE), to name but two, viewed the matter differently, particularly concerning the representations of contemporary "average lives" and "ordinary people." In his 1899 dialogue with Yeats in the *Daily Express* John Eglinton, anticipating an argument Joyce would later make through Stephen Dedalus in *Stephen Hero* that art confronts reality rather than effecting an escape from it, questioned Yeats's turn toward Ireland's mythological past as the basis for an emerging national drama. For Eglinton, the poet who "looks too much away from himself and his age does not feel the facts of life enough, but seeks in art an escape from them."[22] Yeats, who had earlier countered Eglinton's similar charge by adversion to Ibsen in *Peer Gynt* as an example of a modern artist transforming national legend and mythology into a fit dramatic subject, responded that a national drama need not be a "criticism of life" but a "revelation of a hidden life."[23] Intervening between Eglinton and Yeats, AE attempted a defense of Yeats in terms Eglinton might accept: "Mr. Yeats, in common with other literary men, is trying to ennoble literature by making it religious rather than secular, by using his art for the revelation of another world rather than to depict this one. John Eglinton would not, I think, dissent greatly from this as a high aim."[24]

Citing the same debates between Yeats and Eglinton, David Cairns and Shaun Richards maintain that from the 1880s to 1907 Yeats's writings were "unified" in an attempt "to enable the fusion of the Anglo-Irish with the people-nation"; after 1907, they suggest, Yeats became increasingly isolated and thus in letters such as "A People's Theatre" in 1919 to Lady Gregory expresses his intensified sense of marginality by calling for an "exclusive theatre capable of generating 'a bond among chosen spirits, a mystery almost for leisured and lettered people.'"[25] It is important to remember, on the contrary, that Yeats's aversion to popular culture of various media existed long before 1907 and the rioting at the Abbey Theatre over Synge's *Playboy of the Western World*. Moreover, not only was there a pronounced rupture between the literary and the popular, there also existed considerable disagreement about what constituted a *modern* literary drama.

Little disagreement existed among Shaw and the founders of the Irish Literary Theatre, however, that the "unliterary" popular theater resulted from the intrusion of capital, a charge implicit in Yeats's frequent use and disparagement of the term "commercial theatre." In this criticism, the lack of opportunity for literary experimentation originates in the dominance of those popular discourses founded solidly on commercially successful formulas. As Jameson points out, similar hypotheses are invoked to explain today's mass culture: the "atomized or serial 'public' wants to see the same thing over and over again, hence the urgency of generic structure and generic signal." One effect of this construction of audience and emphasis on repetition is already strikingly apparent in attitudes like Shaw's toward the popular theater: "In mass culture, repetition effectively volatizes the original object—the 'text,' the 'work of art'—so that the student of mass culture has no primary object of study."[26] All popular and mass cultural texts are thus valueless, "glaringly artificial" reproductions, degraded replicas of some text long forgotten. By contrast, "literature" is authentic or "original." Writers like Shaw believed that the repetition of popular generic forms, especially of melodrama and spectacularly produced drama of several genres, posed an almost insuperable obstacle to the advancement of modern or more literary drama. This argument is still very much with us today, emerging in discussions both of "legitimate" drama and of the contemporary film industry's relentless production of sequels of commercially successful movies. Robert Gould, the cynical film executive in David Mamet's *Speed-the-Plow* (1985), staunchly defends this practice: "Make the thing everyone made last year" and invest resources only in those projects that will "GET THE ASSES IN THE SEATS."[27] The commodification of artistic texts leads to repetition and intellectual vulgarity, both in Mamet's Hollywood and Shaw's London; as a result, "literature" has little chance of surviving.

Condemned by both Yeats and George Moore as the "theater of the many," the popular theater by their definition attempted to please as many playgoers as it could; artistry, they maintained, required freedom from such potentially coercive consensus. As Moore argues in his preface to *The Bending of the Bough,* produced by the Irish Literary Theatre in 1900, "It is impossible to write plays in England except for money, and all that is done for money is mediocre."[28] The rallying cry of the decadent movement— Wilde's well-known "Art for art's sake"—was expanded to "Art for art's sake and not money's sake" and echoed by the founders of the Irish Literary Theatre as well as by Shaw, Archer, A. B. Walkley, and later O'Casey in their advocacy of a National Theatre for England.

Further, because popular dramatists wrote to as large an audience as they could reach, their works seldom essayed investigations of moral or political truth, instead communicating, to borrow Yeats's phrase, "images of passing fancy." Interestingly enough, after learning of the Irish Literary Theatre's repertory for 1901, Joyce would accuse Yeats and Moore of succumbing too easily to the parochial, narrowly nationalistic interests of the "rabblement." "No man, said the Nolan, can be a lover of the true or the good unless he abhors the multitude; and the artist, though he may employ the crowd, is very careful to isolate himself. . . . The Irish Literary Theatre gave out that it was the champion of progress, and proclaimed war against commercialism and vulgarity. It had partly made good its word [with the production of Martyn's *Heather Field,* which Joyce admired] and was expelling the old devil, when after the first encounter it surrendered to the popular will" (*CW* 69–70). Less concerned than Moore or Shaw with the deleterious effects of capital on art—or with aesthetic "vulgarity"—Joyce nevertheless was adamant that art could never be produced if poets either acceded to the political position of the majority or were shackled by the conventional mores of the public. The "popular devil," he wrote, is "more dangerous than your vulgar devil" (*CW* 70).

Moore makes two other allegations in his "Preface" that Shaw, Yeats, and nearly all deprecators of popular turn-of-the-century drama advance. One resembles Joyce's attack on the Irish Literary Theatre: namely, that the ticket-buying mob dictates its desires to the author of the popular text, who adheres to their wishes or ideological commitments. Another is that popular culture operates successfully only insofar as it facilitates its audience's escape from the real world. Again, as Lowenthal defines this latter view, popular culture is "estranged from values and offer[s] nothing but entertainments and distraction" so as to "expedite flight from an unbearable reality." Moore would certainly have agreed with this appraisal and argued that the twin tyranny of both working-class and bourgeois playgoers made the London stage a stifling climate in which to cultivate dramatic art: "We must look to discover the depths to which an art can sink when it is written and produced at the mutual dictation of the gallery boy, who for a shilling demands oblivion of his day's work, and the stockbroker, who for 10s. 6d. demands such amusements as will enable him to safely digest his dinner." Although obviously not so globally disseminated as the electronic media of postmodern mass culture, the commercial theater in Moore's view surrounded and entrapped aspiring literary dramatists: "The same audience goes everywhere, and the same fare is consequently served everywhere at the same prices."[29] Moore's latter indictment is, in fairness, somewhat accurate because, by the last half of the nineteenth century, the exodus of middle- and upper-class patrons from the theater earlier in the century was reversing. Irving, the Bancrofts, the Kendals, and other "legitimate" stars were amassing an audience of varied social class so that the "popular" was not directed only to the proletariat, a commonly held delimitation of popular culture's appeal.[30] On the contrary, the theater against which Shaw inveighed, the theatrical world that rejected both him and Ibsen, was not the East End playhouse or South London music hall that catered to largely working-class audiences but a theater in which commoners and aristocrats, gallery boys and stockbrokers, wept silently together at the poignant conclusions of plays like W. G. Wills's *Olivia* (1881).

But what of Moore's claim that popular audiences "demand oblivion" of their day's work, by "amusement" and, implicitly, through escapism? The hypothesis gains support from Shaw, who, in his "Preface" to *Three Plays for Puritans* (1901), disparaged the popular theater as a place "people can endure only when they forget themselves" (*CPP* 2:20), an amnesia facilitated by the "jejunely insipid" tastes of audiences who "are at home in a fool's paradise of popular romance" (*CPP* 2:13). Equally important from Shaw's perspective, in a popular theater inimical to intelligence and artistry even literary or "legitimate" drama could be transformed into drivel that deflects the audience's attention from both reality and truth. This "intentional brainlessness," ironically, produced "reckless mutilations" of Shakespeare's texts by Shakespeare's most vocal defenders such as Irving and the American adapter-director Augustin Daly. As "slaughtered" by Daly, Shakespeare could act as a catalyst for escapism through the common editorial practices of "altering, transposing, omitting, improving, correcting, and transferring" lines and entire scenes—or by equipping the fairies in *A Midsummer Night's Dream* with "portable batteries and incandescent lights, which they switch on and off from time to time, like children with a new toy" (*Theatres* 1:171, 178). Why such inanity? It is, Shaw argued, the result of "conducting theatres on the principle of appealing exclusively to the instinct of self-gratification in people without power of attention, without interests, without sympathy; in short, without brains or heart" (*CPP* 2: 20). In this "fool's paradise" in which playgoers forget themselves, conventions of the "popular" theater insinuated themselves into the production of Shakespeare and other "legitimate" drama, effacing the line between popular and literary on the London stage.

More specific and seemingly more durable than literary/popular, the opposition realistic/popular is equally susceptible to deconstruction—and not merely for the reasons Eglinton proposes in parrying Yeats's advocacy of a return to Ireland's past in appropriately "national" drama. Dublin's Gaiety Theatre and Stephen Dedalus's playgoing provide one means of exposing the fragility of this polarity. Even though young Joyce, like Stephen Dedalus, was a "constant god" at the Gaiety Theatre for entertainments as diverting as "Grand Operas" like *Maritana* and pantomimes like *Turko the Terrible,* he is insistent in *Stephen Hero* about the artist's obligation *not* to create worlds of mere wish fulfillment or fantasy. When discussing Ibsen, however, Stephen intimates a paradoxical stance toward the popular that both resembles and differs drastically from the familiar censures of Yeats, Moore, and Shaw. For example, there is one means of escape from the real world in which Joyce's Stephen not only indulges but endorses: attendance at the popular theater. For young Dubliners like Stephen (and Joyce), the popular theater often furthered the project of liberation from what Althusser terms the "ideological state apparatuses" of late nineteenth-century Dublin, especially the church, school, and family.[31]

Of course, the theater itself might serve to reinforce capitalist relations of production and construct subjects compliant to such relations. But for young Joyce and many young Dubliners, the theater subverted the familism promoted so strongly by Irish ideological apparatuses and, therefore, was connected to sexual emancipation, to an escape from repression. The imagery connected to theatergoing in *Stephen Hero* underscores the popular theater's counterhegemonic function. "On his side chastity, having been found a great inconvenience, had been quietly abandoned and the youth amused himself in the company of certain of his fellow-students among whom (as the fame went) wild living was not unknown. The Rector of Belvedere had a brother who was at this time a student in the college and one night in the gallery of the Gaiety (for Stephen had become a constant 'god') another Belvedere boy . . . bore scandalous witness into Stephen's ear" (*SH* 35). In the "Circe" episode of *Ulysses* Bloom recalls an even more "scandalous" encounter on the stairs of the "old Royal," a "dark sexsmelling theatre" that "unbridles vice" (15:3321–22).

Today, we tend to forget the allure the theater once held, and seemingly no longer holds, for the young: the manner in which the theater, especially in a colonial or, in some respects, provincial culture such as that of turn-of-the-century Ireland, serves to counteract political and sexual repression. Recall, for instance, as Richard Rowan in *Exiles* tells Beatrice, that at fourteen he attended the theater to hear *Carmen* the night his father died. Or consider the boy-narrator of Joyce's "Sisters," for whom reading the theatrical advertisements in shop windows constitutes an escape to the "sunny side of the street" from an arena of darkness, death, and the religious mystification of even the "simplest acts" (*D* 12, 13). Similarly, for Stephen and his classmates playgoing furnished a glimpse at a life they were denied, a world opposed to the deathly legislation of the Father. "Wild living," the abandonment of chastity, and "scandalous witness"–the theater promised young people like Stephen both an escape from home and overproprietary clerics and admittance into a world of sensuousness. Even if the activity of theatergoing itself was only a small victory over repression, the above passage hints at the connection in Stephen's (and the young Joyce's) consciousness between drama and sexuality, between the theater and a biological "reality" various ideological apparatuses (public and private) attempted to occlude.

Is this victory accomplished through a flight into fantasy or through a deeper investigation of instinctual realities denied by various institutional discourses? And what of theatrical treatments of sexuality? Is this mindlessly "popular" or more "realistic"? Where, in sum, might such representations reside in discourse on sexuality in Joyce's Ireland? Such distinctions and answers become even more difficult after considering the calendar of plays available to Dubliners at the turn of the century. Pinero's "problem plays" *The Second Mrs. Tanqueray* (1893) and *The Notorious Mrs. Ebbsmith* (1895), to take one example, were hailed by some as both serious and realistic, as harbingers of a new age of modern drama, although Shaw at the time and O'Casey much later in *The Green Crow* (1956) had a more severe opinion of their merits.[32]

For some, the repertory at the Gaiety Theatre offered an attractive array of entertainments; for others, social problem plays catered to the "morbid taste" of a few playgoers. Such was the verdict of the *Irish Playgoer and Amusement Record* concerning John Hare's production of Pinero's *Gay Lord Quex* (1899) in March 1900. Ever a champion of melodrama, the *Irish Playgoer* concluded that because the "popular parts of the house were thinly populated," the presence of royalty and other Dublin socialites suggested that "only the 'eminently respectable' portion of our community . . . really appreciates the unsavoury on the stage."[33] This view, associating as it does sexual perversity with cultural position or advantage, was indirectly alluded to later by Synge in a 1904 letter to Stephen McKenna concerning the representation of "modern matters" on the Irish stage. Here Synge refutes the mythology that Irishmen are too "blessedly unripe" for modern plays and recounts the appearances in Dublin of Madame Réjane, Mrs. Patrick Campbell, and Olga Nethersole in social dramas largely concerned with sex and sexuality. Synge, nevertheless, argues against a "mordid sex-obseded" drama in Ireland, not because of the subject but because it is "bad drama and played out." He similarly disparages an "unmodern" and "Cuchulainoid" National Theatre, endorsing drama that grows out of "the fundamental realities of life which are neither modern or unmodern" and "rarely fantastic or spring-dayish."[34] For Synge, drama must deal with "the entire reality of life," hence a National Theatre must rid itself of the "disease" of "squeamishness" about the representation of certain subjects. Yet another issue resides here—can one escape into "reality" as well as into "fantasy"? If certain realities are denied one, is his or her escape from such confinement a flight from reality? Can drama be more real than the everyday reality some people live? The *Irish Playgoer* implies that the "popular" Dublin audience has little interest in matters of "the unsavoury," a hypothesis resuscitated to explain the riots at the Abbey after Synge's supposed imputation of Irish women in *The Playboy of the Western World*. This manifestation of the "island of the saints" ideology, one finally as spurious as insistence upon the oppositions literary/popular and realistic/popular, rests on the notion that most people are not interested in mundane or sensual realities. Surely some of Moore's stockbrokers and gallery boys were.

Following Yeats and Shaw, Joyce, through Stephen's theories of the art of the dramatist, maintains that real drama does not induce escapism. This art, as Stephen admired in Ibsen's work and outlined to his mother in *Stephen Hero*, emerges directly from life; it does not avoid life by providing some alternative to the "real" world. Like Moore's weary gallery boys, Mrs. Dedalus, a pious Catholic suffering through her son's loss of religious fervor, the financial ruination of her family, and a daughter's fatal illness, uses drama to effect a vacation from reality. She explains, "Sometimes I feel that I want to leave this actual life and enter another—for a time." Stephen quickly and irreverently corrects his mother's misconception: "Art is not an escape from life. It's just the very opposite. Art, on the contrary, is the very central expression of life. An artist is not a fellow who dangles a mechanical heaven before the public. The priest does that" (*SH* 86). Stephen's characteristic attack on Catholicism aside, Joyce's insistence on dramatic art's grounding in this world, not in some contrived heaven, resembles the charges levied against the popular drama Joyce was certainly seeing at the Gaiety.

But does popular drama, by definition, offer its audience a "vacation" from "actual life"? Students of popular culture such as Bernard Sharratt doubt that most viewers of popular drama share Mrs. Dedalus's desire for escape from the world. Concerned largely with melodrama and its production of ideology, Sharratt challenges Michael Booth's thesis that melodrama transports its audiences to an alternative "dream" world totally superior to their own. If this were the only or even primary effect of melodrama and if this world *were* ideal, Sharratt asks, why is "actual or vicarious fear" such an "essential element" of melodrama (and of the entertainments at so many other popular cultural sites—the circus, speedway, cinema)? That is, on one hand melodrama creates a dream world of black-and-white morality, minimal psychological complexity, and—most often—poetic justice after a series of struggles for the heroine and her friends or family. On the other hand, as Sharratt underscores by reference to Booth's own depiction of this putatively superior world, a domain of "'shootings, stranglings, hangings, poisonings, drownings . . . tortured heroines, persecuted heroes and fearsome villains' seems a distinctly odd one to choose to *escape into*."[35] Do gallery boys and factory workers, even those exasperated with their living conditions, always desire to take up residence in such a hazardous place? Sharratt posits the equal likelihood that numerous popular cultural forms, including drama, perform a conservative function by foregrounding an often harrowing world that, albeit exciting, serves the dominant class's interest of inducing the working class's satisfaction with the real world, as unexciting but secure as it is. And subtending all of these hypotheses—Shaw's, Booth's, and Sharratt's rival explanations—are the unexamined assumptions that working-class and bourgeois audiences, dissatisfied with their lived realities, are either eager to escape them or desirous of theatrical worlds sanitized of any vestige of the real.

The notion that popular culture trades in escapist fantasies also rests on two complementary, equally problematic hypotheses: one, as the preceding discussion implies, that the real/popular structure is concrete, thereby hypostatizing the real and the popular as essential, distinct entities and making impossible any rapprochement with their opposites; two, that the reception of popular cultural texts is universal and invariable. Emerging inevitably from most modernists' admiration of Ibsen, the realism/popular art binarism often accompanies—or is offered as a refinement of—the polarization of literature and popular culture.

Recalling the distasteful precedent of Victorian "improvements" of Shakespeare, the literary/popular polarity is extremely difficult to sustain based on the evidence of theater history. For in both London and the provinces Shakespeare was fashioned into a playwright to meet the needs of a diverse audience. In provincial towns like late Victorian Leicester, productions of Shakespeare consistently drew working-class audiences to the theater, although in some instances this phenomenon is attributable to the manipulations of the "higher" social orders. Through reading clubs, as Jeremy Crump has shown, Shakespeare was proffered as an "improving entertainment," a salutary alternative to the "drinking-dominated culture of large parts of the working class." As a result, when Shakespeare's plays were revived in Leicester, audiences "included many who were familiar with his works from various institutional contexts which led to a more serious engagement with them." One alternative mode of reception consisted of the codes of behavior, hence level of involvement, at the popular theater: hissing the "villain," applauding florid oratory, and "reading" a seriocomic moment like the grave-digger scene in *Hamlet* as if it were a burlesque.[36] Shakespeare, then, was *not* so "self-evidently legitimate theatre" because it could be apprehended as literature or as burlesque or melodrama. Lawrence Levine describes an analogous situation in nineteenth-century America: "Shakespeare *was* popular entertainment in nineteenth-century America," Levine insists, but by the early twentieth century Shakespeare (and Italian opera, another popular art form in nineteenth-century America) had become sacralized as "*Culture.*"[37] This background makes Ayamonn Breydon's project of bringing Shakespeare to his fellow workers in O'Casey's *Red Roses for Me* (1942) especially ironic: "They [Breydon's fellow workers] think he's beyond them, while all the time he's part of the kingdom of heaven in the nature of everyman. Before I'm done, I'll have him drinking in th' pubs with them!" (*CP* 3:131). Rather than viewing such a project as a radical intervention on Breydon's part, it might be regarded as restoring a cultural order that modernism displaced.

If the literary/popular opposition is both theoretically and practically impossible to maintain because each pole, no longer safely autonomous, is parasitically eroded by the other, the opposition is no more untenable than the realistic/popular binarism. To be sure, the worlds of science fiction and fantasy, like the magical worlds of *The Tempest* or Victorian pantomime, bear little resemblance to our real world or to Dublin at the turn of the century. And doubtless the alternative worlds of some popular genres *do* offer their ticket-buying "inhabitants" both escapism and wish fulfillment. The "sensation scenes" of Boucicault's plays, to take one example, provided audiences with spectacle to be wondered at, just as melodrama's fast-moving plots promised excitement and, finally, gratification as they closed on a strong note of poetic justice. Both the deconstruction of such structural allegories and common reading experience, however, refute claims that the popular lacks elements of reality or that realism is devoid of popular appeal. On the contrary, as I hope to show in the chapters that follow, the realities of the lives of O'Casey's and Joyce's Dubliners are to a great extent determined, not merely influenced, by popular drama. This includes the lives of Joyce and O'Casey themselves, both as writers and as consumers. And as many critics have pointed out, the Dubliners of Joyce's *Ulysses* may not have produced much, but they were conspicuous consumers of a wide variety of cultural goods.

In addition to the historical rationale outlined above, the theoretical reasons for deconstructing the realism/popular drama polarity include not only the allegorizing potential of binaristic logic but also the need for attentiveness to the ways in which what Nelson Goodman describes as "worldmaking" occurs. For Goodman, the "real world" is merely "one of the alternative right versions (or groups of them bound together by some principle of reducibility or translatability)" of the world; all other versions of that same world differ from the "standard version" in "accountable ways." As Goodman explains, for the phenomenologist the perceptual world is fundamental, while for the physicist the real world may be entirely different. For the "man-in-the-street, most versions [of the real world] from science, art and perception depart in some ways from the familiar serviceable world he has jerry-built from fragments of scientific and artistic tradition and from his own struggle for survival. This world, indeed, is the one most often taken as real."[38] This "version" or construction we deem real—this "jerry-built" world and the fragments that contribute to it—are my chief interests here. And Yeats's and Shaw's denunciations of the popular drama notwithstanding, insofar as this drama constitutes one of these fragments of the real, it is indeed worthy of our scrutiny.

As Crump's example of Shakespeare's popularity with working-class audiences verifies, a dramatic text can be received as something more or less real or valuable than it might initially appear: if certain audiences can transform Shakespeare into melodrama, other audiences can regard a popular drama as revelatory of some great truth or conflict, one of the qualities Joyce valued in Ibsen's plays. The most romantic play might be perceived as realistic, bearing meaningful relationship to that jerry-built world Goodman outlines, or as "literary," a text with some claim to truth. This was the case in Victorian London; it is the case today, as films by directors such as Alfred Hitchcock and John Ford are no longer regarded as mere thrillers or westerns but as artistic texts with complex cinematic languages to be explicated. Similarly, the theater Hugh Hunt declared "best forgotten" was, for such theatergoers such as Joseph Holloway, very much worth remembering. Addressing the Irish Literary Society on 26 March 1900, Holloway, ever the champion of the Queen's Royal Theatre (commonly abbreviated as the Queen's), professed to give a "pittite's" perspective of modern Irish drama that countered the censures of his more educated contemporaries. Of course, literary sophistication is not necessarily required to adopt a critical view of the Queen's, as the narrator in the "Cyclops" chapter of *Ulysses* proves by comparing the inebriate excesses of Barney Kiernan's pub favorably with the Queen's repertory: "Gob, the devil wouldn't stop him [the citizen] till he got hold of the bloody tin anyhow [to throw at Bloom] and out with him and little Alf hanging on to his elbow and he shouting like a stuck pig, as good as any bloody play in the Queen's royal theatre" (12:1843–46). Taking a different position, Holloway advised that "literature must take a back seat to the dramatic effectiveness of the work performed" and admonished "high and mighty" scholars who tend to overlook this: "The non-playgoing high-and-mighty literary critics . . . pretend to know all about what stage work ought to be, and despise all *real* playgoers like myself, for not agreeing in their estimate" (emphasis added). For Holloway, Boucicault's plays were "perfect works of dramatic art in their way" with the theatrical "spirit" and "go" for which the Queen's was famous.

The plays of the Queen's manager J. W. Whitbread, often cited as a poor imitator of Boucicault, were, for Holloway, much more—they broke new ground toward the establishment of a modern Irish drama. This enthusiasm enlivens Holloway's review of Whitbread's *Wolfe Tone* (1898): it marked "a step in the right direction" in attempting to "create a new type of true Irish play without too much of the 'arrah-begorra' element in it." Holloway called on other playwrights to follow this lead: "Why not have educated Irishmen and women, *as in everyday life,* as Mr. Whitbread has endeavored in this play to make them do? We have had enough and plenty of Irish caricatures on the stage . . . let us have a little of the genuine article now by way of change."[39] In sum, though Yeats and Frank Fay during his tenure as a reviewer for the *United Irishman* between 1899 and 1902 cast Queen's melodrama in the role of the nonliterary "other" of literature, some real playgoers regarded these same plays as a significant departure from the old, a move "in the right direction" toward a modern, decidedly realistic, Irish drama.[40] In a sense, then, such judgments concerning a play's "literary" or mimetic value are radically contingent upon factors such as textual production and audience reception for which binaristic categorization cannot account.

The popular theater serves to register the differing ways audiences construct meanings and the manner in which reception is inscribed within class distinctions in Joyce's "A Mother." As R. B. Kershner accurately describes it, the concert in the story, promoted by a "leading bourgeois 'cultural' group," is a "massively over-determined cultural event" meant "to be both 'entertainment' and 'art.'"[41] In addition to the bourgeois presumptions of the concert's organizers, other determinants of the event, or so the narrator implies, are both the nationalist movement and the "higher" forces at work in the Irish literary revival, for Kathleen Kearney is selected as an accompanist in part because of her Nationalist friends and in part because she is a "believer in the language movement" (*D* 138). As the concert ensues, the narrator seems initially to praise Mr. Duggan, the working-class opera singer who had appeared in *Maritana* at the Queen's. Nevertheless, his singing "with great feeling and volume," qualities "warmly welcomed" by the gallery, parallels the excesses of the same qualities in Queen's productions typically denounced by critics; and the image and explanation of the singer's "wiping his nose in his gloved hand once or twice out of thoughtlessness" replicate snide characterizations of the Queen's and its repertory (*D* 142). It is, I think, at this point when the narrator most thoroughly assimilates the voice of the story's unhappy title character, a topic both Kershner and David Hayman broach: Mrs. Kearney's "ivory manners" make her attentive to such details, so the narrator cannot let Mr. Duggan's affront to etiquette pass unnoticed.[42] Yet, however much her own predisposition motivates this censure, the reference to Fitzball's opera and the Queen's Theatre accords with prevailing "literary" opinion. Importantly, in the strained atmosphere backstage during Mrs. Kearney's confrontation with Holohan over Kathleen's contract, Miss Healy asks another *artiste*, "Have you seen Mrs Pat Campbell this week?" (*D* 146). He has not, but has heard that she was "very fine."

For *most* playgoers, Mrs. Campbell and the theaters in which she played occupied a cultural niche much higher than that of the Queen's and its performers, hence this verdict is hardly surprising. But how reliable are such judgments in Joyce's story? How closely tied are they to class issues and cultural hierarchy—or to the colonial context in the case of Madam Glynn, the worn British singer retained to sing "Killarney" to the marked disapproval of "the cheaper parts of the hall" (*D* 147)? Are we to assume, as Kershner perhaps too readily does, that her performance is totally "incompetent"—or, alternatively, that the dense layering of popular theaters and the social levels of their respective audiences in the story introduce uncertainty into seemingly "objective" realities? Does the indictment of the "cheaper seats" merely confirm the elitist rationale of the planning committee in obtaining Madam Glynn in the first place: namely, that amateurish Queen's performers are good enough for the gallery, but only more sophisticated London talent will appeal to the dress circle? And even though the narrator echoes the popular disapproval of Madam Glynn's "old-fashioned mannerisms" and "high wailing notes," should we conclude that all ranks of the audience were similarly disapproving of the singer's antique conceptions of "elegance"? In sum, the story's ambiguous narration and the narrator's specificity about the social backgrounds of performer and audience frustrate our ability to render clear verdicts about such matters. The only performances in "A Mother" that meet with universal applause are those of the Irish tenor and contralto and, predictably enough, the "stirring patriotic recitation" with which the first half of the program concluded.

Perhaps the most compelling demonstration of a popular Victorian play's reception as literature with significant claims to truth, hence a demonstration of a reader's extrapolation of value from what is ostensibly an unpromising source, occurs in *Ulysses* in Leopold Bloom's vivid recollection of his father's affection for Augustin Daly's *Leah the Forsaken* (1862), an adaptation of S. H. Mosenthal's *Deborah*. Most theater reviewers attributed the play's success—its more than three-hundred-night run at the Adelphi and, along with an earlier Italian version starring Madame Ristori, its spawning of a host of imitators—to the role of Leah that provided an emotional tour de force for the many actresses who assumed the part.[43] Henry Morley, for instance, condemned Daly's adaptation as overturning all the original play's dramatic "proportions," grumbling that "very much credit is due to Miss Bateman for succeeding even in a single act." Barton Baker pronounced the work "gloomy and monotonous," its production redeemed only by Bateman's "powerful and original rendering" of the part. Although critics such as Clement Scott lavished considerable praise on Daly, most of the plaudits went to Bateman's performance.[44]

Daly continued throughout the century to forge "modern" adaptations of German drama—some forty-two of these, according to Marvin Felheim—but in Shaw's opinion these could hardly be termed works of modern "literature," as he clarifies in a review entitled "Mr Daly Fossilizes": "What is to be done with Mr Daly? How shall we open his mind to the fact that he stands on the brink of the twentieth century in London and not with Mr. Vincent Crummles at Portsmouth in the early Dickens days?" (*Theatres* 1:163). But those old days were alive for Bloom's father—and for Bloom as well in June of 1904. Hence, recalling Hamlet's metaphor, even if *Leah* were "caviary to the general" audience, Bloom's father "receiv'd" it as an "excellent play," a meaningful drama much more than a convenient vehicle for an aspiring young actress.

For the late Rudolf Virag it was not only the attraction of Kate Bateman in the title role in the Adelphi production he saw in 1865 (actually

1863); rather, much like Holloway's reading of incipient realism in popular Irish melodrama, the elder Bloom saw only profound truth in *Leah*. His son recalls this response as he passes by a handbill advertising Mrs. Millicent Bandmann-Palmer's performance of the part that night:

> Poor papa! How he used to talk of Kate Bateman in that. Outside the Adelphi in London waited all the afternoon to get in. Year before I was born that was: sixtyfive. And Ristori in Vienna. . . . The scene he was always talking about where the old blind Abraham recognises the voice and puts his fingers on his face.
>
> Nathan's voice! His son's voice! I hear the voice of Nathan who left his father to die of grief and misery in my arms, who left the house of his father and left the God of his father.
>
> Every word is so deep, Leopold. (5:197–206)

Maybe not for Shaw or for many modern audiences, but for the late Virag every word of Daly's play was "deep," steeped in truth and reality. Perhaps flamboyant acting *can* produce a "thin beam of light" from melodrama, a "significance" that for Tom Stoppard's arrogant Player in *Rosencrantz and Guildenstern Are Dead* (1966) "melodrama . . . does not in fact contain," but for Bloom's father such was not the case with *Leah*.[45] And though perhaps not modern, Daly's play formed one small part of the Viconian circle of history in Joyce's Dublin in June 1904.

Several issues of significance in *Ulysses* surface in this passage: the relationship of fathers and sons, the son's abandonment of his religion and subsequent estrangement from his family, the motif of the wandering Jew, and so on. But at this preliminary point, it is sufficient to recognize in Bloom's memory the very effects of the popular which Yeats and the proponents of a literary theater deny. Far from communicating the "image of passing fancy," Daly's play provokes both intellectual and emotional responses from Joyce's Blooms. Because *Leah* has probably been forgotten by most of us, a summary here might prove helpful. The narrative centers around the wanderings of a band of homeless Hungarian Jews (including the blind and elderly Abraham, a young mother, and her nursing infant) led by the self-sacrificing heroine, Leah. Fleeing persecution in Hungary, they rest near an Austrian village whose citizens are disinclined to receive them; as the act 1 curtain drops, an angry mob, poised to stone Leah or drown her, is stopped by a local cleric, who appeals to their sense of charity and raises the cross in Leah's protection. As her name and the play's subtitle ("The Forsaken") imply, Leah meets and is forsaken by a young Christian lover, Rudolf, who is misled by his interfering father and the villainous Nathan, a Jew who has renounced his religion and assumed a new identity, into doubting Leah's affections for him. As a result, Rudolf rejects Leah, marries a Christian girl whom his father has promoted all along, and with her has a daughter, whom he names Leah. Enraged at this betrayal, the elder Leah in a sensational moment of high emotion curses Rudolf and leads her followers away from his village. Years later, Leah is again destitute and near the outskirts of her former lover's town. Inherently virtuous, and like all melodramatic heroines maintaining this virtue even in the most desperate situations,[46] Leah saves Rudolf's child from tragedy and returns her to him, magnanimously blessing his family as the final curtain descends.

As important as the play's effect on Rudolf Virag, Daly's popular play exerted a measurable effect on (LEAHpold?) Bloom as well—and, quite obviously, on Joyce himself. The day on which most of the action of *Ulysses* takes place, 16 June 1904, is more than forty years after the premiere of *Leah* in Boston in 1862. Still, *Leah* remained prominent in the repertory of actresses such as Mrs. Bandmann-Palmer, who appeared at the Gaiety Theatre the week of 13–18 June in *Mary, Queen of Scots, East Lynne, Hamlet, Leah,* and *Jane Shore*. Bloom himself, a fact often overlooked, had seen both the play and actress before: "*Leah* tonight. Mrs Bandmann Palmer. Like to see her again in that" (5:194–95). And, of course, *Leah* meant something to Joyce, as Bloom's detailed précis of the plot intimates. As Richard Ellmann recounts, in 1917 Joyce supplemented his reading of 1904 Dublin newspapers by spending "a whole afternoon" quizzing Claud Sykes, an actor he met in Zurich who had formerly acted in Bandmann-Palmer's company, about the play and the production because he intended to "refer to the play, as well as to Mrs. Bandman [*sic*] Palmer's other roles, in *Ulysses*" (*JJ* 411). With the exception of Bloom's wry commentary on Bandmann-Palmer's cross-dressing to impersonate Hamlet ("Why Ophelia committed suicide" [5:196–97]), however, Joyce did not refer to other roles in her repertory. But clearly either the relatively undistinguished player or play was meaningful on some level to him. Was it the play's sympathetic representation of wandering and exile, the fact that Leah like Virag was a Hungarian Jew in search of a home, or the betrayal of a father by his son that attracted Joyce's attention? Was it the manner in which this representation counterbalanced the anti-Semitism of characters such as Deasy, who in "Nestor" tells Stephen that Jews are "wanderers on the earth to this day" because they "sinned against the light" (2:361–63). Or was it something much more theatrical: Leah faced by the angry mob at the end of act 1 or her last-minute rescue of the child? Only one thing is certain: thirteen years after Joyce left Dublin, he remembered the play and the player for his modern-day *Odyssey*. Bloom contemplated both as well and remembered well his father's impressions of Daly's melodrama.

Thus, as Yeats, Shaw, and others disparaged it, the popular theater in turn-of-the-century Dublin and London amounted to one of the most rebarbative symptoms of a Philistinism impeding the advancement of a genuinely literary culture. There exists, additionally, an almost uncanny analogy between modernists' condemnations of the late Victorian drama and present cynicism about postmodern mass culture. As Patrick Brantlinger explains, "mass culture" to its many critics today heralds the advent of a "new barbarism" of pervasive "'vulgarisation and proletarianisation' of the 'arts and sciences.'" Brantlinger examines Robert Sinai's and others' laments that "the old verbal culture is in decline and there is everywhere a general retreat from the word."[47] As the above summary of derisive views of the late Victorian theater confirms, especially Shaw's and Yeats's attacks on the ascendance of the stage picture over language and Fay's analogous complaints about Queen's melodrama, Sinai's is hardly a new complaint. And, given the present cultural moment in which nearly every artistic medium is packaged into music videos and marketed by way of T-shirts and posters, such complaints may seem justified. But at what interpretive cost are they sustained? If the social "real" contains an irreducible component of popular culture, if Joyce's Blooms and O'Casey's Dubliners possess any explanatory power in revealing aspects of this reality, how much longer can we dismiss the nineteenth-century theater as unworthy of attention?

A THEATER REMEMBERED–AND EMBRACED

As Patrick Parrinder observes, for Joyce, popular culture was "something to be collected and exhibited; his work thus functions as a library or archive which confers permanence on the material deposited in it."[48] This notion scarcely seems astonishing, as Joyce and O'Casey as well were less inclined than Yeats or Shaw to enforce distinctions between "literature" and popular culture, between a "high" canonical culture and a "lower," more widely disseminated one (although in essays such as "Ibsen's New Drama" and "The Day of the Rabblement," Joyce contemplated this polarity and criticized accession to the popular). Like Joyce, O'Casey was committed to principles of artistic freedom from commercial or institutional constraints; like his Ayamonn Breydon, O'Casey persisted throughout his career to attack conceptions of art or culture that lacked contact with the people. Similarly, Joyce's youthful critical prose amounts less to a condemnation of the popular than to an exposition of his doctrine of an unfettered artistry and an independent artist. As the inaugural sentence of Joyce's "Day of the Rabblement" implies, however, though an artist might abhor the multitude, he or she might also quite properly "employ the crowd" (*CW* 69). The public "archive" to which Parrinder refers—the "library" of popular cultural forms with circulation desks everywhere in Joyce's Dublin—is therefore much more than a dusty collection of texts and memorial associations for Joyce and O'Casey, but a potent force in the lives of their Dubliners. Any representation of these lives would be incomplete without this archive.

To employ the crowd and replicate the everyday realities of Dublin life, knowledge of popular culture would seem to be a prerequisite. And Joyce and O'Casey were intimately acquainted with the tastes of Dubliners. This familiarity does not lead, in every instance, to representations of "ordinary people" as "cultural dopes," although such butts of parodic derision as Private Carr and the Citizen in the "Circe" and "Cyclops" episodes of *Ulysses,* or Joxer Daly in *Juno and the Paycock* (1924), might qualify as such.[49] Not all of Joyce's or O'Casey's characters, though, reveal the effects or marks of culture so blatantly or so comically. As feminist readers of *Ulysses* have demonstrated, Molly Bloom, like many Dubliners, is very much a product of her society, "bound by the scripts available to women in turn-of-the-century Ireland." So, too, in Suzette Henke's estimation, is Gerty MacDowell, the lame girl Bloom ogles in "Nausicaa," who possesses a "media-controlled self image" produced by turn-of-the-century popular culture.[50] Still, Joyce does not always appropriate from popular media for the purposes of social criticism, parodically transmitted or otherwise, as Cheryl Herr reminds us: "To distinguish between low and high culture is less than accurate and especially inappropriate in studying Joyce, who did not discriminate in his works between the value of an allusion to the popular and a reference to a work of higher social status."[51] More than the value of an allusion is at stake here, however: access to the codes of those cultural discourses, popular or otherwise, which construct subjectivity and sexuality is really the issue. If allusions to popular culture in *Ulysses* and *Finnegans Wake* were traced to their origins, the trek would frequently lead to the theater, the very same theater from which Joyce, O'Casey, and many of their characters derived so much pleasure—and in which Shaw and Yeats discovered so much vulgarity.

The most compelling evidence of these writers' personal investments in popular drama and theater comes from their own accounts, from those of their relatives or friends, and—perhaps most telling—from the experiences of several of their central characters. It is important here to clarify that even though O'Casey and Joyce attended Dublin theaters in the mid- and late 1890s and thereafter, they did not necessarily see the same plays or patronize the same establishments. With the exception of their mutual admiration for Ibsen and Shakespeare, they were attracted to very different kinds of drama, and at various times they were unable to afford the price of a ticket. In particular, O'Casey's poverty well into the 1920s, unrelieved by the beneficence of a Sylvia Beach or Harriet Shaw Weaver as was Joyce's good fortune, prevented him from attending the Abbey Theatre. Reacting in 1919 to the Abbey directorate's charge that one of the main characters of his early play *The Frost in the Flower* resembled those in earlier Abbey plays, O'Casey explained that he had been to the Abbey only twice and therefore could not have modeled his characters in this way. Briefly, I shall turn to O'Casey's and Joyce's theatergoing experiences—and those of Joyce's characters. Before the founding of the Abbey Theatre they frequented Dublin's Theatre Royal, Gaiety Theatre, Queen's Royal Theatre, and in O'Casey's case the inconsistently managed Mechanics Theatre on Lower Abbey Street. It is within these experiences that the popular theater is both remembered and, most often, embraced.

O'Casey's youthful exuberance and enduring affection for Irish melodrama are well documented in his autobiographies and elsewhere. *I Knock at the Door* (1939) and *Pictures in the Hallway* (1942), the first two volumes of his autobiography, contain lengthy expressions of his affection for two playwrights: Shakespeare and Boucicault. In "Touched by the Theatre," a chapter of *Pictures in the Hallway,* he discusses how his brother Archie by 1895 or 1896 was "completely gone on the stage" and how "Johnny [O'Casey employs third-person narration, using his name Johnny Casside for himself] was not far behind" (*Autobiographies* 1:297). O'Casey, who at this time was in his teens (O'Casey was born in March 1880, two years before Joyce), recalls forming the Townshend Dramatic Society with Archie, fashioning sets from materials cast off from the Queen's Theatre, and assuming roles in Boucicault's *Shaughraun, Arrah-na-Pogue,* and *The Octoroon* (1859), a sensational melodrama about slavery in Louisiana widely viewed in the United States during the Civil War era and afterward. In addition to taking parts in these and other dramas from *Dick's Standard Plays,* O'Casey and his brother performed scenes from *Julius Caesar* and *Richard the Third.* One of the highlights of these years was O'Casey's appearance as Father Dolan in *The Shaughraun* (as a replacement for an actor fallen ill) in a benefit performance at the Mechanics Theatre for the popular impersonator of Boucicault's Stage Irishman, Charles Sullivan. Over fifty years later in *Inishfallen, Fare Thee Well* (1949), long after O'Casey's plays were first produced by the Abbey Theatre and he had taken up permanent residence in England, he reminisced nostalgically about these earlier years. "He told no-one that he had known this old stage well, that he had even played a part on it; that one of his brothers had often done so; that he had watched, from the pit below. . . . He had drunk glasses of diluted claret, sweet with sugar, with those who had played the principal parts in Boucicault's *The Shaughraun* in a pub opposite the theatre. . . . All changed now, changed utterly; and here he was now with plays of his own showing themselves off on the very same stage that he himself had trod as a growing youngster so long, so long ago" (*Autobiographies* 2:142–43). Appropriating the refrain "changed, changed utterly" from Yeats's "Easter 1916," a poem he cites several times in his autobiographies and occasionally travesties, O'Casey never forgot the theater or the plays he once loved. The backdrops of the Lakes of Killarney and peasant cottage of *The Colleen Bawn* were gone, but O'Casey's memories of Irish melodrama remained vivid—recall the prominence of patriotic melodrama in *The Drums of Father Ned* (1959)—and extremely influential.

The Queen's Royal Theatre during these years earned with great justification a reputation as the home of both melodrama and Irish drama. In producing drama on Irish subjects, the Queen's stood virtually alone in Dublin. The Theatre Royal typically offered between one and three weeks of Irish revivals a year, most often of Boucicault, and the Gaiety Theatre produced even fewer Irish plays before the Irish Literary Theatre's programs of 1900 and 1901. Under John and Michael Gunn's management, the Gaiety, which opened its doors in 1871, presented Dublin audiences with a varied repertory of light opera, English social comedy and farce, and occasional revivals of "classics" like Shakespeare or Sheridan. Besides mounting the annual Christmas pantomime that routinely ran for seven to eight weeks (well into the following February), the Gaiety's best-known attraction was German opera, with which the Gunns competed some five to seven weeks a year against Italian opera at the Theatre Royal.

By 1880, the "old" Theatre Royal that Bernard Shaw recalled so fondly had been destroyed by fire and was not rebuilt until 1897.[52] When it reopened, it continued to attract London's brightest stars in repertories of classical and modern plays or in musicals and light opera, and it renewed its commitment to Italian opera, for which the old Royal was famous. For a time during the Christmas season, the Theatre Royal pitted Italian opera against the very successful Gaiety pantomimes for holiday audiences. Throughout January 1898, for instance, the Arthur Rousbey Opera Company vied with *Aladdin* at the Gaiety, but by the following year the Royal began producing its own pantomimes in competition for the seasonal box office. At the Queen's at the turn of the century, by contrast, J. W. Whitbread competed successfully with both of his rivals, whether they countered with Shakespeare or opera, pantomime or burlesque, with a consistent series of melodramas. Such was the case both throughout the year and at Christmas, which became an occasion for the revival of older Irish melodrama and the premiere of new ones. At least one-third of the Queen's annual repertory, some fifteen to seventeen weeks a year in a production calendar abbreviated only by Holy Week or, more typically, by longer four-to-six-week Lenten closings, was filled by Irish dramas by Boucicault, Buckstone, Cooke, O'Grady, or Whitbread.

O'Casey gained his early experience of the theater, for the most part, at the Queen's and at the Mechanics Theatre, and he recalled these days with great pleasure. In the judgment of the Abbey Theatre directorate in 1920 and 1921, however, his immersion in popular Irish drama did not serve him well as a fledgling playwright. O'Casey wrote several full-length plays between 1918 and 1920—*The Harvest Festival, The Frost in the Flower, The Crimson in the Tri-colour,* and *The Seamless Coat of Cathleen*—and submitted them to the Abbey with unhappy results (his early one-act play *The Cooing of Doves* suffered a similar fate). Of these early works, only *The Harvest Festival* survives, making difficult any firm evaluation of these plays' aesthetic merits or defects. The Abbey's response to these early efforts, excepting the grounds cited above for the rejection of *The Frost in the Flower,* identifies O'Casey's accession to the conventions of popular Irish drama as their principal failing. An anonymous reader in January 1920 objected that "many" of the characters in *The Harvest Festival* were too "typical," "conventional conceptions" as "unreal as the 'Stage Irishman' of 20 years ago" (*Letters* 1:91). Yeats's critique of *The Crimson in the Tri-colour* similarly indicts O'Casey's capitulation to popular taste: "It is so constructed that in every scene there is a something for pit & stall to cheer or boo. In fact it is the old Irish idea of a good play—Queen's melodrama brought up to date would no doubt make a sensation—especially as everybody is ill mannered as possible, & all truth considered as inseperable [sic] from spite and hatred" (*Letters* 1:90). Yeats's unkind analogy might have been motivated by an antagonism toward popular theater made even more virulent by a historical dilemma he could do little to quell; during the later years of World War I, Irish drama enjoyed a marked increase in popularity in part because of the work of such Queen's favorites as P. J. Bourke and Ira Allen and in part because of the sharp decline of London plays and touring actors in Dublin.[53] Irish drama at the Queen's Theatre was thus enjoying a wide increase in popularity while O'Casey was beginning his career as a playwright. Therefore, although I agree with Robert Hogan that matters of influence where O'Casey is concerned are generally advanced with a "pleasant and genteel fuzziness,"[54] an investigation of the relationship between O'Casey and the popular theater might nonetheless prove valuable.

Rather surprisingly given the avalanche of scholarship on *Ulysses* and *Finnegans Wake* alone, Joyce's record of attendance at the theater, especially during his college years and shortly thereafter, has seldom been examined. Unlike O'Casey, Joyce devoured a wide variety of theatrical entertainments in Dublin before departing with Nora Barnacle for the Continent in October 1904. His avid reading of plays by Ibsen and Gerhart Hauptmann at this time was, unfortunately, not supplemented by theatrical productions of their works because neither writer's plays were much performed in turn-of-the-century Dublin.[55] But the conspicuous absence of Ibsen and Hauptmann from the Dublin stage hardly abated Joyce's desire for drama, both on the page and as viewed from the upper galleries of Dublin theaters. Joyce's younger brother Stanislaus recalls that during his adolescence the Joyce family made "frequent visits . . . to the cheaper parts of theatres, to see Edward Terry in his comedy parts, or [Henry] Irving or [Herbert Beerbohm] Tree if tickets could be had, or the lesser lights, Edmund Tearle as Othello or Olga Nethersole" (*MBK* 59).

As they did when touring the provincial British towns, eminent London players such as Irving, Tree, Frank Benson, Martin Harvey, and Mrs. Patrick Campbell—all of whom appeared at the Gaiety or Theatre Royal during Joyce's years at college—offered repertories in Dublin in which Shakespeare predominated. And in nearly every one- or two-week appearance, the typical stint of touring stars, revivals of Shakespearean drama were complemented by what M. Willson Disher aptly terms the "Victorian Shakespeare": plays like Bulwer-Lytton's *Lady of Lyons* (1838), alluded to in *A Portrait of the Artist as a Young Man,* and Boucicault's *Corsican Brothers* (1852), which had "acquired a prestige denied to others."[56] In the repertories of touring actresses, both those of the reputation of Stella Campbell and less celebrated players such as Lena Ashwell, Olga Nethersole, or Millicent Bandmann-Palmer, roles in Shakespeare's dramas alternated with more contemporary parts by Pinero, Henry Arthur Jones, Herman Sudermann, and others. In late 1897, according to his brother, while Joyce was "seized with an overmastering admiration for Ibsen," he was also apparently taken with Mrs. Campbell's performance in the title role of Sudermann's *Magda* (*MBK* 87). In his recollection of the event, Stanislaus emphasizes the significance of this visit to the theater, linking his brother's admiration for Ibsen with his response to *Magda.* Yet, to my knowledge, although scholars have scrutinized the Ibsen-Joyce relationship, with the exceptions of James S. Atherton's and Herr's work, lesser-known plays like Sudermann's and their considerable effect on the young Joyce have been ignored.[57]

Stanislaus Joyce, Richard Ellmann, and Joyce's boyhood friend J. F. Byrne (Cranly in *Portrait*) all confirm that young Joyce, like his counterpart Stephen Dedalus, was both a devoted playgoer and a voracious reader of plays. One should not infer from this or from Joyce's "overmastering admiration" for Ibsen, however, that all of his interests in the theater were intellectual or even very profound. On the contrary, as his youthful enthusiasm for Sudermann's plot in which Magda rebelliously breaks away from her repressive home intimates, he was attracted to dramas that in one way or another related to his own present-day dilemmas or ambitions. At times, he attended the theater for even less substantial reasons. As Byrne mentions, he and Joyce "went to as many operas as we could afford. In our very youthful days we enjoyed such popular favorites as *Trovatore, The Bohemian Girl,* [and] *The Lily of Killarney.*"[58] And his brother explains that in his rebellion young Joyce was fond of toppling established literary hierarchies, mainly by elevating popular entertainment over so-called literature. In his *The Complete Dublin Diary,* Stanislaus repeats his brother's theory that "the music-hall, not Poetry" is a "criticism of life."[59] Not surprisingly, Joyce's affinity for both drama and theater marks complicated intellectual and libidinal investments, which exert a strong determinative effect on his art, especially on *Ulysses*.

Joyce's characters share his fascination with the theater, as H. C. Earwicker's trip to see a W. G. Wills historical melodrama in *Finnegans Wake* suggests. "The truly catholic assemblage gathered together in that king's treat house [the Gaiety on King's Street] . . . to clap-plaud (the inspiration of his lifetime and the hits of their careers) Mr Wallenstein Washington Semperkelly's immergreen tourers in a command performance by special request with the courteous permission for pious purposes the homedromed and enliventh performance of the problem passion play of the millentury, running strong since creation, *A Royal Divorce*" (*FW* 32:25–33). A Dublin favorite performed often by the W. W. Kelly and other touring companies, *A Royal Divorce* places in the dramatic foreground Josephine's unstinted devotion to Napoleon even after he has divorced her to take a more politically advantageous wife.[60] In this portrayal of idealized love and wifely constancy, such plays as Wills's—and his brother Freeman Wills's and Frederick Langbridge's *The Only Way* (1899), to which Molly Bloom alludes in the "Penelope" episode of *Ulysses*—form a counterpoise to those "modern" dramas of problematic sexuality, insidious double standards, and betrayal like Pinero's and Sudermann's. In addition, Wills's play possessed an especially potent historical appeal in the late 1890s, as Irish devotion to Napoleon grew in fervor along with the increasing number of journalistic and theatrical accounts of Napoleon's sympathy for the project of the United Irishmen. In *Portrait* Joyce hints at Napoleon's resurgence of popularity in Ireland after the fall of Charles Stewart Parnell. Early in the novel, Stephen models his plain attire after Napoleon's sartorial predilection for simplicity, and he was once gratified to learn that the day Napoleon received his first Holy Communion was the happiest day of his life. *A Royal Divorce* was so well supported in Dublin at the turn of the century that it was typically revived twice annually in one-week runs, one production in the spring or summer, another in the fall or winter. In selecting it as Earwicker's "inspiration," therefore, Joyce accomplishes more than the establishment of one more link in the chain of allusions to Napoleon in the novel; he also confirms HCE's rootedness in turn-of-the-century popular culture and outlines the discourses on sexuality and nationalism to which *A Royal Divorce* contributed.

Joyce's female characters are equally familiar with the theater. Gerty MacDowell and both Milly and Molly Bloom are much taken with Martin Harvey in his several highly celebrated appearances in Dublin: Gerty has collected a postcard of Harvey, although in a mocking aside the narrator remarks that she "wasn't stagestruck like Winny Rippingham" (13:418); and Molly remembers with some irritation in "Penelope" having "had" Harvey "for breakfast dinner and supper" because of Milly's infatuation with him (18:1055). Molly complains further of being "squashed" at the Gaiety by the packed house Herbert Beerbohm Tree drew in *Trilby* (1895) and recollects the audience's response to the Kendalls in *The Wife of Scarli* (1897), even though she must have seen it seven years before (there is no evidence of its having been performed in Dublin between 1898 and June 1904).

In *Dubliners* and *Stephen Hero* the same phenomenon obtains. Stephen's mother, struggling to understand her son's reverence for Ibsen and indulging in a "brave prevarication" to disguise her maternal concern with what he is reading, tells Stephen he is "old enough now to know what is right and what is wrong." Though one might doubt the sincerity of this statement, there is less reason to question Mrs. Dedalus's statement of former enthusiasm for drama (or the implication of one substantial cost Irish women often paid as a result of marriage): "Before I married your father I used to read a great deal. I used to take an interest in all kinds of new plays" (*SH* 85). Emma Clery, the girl with whom Stephen is infatuated, shares this interest: "She was awfully fond of the theatre herself and a gypsy woman had once read her hand and told her she would be an actress" (*SH* 67). In "Eveline," Eveline and her suitor Frank enjoy a production of *The Bohemian Girl*, one song from which Maria sings, albeit imperfectly, in "Clay." Eveline's elation at sitting in "an unaccustomed part of the theatre" suggests the powerful attraction of the theater for even Dublin's most impoverished: Eveline frequented the theater enough to become accustomed to the cheaper seats, even though the "invariable squabble for money" with her increasingly brutal father "had begun to weary her unspeakably" (*D* 38). Might we conclude that, like Joyce and his friend Byrne, she went to as many theatrical entertainments as she could afford? More important, to what extent do Frank's "tales of distant countries," song of "the lass that loves a sailor," romantic biography, and "face of bronze" resemble the conventions of popular romantic texts like Balfe's? How much, to borrow Oscar Wilde's observation from "The Decay of Lying," does life resemble art in Joyce's fiction, the theatrical art both Joyce and his characters consumed?

The chronicle of theatergoing continues so strongly in *Ulysses*, particularly for Bloom, that the "Circe" episode, which represents the internal mechanisms of Bloom's consciousness, takes the form of a "psychodrama" shaped by conventions of both the music hall and the pantomime.[61] Like Joyce himself, the Blooms regard the theater seriously, as do several other characters in *Ulysses*. As a canvasser for advertisements and the husband of a local celebrity, Bloom knows a great deal about the local theater: he remembers where Pat Kinsella ran the now defunct Harp Theatre "before [J. W.] Whitbred [*sic*] ran the Queen's" and—like most Dubliners—enjoys recollections of all the "Dion Boucicault business" of popular Irish melodramas. Memories of these plays drift in and out of Bloom's consciousness, at times influencing his response to people he encounters on the street. To take a small example, as he had in "The Lotus Eaters" Bloom in "Lestrygonians" contemplates the Phoenix Park murders by the invincibles and the unfortunate history of political betrayals the incident later came to symbolize, thinking, "Never know who you're talking to. Corny Kelleher he has Harvey Duff in his eye. Like that Peter or Denis or James Carey that blew the gaff on the invincibles" (8:441–43). This reference to Duff, the cowardly informant in *The Shaughraun,* represents the power of the popular theater to insinuate itself into the playgoer's consciousness, in this case mediating between perception and the object perceived—between the real world and the fictional world of the theater. The same passage verifies the thrust of Jack Boyle's wry comment in *Juno and the Paycock* that "real" Dubliners know more about film actors than about religion; here Bloom easily recalls the name of a Boucicauldian villain but is unsure about the name of an infamous historical traitor. Real Dubliners may know more about the theater than about history.

In several episodes of *Ulysses,* Joyce implies that turn-of-the-century Dubliners' broad acquaintance with the theater was almost inevitable. The ubiquity of theatrical advertisements in "The Wandering Rocks" chapter testifies to the virtual omnipresence of the stage in Irish culture. In various locations Father John Conmee, Miss Marion Dunne, Lenehan and M'Coy, Patrick Dignam, and several British aristocrats are greeted by the sight either of Eugene Stratton, popular singer and Negro impersonator, or of Marie Kendall, "charming soubrette," smiling on a poster and raising her skirt ever so naughtily. Even this comparatively minor brush with the theater triggers characters' memorial associations and shapes the content of existential experience in *Ulysses,* thereby revealing popular culture's power to mold the inner lives of its consumers. One such consumer is HCE in *Finnegans Wake,* who names his sons, the twins Shem and Shaun, after characters in plays especially popular in turn-of-the-century Dublin: Shem after James Ralston,

the forger in Charles Young's melodrama *Jim the Penman* (1886), a nick-
name John Joyce frequently visited upon his son; and Shaun after the re-
sourceful native Irishman, Shaun the Post in *Arrah-na-Pogue*.

Joyce's and O'Casey's experiences of the popular theater, then, given
the limited opportunities afforded them in Dublin, were both considerable
and, indeed, considerably different; consequently, their appropriations from
popular plays and manipulation of theatrical conventions are rather different. Questions remain, however, as to what these tell us about both writers
and what interpretive difference this makes in reading their works. One such
question inheres in Joyce's statement in "The Day of the Rabblement" that
the crowd might be employed by the artist: how is the popular theater "employed" by Joyce and O'Casey in their representations of the lives of more
or less average Dubliners? And, in a query more skeptical of the possibility
of authorial autonomy, to what extent do the conventions of popular drama
seem to overwhelm Joyce and O'Casey, hence play a major part in determining authorial consciousness? Finally, what role does the popular theater
play in determining the Irish subject, in shaping the consciousnesses of Joyce's
and O'Casey's countrymen? This last question, in many respects, is unan-
swerable without recourse to a consideration of Dublin's colonial status at
the end of the century. In this chapter's brief concluding discussion and
in the chapters that follow, I shall turn to these matters: representation,
authorial consciousness, and the roles of colonialism and popular theater
in forming subject-positions for Dubliners to occupy.

THE POPULAR THEATERS OF JOYCE AND O'CASEY:
A Critical Remembering

The way we perceive literary texts and their relationships to popular culture is changing as interpretive criticism begins to consider more scrupu-
lously the matrices within which literature is produced. Entire genres and
cultural forms that were once relegated to the distant background of literary
study have now moved into the foreground of our perspective and, albeit
slowly, Irish studies have been reinvigorated by this pronounced shift in
critical perspective. Cheryl Herr's *Joyce's Anatomy of Culture* (1986), David
Cairns and Shaun Richards's *Writing Ireland* (1988), and R. B. Kershner's
Joyce, Bakhtin, and Popular Literature (1989) serve as provocative examples

of this rereading of Joyce and his contemporaries by situating their work within an expanded, redefined cultural context. In addition, therefore, to elucidating the ways in which the popular theater affects representation in Joyce and O'Casey—and to investigating the ways in which the theater helps shape the consciousnesses of their characters—in the chapters that follow I shall also speculate on the manner in which Joyce's and O'Casey's own consciousnesses, hence their artistic production, are also partially determined by Dublin popular culture. For as Franco Moretti explains, "If one wants to keep the couple convention-innovation and give the latter term the full historical and formal weight it deserves, it is all the more important to realize that the first term of the pair has not yet become an 'object of knowledge' in a true sense for literary criticism."[62]

In addition to this issue, Cairns and Richards have laid important groundwork for rereading Irish writing within the colonial history of its production—within the "devastating act of cultural elision" which is Ireland's history. Because of such a history, Cairns and Richards assert, one in which the colonizer speaks continually from a position of government power, "no aspect of the identity of the colonized can safely be assumed to be inherent."[63] How Irish writers and texts respond to this historical situation, whether they allow themselves to be co-opted by colonialist discourses or whether they resist the hegemony of the colonizer, is thus a matter of the utmost importance when discussing popular entertainment. Recently developed theories and strategies of recontextualization in other fields can be usefully adapted to approach such issues. Conceiving of "alternative Shakespeares," to allude to the title of John Drakakis's 1985 anthology, or embarking upon a project of what Stephen Greenblatt terms a "cultural poetics," inevitably "reorients the axis of inter-textuality, substituting for the diachronic text of an autonomous literary history the synchronic text of a cultural system."[64]

Such developments in the study of Renaissance literature form part of a larger movement in the theory and practice of cultural studies exactly opposite that of more exclusionary literary thought or formalist critical practice: namely, a "radical contextualizing of literature which eliminates the old divisions between literature and its 'back-ground,' text and context."[65] *Context* or *con-text*, as some have redacted it, is transformed from a term connoting mere periphery to a viable component of the cultural system in which literature is implicated. Popular culture undergoes a similar change. Fredric Jameson, among others, understands high and mass cultures as dialectically related; and in the following chapters I attempt to combine influence study with a more supple reading method attentive to the ways in which popular drama and performance function as an important intertext for both Joyce and O'Casey. In short, the opposition high culture/mass culture must be reconceived "in such a way that the emphasis on evaluation to which it has traditionally given rise . . . is replaced by a genuinely historical and dialectical approach to these phenomena. Such an approach demands that we regard high and mass culture as objectively related and dialectically interdependent phenomena."[66] One word of clarification: though both "twins" in this relationship must be better understood, my emphasis throughout will be on the particular dependence of the high on the low, of the indebtednesses Joyce and O'Casey owe their less distinguished antecedents and contemporaries.

Because playwrights learn their craft in the theater, even if as in Shaw's case they learn to repudiate the lessons taught there, a study of O'Casey that begins with his experience of popular theater scarcely seems surprising. I am not, of course, the first scholar to undertake such a project. By comparison, the inclusion in this discussion of Joyce, who published only one play in his career, might seem misplaced. Not so. I am inclined to agree with Henry Ward Swinson, who initiates his very useful doctoral dissertation "Joyce and the Theater" with the assertion that "Joyce's interest in the theater was lifelong. More than poetry or even fiction, the theater, in all of its various manifestations, mattered most to Joyce."[67] The theater, therefore, may serve as a powerful influence on Joyce, with *influence,* a potentially mystifying term invoked to pay homage to an author's mastery at redeploying prior texts in any fashion he or she chooses, requiring some elaboration. Richard Brown provides one such critique of orthodox conceptions of influence while examining Joyce's reading and its relationship to his understanding of contemporary research into human sexuality. "One Joyce critic [Marvin Magalaner], discussing the 'influence of Joyce's reading,' says that 'Joyce seems to have been impressed mainly, both as an artist and supreme egoist by analogies to his own life and to books he himself was planning.' Such an approach does not allow the extent to which Joyce must have been conditioned by his reading, or at any rate, bound up by the same kinds of dilemmas."[68] Reconstituting and then employing Joyce's experience of the popular theater thus involve a double difficulty. First, whereas scholars like Kershner, intrigued by Joyce's reading of popular fiction and other prose forms, may pursue this study aided by a number of prior investigations, Ellmann's *Consciousness of Joyce* (1977) for instance, those interested in Joyce's love of drama and theater are not nearly so fortunate. Second, even though this latter, less critically mapped route must be traveled, in part because Joyce *was* impressed by dramas that related to his life and future projects, he was also conditioned by this spectatorship. Such a hypothesis drastically modifies the nature of influence study, necessitating a thorough reconsideration of this critical practice and its most fundamental assumptions.

Brown's notion of Joyce being "bound up by the same kinds of dilemmas" as characters in the books he read parallels a matter I wish merely to introduce here: Joyce (and O'Casey as well) as subject and author. It is one thing to assert that authors illuminate the workings of ideology on and through fictional characters; it is another to claim that they wield this knowledge to gain emancipation from the very apparatuses that operate to construct them as subjects. Of relevance here is the "equivocal process of subjectification" Louis Montrose defines: "on the one hand, shaping individuals as loci of consciousness and initiators of action—endowing them with *subjectivity* and with the capacity for agency; and, on the other hand, positioning, motivating, and constraining them within—*subjecting them to*—social networks and cultural codes that ultimately exceed their comprehension or control."[69] I agree with Brown that most Joyceans concern themselves solely with the first half of Montrose's definition, routinely attributing to Joyce unlimited potential for agency and creative autonomy. In this attribution, Joyceans thereby position themselves diametrically opposite Michel Foucault in such essays as "What Is an Author?" and Roland Barthes in "The Death of the Author," both of whom deny authors such powers of self-determination. When Foucault and Barthes scrutinize homologies between the overstatement of authorial power and a godlike creative agency —when they illuminate the conditions "that fostered the fundamental category of 'the man and his work'"[70]—they are questioning with particular force, though quite unaware of it, orthodox critical opinion of Joyce and O'Casey.

Consider, for example, Frank Budgen's conscious invocation of the Old Testament when framing a comparison between Joyce's intricate plan for *Ulysses* and God's creation of the world: "Joyce composes with infinite pains, but he looks on his handiwork when he has done it and finds it good."[71] Or consider the refrain in conventional readings of O'Casey that uncovering connections between O'Casey and any particular cultural form is complicated because he was so much "his own man."[72] In what Brown perceives to be their detrimental isolation, Joyceans routinely cast Joyce as the "man of genius" Stephen Dedalus describes in the "Scylla and Charybdis" episode of *Ulysses:* "A man of genius makes no mistakes. His errors are volitional and are the portals of discovery" (9:228–29).[73] Joyce, in a now familiar variation of a reverence upon which much Joycean criticism is based, wears the mantle of the great appropriator, transforming everything he read and saw with the ease and mastery that accompany genius. This, for instance, is the premise from which Jean Kimball proceeds in delineating the relationship between Sigmund Freud's study of Leonardo da Vinci and representations of infancy and artistry in *Portrait* and *Ulysses:* "For Joyce's great and unique gift is his uncanny ability to recognize and appropriate insights and ambiences not his own and to transform them into an integral part of his own symbolic statement without sacrificing their own integrity."[74] Such endorsements hence perpetuate the myth of the godlike artist who fashions whatever materials he or she finds into the masterworks we study.

Less often in Joyce studies does one find a reversal of this depiction of authorial power, a recharting of the circuitry of creative energy that demonstrates how an influence possesses more power than that with which it is normally imbued. This alternative, more skeptical understanding of authorial empowerment, finds its strongest articulation in Foucault's postulation of the authorial function: "to characterize the existence, circulation, and operation of certain discourses within society." In his reconsideration of authorial functioning, Foucault maintains that as readers and exegetes we betray our need for a figure of authority by our construction of a "rational entity" in whom we invest enormous creative and originary power. Challenging this formulation, Foucault questions the privileges we bestow upon the subject, not necessarily to abandon the notion of the subject but rather to "seize its functions, its interventions in discourse, and its system of dependencies."[75] Stating the case more baldly (at least Foucault acknowledges both "interventions" and "dependencies"), Barthes maintains that "we know now that a text is not a line of words releasing a single 'theological' meaning (the 'message' of the Author-God) but a multi-dimensional space in which a variety of writings, none of them original, blend and clash. The text is a tissue of quotations drawn from the innumerable centres of culture."[76] The ramifications of Foucault's and Barthes's interrogations of authorship thus counter the premises of much Joyce scholarship: from author as maker to author as scriptor, epigone, or subject with limited agency.

Prominent exceptions to the critical tendency to endow Joyce with absolute authorial power are contained in readings like Jennifer Schiffer Levine's of originality and repetition in *Finnegans Wake* and *Ulysses.* Levine extrapolates the precedent from Joyce's own work for uncertainty about the authenticity of any writing or the empowerment of any author as creator. Shaun, as Levine points out, serves as the principal deflator of such ideal-izations in the *Wake,* referring disparagingly to Shem's "most venerated pub-lic impostures," his "pelagiarist pen," and his "piously forged palimpsests" (*FW* 182:1–3). Earlier in the novel, as Levine emphasizes, the author of the lost letter retrieved from the dungheap is dubbed "our copyist" (*FW* 121:29–30), and later the description of Shem's house underscores its lit-tered (literary) borrowings from a variety of sources. For Levine, in *Finne-gans Wake* Joyce suggests with an insistence we "cannot dismiss" that a writer is a con man and a thief, much like Ralston in Young's popular play and "Dublin favorite," *Jim the Penman,* and indeed she does not dismiss the idea: "If writing is largely quotation, then the notion of originality has to be rethought." One reason for Levine's and, if her thesis is accurate, Joyce's skepticism about originality resides in the nature of language itself: "Total originality, given the shared nature of language, is impossible."[77]

Surely there must be some space between innovation and conven-tion, between Montrose's two senses of subjectivity as capacity for action and a condition of subjugation – some critical ground between Joyce's god-like genius and the Wakean dungheap. Although she is not discussing the conditions of colonialism per se, Levine might have been, for the colonial-ist (frequently the anticolonial or antihegemonic) ramifications of Irish lit-erature form one aspect of such a critical site. Especially in the next chapter on Irish melodrama, the issue of Irish writing within a colonial history will surface frequently. From Cairns and Richards's perspective, through vari-ous cultural discourses the "making and remaking of the identities of the colonized and colonizer have been inflected by this relationship."[78] And a host of contemporary playwrights would seem to agree, as the effects of colonialism not only form the basis of action in Brian Friel's *Translations* (1980) but also receive stark representation in some of the contemporary stage's most intriguing plays: David Hare's *Fanshen* (1976), Bernard Pomer-ance's *Elephant Man* (1979), Caryl Churchill's *Cloud 9* (revised edition, 1980), Anne Devlin's *Ourselves Alone* (1985), several plays by John Arden and Margaretta D'Arcy, and others.[79] In *Translations,* Owen O'Donnell's in-sistence that his being renamed by British soldiers exerts no effect on his self-identity becomes, by the end of Friel's drama, a hollow and self-deluding

claim. And the monstrously repressive actions threatened by a British officer against Baile Beag, the small Irish-speaking community in County
Donegal in which the play's action takes place, seems puny indeed when
compared with the greater damage done by the British geographers' project
of Anglicizing the names of nearby landmarks and villages, the cultural
"translations" to which Friel's title refers. The issue of Ireland's colonialism
is thus relevant, albeit perhaps less so than in examinations of popular melodrama, to readings of Joyce and O'Casey as well.

One tellingly pointed dialogue over an analogous supposition appears
in *Marxism and the Interpretation of Culture* (1988), a valuable anthology of
papers given at a conference at the University of Illinois. Here Moretti reiterates the position he had articulated earlier in "The Long Goodbye: *Ulysses*
and the End of Liberal Capitalism," from which the following is taken: "I
have dealt – and shall continue to deal – with Joyce and *Ulysses* as expressions
of English society and culture. Of course, it is a well-known fact that Joyce
is Irish and that *Ulysses* takes place in Dublin. But if Joyce were an Irish
writer, . . . if the city of *Ulysses* were the real Dublin at the turn of the century, it would not be the literary image *par excellence* of the modern metropo-
lis."[80] Moretti goes on to ask, "What ever has emerged from the studies that
interpreted Joyce on the basis of Ireland?" and continues to dislocate Joyce's
Dublin from its historical referent. He does so by way of two interpretive
moves: by elevating the private, "possible" world of Bloom's daydreaming
over the public, "actual" world in which he lives; and by alleging that Joyce's
"more significant and typically modernist innovation" manifests itself in a
dissolution of the connection between "possibility" and "anxiety." Specifically, because adultery amounts to a "harmless pastime" in *Ulysses* rather than
the "possible" second "world" of the nineteenth-century novel, the "meaning of life" for Joyce's Dubliners is no longer vested in the public or social
domain but relegated to the private realm of consumption and fantasy. Ergo,
because such novels as *Ulysses* depend little on the public or on cultural specificity, Joyce and *Ulysses* are "expressions of English society and culture."[81]

Responding to Moretti, Colin MacCabe expressed his incredulity that
"those who invoke 'comrade history' never pay much attention to particular histories," in this case, the relationship between adultery and art in *Ulysses* and the consolidation between the Catholic church and the nationalist
movement in Ireland in 1922 that effectively denied Joyce a public voice
in his own country.[82] In another rejoinder of Moretti, Herr maintains that
there is "something reductive in turning so fully to the English context of

Joyce's works. Especially in regard to theatrical experience, the point to be made is rather that 'Irishness' was for Joyce a relational and contested category." For Herr, Ireland's "derivative, colonial status . . . accounts for much of the mood of decline and crisis in *Exiles*."[83] In terms of colonialism's effect on theatrical experience, the point might be pressed even further. Surely Ireland's colonial status at least partially accounts for the annual resuscitation of Boucicault in Dublin and the consistent repertory of Irish drama at the Queen's Royal Theatre, a drama replete with anti-English conventions and overturnings of Victorian stereotypes of native Irishness. What other theatrical conventions, audience expectations, and broader cultural effects of the theater event in turn-of-the-century Dublin might one attribute to colonialism? By *theater event,* I mean, following Timothy Wiles's definition, the "creative interaction of literary text, actor's art, and spectator's participation."[84]

Colonialism led to Dublin's status as a cultural satellite of the London stage, a status shared by English and Irish provincial towns alike. Provincial theater managers tended to book touring players who had previously drawn large audiences, frequently by reviving popular roles in older plays, so Dubliners saw many of the same actors year after year in the same or similar roles. Like English provincial audiences, Dublin theatergoers developed especially strong attachments to certain actors, often supporting their appearances in an extravagantly emotional fashion inside and outside the theater.[85] One reason for such enthusiasm seems quite simple: during the last decades of the nineteenth century, Londoners could see William or Madge Kendal, Ellen Terry or Henry Irving, on most nights of the theater season. Dubliners were not so fortunate. The brightest stars seldom played in provincial towns more frequently than twice a year, and most English touring players annually scheduled a single one- or two-week visit to Dublin.

The effect on playgoers of such fleeting contact with greatness should not be underestimated—and Joyce does not. As Disher explains, provincial audiences developed a "steadfast loyalty" to their favorites, a steadfastness tinctured by wonder at the arrival of familiar, yet still mysterious, visitors. Moreover, given the large audiences who flocked to provincial theaters, actors played to a greater percentage of the population on tour than they did in London: "In the West End a star acted to playgoers—in the provinces to populations."[86] Consequently, actors' arrivals in cities like Dublin occasioned public celebration, and actors were often called upon to grace Dublin social functions. Martin Harvey presented talks to the Dickens Fellowship, and Frank Benson's company, whose productions of Shakespeare were well supported in Dublin (Benson himself also played in Yeats's and Moore's *Diarmuid and Grania* in 1901), competed in field hockey and soccer against local teams.[87] In sum, because of the provincial and colonial dimensions of the theater event in Dublin – these dimensions are sometimes identical, sometimes not – any assessment of the role of drama and theater in Joyce's work (and O'Casey's as well) must acknowledge its specific sociohistorical context. As MacCabe insists, attention must be paid to "particular histories."

Both the establishment of a record of theatrical consumption and an assessment of influence are aspects of my remembering of a now largely forgotten "particular history." In addition, and perhaps more important, what concerns me here is theatrical representation and what Raymond Williams, speaking of drama in the twentieth century, refers to as the "dramatization of consciousness itself." "The specific conventions of this particular dramatization – a country, a society, a period of history, a crisis of civilization; these conventions are not abstract. They are profoundly worked and reworked in our actual living relationships. They are our ways of seeing and knowing, which every day we put into practice."[88] Or, to echo Brown, they present dilemmas in which we are bound. Among others, Shaw recognized the power of the theater to shape consciousness, to create false stereotypes and to theatricalize reality, as Lawrence Doyle explains Tim Haffigan's assumption of the role of Stage Irishman to his duped colleague Broadbent in *John Bull's Other Island* (1904): "No Irishman ever ever talks like that in Ireland, or ever did, or ever will. But when a thoroughly worthless Irishman comes to England . . . he soon learns the antics that take you in. He picks them up at the theatre or the music hall" (*CPP* 2:905–6). "Antics" can be learned at the theater, but they can only be manipulated to advantage – the Broadbents of the world can only be duped – because consciousness is shaped there as well. A complementary aspect of the "popular" informs the argument Doyle later addresses to Broadbent about the unhealthy relationship of Irish imagination and "reality." Doyle's examples of the destructiveness of imagination seem derived from, among other places, Shaw's animosity toward the melodramatic stage: "At last you get that you can bear nothing real at all: . . . you nag and squabble at home because your wife isn't an angel, and she despises you because you're not a hero" (*CPP* 2:910). Here Doyle is not merely proffering an extreme example of the profound ways in which expropriations from popular culture intrude upon the interactions of husbands and wives; he is also alluding to the pervasive operation of a semiotic mechanism in culture which constructs imagination or consciousness, just as it makes possible and delimits certain kinds of knowledge.

My thesis, then, is that Joyce and O'Casey—and many of their most important characters as well—in crucial respects "see" and "know" the world in ways determined by popular dramatic and theatrical conventions of the turn-of-the-century stage, even as these writers in many instances parody or through other means overturn these very conventions. There resides in this assertion at least one paradox that will lead us to an examination of a problematic integral to this book: namely, if these writers and their characters "see" and "know" *only* what this culture allows them to, how can they be capable of parody, of getting out of cultural constructs and into a deconstructive irony? Both parody and irony assume the possibility of resistance and the existence of an authorial consciousness capable of breaking free from powerful chains of signification to the class interests they serve. These moments of authorial emancipation must be isolated and examined, along with those instances of myopia or co-optation which inevitably accompany them. My thesis may strike some as eccentric, perhaps reckless, for more commonsensical reasons. After all, unlike Shaw, who wrote prolifically as a novelist, reviewer, and playwright in the 1890s, O'Casey and Joyce were just leaving their teen years at the beginning of the century. Nonetheless, I hope to demonstrate that these ways of knowing, originating in the popular theater, are put into practice in some of their greatest achievements. If critics today have largely forgotten this "arid wasteland" of drama and theater, it seems that O'Casey and Joyce never did.

The Queen's Royal Theatre and the Politics of Irish Melodrama

> BENEFIT! AT THE QUEEN'S THEATRE! It is the custom each year before the theatre closes for Lent that the popular manager [Whitbread] should have two nights devoted to his benefit. . . . no incident in connection with Dublin theatres is more worthy of public patronage and support.
>
> — *The Freeman's Journal,*
> 26 February 1895

IF POPULAR TURN-OF-THE-CENTURY IRISH DRAMA has been dismissed in terms like Hugh Hunt's quoted in chapter 1—as fatuous plays chockablock with "blarney and blather" that, like a child's bad dream, are "best forgotten"[1]—so too has the Queen's Royal Theatre, which by the 1890s had become known as the home of such drama in Dublin. When Bernard Shaw in the 1940s reminisced about his boyhood in Dublin, his opinion of the theater differed only in its greater verbal sophistication from that of Joyce's ungenerous narrator in the "Cyclops" episode of *Ulysses*. Shaw's warmest memories were of spectacular Christmas pantomimes—still enormous attractions at the Theatre Royal and the Gaiety Theatre during Joyce's and Sean O'Casey's adolescences—and of Barry Sullivan playing Shakespeare, as he did almost annually in Dublin for some forty years.[2] Shaw's worst memories were re-

48

served for the Queen's Theatre. As he said, "respectable people then did not frequent it, as it served not only as a theatre for crude melodrama but as a market for ladies who lived by selling themselves."[3] At the time of the theater's closing in 1969 and demolition in 1970, Dublin newspapers followed Shaw's lead by indicting it not only on aesthetic counts but on its encouragement of moral lapses as well. The *Irish Press* (24 February 1970), for example, alleged that between 1887 and 1907 patrons of the Queen's enjoyed not only "Boucicault-type melodrama uproariously presented" but also the "supplementary entertainment" of "easygoing ladies." In the *Evening Press* (24 February 1969), Andrew Marsh opined that though the "matrons of Rawthmines and Rawthgar shunned the place . . . no doubt their menfolk slipped in there now and again." If some "ladies" who frequented the "old Brunswick Street house" were "easygoing," one might infer from such animadversions upon the Queen's as these, so too were the theater's standards of production and its principal dramatic attractions: melodrama and, especially, Irish nationalist drama.

At the turn of the century, this opinion was shared by Yeats, George Moore, and Frank Fay writing in the *United Irishman*. In 1900, when reviewing Edmond Rostand's *Fantasticks* at the Theatre Royal, Fay praised the poetic dramas "common enough on the boards of Parisian theatres" but lamented that these "are not beloved by English-speaking audiences, and I grieve to say that the majority of Dublin playgoers are in the same category" (*United Irishman*, 8 September 1900). A month later, he resumed his diatribe against the contemporary stage. "In these days it is getting a confused question as to what is drama at all. To some it is the lofty expression of noble thoughts or the tragic exposition of keen emotions. To others it is a ten-ton tractor engine with perhaps a boiler explosion as a subsidiary effect. . . . True literary drama is dead, and we are now living under the reign of a triumvirate of actor, scene shifter, and lime lighter" (20 October 1900). For Fay, the Queen's was the provenience of many such plays and inartistic staging practices. Commenting on a revival in 1899 of J. W. Whitbread's *Irishman* (1889), Fay termed the popular drama a "crude piece of unconvincing conventionalism."[4] A production of Dion Boucicault's *Shaughraun* in May 1900 fared no better, as Fay complained that Boucicault's Irish dramas are "nowadays used simply to show off the Irish comedian or the Irish character actor." Importantly, in this objection Fay is not deprecating the acting practices at the Gaiety Theatre or the Theatre Royal, neither of which produced many Irish plays during these years. It is thus worth re-

membering, when reading critical reportage like Fay's, that although the
Queen's, its plays, players, and audiences were frequently the targets of censure or roughshod parody as in Joyce's "Cyclops," it nonetheless was the
only theater in Dublin that consistently produced Irish and other dramas
of especial interest to popular audiences.

Not surprisingly, both the Queen's and its repertory at the turn of
the century claimed its portion of supporters. The *Freeman's Journal* and
Joseph Holloway writing for the short-lived *Irish Playgoer and Amusement
Record* (1899–1900) were two of these, not to mention O'Casey. As the epigraph from the *Freeman's Journal* implies, the Queen's, particularly during
the management of James W. Whitbread (known as J. W.) from 1884 to
1907,[5] ascended from the checkered reputation Shaw recalls to an institution with widespread popular support. Holloway's aesthetic judgment, albeit not so keen as his factual knowledge of the Dublin theatrical world,
verifies this when, in an 1899 chronicle of the theater's past season, he exclaims that Whitbread has "worked wonders" during his tenure at the
Queen's: "Now a playgoer is sure to see an exciting well-staged drama, or
an Irish play in progress if he drops into the theatre any evening casual like."[6]
Joined by Kennedy Miller, a longtime associate who, in 1899, was formally
appointed general manager of the theater and whose acting company was
particularly suited for Irish plays, Whitbread and the Queen's grew in popularity throughout the 1880s, 1890s, and first decade of this century.[7] By
the Christmas season of 1906, when the Queen's again faced the formidable
competition of pantomimes at the other theaters, the *Freeman's Journal* remained unwavering in its support, maintaining that "Christmas would
scarcely be itself in Dublin" without a new play by Whitbread at the Queen's
(combined issue, 25 and 26 December 1906). More recently, Séamus de
Búrca has affectionately proclaimed it *the* "Irish National Theatre" until Whitbread's retirement in 1907.[8]

My respect for Shaw's wisdom on theatrical matters notwithstanding, critical opinions like his have helped induce the critical neglect of Irish
popular culture outlined in the preceding chapter. As after Sheridan, the
notion goes, the British stage anxiously awaited Shaw's arrival, so in Dublin, Yeats, Synge, and O'Casey marked the arrival of the Irish playwright
in Ireland. But as Shaw built on a solid foundation of Victorian popular
theater, so O'Casey and Denis Johnston—and later, contemporary playwrights such as Brian Friel, John Arden, and Margaretta D'Arcy—grounded
their plays in a distinctive tradition of Irish drama, which they perpetuated

and continued even as they transformed it into a more modern drama.[9] Unfortunately, those few theater historians who have recognized the importance of Irish popular drama have tended to focus on romantic comedies such as Boucicault's *Colleen Bawn* at the expense of a parallel and equally popular tradition of nationalistic dramatizations of Irish history.[10] Historical dramas such as Boucicault's *Robert Emmet* (1884, a revision of an earlier, incomplete script by Frank Marshall), Whitbread's *Wolfe Tone*, *The Ulster Hero* (1903), and *Sarsfield* (1905), and several later plays by P. J. Bourke and Ira Allen constituted one of the major streams that fed into the creation of the modern Irish history play—and both types of Irish drama contributed substantially to O'Casey's ironic representations of history and Dublin life in the second and third decades of this century.

The most popular plays in the Queen's repertory—those of Boucicault, Whitbread, and Hubert O'Grady—operate in a manner similar to that of other popular cultural forms during this crucial period on the berm between Victorianism and modernism, if such essential terms of periodization can be tolerated for the moment. Like other popular genres, Irish drama at the Queen's presented its audience with a variety of spectatorial pleasures and ideological satisfactions, many of which pertain to Ireland's colonial subjugation and the often invidious English representations of Irishness that served as justification for stern colonial governance. Moreover, the Queen's Irish drama corroborates Stuart Hall's revision of critiques like Bernard Sharratt's that insist upon popular culture's co-optation by the dominant class in perpetuating its social advantage. On the contrary, Hall urges, "In the study of popular culture, we should always start . . . with the double-stake in popular culture, the double movement of containment and resistance, which is always inevitably inside it."[11]

This combination of political tendencies in popular Irish dramas helps to explain both their simultaneous box-office success in England and Ireland and their censorship in times of especially violent political unrest between the countries. Much of the popularity of these plays depends, therefore, on the historical and cultural contexts of their performance, phenomena orthodox theater historians overlook when typically advancing two elements of Boucicauldian melodrama as responsible for its success: Boucicault's ingenuity at devising sensational staging techniques and his creation of entertaining Stage Irishmen.[12] Though Boucicault's considerable talent is beyond debate, such analyses invariably posit an unchanging or "bounded" text and universal spectator, foreclosing from consideration the possibility that audiences' constructions of the text might differ significantly from one moment to the next, from one locale to another. It is difficult to imagine, however, that Irish audiences reacted to Boucicault's plays in ways that merely replicated London theatergoers' responses. Yet another similarly durable hypothesis emphasizes the attraction of specific actors, such as Boucicault himself, who until 1881 played the roles of his Stage Irishmen. He was succeeded in these roles by Hubert O'Grady and Charles Sullivan, and such skilled impersonators of villains as Shiel Barry and Frank Breen also helped draw crowds to Dublin theaters. Unquestionably, both in the production of Irish drama and in the annual returns at the Gaiety and Theatre Royal of popular London actors, specific plays became associated with familiar players, whose presence alone attracted a crowded house. But the celebrity of well-known actors cannot finally account for the persistent production of new Irish plays and revival of older ones during this period.

Boucicault himself identified yet another potential source of these plays' popularity—Irish history and romance.[13] Keenly aware that English plays based on Irish subjects routinely depicted Irishmen as drunken comedians, he was quick to distinguish his Irish characters from their cousins on the London stage: "The fire and energy that consists of dancing around the stage in an expletive manner, and indulging in ridiculous capers and extravagancies of language and gesture, form the materials of a clowning character, known as the 'Stage Irishman,' which it has been my vocation to abolish."[14] In this project, Boucicault anticipates Stephen Dedalus's meditations in the "Nestor" episode concerning Buck Mulligan's and others' comic performances for Englishmen like Haines: "A jester at the court of his master, indulged and disesteemed, winning a clement master's praise. Why had they chosen all that part?" (2:43–45). Commentators such as R. B. Graves insist that Boucicault's putative abolition of the Stage Irishman's motley is largely self-deception: that Myles-na-Coppaleen, Shaun the Post, and Conn are indistinguishable from their foppish predecessors. Of singular importance to the popularity of Boucicault's plays in Dublin, according to Graves, is Dubliners' critical reaction to the Stage Irishman: there, the Stage Irishman's "laziness, scheming, and whatever else he can be accused of are not identified with Irishness," as was the case in London, but "serve rather to underline the moral code of the majority of Irish by contrast."[15] Like Graves, D. E. S. Maxwell valorizes Boucicault's Stage Irishmen as the principal reason for his popularity, but he defines their attractions quite differently: the "interest" of these plays resides in their "inverting the stupid and unreliable

Stage Irishman into the charming and patriotic Stage Irishman, a reversal which Dublin took to its heart."[16] History, in both readings, would seem to have little to do with Boucicault's popularity; rather, theatrical stereotyping (or its undoing) is responsible. The question begged here, it seems to me, is why, at this particular moment, would Dubliners be especially welcoming of such characters—and how, then, are we to understand the popularity of the very same characters in England? In sum, stereotyping is a historical and malleable practice, stable enough to produce deeply entrenched, hence repetitive, racial and ethnic slurs, yet protean enough to create variations as the colonialist or hegemonic need arises.

Maxwell's observation is nonetheless valuable, especially after comparing Boucicault's Irishmen with such low-comic antecedents as Wild Murtogh in John Baldwin Buckstone's *Green Bushes* (1845). In contrast to the expanded, in some ways heroic roles of Boucicault's Irishmen, Wild Murtogh is a minor comic figure through which Buckstone furthers the stereotype Boucicault reviled: a conniving, fractious, but entertaining drunkard who wields both a mean shillelagh and a "darlin'" brogue. Yet surely more compelling explanations might be formulated for Boucicault's virtually unrivaled popularity in Dublin. Following his own suggestion, one source of popular acceptance resides in Ireland's history, especially in its colonial status; another, in Hall's conception of cultural texts as "deeply divided" commentaries on the social matrix in which they are produced: "We tend to think of cultural forms as whole and coherent: either wholly corrupt or wholly authentic. Whereas, they are deeply contradictory; they play on contradictions, especially when they function in the domain of the popular." In such texts, Hall concludes, tensions exist between "what belongs to the central domain of elite or dominant culture"—English colonial power in Ireland—and "the culture of the periphery"—native Irishness.[17] As a result, the melodramatic text at this moment of especially intense Anglo-Irish division might be received in widely divergent ways: as an acquiescence to England's domination that tamely recalls a simpler, more idyllic past, or as a statement of resistance, a summons to continue the struggle against colonial governance.

The plays of O'Grady, Boucicault, and Whitbread thus constitute chameleon-like responses to the historical situation of colonial rule, possessing elements of both containment and resistance and thereby appealing to audiences of various political sympathies. The opposite of conservatism and nostalgia, in this instance, is the counterhegemonic discourse of anticolonialism to which Irish drama at the Queen's contributed mightily. That is, as Cairns and Richards describe, as a result of England's colonial enterprise in Ireland, many Victorian discourses—scientific, medical, literary—constructed native Irishness in reductively disparaging ways. Cairns and Richards point to, among others, Matthew Arnold's feminization of the native Celt and L. Perry Curtis, Jr.'s study of Victorian journalism and physiognomy, the latter of which authorized "scientific" homologies between Irishmen and apes.[18] As Curtis describes, popular journalism, especially through cartoons in such periodicals as *Punch* and *Puck,* furthered this process of simianization, which became accelerated in the years following the Fenian uprising in the 1860s: "However brutish the faces of Irishmen found in British cartoons and illustrations during the 1840s and 1850s, Paddy remained essentially human in outward form until the 1860s, when the era of acute midfacial prognathism began to turn into the age of the simianized Celt."[19] Such vilifications continued to be applied to Irish nationalists, to members of the Land League in the 1880s for instance.

These shifts in English representations of Irishness are inscribed in various cultural forms and political discourses throughout the mid- and late Victorian period, even in the thought of social critics extremely sympathetic to Ireland's historical suppression such as Karl Marx and Frederick Engels. Engels in particular, who draws such heartrending pictures of the squalid urban conditions in which Irish (and other) workers suffered in *The Condition of the Working-Class in England* (1844), betrays a tendency to colonialist characterizations of Irishness that undergoes an alteration after the Fenian uprising. In an 1843 letter, Engels praises the "wild, fanatical Gaels" with whom Daniel O'Connell surrounded himself and offers an astonishing appraisal of Irishmen's closeness to nature: "One who has never seen Irishmen cannot know them. . . . The Irishman is a carefree, cheerful, potato-eating child of nature," whose "half-savage upbringing" clashes so sharply with a "completely civilised environment" that Irish workers in the empire's "Great Towns" are in a psychological state of "continually smouldering fury."[20] The predictable binarism civilization/barbarism underlying these remarks grows in force in Engels's later letter to Marx after the episode at Clerkenwell prison. In a letter of 14 December 1867, Marx criticized the bombing as a "very stupid thing" and labeled Fenianism as a "melodramatic sort of conspiracy"; Engels responded by terming the Fenians "fanatics," "cowards," and "cannibals."[21] The "child of nature" in 1843 has, by 1867, evolved in Engels's writing into a cannibalistic savage; one of the authors of important interventions into the ideologies of colonialism and industrial capitalism reveals firsthand the power of these ideologies to shape even the most resistant thought.

In addition to these processes of feminization and simianization, incredibly ugly words that match the operations they describe, a process of negricization also influenced representations of various Caucasian colonial subjects, including Irishmen. As Sander L. Gilman and Abdul R. Jan-Mohamed have discussed, and I learned by investigating the mythologies surrounding the late Victorian sideshow performer John Merrick, commonly known as the "Elephant Man," the operation of negricization brought with it a host of supposed racial traits, most especially those concerning bestial sexuality and a corresponding anatomical exaggeration.[22] Victorian "freak" shows, another term as hideous as the entertainment it denotes, and pornographic entertainments typically featured colonial performers and, if these performers happened to be English, as Merrick was, a colonial mythology was often contrived to explain their "otherness": their disfigurement, unique physiology, and so on. Heaped upon this base of physical difference–this "otherness" so essential to England's self-definition as civilized and human, appropriately holding its instinctual desires in check–were generalizations about racial identity, cognitive capacity, level of articulateness, and sexuality. Colonialism, in short, manufactured a constellation of representations that Irish popular cultural forms at times endeavored to refute, frequently by supplanting one extreme depiction and replacing it with its polar opposite.

Insofar as stereotyping is an essential ideological instrument in colonialist discourse, I am especially interested in the methods by which Irish dramatists overturned stereotypes and in the ways in which melodrama taught historical lessons to its audience, lessons that functioned as rubrics through which Irishmen could interpret contemporary events. My interests, quite obviously, revolve around the growing unease between England and Ireland at the turn of the century, and I construe popular entertainment as an aesthetic confrontation of the domestic, economic, and political predicaments resulting from England's colonial domination. From the time of *Arrah-na-Pogue* until the Easter 1916 uprising, Anglo-Irish relations grew increasingly strained. The Fenian insurrection in the 1860s, the Land League and Home Rule movements, and the Boer War all contributed to an increased hostility between the two countries. Boucicault's, O'Grady's, and Whitbread's Irish plays, although viewed today and by many then as trifling dramas of excitement and humor, addressed issues of contemporary concern to Irishmen, either working toward a resolution of these issues or amounting to a call to arms. In the readings that follow, therefore, Hall's conception of the "double-stake" in popular cultural forms, the paradoxical co-presence of containment and resistance inherent to them, and the issue of dramatic conventions constituting an anticolonial refutation will be placed prominently in the foreground. In the former case of containment and re- sistance, I shall elaborate the characteristics of two myths, one conservative and one more radical, that informed popular Irish drama at the turn of the century. Before doing so, however, the plays and playwrights that domi- nated this popular theater, some of which must surely have been forgotten along with the bad dreams of our childhood, require some brief attention.

HISTORY AND MELODRAMA: Boucicault, Whitbread, and O'Grady

Ireland's most widely supported dramatists at the turn of the century, par- ticularly Boucicault, found ingenious ways of linking history and melodrama; so too did populist Dublin newspapers. Most students of Irish drama tend to agree that Boucicault's so-called Irish plays—*The Colleen Bawn, Arrah-na- Pogue,* and *The Shaughraun*—mark the pinnacle of his prolific writing career that began with *London Assurance* in 1841. Although they were certainly devised to entertain, these plays and their Irish characters reflect his in- creased awareness of Irish history and contemporary political tensions. Even though Boucicault spent his later years in the United States, his nationalist sympathies grew in intensity, leading to his brief historical essay *A Fireside Story of Ireland* (1881) and later to his tragic historical drama *Robert Emmet.* The former work delineates his aversion to English dominance in Ireland, revealing a polemical side of the famous melodramatist very different from the one he exposed to his audiences. The explicitly nationalist tone of the early paragraphs of *A Fireside Story of Ireland* clarifies the political position that his Irish melodramas generally only imply:

> While other nations were thus advancing, by experiment and experience, towards a higher state of civilization . . . Ireland was not permitted to share in the progress. Her elder sisters of the British family seemed to regard her with indifference and contempt, as one fitted for a sordid life of servitude. . . .
>
> Thus, like an untutored, neglected, ragged Cinderella, she has been con- fined in the out-house of Great Britain.[23]

1. The "Sensation Scene" of Dion Boucicault's *Colleen Bawn*. Courtesy of the Raymond Mander–Joe Mitchenson Theatre Collection.

2. Dion Boucicault. Courtesy of the University of South Florida Library, Special Collections, Tampa campus.

3. Sensation scene from *The Shaughraun*. Courtesy of the University of South Florida Library, Special Collections, Tampa campus.

4. Conn and his dog and scene from *The Shaughraun*. Courtesy of the University of South Florida Library, Special Collections, Tampa campus.

THEY DID THIS KIND OF THING FOR SHAKSPEARE; WHY NOT FOR BOUCICAULT?

5. Caricature by Alfred Bryan of Boucicault as Shakespeare (ca. 1870). Courtesy of the Raymond Mander–Joe Mitchenson Theatre Collection.

6. Drawing by Harry Ireland of Frank Breen, veteran character actor at the Queen's Theatre, as Michael Feeney [*sic*] in Boucicault's *Arrah-na-Pogue* (ca. 1895). Courtesy of the Irish Theatre Archive, Dublin.

7. J. W. Whitbread. Courtesy of Séamus de Búrca.

8. Cartoon by "Spex" of Hubert O'Grady as Conn in Boucicault's *Shaughraun* (from *Zoz*, April 1877). Courtesy of the Irish Theatre Archive, Dublin.

9. Hubert O'Grady as
Sadler, the villainous time-
keeper in *The Famine*.
From O'Grady's obituary
in the *Irish Playgoer*,
December 28, 1899.

10. John Baldwin Buckstone. Courtesy of the Irish Theatre Archive, Dublin.

11. P. J. Bourke, second from left, from *Waterfront* (June 1903). Courtesy of Séamus de Búrca.

Boucicault's comedies, albeit in much more exciting fashion than his *Fire-side Story*, address the same tensions as his own and Whitbread's histories present, yet they also advance a myth of the reconciliation of English/Irish opposition that both complements and opposes the myth of nationalist martyrdom promoted by Irish historical melodrama (and eventually deconstructed by O'Casey).

As successful as Boucicault in Dublin and provincial towns but scarcely remembered today is Hubert O'Grady (1841–99), whom Peter Kavanagh termed "the most popular dramatic author in Ireland during the last decade of the [nineteenth] century."[24] Kavanagh also installed O'Grady's *Famine* (1886) as the country's most popular play during this time, a ranking well supported by its long history of productions at the Queen's alone. Born in Limerick and trained as an upholsterer before turning to acting and writing plays, O'Grady achieved public acclaim as Conn in an 1876–77 Dublin revival of *The Shaughraun* that ran for an exceptional seven weeks at the Gaiety Theatre. A favorite in Dublin after this, O'Grady did not relinquish his celebrity until his death in Liverpool of pneumonia on 19 December 1899. Even after his death, his wife and other Irish companies continued to tour in repertories of his plays. Like *The Famine*, set in rural Ireland in 1881 at the time of the "No-Rent Manifesto" authored by founders of the Land League, O'Grady's best-known plays deal comically either with specific historical moments of tension between the English and Irish or with the unfortunate socioeconomic circumstances devolving from them. *The Eviction* (1879), *Emigration* (1880), and *The Fenian* (1888) are among the most enduring of O'Grady's Irish melodramas; much like *The Famine*, they were revived frequently during the 1880s, 1890s, and first two decades of this century.[25] As one indication of the longevity of O'Grady's work in Dublin, in 1902 W. Faulkner Cox's Company appeared at the Queen's in January in *Emigration;* Robert Barton's Company presented O'Grady's *Wild Irish Boy* (1877?) in July and *The Fenian* in November; and Mrs. O'Grady's Company performed *The Famine* in October.

Newspaper reports of O'Grady's death lauded his ability as a comic actor and, reluctant to pronounce his plays literary masterpieces, stressed their sociopolitical relevance. Calling his dramas "rough and ready bits of Irish sentiment," the *Evening Herald* (22 December 1899) nevertheless recognized that plays like *Eviction* amounted to a "sermon preached from behind the footlights, and appealed to popular feeling in a curiously successful fashion." As the *Irish Playgoer* warmly recalled in its obituary of O'Grady, in his plays "latterday politics . . . were unblushingly mixed up with the events of thirty years ago in delicious unconcern of the sequence of events."[26] Regardless of this intimation of the unhistorical nature of O'Grady's melodramas, Dublin Castle anticipated their incendiary potential and, as Dublin newspapers reported, threatened *The Eviction* in 1881 with a censurious "Notice." To perform his plays in England, of course, O'Grady was required to submit playscripts to the Lord Chamberlain's reviewer for a license, where again the issue of melodrama's political potential surfaced, raised in one instance by O'Grady himself. In his preface to *The Fenian,* he indicates the delicate balance between so-called "unblushing" melodrama and historical commentary. "This drama is simply a Romantic Irish Love Story and has nothing to do with *Patriotic, Political,* or *Social* evils. It takes its title from the fact that the scene is laid in Ireland – and is supposed to take place during the Fenian movement which gives the opportunity for the *villain* to accuse the hero (Lieutenant Tracy) of complicity with the Fenians" (O'Grady's capitalization and emphasis).[27] Although his protestations of the drama's distance from historical fact are accurate, O'Grady's vigorous defense of the inherent fictitiousness of *The Fenian* betrays his fear of being denied a license because of the play's covert reflection of less material realities. Melodramatic excess and historical representation resided just this closely in many of O'Grady's plays, no matter how "unblushingly" fantastic or comic.

What we know today as "heroical" history plays in the Renaissance, Shakespeare's *1 Henry VI* or the anonymous *Edward III* for example, bear strong resemblance to numerous plays of J. W. Whitbread (1847–1916), the most prolific historical dramatist in Dublin at the end of the nineteenth century. There is some irony in Whitbread's self-assumed vocation as an author of Irish historical drama, given that he was English, born at Portsmouth and deceased at Scarborough. Nevertheless, as the epigraph from the *Freeman's Journal* confirms, by the early 1890s the Queen's and Whitbread's plays had become Dublin institutions. When he was not hosting touring companies (often Irish ones like O'Grady's) or reviving Boucicault's plays, Whitbread was usually producing his own. The majority of these are "historical," a term both critics and Whitbread himself used to categorize his plays. These include *Shoulder to Shoulder* (1886), *The Irishman* (1889), *The Nationalist* (1891), *Lord Edward, or '98* (1894), *The Victoria Cross* (1896), *Wolfe Tone, Rory O'More* (1900), *The Insurgent Chief* (1902), *The Ulster Hero, The Irish Dragoon, Sarsfield,* and *The French Hussar* (1906).[28] Although Whitbread did dabble occasionally in comic melodrama (*Shoulder to Shoulder, The Nationalist,* and *Willy Reilly* [1905]) and less frequently in burlesque (*Miss Maritana*

[1890]), his plays can generally be divided into two groups: those which like Boucicault's *Robert Emmet* deal tragically with Ireland's historical revolt against England (*The Ulster Hero*) and those which glorify fictional heroes fighting abroad in historical conflicts and end comically (*The Irish Dragoon*).[29] Both types depend heavily on melodramatic conventions, including sensational escape and battle scenes; both relate closely to contemporary political turmoil or interests; both furnish ample dramatic "opportunities" for patriotic speechmaking, usually by the historical hero or, in the case of *Wolfe Tone,* by the hero's equally eloquent wife. Most important, Whitbread's best plays such as *Wolfe Tone* and *The Ulster Hero* advance a myth of Irish heroism that reigned for decades in the popular imagination.[30]

Dublin newspapers during the years Whitbread managed the Queen's document the extent to which Irish interest in national history grew, particularly from 1898 through 1907, the year of his retirement. To the readers of these periodicals, history often consisted of a series of melodramatic incidents. For example, two celebrated anniversaries occur within this span — the one hundredth anniversary of the 1798 uprising and the one hundredth memorial of the death of Robert Emmet in 1803 — which prompted numerous journalistic reconstructions of famous and infamous episodes of English/Irish hostility. To commemorate Emmet's heroism, the *Weekly Freeman* published Robert Donovan's biography of Emmet in installments from Christmas 1902 through 4 July 1903. In a special St. Patrick's Day edition in 1903, the *Weekly Freeman* also printed Donovan's biography of Anne Devlin (also spelled "Ann," by Boucicault, for instance), the brave woman who aided Emmet in his attempts to escape his British pursuers and who suffered severe punishments herself, including being hanged until almost unconscious, for refusing to betray him. Here Donovan unravels in grisly detail the sadism of English methods of interrogation and confinement, comparing Anne Devlin's torture with methods of "extracting information" commonly employed by English soldiers and defended by British parliamentarians during the uprisings of 1798. This variety of historical account became common in Irish populist newspapers, and the last sentence of Donovan's biography of Anne Devlin serves as a small example of the melodramatic history many Dubliners read: "So, whenever and wherever the story of Robert Emmet's *sacrifice* is now told, there is also recalled the *faithfulness* and the *martyrdom* of Anne Devlin."[31] History thus presented was often a drama of martyrdom and sacrifice, and numerous Irish plays at the Queen's interpreted history for their audiences in precisely the same way.

Donovan's paralleling of the events of 1798 as analogues both to incidents in Emmet's life and to battle reports from the Boer War marks a crucial conjunction in Irish thought between past and present, between history and historical drama. As Whitbread's canon and the settings of *Arrah-na-Pogue* and even Yeats's later *Cathleen Ni Houlihan* (1902) suggest, the 1798 uprising provided Irish dramatists with a readily identifiable corpus of heroes, villains, and historical events. (The Fenian uprising in the 1860s, the Land League movement, and the downing of Charles Stewart Parnell similarly served as ready historical material for Irish melodramatists.) At the same time, 1798 provided historians and nationalist groups with enough ideological material to create stark narratives of English atrocity both past and present, present here being the Boer War. Not surprisingly, Henry Joy McCracken, Wolfe Tone, and Lord Edward Fitzgerald–main characters in Whitbread's dramas of 1798–appeared in many of these popular histories written for Dublin newspapers.

Several histories of non-Irish subjects written for newspapers during these years reinforced the melodramatic interpretation of history that Donovan's biographies and popular Irish drama encouraged. Calma's three-part biography of Napoleon published in the *United Irishman* on 10, 17, and 24 November 1900, for instance, concretizes the relationships between past and present and between drama and history so prevalent in Dublin at the turn of the century. Calma recalls how Napoleon wished to separate England and Ireland, making Ireland an independent republic, how the French Directory foiled Napoleon's plan to aid Wolfe Tone in liberating Ireland, and how the "merciless English" fettered the heroic Bonaparte. In the last two installments of this history, Calma articulates a historical maxim echoed by opponents of Irish participation on the side of the British in the Boer War: "The enemies of England are the friends of Ireland." He argues persuasively that "history will supply the proofs" of this assertion.[32] And Dublin theaters, most notably the Queen's, produced plays about Napoleon, especially those that romanticized his dealings with Irishmen: W. G. Wills's *Royal Divorce;* Whitbread's *Wolfe Tone* and *The Irish Dragoon;* Frank Thorne's *Napoleon the Great*, a consistent attraction at the Queen's; and Lloyd Osbourne's and Austin Strong's *Exile* (October 1903), a tragedy concerning Napoleon's final days at St. Helena in which Martin Harvey appeared at the Theatre Royal. In addition, a colored photography display, "The Rise and Fall of Napoleon," was featured at the Tivoli Theatre of Varieties in November 1903.

Irish involvement in the Boer War cemented in Irish thought the melo-dramatic nature of Ireland's historical struggle against England. Speaking before the House of Commons in October 1899, Michael Davitt condemned the Boer War as motivated by "the meanest and most mercenary of ends and aims which ever prompted conquest or aggression, and it will rank in history as the greatest crime of the nineteenth century."[33] Perhaps more than any other single event, the Boer War reaffirmed the nationalist position that fighting against England in a foreign war was, as Calma's history of Napoleon avers, striking a formidable blow for Ireland. For this reason, many Irish nationalists went to South Africa to aid the Boers. Still, British recruiting officers scoured Ireland in search of enlistees to oppose the Boers. As a consequence, the nightmarish situation emerged on South African battlefields of Irish nationalists confronting their own countrymen who had enlisted in the British army. From October 1899 through most of 1900, the Irish Transvaal Committee ran emotionally charged and ideologically rich notices in Dublin papers exhorting Irishmen at home to thwart recruiting officers' efforts. Many of their arguments mirror both the sentiment and politics of popular drama:

> Fellow Countrymen –
>   The Irishmen in England's service who are sent to South Africa will have to fight against Irish nationalists who have raised Ireland's flag in the Transvaal, and have formed an Irish Brigade to fight for the Boers against the oppressor of Ireland.
>   Remember Ninety-Eight!
>   Remember the Penal Laws!
>   Remember the Famine!
>   England's army is small. *Englishmen are not good soldiers. England has to get others to do her fighting for her.* In the past Irishmen have too often won battles for England, and saved her from defeat, and thus have rivetted the chains upon their motherland. Let them do so no more.[34]

Much like popular Irish drama, this advertisement not only reveals the growing surge of nationalism that swept turn-of-the-century Dublin but also foregrounds Irish determination to counter several specific colonialist representations of Irishness (not the least of which was inherent criminality, so pointedly adverted to by Davitt).

For example, in its interventions in British recruitment efforts for the Boer War, the Transvaal Committee manipulated the colonialist practice of feminizing Irishness to a very different ideological end. That is, the committee cleverly feminized Englishmen by maintaining that their inherent ineffectualness as soldiers necessitated the assistance of stronger and, by implication, more manly Irish recruits. In its plea to "Remember Ninety-Eight" and the patriots who resisted England then, the Transvaal Committee was to find strong allies in Boucicault and Whitbread; since many of Whitbread's plays were set in 1798, patrons of the Queen's Theatre were not likely to forget this moment in Irish history. Later, in 1915, similar lessons were being taught by P. J. Bourke's *For the Land She Loved*, a historical drama set in 1798 and performed in November for the Defence of Ireland Fund at the Abbey Theatre. Reversing feminizing representations and recalling patriotic historical personages, many known for their bravery and oratorical skill, supplemented yet another nationalist inversion of British stereotyping during the Boer War years: namely, the representation of British soldiers, not animalistic "natives," as possessing unbridled or bestial sexual appetites. One hint of this overturning flickers in Bloom's imagination after he notices a British recruiting poster in "The Lotus Eaters": "Maud Gonne's letter about taking them off O'Connell street at night: disgrace to our Irish capital. Griffith's paper is on the same tack now: an army rotten with venereal disease: overseas or halfseasover empire" (5:70–72). Here Bloom refers to Maud Gonne and the Daughters of Ireland urging Irish women not to consort with those British soldiers released from their barracks at night for a time during the Boer War to encourage recruitment. Military finery, for Gonne and the *United Irishman*, could not disguise the degenerate sexuality of the colonizer, another inversion of a colonialist stereotype (in this instance, of the promiscuity and bestiality of colonized peoples).

Reports of the fighting in South Africa verify that so-called objective historical facts can be rendered in melodramatic ways. Like the histories of Emmet, Anne Devlin, and Napoleon serialized in Dublin newspapers, reports from the Boer War in the *United Irishman* reinforced the implications of the Transvaal Committee's advertisements, with their English villains, Irish martyrs, and cowardly pro-British Irish traitors. Gallows and firing squads appeared in newspaper headlines nearly as often as they did on the stage. On 13 January 1900, to cite one example, the *United Irishman* angrily related how General Lord Methuen of the British army captured five Boers and two Irishmen, executed them, and then forced Boer prisoners to bury them. The newspaper fumed at these atrocities, terming them "a picture of unslaked, savage, cowardly hate and vengeance which entitles General

Lord Methuen to a rope and gallows in every civilized army in the world."
Other stories of Irish "scoundrels" bayoneting unarmed Irish nationalists,
of "English Skulkers Behind Irish Regiments," and of "Three Irish Regiments Butchered in a Trap" appeared in the *United Irishman* in January and
February 1900.[35] Here, again, a clear inversion of English stereotyping of
Irishness is achieved: the English, in these accounts, are "savage" and bar-
baric, something less than civilized in their military comportment. No doubt
the narratives of many of these reports were shaped from material fact, regardless of the political stance of the reporters. The point of importance
here is that in several ways these melodramatic renderings of history paral-
leled the instruction Dubliners received at the theater. Whitbread's and
others' history plays, therefore, albeit often sensational, were no more so
than the historical narratives circulated in the press. Further, their representations of "native" Irishness and Englishness consistently countered the
invidious characterizations of Irishmen promulgated by a number of Victorian texts, theatrical or otherwise.

To this point, I have used the term "melodrama" in very general ways.
My appropriation of the term insofar as it describes history or a means of
relating historical materials merely calls attention to the ways in which melodramatic and historical texts tend, unlike tragedy, to locate opposition in
a public world rather than in the internal conflicts of a tragic hero. Like
most varieties of nineteenth-century melodrama, historical drama is irreducibly public, making it vulnerable to the kinds of representations I have
described. Melodrama also slips "readily into the facile" because "man's impulse to think well of himself" renders him "susceptible" to act as a "par-
tisan against oppressive men or defective principles."[36] At the turn of the
century, the Fenian uprising of the 1860s, the Home Rule movement,
and the Boer War—to name but three—predisposed Dubliners to see the
English as "oppressive men" and British rule as replete with "defective principles." Consequently, melodrama's popularity suggests the extent of social division in Ireland at this time, for melodrama typically signals the
"breakdown" of a reality in which the individual and society cohere.[37] The
local and topical implications of Boucicault's and Whitbread's plays are there
to be read, and these finally amount to two interpretations of the historical
English/Irish opposition: Boucicault's comic plays advance an optimistic,
inherently conservative myth of reconciliation, while Whitbread's for the
most part form a tragic, at times potentially emancipatory chronicle in which
this opposition will inevitably continue. Equally important, both playwrights

create dramas in which the status of native Irishness is elevated, offering effective counterrepresentations to especially loathesome Victorian caricatures of Irishmen.

HISTORY AND THE MYTH OF RECONCILIATION

In their magnification of the historical hero, Whitbread's plays are more closely aligned with traditional notions of historical drama. By comparison, Boucicault's Irish plays might appear far removed from historical or political drama.[38] Not so. Even *The Colleen Bawn*, the least political and historical of Boucicault's three best-known Irish plays, is composed of elements that an Irish audience would find of political interest. Admittedly, in many respects, *The Colleen Bawn*, based on Gerald Griffin's novel *The Collegians* (1828), differs very little from popular French plays of intrigue and from the sensational melodrama for which Boucicault would become famous, indeed. Like his earlier play *The Octoroon*, O'Grady's *Eviction*, and Whitbread's *Nationalist*, *The Colleen Bawn*'s plot centers on dispossession and love: Hardress Cregan, secretly married to Eily O'Connor, must find some way to escape the marriage and marry the wealthy Anne Chute if he is to save his family home from foreclosure by the merciless Corrigan, who holds a mortgage on the Cregan property and is eager to seize it. Typical of the melodramatic villain's corrupt sexuality, Corrigan would reconsider if Hardress's widowed, hence powerless, mother agreed to marry him. Misunderstanding Cregan's plans to save his home, his friend Danny Mann attempts to intimidate Eily into forsaking her marriage certificate, one of several important documents upon which the play's action depends. Eily refuses and Danny hurls her into one of the lakes of Killarney. Fortunately, Myles-na-Coppaleen, Boucicault's Stage Irishman, is nearby attending his still; when he hears Eily's scream of distress, he shoots Danny Mann (almost accidentally) and in the most sensational scene in the play saves the girl's life. By the end of *The Colleen Bawn*, Corrigan's villainy is exposed; Hardress repents of his callous treatment of Eily, and his mother also apologizes for her class-based antagonism toward Eily; and Anne Chute chooses Hardress's best friend, Kyrle Daly, as a husband, the man she has loved all along and misjudged too often. The world of the play will finally not admit too much unhappiness.

But *The Colleen Bawn* goes beyond melodrama and sensationalism to touch upon issues of contemporary importance to Irishmen. One of these is the preservation of Irish dialect, a greater issue later in the century during the Gaelic movement. Important to this preservation is Myles-na-Coppaleen, who is more closely related to the drunken, shiftless Stage Irishman than are Boucicault's later Irishmen. Loaded with song, poteen, and expressions like "begorra," "avourneen," and "acushla," Myles is the antithesis of Hardress Cregan, the young, serious-minded, and Anglicized protagonist. What is endearing in Myles, however, is not in Eily, at least in Hardress's view, as her Irish pronunciation causes him embarrassment early in the play. Try as she may, Eily cannot speak the Anglicized vernacular of Hardress's middle class. Even the more refined Anne Chute expends considerable effort suppressing her Irishness: "When I am angry the brogue comes out, and my Irish heart will burst through manners, and graces, and twenty stay-laces" (*DB* 73). For Myles and his old friend Father Tom, song, whiskey, and blarney are all that remain of old Ireland; thus when Eily dejectedly reports to the good priest that Hardress has demanded she not sing Irish songs because the words are "vulgar," Father Tom prescribes a remedy echoed by countless Stage Irishmen: "Put your lips to that jug; there's only the sthrippens left. Drink! and while that thrue Irish liquor warms your heart, take this wid it. May the brogue of ould Ireland niver forsake your tongue—may her music niver lave your voice—and may a true Irishwoman's virtue niver die in your heart!" (*DB* 65). The play's comic conclusion celebrates the legitimization of Irish speech as Eily is reunited to a husband chastened by Myles's devotion and newly appreciative of his wife's Irishness:

> EILY (to Hardress):   And ye won't be ashamed of me?
> ANNE: I'll be ashamed of him if he does.
> EILY: And when I spake—no—speak—
> ANNE: Spake is the right sound. Kyrle Daly, pronounce that word.
> KYRLE: That's right; if you ever spake it any other way I'll divorce ye—mind that. (*DB* 103)

Myles's heroics make such an ending possible. He has, therefore, not only entertained the audience and saved the heroine but also helped restore native dialect to his fellow countrymen.

Perhaps not so clearly emblematic of Irish nationalism as the characters in historical drama, the male and female leads in *The Colleen Bawn* anticipate their virtues. Indeed, Eily O'Connor functions emblematically as both Virtue betrayed and Ireland forsaken, lacking both the earthy self-reliance of Anne Chute and the courage of Anne Devlin. Yet as idealized by Danny Mann, Eily combines Irish beauty with angelic perfection: "The looking-glass was never made that could do her justice; and if St. Patrick wanted a wife, where would he find an angel that 'ud compare with the Colleen Bawn. As I row her on the lake, the little fishes come up to look at her; and the wind from heaven lifts up her hair to see what the devil brings her down here at all–at all" (*DB* 57). The "devil" in this play is Corrigan, unwittingly aided by Mann himself; together they very nearly destroy virtue in this play, in part because Cregan cannot act decisively. In contrast to Cregan's weakness, Myles's heroism, albeit cloddish, shines as brightly as Eily's ethereal beauty. This heroism finds a more grandiloquent vehicle for expression in the Irish history play and replaces hard-drinking and comical vernacular as the primary characteristic of Whitbread's historical Irishmen. The reunion at the end of *The Colleen Bawn*, then, signals not only a happy future for the young lovers but the restoration of a native Irishness threatened by dispossession of both home and language. Eily's vernacular may not be Irish, but it is a variety of English which Boucicault's peasants can claim as their own.

But these are merely general indications of Boucicault's sociopolitical vision and nationalist sentiment in *The Colleen Bawn;* historical references to the Irish uprisings in 1798 or the Act of Union which prompted them are absent from the playscript. In fact, the only character and action in the play that can be construed as having a historical base–an extratextual referent in contemporary Irish politics or history–are Corrigan and his land-grabbing tactics. Avaricious Irish landlords and process servers were almost always connected in Irish thought to England's colonial oppression. In a meeting of Irish leaders in April 1903 to discuss the Land Bill, Michael Davitt argued that Irish landlords "have been England's mainstay in Ireland and the deadliest enemies of the Irish national cause." He added that he greatly preferred to fight an Englishman, whose motives he could understand, than to do battle with a "gang of recreants who have been false to their blood and to their country."[39] Corrigan clearly qualifies as one of these, and his employment of British soldiers in an attempt to enforce his villainy places him squarely on the England side of the England/Ireland opposition that evolves much more fully in *Arrah-na-Pogue* and *The Shaughraun*.

Arrah-na-Pogue, Boucicault's next Irish play, more explicitly reveals his concern with Ireland's history under colonial rule, even though it resembles *The Colleen Bawn* in several respects: the plots of both plays center around pairs of lovers, a pair of obstructing villains, and the vitality and heroic potential of the Stage Irishman. Both plays end comically with the promise of marriage and freedom from the legal problems that loomed ominously earlier. Yet essential differences in characterization distinguish these two similar plays, the most significant of which concerns Shaun the Post, Myles-na-Coppaleen's counterpart in *Arrah-na-Pogue*. In *The Colleen Bawn*, Myles tends his still in a cave, returning to Irish society only long enough to give Father Tom a keg of liquor. His saving of Eily results from chance as much as anything else: had Danny Mann not led her to a remote cave by one of the lakes, Myles could not possibly have helped her. Shaun, by contrast, leaps into the thick of the action in *Arrah-na-Pogue*. He trusts Arrah's virtue and is imprisoned for confessing to a crime he did not commit. Further, while Myles's function as the agent of comedy and song includes the singing of ballads extolling the beauty of Ireland and its women, Shaun's similar position includes the more direct articulation of nationalistic sentiment. For this purpose, Boucicault adapts the famous anthem of the 1798 rebellion, "The Wearing of the Green," and Shaun's singing of it in act 1 associates him with the nationalist movement. (This song was excised from many productions of the play in the British Isles because its singing appeared subversive of British colonial authority.) In addition, Shaun's language occupies a middle position between Myles's Gaelicisms and Cregan's Anglicized vernacular; he seems equally skilled at "natural" wit and rhetorical sophistication. At Shaun's trial in act 2, O'Grady makes this very point in deciding upon his guilt:

> O'GRADY: I'm for letting him off.
> MAJOR COFFIN: On what grounds?
> O'GRADY: The eloquence of his defense.
> MAJOR COFFIN: I regret to say that we cannot admit so Irish a consideration. (*DB* 153)

In a manner in which Myles's discourse would not permit him, Shaun becomes one of the first in a long line of Irish heroes in historical drama to speak at the dock, invigorating a more refined eloquence with the liveliness of Irish dialect. Oratorical skill and rhetorical sophistication become encoded later in popular Irish drama as civilizing attributes of both histori-

cal heroes like Robert Emmet and Wolfe Tone *and* comic Irishmen like Shaun
the Post (and also reign as a prime topic for debate, as is the case in the
"Aeolus" episode of *Ulysses*).

It is, I believe, the increasing verbal sophistication of characters like
Boucicault's Shaun and Conn that distinguishes them from the more broadly
comic character featured in a number of Whitbread and O'Grady plays, the
"Wild Irish Boy," who in significant ways serves as a prototype for several
characters of both O'Casey and Synge. In his early play *The Gommock* (1877),
for example, O'Grady develops such a character: "a quare boy, fond of fairies,
fortune-telling, fighting, and fun. For draming [sic], dancing, singing and
jumping there isn't his match in the county." Similarly physically adept,
especially at thrashing lecherous process servers, are Hughey in O'Grady's
Emigration and Denny O'Hea in Whitbread's *Nationalist*. All of these
characters also possess linguistic gifts equal to their pugilistic endowments –
but sophistication is not one of them. Rather, such characters delighted
audiences by bettering their adversaries with puns and native wit, just as
they trounced them with their superior physical skills. In *The Gommock* Larry
warns the villainous Hickey, "I'll put my fist through you and shake hands
with the wall"; in *Emigration,* Hughey promises Jerry Naylor, who attempts
to prevent a peasant family from emigrating to America, that he will be "flat-
tened like a pancake" if he continues his selfish obstruction; in *The Nationalist* Denny catches Paddy Flynn, a leering land agent and attorney, forcing
a kiss from an innocent country girl. Administering a "kiss ov anodther sort,"
Denny knocks Flynn to the ground. While throwing the villain in a wash-
tub and generally knocking him about, Denny promises him a "taste ov
the science ov boxology" before the coward runs off.[40] Then Flynn's partner
Matthew Sheehan stumbles upon the scene, his pockets brimming with
"writs of ejectment" and his mouth running with calumnies about Denny's
beloved, Peggy Donohue. When Flynn reappears saying he has had an "ocu-
lar demonstration" of Peggy's infidelity, Denny punches him, adding that
Flynn has now received a "knockular demonstration" to the contrary. Such
scenes with their knockabout humor combined vigorous stage action with
punning figures of speech to amuse Irish audiences and to give them the
satisfaction of seeing strapping rustic boys box the ears of greedy lawyers
and unscrupulous landlords. But this variety of comic Irishman, closely related to Boucicault's, seems less heroic, less nationalistic than Shaun the Post
or Conn.

More significant, at least for my purposes, are the anticolonial dimensions of such scenes and characters. Craven process servers and barristers like Flynn and Sheehan appear routinely as informants and traitors to the Irish cause in Whitbread's historical dramas, typically claiming legal authority and the power of Dublin Castle in enforcing their self-interest. Beyond their cowardice, duplicity, and rhetorical enfeeblement, such characters are frequently effeminate or physically inferior to both comic and historically significant Irishmen. In Whitbread's *Wolfe Tone,* for instance, Joey Rafferty, an attorney at law in "castle pay" who serves as an accomplice to Samuel Turner, a barrister and informant who has gained admission to the United Irishmen, is described as puny and almost pesky, an "imp of inequity" and a "monkey faced villain." When Shane McMahon, Tone's loyal and heroic servant, confronts Rafferty in act 1, he threatens "to lave the stamp ov me knuckle" on Rafferty's "ugly nose." Shane is urged on by Peggy Ryan, who becomes Mrs. Tone's maid and later Shane's wife, with "Ye're a better man than I thought ye were. Hit him hard." Here the native Irishman is manly, the villain effeminate; the Irishman attractive, the villain "monkey faced"; the Irishman verbally clever, the villain more pedestrian – and the Irishman morally correct, the villain, a representative of a ruthless colonial authority. The villain's feminization is completed later in the play when Peggy, finding herself alone and flourishing a menacing broom, threatens to "spiflicate" one of Rafferty and Turner's accomplices.[41] A "wild Irish girl" is more courageous than an effeminate adversary, and many colonialist representations of native Irishness are effectively refuted.

Like the more sophisticated Stage Irishman, the leading male and female characters in *Arrah-na-Pogue* reflect Boucicault's heightened emphasis on history and nationalism. Not surprisingly, given the play's political tone, the truly eloquent figure in *Arrah-na-Pogue* is not Shaun but Beamish Mac Coul, the young Irish hero who has returned from America to lead Irish rebels against the English. Compared to his predecessor Hardress Cregan in *The Colleen Bawn,* Mac Coul is a patriot who can also articulate his nationalist ardor in eloquent English. Mac Coul's impassioned speeches early in the play prefigure the ascendance of this character in Irish history plays: "Oh, my land! My own land! Bless every blade of grass upon your green cheeks! The clouds that hang over ye are the sighs of your exiled children, and your face is always wet with their tears" (*DB* 115). In his patriotic fervor and courage, Mac Coul overshadows the Anglicized and cowardly Hardress Cregan. As was the case with the patriotic hero, Arrah, the active, patriotic woman, will replace in many history plays the helpless Eily O'Connors around whom the dramatic action of various types of melodrama revolves. Like Eily, Arrah will sacrifice her life if it means the safety or happiness of the people she loves, and she *does* faint at moments of high dramatic tension. But she would also "be proud to stand anywhere," even the gallows, with her half-brother Mac Coul—sentiments she hurls at his British pursuers. Like Shaun and Mac Coul, Arrah, the inheritor of many of the characteristics of her melodramatic ancestors, might better be regarded as an early example of a new Stage Irishwoman. Neither a shrew leading comic Irishmen by the nose nor a hapless victim, Arrah is a more complex woman who is part Eily O'Connor and part Anne Devlin.

The villains in *Arrah-na-Pogue*, Michael Feeny and Major Coffin, serve also to anticipate even more reprehensible figures in the popular Dublin history play: the avaricious Irishman in the service of the British government and the overzealous British officer. As malicious as both Coffin and Feeny are, however, this type of character evolves even more sinisterly into Harvey Duff, the police informer in *The Shaughraun*, and into the Judas-like betrayer in both Victorian historical drama and Whitbread's Irish plays. To attract audiences to the Queen's Theatre, touring companies entrusted the roles of villains to their most skilled character actors. In an 1884 revival of Boucicault's plays, for example, Shiel Barry as Feeny and Harvey Duff shared the limelight with Charles Sullivan (one of O'Casey's favorites) as Shaun and Conn. Playgoers loved to boo these characters, and Dublin critics in the 1880s were often generous in their praise of actors who could so thoroughly provoke an audience's hatred. One review in the *Freeman's Journal* of Shiel Barry as Feeny makes this critical admiration clear: "In Mr. Shiel Barry the ideal Michael Feeny is found, and it is the highest praise this sterling actor could desire to trace the deep hatred and disgust which his master villainy—in the play—excites among the gods" (15 July 1884). These commendations indicate precisely where theater managers placed the *theatrical emphasis* of Boucicault's plays—squarely on exaggerated portrayals of the Stage Irishman and the villain. But it would be misguided, I think, to assume that Boucicault's *dramatic emphasis* remained either solely sensational or constant throughout the writing of his three major Irish dramas or that audiences were unaffected by political events of the latter half of the nineteenth century. The politically turbulent years spanning the composition of *The Colleen Bawn* and *The Shaughraun* effected particular strain on relations between England and Ireland. Boucicault's Irish dramas reflect this strain and communicate with particular force to Dublin audiences all too aware of their subordinate political status and the everyday hardships caused by economic conditions at home.

The Shaughraun, in which Boucicault weaves contemporary events and tensions into the texture of his comic melodramas, carries the nationalist trajectory of his work even further. The play is set in Ireland immediately after the Fenian uprising in 1867 and two widely publicized episodes of Fenian attacks in England: the bombing at Clerkenwell prison and the rescue attempt at Manchester in which the release of imprisoned Irishmen resulted, ironically, in the capture and ultimate execution of their nationalist rescuers. By August 1875, when *The Shaughraun* began a successful run at London's Drury Lane Theatre (it had opened the previous November at Wallack's Theatre in New York), the harsh British response to both the Fenian bombing at Clerkenwell and the raid at Manchester had dissipated. But as Norman McCord points out, and Marx's and Engels's reactions to the Clerkenwell episode indicate, shortly after these incidents public opinion in London concerning Irish nationalism was bitter indeed. Editorials in the *Times* and elsewhere indicted the Fenians and called for sharp reprisals against them: "As to the Fenian conspiracy itself, it must be evident that the time is past for clemency and forebearance. With traitors and assassins there can be but one course."[42] British newspapers condemned Fenianism as indicative of "the outrageous egotism, the shortsightedness, and downright folly of an exaggerated national sentiment," and in 1869 the *Quarterly Review* censured Gladstone's "ill-judged lenity in dealing with Fenian criminals."[43] From comments such as these, McCord accurately infers that there existed a "great deal" of "clear evidence of anti-Irish feeling" in Britain in the late 1860s and 1870s; and, as Curtis demonstrates, this feeling led to the 1860s becoming a "pivotal point" in the alteration of stereotyping of Irishmen from the humble and always entertaining Paddy to the more sinister, decidedly apish, nationalist prepared to commit whatever atrocity necessary to liberate his country.[44] Yet, at the same time, *The Shaughraun* did exceptionally well in London, even though it encourages audiences to cheer at Conn's escape from the violent end many felt Irish nationalists deserved. In fact, Kinchela and Harvey Duff, the play's villains, count on an increased English hostility toward Irish nationalists after the Fenian raids to rid them of the meddlesome Conn:

> DUFF: Oh! whew! The soldiers will not dhraw a trigger on him barrin' a magistrate is by to give the ordher.

KINCHELA: But the police will. You will go at once to the police barracks at Sligo, pick your men, tell 'em you apprehended an attempt at rescue. The late attack on the police-van at Manchester, and the explosions at Clerkenwell prison in London will warrant extreme measures. (*DB* 200)

Of course, characters like Conn are scarcely so terrifying as Fenian bombers, and evidently Londoners felt Conn deserved better than the "one course" of punishment for which the *Times* clamored. He could not be taken too seriously as a menace to the empire.

Boucicault, however, took these matters seriously. In January 1876, in what may have been partly a publicity stunt, he wrote an open letter to Prime Minister Benjamin Disraeli demanding the release of Irish political prisoners from British prisons. When touring companies carried *The Shaughraun* to the provinces, Boucicault asked that they give special benefit performances to aid the families of imprisoned Fenians.[45] Some may be tempted to object that, after all, *The Shaughraun* is a comic melodrama and for this reason bears little relationship to Boucicault's more serious sympathy for Irish nationalism. Perhaps, but in the cases of Boucicault's three Irish plays, it is possible to detect behind these plots his growing awareness of Ireland's long struggle against England. The world of *The Colleen Bawn*, for instance, includes no police spies, no exiled nationalists, no overt fears of atrocities to prisoners—in short, no deep chasm between England and Ireland, although desperate financial problems exist for Cregan and his mother, and Corrigan, the "scalpeen" who would profit from his countrymen's dilemmas, seeks the assistance of an English constabulary force in pursuing his avarice. The world of *The Shaughraun* is decidedly more politicized, more concerned with recent historical events and English/Irish opposition.

In short, Boucicault's *Arrah-na-Pogue* and *The Shaughraun* contain ideological material and historical perspective that most comic melodrama lacks. If this were not the case, why were efforts made to block their production in England at moments of unrest between England and Ireland? Again, although both plays provide exciting escapes and rescues, frolicking comedy, and all the resolution and closure that traditionally draw audiences to melodrama, none of these attributes alone or in combination explain the enduring popularity of these plays in Dublin. As I have described, part of this appeal results less from the theatrical vividness of melodrama—the principal means by which audiences are putatively transported out of their sociohistorical "real" and relocated in an escapist fantasy supposedly divorced from the "real"–than from the plays' political immediacy and historical grounding, several features of which distinguish Boucicault's Irish dramas from traditional comedy and melodrama and bring them closer to the generic domain of the history play.

First, comedy (and, by extension, much domestic melodrama), as Herbert Lindenberger maintains, is for the most part "set not only in the historical present but in the very cities in which their audiences are assembled."[46] With the notable exceptions of Shakespearean romantic comedy and of Elizabethan comic fantasies like *Endymion* or *Mucedorus,* Lindenberger's point seems well taken. Jacobean city comedy, most comedies of manners, and much modern comedy–T. W. Robertson, early Shaw, much of Pinero and Wilde, for instance–serve to a significant extent to verify the insight of Lindenberger's observation. Many of Noël Coward's or Neil Simon's comedies and the "screwball comedy" films of the 1930s and 1940s– *The Awful Truth* (1937), *The Philadelphia Story* (1940), *His Girl Friday* (1939), and others–might also be added to this list. Conversely, both of Boucicault's plays are set during key historical periods in the history of Irish rebellion, *Arrah-na-Pogue* in 1798 and *The Shaughraun* during the Fenian uprising in the 1860s. Each play is also set primarily in the Irish countryside, not in Dublin, and the association of Irish insurgence with the pastoral values of the "green world" is reinforced throughout both plays.

Second, although *Arrah-na-Pogue, The Shaughraun,* and Edmund Falconer's popular *Peep o'Day* (1861) all end in ways typical of romantic comedy–with festivity, the renewal of love or the promise of marriage (the promise of multiple marriages in *The Shaughraun*), and the resolution of difficulties that prevented the lovers' relationship–the nature of reconciliation in these plays differs significantly from that of romantic comedy. The dominant opposition in most romantic comedy is youth/age; by the end of a romantic comedy, young lovers finally overcome parental or archaic social objections to their union. Although the youth/age opposition contributes in some ways to the conflict in these plays, the most formidable opposition to Boucicault's lovers joining is English/Irish. To be sure, Boucicault's plays have their share both of Irish informants and of more traditional blocking *senex* figures, also Irish, who will exchange mortgages or monetary gain for the sexual favors of pure Irishwomen. But these characters–Michael Feeny in *Arrah-na-Pogue* and particularly Corrigan in *The Colleen Bawn*–are linked explicitly to an English/Irish opposition that must be collapsed. And in Boucicault's myth of reconciliation they are. In *Arrah-na-Pogue*, O'Grady, an Irish official, secures pardons for Beamish Mac Coul and Shaun from a generous British secretary. The pardon ultimately allows Shaun to marry Arrah. Casting the colonial government in Dublin Castle in such a favorable light represents one instance of the breaking down of English/Irish tension in the play.[47]

The situation is somewhat more convoluted in *The Shaughraun*. Robert Ffolliott, attempting to escape British troops, is pardoned by "Her Majesty," but the Irish villains Duff and Kinchela conceal the pardon, then abduct Ffolliott's betrothed, Arte O'Neal, and Moya Dolan, Conn's lover. With the help of Captain Molineux, an exemplary young British officer in love with Ffolliott's sister Claire, Conn rescues the women and apprehends the villains. Molineux's heroism outweighs his Britishness, and Ffolliott consents to Molineux's marriage to Claire. In a similarly magnanimous way, Molineux's dealings with Ffolliott are devoid of the hostility with which many Britons regarded the Fenian movement. *Peep o'Day* continues the flow of pardons for nationalist insurgents, this time awarded at the close of the play by yet another gracious British officer. Harry Kavanaugh, the leader of the rebels in *Peep o'Day*, wins not only a pardon but also the hand of Mary Grace because of his "noble conduct" in laying down his arms in surrender to British officers. The comic endings of these plays thus rely heavily on a resolution to the British/Irish opposition.

Third, Boucicault neutralizes specific instances of social and historical division other than the English/Irish polarization in these plays. One of these, the at times adversarial stance of the Catholic church toward nationalism, Jack Boyle explains vehemently to Joxer Daly in O'Casey's *Juno and the Paycock:* "I'm goin' to tell you somethin', Joxer, that I wouldn't tell to anybody else – the clergy always had too much power over the people in this unfortunate country" (*CP* 1:24). Boyle continues, "Didn't they [the clergy] prevent the people in '47 from seizin' the corn, an' they starvin'; didn't they down Parnell; didn't they say that hell wasn't hot enough nor eternity long enough to punish the Fenians? We don't forget, we don't forget them things, Joxer" (*CP* 1:24–25). Later in *Juno and the Paycock*, after he thinks he has inherited a substantial sum of money, Boyle will find it quite easy to forget "them things." So do the audiences of Boucicault's plays (though of course Boucicault wrote these before the Parnell–Kitty O'Shea scandal). Many powerful churchmen (Archbishop Paul Cullen of Dublin for instance) denounced the Fenians, however, and Boyle correctly attributes the infamous

"Hell is not hot enough" condemnation to a cleric, Bishop David Moriarty of Kerry.[48] None of this vituperation taints Father Dolan's actions in *The Shaughraun;* and, indeed, Irish priests appear in the vanguard of patriotic insurgence in the Queen's Irish drama, Father Kelly in O'Grady's *The Fenian* and Father John Murphy in Bourke's *When Wexford Rose* (1910), for instance. In O'Grady's play the alliance of the clergy and nationalist movement is made explicitly by Father Kelly who, while being arrested so as to be unable to marry the play's aristocratic young hero to his beloved of the peasant class, urges an angry crowd to restrain itself. He does so by proclaiming his readiness to suffer for his cause, following in the steps of self-abnegating clerics and Irish nationalists alike: "My good people, I beg you to restrain your feelings. . . . I am not afraid to face the prison cell or the plank bed as many of my countrymen have done before for daring to do their duty to their country or their creed."[49] Throughout *The Shaughraun,* in fact, Dolan's affection for Ffolliott supersedes any clerical or official concern about membership in a secret society or the use of violence to achieve emancipatory ends, two of the Church's objections to Fenianism. In a more general sense, Father Tom in *The Colleen Bawn* stands as a figure of consolation and even good humor. Both priests playfully admonish the Stage Irishman for his human frailties, but neither priest hesitates to share a drink with him or to offer sanctuary to a nationalist friend.

Excluding perhaps military spectacles and lavishly produced melodramas about Nelson and Napoleon at London's Astley's Theatre or Royal Circus, Boucicault's Irish dramas seem more politically and historically constituted than most varieties of melodrama or romantic comedy. Perhaps most modern readers fail to recognize this because, as Lindenberger asserts, "we rarely think of history as comedy"; modern readers are much more accustomed to see "tragedy as an action in historical dress."[50] For this reason, plays like Boucicault's appear completely unrelated to history as it is usually depicted on the stage. In *Arrah-na-Pogue* and *The Shaughraun* just the opposite is the case: underlying both plays resides the history of Ireland's struggle and a mythology that Ireland can be unified socially, politically, and religiously. This myth is usually transmitted in plays whose narrative posits the peaceful coexistence of England and Ireland—and implicitly asserts the power of humanity and truth to topple national, social, and economic barriers. This myth of optimism and cohesion obviously appealed to an Irish audience that had confronted far too many insurmountable difficulties outside of the theater and, recalling Hall's point, offered a nostalgic, in part politi-

cally conservative retreat to Dubliners. The threads of a more radical, emancipatory ideology are also visible in the fabric of such plays, however, ones
made even more apparent in more tragic Irish drama at the Queen's.

THE MYTH OF THE HISTORICAL HERO

When J. W. Whitbread assumed the management of the Queen's Theatre
in 1884, popular Irish drama gained an important ally. Until his retirement
in April 1907, Whitbread frequently revived Boucicault's and such other Irish
comedies as Buckstone's *The Green Bushes*, Falconer's *Eileen Oge* (1871), and
Peep o'Day. Yet, at the same time that Dublin audiences supported performances of these and similar plays, Boucicault and Whitbread turned away
from the essentially comic conventions of *Arrah-na-Pogue* and *The Colleen
Bawn*, appropriating material instead from Ireland's often unfortunate, even
tragic, history. Whitbread wrote some comic melodrama – *Willy Reilly* and
quasi-historical adaptations of Irish novels like *The Irish Dragoon* – that alternated in repertory with more political or historical dramas. But plays like
Boucicault's *Robert Emmet*, albeit not a commercial success in 1884 when
Boucicault wrote it, and Whitbread's extremely popular *The Ulster Hero* represent the new direction dramatizations of Irish history took at the turn
of the twentieth century.

Before Whitbread's management, the Queen's produced Irish entertainments of the crude "blarney and blather" variety that Bernard Shaw reviled in his later memories of the Dublin theater of his boyhood. From its
first year of operation in 1844 under the management of John Charles Joseph, the Queen's financial condition seemed almost always precarious.
Joseph, whose management was marked by failure, let the theater first to
John Harris and then to Charles Dillon in 1852, who later was followed
by Henry Webb and finally Whitbread. In 1854, for example, under Dillon's
management the Queen's produced S. C. Hall's *The Groves of Blarney*, advertised as "illustrative of Irish love and life in 1720." The play included such
songs as "The Blarney," "Aileen Mavourneen," and "Irish Invitation" and
seemed to present a "mythical land" completely divorced from the turmoil
and harsher realities of nineteenth-century Ireland. But lumping this kind
of play together with O'Grady's more topical melodramas, Whitbread's often
heroical history plays, or even Boucicault's Irish comedies ignores the shift-
ing political and theatrical realities of late nineteenth-century Ireland. In

this more volatile atmosphere charged with nationalist sentiment, the clod-hopping Stage Irishman, too much indolence and shiftiness, were unmarketable theatrical commodities. And when the Queen's Theatre ventured too near this retrograde figure or those stereotypical defects of Irish character which he communicated, reviewers' censures were immediate and direct. During Easter Week of 1903, for example, Whitbread sponsored a playwriting competition and awarded Robert Johnston one hundred pounds for creating the best drama on a patriotic theme. Whitbread produced Johnston's play (*The Old Land*), which unfortunately included a rowdy scene at a public house. Even critics generally laudatory of Whitbread's productions were quick to denounce such denigrating pictures of Irishmen. The reviewer for the *Freeman's Journal* suggested that a "table covered with bottles, presumably of strong drink, and suggestive of deep potations, is an accessory that might very well be dispensed with." He also objected strenuously to scenes in Johnston's play which "display a tendency to follow on the line of the conventional Stage Irishman and Irishwoman, a creation never popular among Irish audiences, and now perhaps less so than ever." For, in fact, the drunken caperer led by the nose by his shrewish wife *did not* attract crowds to Whitbread's theater—nor, to any great extent, did blarney, blather, or mythical lands.

Large audiences were attracted to Whitbread's theater by entertainments they were not able to enjoy at either the Gaiety Theatre or Theatre Royal. To begin, both Boucicault's *Robert Emmet* and Whitbread's plays about Henry Joy McCracken, Michael Dwyer, Wolfe Tone, and other heroes of Ireland's past contain nationalist and tragic sentiments common to their antecedents in other eras and cultures when historical drama thrived. In several respects Whitbread's emphasis on the national hero resembles the emphases of the heroical history plays of Elizabethan England, although adducing similarities in literature from two so widely divergent cultures is often a risky enterprise. Nevertheless, Wolfe Tone, Michael Dwyer, Patrick Sarsfield, and Henry Joy McCracken in Whitbread's plays fight for a free Ireland as valiantly and unselfishly as Talbot in Shakespeare's *1 Henry VI* and Edward the Black Prince in the anonymous *Edward III* fight for England. Bravery and self-sacrifice are conventional attributes of Whitbread's historical Irishmen—and, in some cases, of their loyal and usually entertaining servants, a vestige both of comic melodrama and of numerous nineteenth-century novels (Mickey Free in Charles Lever's *Charles O'Malley* [1840], for instance, which Whitbread adapted in his *The Irish Dragoon*).

Sarsfield, for example, begins with a villainous Dutch nobleman's disparagement of the Irish general. His malevolence is quickly answered by a loyal Irishwoman, whose retort typifies the way Whitbread depicted Ireland's historical heroes: "I know that he has sacrificed Home, Estates, Money, for the cause he has at heart—Ireland's good. Three years ago he was a rich man. Now he has but his sword with which to carve his way to fortune. . . . The man you malign is an honourable Irish Gentleman and deserving of a commendation, not contumely, even from a foe."[51] In addition to such rhetoric, the opening act features curtain-lowering excitement: just as the curtain drops, Sarsfield's loyal servant "Gallopin'" Terry Hogan and his fellow nationalists save the general from a Dutch trap. Act 2 closes with a similar rescue preceded by similar praise of the general, this time in reference to Sarsfield's considerable and class-blind ability as a leader of men: "Surely Ireland ought to be proud of such a general. And as for the soldiers, Terry says they fairly worship him—he's that good and kind to them." *Sarsfield* concludes in 1691 with the fall of Limerick and, sadly, with Sarsfield's forced departure for France. His comic servant, the counterpart of such clever and heroic servants as Mickey Free in *The Irish Dragoon* and Shane McMahon in *Wolfe Tone*, here is reduced to a minor character who is unable to wrest a comic resolution from this particular historical episode—one in which thousands of Irishmen emigrated to the Continent after the signing of the Treaty of Limerick. Rather than enjoying the kind of closure engineered in Boucicault's comic plays by such characters as Myles and Shaun, therefore, an Irish audience receives somewhat different satisfactions from many of Whitbread's plays: theatrical excitement, to be sure, usually derived from the same sources as in Boucicault's dramas, and also a myriad of reasons for nationalist pride, the historical hero's bravery and self-sacrifice being paramount among these.

Because Irish patriots actually conspired to overthrow an oppressive English regime, Whitbread and Boucicault frequently employed the secret meetings, sacred oaths, and betrayals of trust that commonly appear in historical dramas of conspiracy and resistance (*Julius Caesar*, Thomas Otway's *Venice Preserved*, Georg Büchner's *Danton's Death*, and the like). Such is the case in *Lord Edward, or '98* when in act 1 Napper Tandy, Lord Edward, and other United Irishmen meet in Paris to secure the assistance of the French Directory. By act 2 Edward has married and moved back to Dublin, and news arrives that French soldiers are on the move to support the Irish nationalists. This good news, however, is carried to Dublin Castle by the treacherous Francis Magan, a trusted friend of Lord Edward. For the next two acts, Edward seeks refuge from his relentless pursuers, who, aided by Magan's intelligence, are never far behind him. The play ends with the title character's receipt of a mortal wound during a confrontation with his opponents, his incarceration at Newgate Gaol, and his demise sixteen days later. Through all this, the Irish historical hero remains a figure in which Dubliners could take pride, deciding nobly like many of his tragic predecessors between love and duty, personal safety and the risks entailed with nationalist insurgence.

Plays like *Robert Emmet* provided all of these theatrical and ideological attractions and more. Although it relies heavily on the melodramatic opposition between Irish nationalism and its typical opponents (Irish traitors and British tyrants), this is perhaps its only resemblance to Boucicault's earlier work. Most important, *Robert Emmet* is essentially a heroical tragedy. That is, only Danny Mann in *The Colleen Bawn* dies during the course of the comedies; in *Emmet,* the informer Quigley, the noble Lord Kilwarden, Emmet's loyal friend Andy Devlin (Anne's brother), and Emmet himself are killed. To provide a comic ending for any of his characters, Boucicault was forced to alter well-known historical fact, which he does in the case of Michael Dwyer and Anne Devlin, who escape to America in Boucicault's play before Emmet is executed—but only after Anne has suffered brutal treatment by the villainous Major Sirr and helped Dwyer kill Quigley. The play contains no Conn or Myles to rescue young rebels or hapless heroines at the last minute. In fact, the simple world of Myles-na-Coppaleen with its ballads and jugs of whiskey is replaced by one in which wholesale betrayal and sadistic punishment dominate. Like many Victorian history plays, W. G. Wills's *Charles the First* or Tennyson's *Becket* for instance, *Robert Emmet* centers around a historical character's staunch sense of values and the high price of martyrdom he must inevitably pay. Blarney becomes eloquence in this play, an eloquence aspiring to that of conspiratorial heroes of other serious historical drama, Shakespeare's Brutus or Otway's Pierre for instance. One such instance is Emmet's comparison of the present rebellion with Ireland's heroical past. "If you [Emmet's men] stand by me you must march as children of Erin, as United Irishmen, whose one hope is freedom; not as banditti, whose sole object is plunder. The green flag that led our countrymen at Fontenoy under Sarsfield has never been dishonored, and it shall not be so under Robert Emmet, so help me God" (286).[52] Emmet's allusion to Sarsfield's heroics locates the rebellion within the chronicles of a glorious national past. Moreover, throughout the play Emmet compares Irish rebellion to the French Revolution, to America's struggle for independence, and to other appropriately honorable uprisings. Far from living in a world of blather and comedy, therefore, Robert Emmet stands as a Christ figure betrayed by some of his own men, as a Napoleon, Brutus, or Washington in the midst of a battle for freedom, as an Irish hero descending from Sarsfield and Irish chronicle—*not* from Myles-na-Coppaleen.

Although the central focus in *Robert Emmet* is on Emmet, other characters common to Boucicault's earlier plays appear as well. In her courage and nationalistic sentiment, Anne Devlin resembles Arrah; however, her assistance in murdering Quigley *and* her enforced emigration eradicate the idealism of Boucicault's earlier plays. Similarly, Sarah Curran, Emmet's romantic opposite, and Tiney Wolfe demonstrate their courage throughout the play. There is no Stage Irishwoman here leading a besotted husband by the nose—only brave women whose loyalty and values parallel Emmet's. Clearly, the stage villains in *Robert Emmet* originate from Boucicault's earlier plays; however, their success in bringing Emmet to the firing squad and their Judas-like betrayal distinguish them even from scoundrels like Harvey Duff. And Major Sirr, opposed by the noble British officer (Norman Claverhouse) who often appears in these plays (and in *Arrah-na-Pogue*), is the darkest of all of Boucicault's villains, particularly in his readiness to abuse Anne Devlin. Foreclosing on mortgages is one thing; torturing women is quite another.

Many of Whitbread's plays follow a formula similar to that of *Robert Emmet*. Plays like *The Ulster Hero*, for instance, cannot dispense happily with the unfortunate predicaments of historical personages well known to most Dubliners. The happier fates enjoyed by fictional heroes in plays like *The Irish Dragoon*, in which Napoleon refuses to execute a brave Irish soldier for "being true to his country," are therefore seldom accorded to Whitbread's historical heroes.[53] In several respects, *The Irish Dragoon* serves as an illuminative counter or contrast to more serious historical dramas like *The Ulster Hero*. From the very beginning of the former play, the exaggerated attractions of Lever's novel are evoked: the villain Hammersly expresses his hatred of Ireland ("this hole of a place"); the young hero Charles, his servant Mickey Free, and the lovely heroine Lucy Dashwood are introduced as the familiar character types they are; and the talk is of a duel Charles is to fight with Hammersly. Lucy shows her love of Charles here by offering to sacrifice her happiness with him if he will not fight the foes whom she believes will murder her beloved. Hammersly views Charles as a social inferior, hence an unsuitable foe for a duel, and the opening scene concludes with

Charles's receiving notice of his commission in the dragoons–the matter of his social station is hence addressed and the audience is prepared for future excitement.

Such pleasure is never slow in coming in plays like *The Irish Dragoon*. Dramatic excitement is buoyed as well by a comic subplot in which Mickey Free clumsily woos Susie Dogherty, Lucy's very Irish maid (a conventionally comic predicament and resolution, used by Whitbread in *Wolfe Tone* and other plays). Charles is wounded, later betrayed to Lucy's father by Hammersly, although her father finally recognizes the villain's duplicity, and finally captured by Napoleon's men. The audience even receives a humorous history lesson when Mickey Free meets Napoleon in act 3.

> NAPOLEON: You are witty, sare. It is easy to see you come from Ireland.
> MICKEY: Aye, an' if you had come to Ireland when ye promised, you wouldn't be here in the pickle ye are.
> NAPOLEON: What zat you say? . . . I always keep my word.
> MICKEY: Well, ye didn't in '98 anyways.

Mickey helps O'Malley escape from the French and, after Hammersly's several successful manipulations and strategically misunderstood letters, the play ends dramatically and happily: young O'Malley rescues Lucy from Hammersly, and we are assured of the impending marriages of both O'Malley and Mickey to their respective mates.

Things fail to work out so neatly in *The Ulster Hero,* where Henry Joy McCracken, like Robert Emmet, is eventually betrayed, imprisoned, and martyred while fighting for Ireland's independence. And although Whitbread employs conventional characters and sensational scenes typical of Boucicault's *Robert Emmet* and earlier plays–police spies, traitorous informants, villainous British officers, multiple romances, strong curtain scenes, and eloquent nationalistic rhetoric, to name but a few–reviewers often cited the play's historical accuracy as one of its most prominent virtues. For example, the *Dublin Evening Mail* on 13 January 1903 reviewed the play's opening performance with high praise for the "extensive and lucid manner" in which *The Ulster Hero* traces with "historical precision" McCracken's eventful career. To many Dubliners, therefore, as I have tried to demonstrate through popular newspaper biographies and news accounts of the Boer War, history *was* melodrama–and melodrama was often the vehicle for a historically "precise" account.

The center of attention in *The Ulster Hero* is occupied by the young hero (McCracken), his "Colleen Bawn" (Norah Bodel), McCracken's brave sister Mary, and a coterie of villains. The most unctuous of these is the informant Danny Niblock, whose smug villainies form a counterpoint to McCracken's courage. The play opens with Niblock rifling through James Hope's (McCracken's colleague) desk and laying bare his antinationalistic treachery to the audience: "United Irishmen are ye? Well, me boy, you'd better be more careful of yer papers or it's insoide the four walls of a jail ye'll be."[54] The first scene ends with Niblock vowing to send McCracken to the gallows, a vow which he, Captain Fox, and the traitorous Hughes eventually keep. In act 1, Fox offers five hundred pounds for evidence leading to the conviction and death of the United Irishmen, a bribe Hope refuses but John Hughes, another of McCracken's close associates, quietly accepts. Unlike the broadly comic subplots of plays like *The Irish Dragoon* or *The Nationalist*, whatever humor exists in *The Ulster Hero* emanates darkly from Niblock's comparison of himself and Hughes, McCracken's betrayer: "The parvarsity of human nature is astonishing. Why can't men be honest? I'm a loyalist, and it's legitimate business on my part to be a spy: but that fellow professes patriotism when all the time he's a blayguardly informer." Like Niblock, Hughes and Fox have several dramatic opportunities to reveal their scurrilous intentions to the audience.

McCracken's Anglicized eloquence, like Emmet's, provides the sharpest contrast to Niblock's very vernacular speeches. In most of these, he espouses his love of country and his willingness to die for Ireland. One of these should serve to illustrate the point: "Better that every Irishman in this fair land of ours should shed the last drop of his life blood to throw off the yoke of serfdom, than to rot and die the slaves of a mischievous party of miserable aristocrats." McCracken meets with Wolfe Tone at the end of the first act and, along with other patriots, kisses his sword while heroically vowing to fight against England, "that country that has been and is the never failing source of all our political ills." In this way, Niblock's vow to destroy McCracken is juxtaposed to the heroical oaths of the United Irishmen, and much of the play is organized around this parallel structure—and around the various dilemmas of separated lovers and unrequited love which popular dramatists like Whitbread felt compelled to interweave into the fabric of their history plays.

The love triangles in the play bring with them both the sentiment of Eily O'Connor's love for Hardress Cregan and a social class conflict that seems more essentially modern than the narrative tendency toward utopian social equality in Boucicault's Irish plays. McCracken manages a factory in Ulster and falls in love with Norah Bodel, a common laborer. Such an attachment breaches accepted social codes, and at one point in the play Norah's fellow workers attack her for her presumption of social superiority. Sorely misjudged, Norah, the "angelic" heroine of the play, humbly considers herself to be "a poor, ignorant factory girl" unworthy of the "honor" of marrying McCracken. But her co-workers, unaware of her real humility, castigate her as a social-climbing opportunist. Rescuing her at the very moment she is in true danger (appropriating Myles-na-Coppaleen's job in this instance), McCracken admonishes his workers that Norah is "fit for a better place than the factory—better company than yours—because she is fit to be by my side—fit to become my wife!"

Twenty years later, the aristocratic, wealthy Irish hero virtually disappeared from the Dublin stage, most likely because economic conditions in Ireland and labor movements made such a character something less than attractive. In Whitbread's play, however, characters like McCracken are nationalists before they are capitalists, and criticisms of their economic status are merely addenda to villains' asides. In the first scene of the play Niblock hears workers laughing on the way to the factory and condemns McCracken for profiting from the labor of his workers: "Who ever heard 'ov boys and girls laughin' when goin' to work? It's cursin' ye should be the man who's growin' fat an' rich an' affluent on the labour ov' your bones." Such criticisms from spies like Niblock hardly amount to credible readings of the crisis occasioned by industrial capitalism; rather, they become associated with the laziness that prompts men to eschew real labor and earn their living as informers. McCracken, the new Stage Irishman, is not only a nationalist and a martyr but a humane businessman similar to the title character of *Sarsfield,* whose soldiers worship him because of his kindness and compassion. Thus the shiftlessness and scheming associated with the Stage Irishman in London are projected onto the villain in *The Ulster Hero.* The Gaelic "blather" or "parvarsity" of language, too, becomes commonly associated with characters like Niblock, not with eloquent heroes like McCracken. As he marches to the gallows, noble, oratorical, and betrayed, McCracken represents the essence of the new Stage Irishman and the Irish historical hero.

Unlike Boucicault's comedies, then, and again with some exceptions, comic Irishmen or priests seldom emerge as deus ex machina figures in Whitbread's histories, nor do benevolent British soldiers or officials. In those

plays that do not end tragically—*Wolfe Tone* and *The Irish Dragoon* for instance—Napoleon, victorious Irish soldiers, or French troops contribute to
comic endings, but in France's historical opposition to England the ends
of these plays do not herald an optimistic resolution to Anglo-Irish conflict.
The almost pastoral environment of Boucicault's plays gives way in these
history plays to urban settings—Belfast and Dublin—and absent too from
several of Whitbread's plays are the blarney, drinking, and singing that enliven the Irish comic melodrama. Most important, the myth of cohesion—
of the bringing together of disparate strands of Irish society or the abolition
of social divisiveness and the defeat of avaricious landlords by native Irishness—disappears from the majority of Whitbread's plays. The English/Irish
opposition remains, constituted of unmediated conflicts that emerge in
Irish history plays in several ways.

First, the Irish stage villains in these plays become increasingly politicized, more similar to Harvey Duff and Corey Kinchela of *The Shaughraun*
than to Michael Feeny of *Arrah-na-Pogue* or Corrigan of *The Colleen Bawn*.
Irish villains in plays like *The Ulster Hero* and *Robert Emmet* typically come
in two varieties: police informers like Danny Niblock in *The Ulster Hero* and
associates of the hero who eventually betray him, like James Hughes in
Whitbread's play and Quigley in *Robert Emmet*. It is almost axiomatic in
these plays that the former friend of the hero will emulate Judas by turning traitor for money rather than out of reverence for England's colonial
government. And though most of these characters are fictive, they are modeled after historical traitors, the most infamous of whom is Francis Higgins
(known as "the Sham Squire"), who plotted the destruction of Edward Fitzgerald during the 1798 uprisings. These villains also offered dramatic rein-
forcement of the existence of scores of real informants employed both by
Dublin Castle and the Royal Irish Constabulary (RIC), whose job it was
to keep British officials apprised of the activities of Irish nationalist groups.

Second, plays like *Robert Emmet* and *The Ulster Hero* also present particularly reprehensible British soldiers that the comic melodrama, for the
most part, lacks. In *Robert Emmet* the villain is a historical figure, Major
Sirr, and in *The Ulster Hero* it is Captain Fox. Both use their position of
power and their well-lined pockets to coerce or bribe informants, and both
are capable of the most brutal cruelties: Sirr threatens to hang Anne Devlin
if she won't betray Emmet and advertises to the audience through asides
his eagerness to punish her; Fox flogs beggars, cowardly orders his men to
gun down McCracken after they have surrounded him, and threatens Mary

Tombe with scandal if she refuses to marry him. Coercing Irishwomen to marry them or otherwise demonstrating their perverse or sadistic sexuality was standard operating procedure for these characters. Even this convention finds multiple historical referents in Tim Healy's 1883 allegations of homosexuality and sexually deviant behavior in the detective division of the RIC and in the infamous nightly prowls of British soldiers in search of "recruits" during the years of the Boer War.[55] To combine oppressive government policy with such odious personal behavior in these plays was, in effect, to foster nationalist sympathy and anti-English sentiment. No reconciliation or myth of optimism here.

Third, the disparate elements of Irish society in Boucicault's comic plays—religion, patriotism, and economic position—represented by such characters as the priest, the rebel, and the mortgage holder or process server become subsumed by the magnitude of the historical hero. That is, the historical hero unifies these in Whitbread's *Ulster Hero* and in Boucicault's *Robert Emmet*. Emmet is a product of the Irish aristocracy and McCracken is a beneficent factory owner; because of this, the economic emphasis of melodrama based on possession/dispossession of land is replaced by nationalism and a dramatic emphasis on the English/Irish opposition. In these plays, the hero is quick to defend Ireland from British tyranny, and he vows to give his life for the liberation of Ireland. As I have mentioned, he continually exhorts his colleagues (and by extension the audience) to do the same in a series of eloquent speeches. In addition, in these plays the historical hero usually manifests a profound religious conviction, as religious faith and nationalism become linked in the hero's discourse, especially in Robert Emmet's. "Oh, ye spirits! You immortal band of heroes who suffered for your faith! Bodyguard of Him who died for the human race! Accept into your ranks the humble life of one, who, loving his land not wisely but too well, followed in your footsteps upward to the throne where sit the Eternal Trinity of Truth, Light, and Freedom" (293). The dramatic focus throughout *Robert Emmet* and *The Ulster Hero* remains sharply on a passionate nationalism analogous to religious fervor (or amatory devotion in the instance of Emmet's allusion to Othello's "loved not wisely, but too well"), and most Irish historical drama provides numerous justifications for such sentiment. The noble British soldiers and magistrates of *The Shaughraun, Arrah-na-Pogue,* and *Peep o'Day* surface in these plays—Claverhouse in *Robert Emmet* and Ellis in *The Ulster Hero*—but are finally ineffectual at stemming the villainy of their more powerful and sinister colleagues. The consequences are clearly delineated in this variety of historical melodrama: English/Irish opposition grows; loyal Irishmen like Andy Devlin in *Robert Emmet* die gladly for their country; and martyrdom for the hero punctuates the spectacular conclusions of both plays.

Fourth, as often obtained in historical dramas on the late nineteenth-century London stage,[56] the narratives of many of these plays are closed by grossly sensationalistic executions. *Robert Emmet* and *The Ulster Hero* prove no exception. Emmet is shot immediately after speaking "God bless my country." Bells toll and a black flag is raised. The figure of Ireland, dressed in green "with a coronet of shamrocks" in her hair, descends and kneels by Emmet's fallen body. The last scene of *The Ulster Hero* seems equally spectacular and, as the reviewer for the *Freeman's Journal* hypothesizes, seems intended to "rouse feelings of fierce anger in the spectator." "In the closing scene the brave Northern leader [Henry Joy McCracken] is seen upon the scaffold, on which also stands the hangman with the fatal rope. Then the curtain is lowered for a few moments, and when it is raised again the gallant soldier who has given his life for Ireland is seen lying dead beneath the grim instrument of his execution" (13 January 1903). To some, including the reviewer for the *Freeman's Journal*, the scene invited comparison with Ireland's recent past, in particular the mistreatment and murder of Boer soldiers by the British in South Africa: "By an easy transition, fancy travels to some of the scenes enacted recently in South Africa, and one is forced to the conclusion that the march of a century has not altered England very much in her treatment of *gallant foes*, be they Irish or Boer." "Gallant foes" and vindictive English officers—in Irish history plays at the Queen's, English/Irish opposition is finally articulated theatrically in just these terms.

In sum, plays like *The Ulster Hero*, which conveyed history to Irish audiences by way of melodrama, were largely responsible for Whitbread's success at the Queen's Theatre. Alternating in repertory with Boucicault's plays and those of other Irish writers such as Hubert O'Grady, Whitbread's history plays became vehicles for a heroical figure vastly different from the comic Stage Irishman in London. Because of their concomitant anti-British bias and generally more serious tone, Whitbread's plays, to my knowledge, were not produced in London. Indeed, *The Irish Dragoon* and *The Ulster Hero* were licensed by the Lord Chamberlain's reviewer and produced, respectively, at the Queen's Theatre in Liverpool and the Metropole Theatre in Glasgow. And when British writers *did* delve into dramatic topics similar to *The Ulster Hero*—as, for example, Walter Howard did in *The Wearing O' the Green* in 1898 – there were generally featured parts for the "Irish Comic Lead" and his female counterpart. Howard's play follows the Boucicault-Whitbread formula with the very important addition of the old Stage Irishman and Irishwoman. I hope to have demonstrated that such additions would not have been welcome in Dublin by the turn of the century, or perhaps a bit earlier.

That Boucicault's plays were still popular at this time may attest to the power of an old "classic," to the attractiveness of a trip back into a less complicated past. Or, as I have argued above, this popularity might confirm the timeliness of Boucicault's soothing myth of the reconciliation of very real historical division, which, along with the myth of the historical hero, dominated repertories in the Queen's Theatre at the turn of the century. These plays continued to attract playgoers in Dublin even as late as the 1920s, the decade in which O'Casey's *The Plough and the Stars* rocked the intellectual calm of the Abbey Theatre: Holloway reports in his diaries that *The Octoroon* and *Arrah-na-Pogue* ran for a dozen performances each in 1923, and *The Octoroon* and *The Shaughraun* matched this feat the following year.

Yet another explanation of the appeal of such plays resides in Stuart Hall's conception of the contradictorily conservative and radical nature of popular texts. Irish dramas like Boucicault's evoked profound nostalgia for a rural or "green" world of community and cohesion, a utopian world, regardless of real economic concerns, in which dispossession or emigration, foreclosure or familial ruin, could be delayed or interrupted through the goodwill and works of one's neighbors or priest. Secular and imperial law, a weapon in the hands of avaricious or lecherous process servers or barristers, could be subsumed under a broader, more potent ethical law – or comically overturned in a carnivalesque inversion of established order, the stock-in-trade of Wild Irish Boys and Boucicault's Irishmen alike.[57] Or England's colonial power could be resisted more directly by young nationalists and their comic sidekicks, hence the coterminous radical and conservative dimensions of Boucicault's and O'Grady's melodramas. Whitbread's plays, by contrast, frequently evoked a different world: more urban, more complicated, more tragic. Still, the sparks both of nostalgic longing for old Ireland, of carnivalesque transgressions, and of emancipatory nationalism glowed in them; and surely the courage, eloquence, and sophistication of Whitbread's Wolfe Tone, Sarsfield, and McCracken toppled all Victorian stereotypes of Irish nationalists as criminals, effeminate traitors, or inchoate brutes. In sum, Irish drama at the Queen's Royal Theatre offered a mixture of ideological and theatrical pleasures that Dublin popular audiences at the turn of the century could not resist.

Most important, when assessing the ramifications of the rise of the Abbey Theatre and of the various riots its plays provoked, especially those caused by O'Casey's *Plough and the Stars,* and when studying the widely different dramatic forms of Yeats, Synge, and O'Casey, we must not forget the popular tradition that preceded them. Yes, there *was* an Irish drama before Yeats: a political, in numerous respects anticolonial, drama that emerged both from the most serious events in the lives of historical Irishmen and from the lively exploits of a clodhopper brewing liquor in a cave by the lakes of Killarney.

Joyce:
Sexuality, Artistry, and the Popular Theater

> IRENE: I exposed myself wholly and unreservedly to your gaze
> [*more softly*] and never once did you touch me. . . .
> RUBEK: (*looks impressively at her*). I was an artist, Irene.
> IRENE: (*darkly*). That is just it. That is just it.
>   —Henrik Ibsen, *When We Dead Awaken*

> Only at times, in the pauses of his desire, when the lux-
> ury that was wasting him gave room to a softer languor,
> the image of Mercedes traversed the background of his
> memory. . . . At those moments the soft speeches of
> Claude Melnotte rose to his lips and eased his unrest.
> . . . Such moments passed and the wasting fires of lust
> sprang up again. (*Portrait* 99)

THESE TWO PASSAGES—the first from Ibsen's *When We Dead Awaken*,[1] the second from Stephen's "wanderings" in *A Portrait of the Artist as a Young Man*—are revelatory of a problematic within which Joyce, Stephen Dedalus, and the Blooms exist and struggle.[2] That is, as the passage from *Portrait* indicates, Joyce's Dublin culture, like young Stephen himself, suffered the opposing pressures of an aging yet still prominent romanticism with its displacement of physicality and desire, and a nascent, unruly modernism with, among other agendas, its more expansive representation of human sexual-

89

ity.[3] This problematic informs much turn-of-the-century drama and theatrical conventions, the specifics of which are recuperable through a reconstruction of Joyce's playgoing experience, a reconsideration of the issues contained in the plays he saw, and an interrogation of the conventions through which the late Victorian theater actualized the dramatic text on stage. Certainly, many of these issues, those involving gender distinctions and sexuality in particular, were transmitted in other vehicles such as fiction and the emerging sexology of the late nineteenth and early twentieth centuries as Richard Brown, among others, has shown.[4]

Stephen's internal conflict cited above, however—with allusions to Alexandre Dumas *père*'s novel *The Count of Monte Cristo* (1844–45) and Edward Bulwer-Lytton's romantic drama *The Lady of Lyons* (1838)—verifies the key roles both the nineteenth-century novel and Victorian drama played in shaping the consciousnesses of Joyce's Dubliners. The passage also graphs the thematic proximity of genres at this time, intimating the precariousness of privileging one source of influence on Joyce's work and life over others. Throughout the following, therefore, my efforts are *not* designed to elevate this or that play, this or that theatrical convention, as *solely* determinative of an instance in *Ulysses;* rather, I hope to promote the late Victorian theater and its representative plays as an instrument through which we might read more fully the effects of culture on Joyce and *Ulysses,* raising popular theater to the explanatory level that, say, popular fiction and music have occupied in Joyce studies.[5]

My intention is premised on the notion that Joyce's Dublin, at least insofar as it relates to the popular theater and theatergoing, bears strong resemblance to its historical referent. Of particular interest are both Joyce and his characters' reactions to works in the repertories of Dublin's Theatre Royal and Gaiety Theatre. We should, moreover, be ever vigilant to monitor the ways in which Joyce's narrative maneuvers do not merely reflect but also construct "reality" in *Ulysses,* a concern of readers with such diverse theoretical projects as Alick West and Wolfgang Iser, to name but two. Still, sociocultural realities *do* exist in Joyce's works to be recovered. Dominic Manganiello advances this supposition as crucial to viewing Joyce as a political writer, as I do: "To regard Joyce as a dweller in an ivory tower . . . does not jibe with the attempt to picture totally the situation of man and woman. The portrayal of Bloom and Molly, for instance, can hardly be said to be idealised or sentimentalised. Joyce insisted that we must accept life 'as we see it before our eyes, men and women as we meet them in the real world, not as we apprehend them in the world of the faery.'"[6] Aspects of the "common, the average, the everyday" inevitably replicate parts of the late Victorian English and other "worlds," thus accounting for Franco Moretti's view of Joyce's Dublin as "the literary image *par excellence* of the modern city." Nonetheless, the Blooms' world is in crucial respects an Irish one, a cornerstone of recent feminist readings of Joyce.[7] The popular theater must, by this logic, play both a general and a culturally specific part in Joyce's "attempt to picture totally" the *public and private* lives of Dubliners. Understanding this part is an endeavor of this chapter.

The problem is, of course, that not everyone agrees with the premise that Joyce's Dublin bears any relationship to the historical "real" of 1904, regardless of the novel's myriad allusions to contemporary facts and cultural events. Perhaps this superfluity of inessential detail merely creates what Roland Barthes labels *l'effect du réel*.[8] More generous than Moretti on the topic of the realism of *Ulysses*, Alick West discovers a revolutionary style in "Sirens" and "Nausicaa," where "Joyce shows the individual actions within the totality of relations existing at the moment." Therein the "traditional unity is broken" and "in its place is the unity of Dublin"; in the process of effecting this social substitution, West lauds Joyce's totalizing achievement: "This technique [originating in Joyce's 'new vision of society'] is an expression of those forces to which Marx gave formulation when he said that society is the totality of relations."[9] Somewhat contradictorily, however, West also charges that, because of the active agency of the author or the "principle of selection" that governs the content of Joyce's narrative, those who regard *Ulysses* to be "about Dublin" might just as well say "life is life."[10] Events in *Ulysses* connect "directly or indirectly" to the lives of Stephen and Bloom – and ultimately to Joyce's own crisis of refusing to serve the Catholic church, English imperialism, or the nationalist movement. Hence Joyce's plan of resistance contained a built-in contradiction, as *non serviam* in the nationalist enterprise served both the church (which regarded membership in secret nationalist societies as antithetical to Catholics' commitment to their faith) and the empire, the two masters Stephen in the "Telemachus" episode identifies and reviles. The *non serviam* crisis, in West's view, affects Joyce's selection of incidents in the novel, thereby undermining any claim of "realism" in *Ulysses*.

A similar paradoxical appraisal of realism in *Ulysses* links West's critique with that of Wolfgang Iser, although the latter's interpretive aims differ diametrically from West's. Iser, on the one hand, refers repeatedly to the "restless monotony" of Bloom's "everyday life," to the "seemingly opaque chaos of everyday life" in the novel, to the "apparent senselessness of everyday life," and so on. On the other hand, Iser maintains that "the novel cannot be described as a realistic depiction of ordinary life in Dublin despite the vast number of verifiable details that run through it." For Iser, the novel's great "wealth of details" no longer "stabilize the illusion of reality," and the varied narrative styles of the novel's eighteen chapters only create indeterminacy, leaving matters of meaning and the interconnection of novelistic incidents up to the reader: "The implication of a novel written in several different styles is that the view expressed by each style is to be taken as only one possible facet of everyday reality. . . . The novel refuses to divulge any way of connecting up this interplay of perspectives, and so the reader is expected to provide his own liaison."[11] The obviously parodic dimensions of conflicting styles of narration in the "Oxen in the Sun" chapter aside, such a plurality of styles also tends to place frames of perspective within *Ulysses* under erasure, marking each frame as incomplete and temporary. One result of this deconstructive process is that novelized action becomes more like dramatic action, which forces its audience to operate selectively on the representation before it.[12] Readers of Joyce, like playgoers and more so than the readers of other modes of fiction, are required to participate in an always provisional conventionalization of signs and, further, to recognize the conventions of various discourses which form or overdetermine signs. That the sheer abundance and diversity of such conventions "overtax the reader's vision," as Iser claims, is self-evident; that this amounts to an annulment of reality in the novel is less clear.

In this essay, then, oppositions such as Joyce as author/Joyce as consumer, Dublin as reflected reality/Dublin as authorial construct are, inevitably, placed in tension. One must be attentive to these polarities and, in any given instance, determine when Joyce is manipulating or parodying a convention, subverting it or opposing it, and when a powerful discourse is working on him. And, recalling Iser's concerns, to what extent does popular drama and theatergoing in turn-of-the-century Dublin help overtaxed readers in need of interpretive direction fill the "'empty spaces' between chapters in order to group them into a coherent whole"?[13] I will begin this investigation by considering several conventions of the plays Joyce saw and the constructions of sexuality and subjectivity they offer, leading both to a fresh contextualization of *Ulysses* within which Molly is inscribed and to an illustration of the paradoxical representations of artistry and sexuality on the late Vic-

torian stage. Finally, I shall locate moments of distinctly theatrical spectatorship in the novel, especially Bloom's and Gerty MacDowell's in "Nausicaa."

MOLLY AND THE "FALLEN WOMEN":
The Theatrical Origins of Joyce's Revision of the Home

In his biography of Joyce, Richard Ellmann echoes Stanislaus Joyce's emphasis of his brother's nearly simultaneous rejection of Catholicism and growing enthusiasm for drama and theater: "As his faith in Catholicism tottered,
a counter-process began: his faith in art, which is written by and about people with faults, grew great" (*JJ* 50). This "counter-process" and these writers
and characters are, in one sense, widely known: Ibsen and his angst-ridden
doctors, wives, and architects; Gerhart Hauptmann's characters; George
Moore's bohemians living in the Paris of *Celibates* (1895) and *Confessions of
a Young Man* (1889), and so on. Less frequently discussed are the popular
plays Joyce saw at the turn of the century, especially late Victorian romantic
drama and more realistic social dramas. The effect this viewing had on Joyce
is both centered around and complicated by theatrical representations of
the artist's sexuality. More precisely, Joyce's trips to the theater and to the
pages of the drama he devoured with increasing avidity carried him into contradictory representations of sexuality and artistry that took *Ulysses* to rec-
tify. He discovered in the drama he viewed a concomitant valorization of
a sexuality (and attendant social iconoclasm) he could no longer deny—
sexuality as an overdetermined symbol for a variety of rebellions for which
Joyce had sympathy—*and* representations of the artistry to which he aspired
as above matters of the body.

To test these assertions, we might first review the several connections
between drama, sexuality, and the body for the young Joyce. One of these,
which I mentioned in my opening chapter and bears repeating here, comes
from Stanislaus's account of the Joyce family's viewing of Mrs. Patrick Campbell in the title role of Sudermann's *Magda:* "Mrs. Patrick Campbell had
at least one listener for whom the play was not just an interesting postpran-
dial pastime." The analogy he offers to explain his brother's devotion to drama
is, in this regard, significant: "For my brother the drama had become a thing
of supreme importance, what the Mass had been" (*MBK* 87). By this time,
his last year at Belvedere in 1898, Joyce, much like Stephen in *Portrait,* had

once and for all become reconciled to his loss of religious faith. His last attempt at reformation, which lasted "well into 1897" according to Ellmann, had by later that year failed, and the young Joyce now turned to the secular creed of Ibsen's plays and others performed popularly in Dublin.

But why had the drama become so significant to Joyce? One of Stephen's meditations in *Stephen Hero* suggests an answer. "In a stupor of powerlessness he reviewed the plague of Catholicism. He seemed to see the vermin begotten in the catacombs. . . . Contempt of [the body] human nature, weakness, nervous tremblings, fear of day and joy, distrust of man and life, hemiplegia of the will, beset the body burdened and disaffected in its members. . . . Exultation of the mind before joyful beauty, exultation of the body in free confederate labours, every natural impulse towards health and wisdom and happiness had been corroded by the pest of these vermin" (*SH* 194). The Catholic church, in the metaphor developed here, is a house built over a cellar of verminous corpses, a fatal architecture in which saintly relics exude a moral disease deleterious to the living. The body viewed with contempt, the body constrained from participating freely in nature – Joyce's metaphors encapsulate the uneasy relationship between his growing disillusionment with the church and his recognition of his own burgeoning desire. Like Ibsen's plays in which Joyce was absorbed at the time, the so-called Fallen Women or Edwardian problem plays exemplified by Sudermann's *Magda* enact a secular ritual wherein the demands of the body are recognized.[14] It is within the context of such plays that the rupture in Joyce's family on the occasion of his leaving home in 1904 is most fruitfully understood, "home" being an especially meaningful term in Joyce's project of individuation. The same context also illuminates Molly's character and the comic function of the "Penelope" chapter.

A revolt from the repressive law of the church and the tyranny of the father, representations common to Fallen Women plays and to Joyce's early writing alike, invariably meant an acceptance of the demands of the body and a rejection of institutional moralities complicitous in the patriarchal control of women's bodies (and young men's as well where sons are concerned).[15] In provincial repertories conspicuously absent of Ibsen, these plays – Sudermann's *Magda*, adaptations of Dumas *fils*'s *La Dame aux Camélias*, Clyde Fitch's adaptation of Alphonse Daudet's novel *Sapho* (1899), Pinero's *Second Mrs. Tanqueray* (1893) and *The Notorious Mrs. Ebbsmith* (1895), and Jones's *Mrs. Dane's Defence* (1900) – achieved a special notoriety and reputation of modernity in turn-of-the-century touring stops like Dublin.

Theatergoers could expect to see these and similar plays as frequently as three to four weeks a year and more often if major actresses happened to be booked in Dublin during a given season. By convention, fallen women like Paula Tanqueray, Agnes Ebbsmith, Felicia Hindemarsh (Mrs. Dane), or Magda (Magdalene) Schwartze are haunted by past indiscretions, usually secret relationships with former lovers. In these dramas, and in generically similar ones like Jones's *Case of Rebellious Susan* (1894) and *The Liars* (1897), in which a wife contemplates paying back an unfaithful husband in kind, marriage is nearly always put on trial. The typical result is that even if troubled marriages survive, as they appear to by the conclusions of Pinero's *Notorious Mrs. Ebbsmith* or Jones's *Case of Rebellious Susan,* they do so largely as rather pathetic social accommodations. Bereft of all romantic or idealistic qualities, marriage is seen as a wretched institution or, at best, as Sir Richard Kato, the experienced Divorce Court lawyer in *Rebellious Susan* describes it, a "perfect institution . . . worked by imperfect creatures."[16] This demythologizing work is accompanied by other interrogations and moral reformulations, all of which Joyce "read" in Sudermann's drama. Stanislaus Joyce confirms this attraction by quoting his brother's interpretation of *Magda,* addressed to his parents after seeing Mrs. Campbell in the title role, in which Sudermann's original title—*Heimat* (Home)—ironically resonates: "The subject of the play is genius breaking out *in the home* and *against the home.* You needn't have gone to see it. It's going to happen in your own house" (*MBK* 87; emphasis added). By 1904, Joyce's genius *did* break out when he and Nora left Ireland for the Continent.

In plays like *Magda,* the heroine's struggle against the father or other male embodiment of the law is accompanied by other conventional oppositions: social acceptance/rejection (based in part on class distinctions between an aristocratic male and a woman of lower social station), institutional morality/individual morality, present/past, father/son (daughter), repression/desire, and so on. No mere coincidence, Jones's restless housewives or "bad women" are typically opposed by clever barristers—Richard Kato in *The Case of Rebellious Susan* and Sir Daniel Carteret in *Mrs. Dane's Defence,* for instance —and these women are frequently the daughters of clergymen, military officers, and the like. The central battles in these plays are thus waged between a male-dominated society and the women who threaten its continued hegemony, either through their unconventional pasts or by their emancipatory projects for the future. Any attempt by women to usurp male prerogatives —which include adultery and excusable premarital intimacies—marks them as unwomanly and socially unacceptable. Such women are at times contrasted with chaste daughters and wives (and therein the "no-win" situation for women in late Victorian representations of sexuality is revealed): although Aubrey Tanqueray's first wife is, at times, disparaged by his friends, she is at other times praised as a saintly "iceberg" made of "marble," and his daughter Ellean has entered a convent; Magda's younger sister, Marie, has remained at home as a dutiful daughter (and suffered mightily because of it); and Lucas Cleeve's wife in *The Notorious Mrs. Ebbsmith* selflessly pleads with Agnes, her husband's lover, to release him so he might resume his career. That Joyce, as represented by Stephen, was rapidly developing sensitivity to these very oppositions is apparent in both *Stephen Hero* and *Portrait*. Also, as he contemplated leaving Ireland, his privileging of home, familism, and repression in his correspondence to Nora reiterates his reading of *Magda:*

> My mind rejects the whole present social order and Christianity—*home*, the recognised virtues, classes of life, and religious doctrines. How could I like the idea of *home?* . . .
>
>   Six years ago I left the Catholic Church, hating it most fervently. I found it impossible for me to remain in it on account of the impulses of my nature.[17]
> (emphasis added)

Like Magda, the young Joyce found home and its orthodox morality stifling. Their escapes amount to victories, whereas less fortunate characters like Eveline Hill in "Eveline" or Chandler in "A Little Cloud" are never quite able to take this decisive step.

Such major actresses as Mrs. Campbell and Sarah Bernhardt played these roles in the Dublin of Joyce's and O'Casey's adolescence, but so too did lesser-known touring players including Olga Nethersole, Lena Ashwell, and Emma Hutchinson at the Gaiety Theatre and Theatre Royal. Mrs. Campbell's appearance as Paula Tanqueray attracted a "densely crowded audience" to the Gaiety Theatre in April 1898; she returned to Dublin as Magda, Agnes Ebbsmith, and Paula in 1899 and repeated substantially the same repertory in 1900, with Maeterlinck's romantic *Pelléas and Mélisande* replacing *Mrs. Ebbsmith*. She played in *Magda* and Jose Echegaray's *Mariana* in 1901 and returned as Paula and Beata in Sudermann's *Joy of Living* in 1903. Although the *Freeman's Journal* reported that Johnston Forbes-Robertson's assumption of the role of Aubrey Tanqueray added to the public's already whetted appetite for the play, "the importance of the occasion derived from the presence of that lady who so transcendently surpassed all preconceived anticipation by her impersonation some five years ago as 'Paula' in this same play."[18] Stella Campbell played other roles, to be sure, but in Dublin her Paula Tanqueray and Magda had clearly captured the public's imagination. When she attempted in July 1901 to expand her repertory with *Mariana,* two performances of *Magda* were added by "special request" to her week-long stay. She continued to impersonate Magda and Paula well into the new century, playing both in 1910, for instance, and returned triumphantly to Dublin in 1930 as Mrs. Alving in Ibsen's *Ghosts.*

Magda serves as an emblematic drama for my purposes, not only because its central character expresses her sexual freedom openly but also because her antagonists combine to form what Joyce perceived as obstacles in his own life to artistic and personal growth. *Magda,* moreover, contains numerous similarities to *Ulysses.* As Sudermann's play opens, news arrives that Magda, the older of two daughters of Lieutenant-Colonel Leopold Schwartze, is returning to her hometown after a twelve-year absence. Now a celebrated opera singer, she has in effect been disowned by her rigidly authoritarian father. The opening act is designed to establish the opposition between home and world, between the secluded German province where Magda's family resides and the larger world of artistic celebrity in which she moves. Schwartze's friends, several of whom are political leaders in the province, extol the value of rural seclusion and tradition, declaring "how much better it would be to know nothing of the outer world" (199).[19] In the "world in general," Schwartze laments, where "all the ties of morality and authority seem strained to bursting, it is doubly necessary that those who stand for the good old patriarchal order should hold together" (204). The real culprit, as Schwartze sees it, is the "modern age" and its planting of "rebellion in children's hearts." Magda has fled from the tyranny of "old-fashioned paternal authority" and sought a career in the city; now she returns in triumph as a well-known artist. The exposition of the opening act, however unsubtle, leaves little doubt as to the nature of the conflicts she will confront.

Not surprisingly, when Magda characterizes the "larger" society in which she has risen to prominence, she does so through the same metaphor used by her father: that of the "world." In act 2, when her father questions the propriety of a single woman traveling with a young male assistant, Magda undauntedly outlines the differences between her life and that her irascible father might deem appropriate:

MAGDA: In my world we don't trouble ourselves about such things.
SCHWARTZE: What world is that?
MAGDA: The world I rule, father dear. I have no other. There whatever I
do is right because I do it. (223)

One of things Magda does—or did in Berlin some years before her home-coming—is to have an affair with von Keller, a friend of her father's. This liaison produced a son, whose existence at the play's beginning is known only to Magda. When she informs von Keller of his paternity in act 3, he recoils in fear lest someone might overhear this disclosure and destroy his "quiet world, where scandals are unknown." In the last act Schwartze almost persuades his daughter to marry von Keller, who offers marriage as a "holier and more auspicious resolution" to the dilemma of illegitimate motherhood. In von Keller's scheming proposition, all Magda has to sacrifice is her career and her child, whose presence might damage von Keller's political aspirations. This dramatic situation, one in which the career of a seemingly moral and staunchly conservative politician is threatened by past indiscretions, is repeated by Sudermann in *The Joy of Living*, which Stella Campbell added to her repertory. Unlike Beata in this play, who commits suicide both to atone for her sin and to save the reputation of her former lover, Magda has no such self-sacrifice in mind, nor will she abandon her son. She refuses von Keller's proposal. The melodramatic climax comes near the end of the play, when her overwrought father is determined to force the marriage between Magda and the presumed father of her illegitimate child. She tauntingly asks her father how he is so certain von Keller is her only former lover, which provokes the outraged colonel to castigate her as a "Jade!" and to reach for his pistol case. Training a pistol on her, he suffers a stroke and dies moments later. The final curtain lowers with the rest of the Schwartze family circling the fallen colonel and Magda preparing to mourn his passing.

In an essay on *The Second Mrs. Tanqueray*, Austin Quigley describes how in *pièces bien faites* "worlds" collide in a peculiarly theatrical way, and his reading of Pinero seems equally illuminative of *Magda*. The dramatic action of *The Second Mrs. Tanqueray* amounts to a confrontation of separate "worlds," parallel domains of ethics and values more distinctly drawn and complete than one finds them outside the theater, represented by Aubrey Tanqueray's male social circle, his daughter Ellean's secluded life in an Irish convent, and the decadent Continental society in which Paula formerly resided. The "ultimate focus" of Pinero's play is not necessarily "on the rightness or wrongness of any of these worlds, but on the nature of the social transactions that occur between them."[20] Quigley, I think, is correct on all counts here: Pinero constructs differing spheres of values, giving none primacy over the others (though both Ellean and Aubrey, by the end of the play, appear to renounce their respective worlds and to sympathize with Paula's now fatal predicament).

Magda, by contrast, develops the same metaphor of colliding worlds and elicits the audience's ratification of Magda's world over the despotism of her father's. As orthodox critics in London, Dublin, and New York readily observed, an agenda of social reformation underlies Sudermann's drama, especially as played by Mrs. Campbell. Stella Campbell recalls in her biography that critics despised the very dimension of the play which Joyce admired. The *Daily Telegraph*, for example, while finding nothing inherently "disagreeable" or "unlovable" in Sudermann's development of his title character, held that "Mrs. Campbell in every line and accent suggests a revolt, a tirade against constitutional society."[21] William Winter, the patriarch of New York drama critics at the turn of the century, expressed even greater disdain for the play and character in January 1902 after seeing Mrs. Campbell on one of her many American tours. "The character of *Magda* typifies "the new woman"—that is to say, the woman who proposes to take an independent course in all things, and, as far as possible, to act as if she were a lawless man. . . . This young woman represents conceit, perversity, mulish self-will, bad temper, an ill-balanced mind, unprincipled conduct, the self-indulgence of a capricious voluptuary, and the spirit of revolt against all constraints, whether of convention, duty, or common sense."[22] Even though by 1902 *Magda* had been a prominent part of major actresses' repertories for over fifteen years, many reviewers still reviled the play, largely for the reasons they hated Ibsen—and these critical attacks reveal precisely the attractions that most captivated Joyce.

In the harshly drawn antagonism to the central character's desire, especially in its delineation of this opposition along both age and gender lines, Sudermann's play resembles Pinero's *Second Mrs. Tanqueray, The Notorious Mrs. Ebbsmith,* and Jones's *Mrs. Dane's Defence.* But the central characters of these generically similar plays are quite different as well. Unlike Paula Tanqueray or Mrs. Dane, Magda is not a "woman with a past" seeking marriage or untoward intimacy with an aristocratic gentleman. In fact, Magda returns home hoping only for reconciliation with her father and reunion with her younger sister, of whom she is very fond. Neither is she a betrayed wife, like Jones's Lady Susan Harabin in *The Case of Rebellious Susan,* nor one married to an inattentive boor, as is Lady Jessica Nepean's misfortune in *The Liars.* Magda also differs from "bad women" like Agnes Ebbsmith or Herminia Barton in Grant Allen's novel *The Woman Who Did* (1895), who possess a political motive: as Mrs. Ebbsmith describes it, to lead the march for a "Free Union" between men and women outside of marriage and to defend "our position, and the positions of such as ourselves" (296). Indeed, Allen's Herminia Barton, like Shakespeare's Archbishop of York in *2 Henry IV,* turns "insurrection into a religion," in this instance a religion devoted to eradicating the spiritual and physical enslavement of marriage. A "moral pioneer" and finally a "martyr" (42), Herminia lived "in her own world of high seraphic harmonies" and possessed a "stainless soul" that would not permit her to compromise her principles and marry the man she loved (48–49).[23] (Recall that in the "Cyclops" chapter one of the "tribal images of many Irish heroes and heroines of antiquity" on the Citizen's "girdle" is of "The Woman Who Didn't.")

As Richard Brown and Bonnie Kime Scott have shown, attacks on marriage similar to Pinero's and Jones's, those by Ibsen, Hauptmann, Balzac, and George Moore for instance, made a strong impression on Joyce, who in the late 1890s was formulating his own critique of this institution.[24] Certainly this criticism devolves from the action of *Magda,* as do other issues such as equality of the sexes and the generational conflict which Joyce's response to *Magda* makes clear. The former topic, equality of the sexes and the conceptions of gender prerequisite for it, is also very revelant here. In Fallen Women plays, as Winter's criticism of *Magda* underscores, a woman's expression of desire brands her as wishing to act "as if she were a lawless man." In *Mrs. Ebbsmith,* Lucas Cleeve, Agnes's married and younger lover, tells her, "There's something of the man in your nature" (237); in *Rebellious Susan,* Sir Richard Kato tells Elaine Shrimpton that "Nature," not man, is "ungallant and unkind to your sex" and accuses progressive women of being so "evidently dissatisfied with being women" that they apparently want to change their gender (153). In similar attacks on Ibsen's plays, *Rosmersholm* for instance, one London critic opined that the characters were "neither men nor women" but "ghouls," and another complained of Ibsen's admirers being limited only to the "Socialists and the sexless."[25]

The major difference between Magda and her counterparts in Jones's and Pinero's social dramas—and the strongest of her several similarities to

Molly Bloom and to Joyce himself—is that she is an artist. For Margot Peters, Magda's artistry becomes a central issue in Sudermann's play because she is "punished not only for her sexual freedom . . . but for aspiring to a career in the male realm of art."[26] But Magda, in fact, is never *really* punished at all: she simply becomes objectified and sensationalized in male conversation, hence controlled, because she poses a threat to male authority both in the public domain and in homes like Colonel Schwartze's (and John Joyce's as well). The "realm of art" is scarcely represented in the play: no male artists appear as rivals and, in any case, the late nineteenth-century European stage was graced by many strong women performers who, if moving in a man's world, exercised uncommon levels of professional power. Rather, at issue here is Magda's position in the "large world," a foreign world vaster than that of art and diametrically opposite that constituted by her home, and her arrogation to herself all the heretofore male privileges that accompany preeminence in this world. In this respect, the relationship between Molly and Magda is most evident. As Molly complains, men can "go and get whatever they like from anything at all with a skirt on it and were not to ask any questions" (18:298–99). And as Sir Richard Kato finally convinces Susan in Jones's *Case of Rebellious Susan*, "what is sauce for the goose will never be sauce for the gander. In fact, there is no gander sauce" (112). Both women desire this sauce, as Joyce did, for there is no artistic creation without it.

Both women, like all the central characters in the plays discussed above, are no longer "girls," and both harbor desires appropriate to their maturity. Most are between the ages of twenty-seven and thirty-three: Susan Harabin, Jessica Nepean, Felicia Hindemarsh, and Paula Tanqueray are twenty-seven; Agnes Ebbsmith is thirty-three, the age Molly claims she will reach in September, though she will actually be thirty-four. Confused about this, Molly says, "Im what am I at all Ill be 33 in September will I" (18:475). In any event, Magda must be about thirty, although Sudermann does not specify, because her sister mentions that Magda left home twelve years ago, and Magda describes her imprisonment for some seventeen years in this "paternal" house "of bondage." Such a life, if Marie is any example, is inimical to success in the outside world and, perhaps, as Molly laments, so too is marriage: "I could have been a prima donna only I married him" (18:896). Both seem most similar in their frank acknowledgments of desire, although Molly's admission is the more explicit of the two. Still, Magda admits her sexual precocity, one analogous to Molly's boast that she "knew more about men and life when I was 15 than theyll all know at 50" (18: 886–87). In verbal combat with von Keller, Magda unblushingly recalls her youthful passion, which was given expression only after she left her father's home: "I had left my home; I was young and innocent, hot-blooded and careless, and I lived as I saw others live. I gave myself to you because I loved you" (253). Recognizing the strength of her passion, Magda tells von Keller, "I might perhaps have loved any one who came in my way" (253). Molly expresses her desire similarly and in so doing creates the strongest parallel between the two characters. "Of course a woman wants to be embraced 20 times a day . . . no matter by who so long as to be in love or loved by somebody if the fellow you want isnt there sometimes by the Lord God I was thinking would I go around by the quays there some dark evening where nobodyd know me and pick up a sailor off the sea thatd be hot on for it" (18:1407–12). At such moments when, as Molly describes it, "you feel that way so nice all over you you can't help yourself " (18:103–4), Magda rather angrily asks her father, "Shall we not once dare to give what we have of youth and strength to the man for whom our whole being cries?" (276). Both women, therefore, are mothers and artists; both have grown critical of men's unfair advantages, especially in their socially authorized pursuit of adultery; both acknowledge their desire, in Magda's case with a candor that surpasses similar articulations in other plays.

Stanislaus Joyce's emphasis on the effect *Magda* exerted on his brother is reason enough to privilege this genre in reconstructing the popular theater of Joyce's Dublin, but other evidence exists as well of his interest in Fallen Women dramas. One indirect but significant example can be inferred from Stanislaus's memories of his brother's winning twenty pounds for his Preparatory Grade exhibition, and though I have alluded to this passage earlier, it bears closer scrutiny here: "He bought presents for all of us . . . and there were frequent visits, in which I was occasionally included, to the cheaper parts of theatres, to see Edward Terry in his comedy parts, or Irving or Tree if tickets could be had, or the lesser lights, Edmund Tearle as Othello, or Olga Nethersole" (*MBK* 59). As I have mentioned, stars of Irving's and Tree's magnitude played "to populations" in the provinces, typically drawing packed houses in Dublin. For Tree, whose biggest financial success in London and on tour was *Trilby* (1895), this generalization might be pressed even further. As Molly's complaint about the huge crowd Tree drew to the Gaiety Theatre suggests—"the last time Ill ever go there to be squashed like that for any Trilby" (18:1042–43)—the adaptation of the George Du Maurier

12. The Gaiety Theatre, Dublin (ca. 1896). From *1871–1971: One Hundred Years of Gaiety*, souvenir program.

13. Galaxy of touring stars who played the Gaiety Theatre, Dublin, at the turn of the century. From *1871–1971: One Hundred Years of Gaiety*.

14. Stella (Mrs. Patrick) Campbell as Paula Tanqueray with George Alexander as Aubrey in *The Second Mrs. Tanqueray.* Courtesy of the Raymond Mander–Joe Mitchenson Theatre Collection.

15. Miss Kate Bateman as "Leah the Forsaken" (1863). Courtesy of the Raymond Mander–Joe Mitchenson Theatre Collection.

16. Olga Nethersole, from a picture postcard (ca. 1898). Courtesy of the Irish Theatre Archive, Dublin.

17. Mrs. (Millicent) Bandmann-Palmer (1845?–1923) as Hamlet. Courtesy of the Folger Shakespeare Library.

18. Martin Harvey as Sydney Carton (ca. 1900), from a picture postcard. Courtesy of the Irish Theatre Archive, Dublin.

19. Martin Harvey as Hamlet, played for the first time at the Theatre Royal, Dublin, 21 November 1904. Courtesy of the Irish Theatre Archive, Dublin.

20. Martin Harvey as Sydney Carton in Freeman Wills and Frederick Langbridge's *The Only Way*. Courtesy of Hutchinson Publishing Company.

novel created a mania in Dublin, as the *Irish Playgoer* in 1900 remembered: "What playgoer can ever forget the *furore* created by 'Trilby' when the play was first presented at the Gaiety some few years ago by Mr. Tree [1895]? Everyone was crazy to see it, and there was nothing but Trilby spoken of for months afterward in the city."[27] That Joyce's family should go to see Tree – or that Molly should as well – verifies their rootedness in Dublin culture (as "English" as the cultural object might have been originally).

Not so gripping as Tree's Svengali, Edward Terry's drunken but good-hearted attorney Dick Phenyl in Pinero's *Sweet Lavender* (1888) was seen in Dublin nearly every year between 1897 and 1904 (though Terry succeeded in other roles as well). In this urban fairy tale, Lavender, the wronged then redeemed heroine, serves eventually as an exemplar of virtue rewarded in modern London. Her future father-in-law remarks, "Yes, yes, we'll speak well of London. For in this overgrown tangle some flowers find strength to raise their heads – the flowers of hope and atonement." When asked about this sanguine perspective, Lavender responds: "I think, sir – what ever Clement [her fiancé] thinks, always" (183).[28] As lines such as these indicate, it was not a socially reformative trajectory in *Sweet Lavender* that attracted the young Joyce.[29] Comically analogous to Martin Harvey's impersonation of Sidney Carton in *The Only Way*, Terry's representation of an amicably inebriated law, rather than the unyielding law with which villains were allied in melodrama, might have been received by Irish audiences as a comic subversion of power or legal authority. Such a "colonial" rereading of Pinero would resituate plays like *Sweet Lavender* in proximity to David Krause's "profane book" of Irish comedy, a desacralizing and parodic comedy (like those of O'Casey and Synge) used as a compensatory strategy by subject peoples to achieve paradoxical victories over their oppressors.[30] Unquestionably, Joyce would have relished such a victory achieved through parody or travesty. This explanation might also account for the enduring and, in this context, ironic success with Joyce and Dublin audiences of a play that concludes by romanticizing London.

But Olga Nethersole, whom Stanislaus Joyce specifically identifies, is another story entirely. As the Dublin theatrical calendar confirms, Nethersole made frequent trips to Dublin's Gaiety Theatre, playing *only* fallen women in *Camille, Magda, The Second Mrs. Tanqueray,* and, her most famous role, the title character in Clyde Fitch's *Sapho*. She appeared as Marguerite Gauthier in October 1897, as Fanny LeGrand in *Sapho* in October 1902, and as both Fanny and Magda in October 1903. The news of her arrest in New

York for public indecency occasioned by a performance of *Sapho* in March 1900 spread to Dublin and prompted an eloquent defense of Fitch's play in the *Irish Playgoer.* It was not only the content of *Sapho* that incited police to halt its performance in New York but also Nethersole's demonstrative, some argued "suggestive" and "indecent," style of acting. It was, then, almost certainly both the plays and strong performances of Nethersole as Marguerite, Magda, and Fanny that drew Dubliners to the Gaiety Theatre. Indeed, as reviewers document, it was more the latter–what Shaw termed Nethersole's "accentuated and conscious" acting style (*Theatres* 1:127)–that grabbed the attention of the "gods" in the galleries when she was playing in Dublin. And here, too, parallels exist between this lesser-known actress and Molly.

The Daudet novel Fitch adapted for the stage bears generic resemblance to *Magda,* to *La Dame aux Camélias,* and to chapters of Moore's *Confessions of a Young Man.* Daudet's *Sapho* is set in Paris of the 1870s, Moore's in the Parisian art community of the 1880s. Like Marguerite Gauthier who develops a relationship with the young student Armand Duval, Fanny at the beginning of the novel begins a passionate affair with Jean Gaussin, a "serious, hard-working youth" laboring toward advancement in the Department of Foreign Affairs. In some ways like Stephen Dedalus in *Portrait,* Gaussin aspires to the status of "exile," except that here exile signifies government service and the upholding of family tradition rather than escape from home. The respective ages of the lovers are established by the novel's first lines when Gaussin's age is revealed: twenty-one. Fanny is thirty-seven. Similar to Magda's and Molly's candid admissions of desire, Fanny's ardor for Gaussin manifests itself quickly: after meeting him at a party, she returns with him to his students' lodging house–and stays for two days. From a physically prodigious start–the lovers' tryst begins with Gaussin's carrying Fanny up four flights of stairs–their long, intimate congress evolves. We learn later that Fanny has served frequently as a sculptor's model during her some twenty years in Paris and that Gaussin is not her first conquest. Like Molly's flirtations, Fanny's amours are staple topics in male conversation. Also like Molly and Magda, Fanny became sexually active while still quite young, about the time she started her modeling career. When she was seventeen, she posed for a famous statue of *Sapho,* a replica of which Gaussin saw every day on his father's mantel. Now, like Galatea's animation in W. S. Gilbert's *Pygmalion and Galatea* (1871), which was produced frequently in Dublin, the statue has come alive for Gaussin with an extraordinary vitality: "the capacity for pleasure there was in her, the fire in that stone, that harpsichord in which not a note was missing!"[31]

Act 1 of Fitch's four-act adaptation follows the beginning of Daudet's novel, ending with Gaussin carrying Fanny up to her room and not returning, the suggestiveness of which was partially responsible for the police action in New York. In act 2, Fanny returns to care for Jean while he is ill, and friends of Fanny's former lover, a forger named Flamant who has been arrested earlier, come seeking Fanny's assistance. Jean learns of Fanny's past indiscretions and becomes angry but is gradually convinced by Fanny's emotional burning of old love letters, among other acts, that she has finally reformed. They enjoy a brief respite of happiness secluded in the country away from Paris, but by act 3 Jean begins to regret his indiscretion and is prepared to end the relationship. As Joy Reilly, who has conducted an extensive study of Nethersole, observes, Fanny at this point decides to atone for her past life, in part by devoting herself to the child Flamant fathered — and whom Fitch prominently places in the foreground to elicit the audience's sympathy. By act 4, after an unsuccessful attempt at suicide, Fanny grows both wiser and more sympathetic. Jean returns to her, unable to live without her, and it is clear Fanny returns his love. In a final act of self-sacrifice, she writes Jean a love letter and steals away into the night to return to Flamant, thus allowing her young lover to further his career. Echoing a critic at the time, Reilly notes that Daudet's novel, a cautionary tale about a young and weak-willed man falling for a more experienced woman, becomes for Nethersole a vehicle to "soak the star with sympathy." Another redaction of the novel, as Reilly points out, concerns the act 1 seduction: in Daudet's novel Fanny clearly seduces her young lover, while in Fitch's play a "country boy" falls for "a soft-hearted temptress who made a half-hearted attempt to ward him off."[32]

The admixture in *Sapho* of artistry and sexuality, maternal impulse and sexual desire, resembles similar relationships in *Magda* and *Ulysses,* especially Molly's expression of maternal affection for Milly and sexual desire for Stephen. But the most obvious parallel between *Sapho* and *Ulysses* concerns an older woman's seduction of a younger man, an issue that emerges in tamer form in dramas such as *The Notorious Mrs. Ebbsmith* and *Mrs. Dane's Defence.* In these works, however, the differences in age are not nearly so extreme as that between Fanny and Jean — or Molly and Stephen. At thirty-three, Agnes Ebbsmith is five years older than Lucas Cleeve, an unhappily married man with whom she resides in Italy; in *Mrs. Dane's Defence* Sir Daniel Carteret, Mrs. Dane's crafty adversary, advises his adopted son, age twenty-four, not to forge an alliance with an older woman (in this case twenty-seven, though Carteret suspects the lady might be older). Both dramas suggest, albeit less dramatically than Daudet's novel, that older women exert an "un-naturally" strong influence over their younger lovers, a thesis to which Stephen would seem to subscribe. His interpretation in "Scylla and Charybdis" of Shakespeare's relationship with Ann Hathaway punningly stresses the twenty-six-year old's sexual power over her younger lover, eight years her junior at the time of their marriage in November 1582. "He chose badly? He was chosen, it seems to me. If others have their will Ann hath a way. By cock, she was to blame. She put the comether on him, sweet and twenty-six. The greyeyed goddess who bends over the boy Adonis, stooping to conquer, as prologue to the swelling act, is a boldfaced Stratford wench who tumbles in a cornfield a lover younger than herself" (9:256–60). Joyce was at times almost obsessed with infidelity (during the late summer and fall of 1909, for instance, when he was convinced of Nora's intimacy with Vincent Cosgrave five years earlier) and employs Ann Hathaway's "tumbling" of Shakespeare – she was some three months pregnant with Susanna at the time of their marriage – as a key to reading Gertrude's "incestuous" marriage to Claudius in *Hamlet*. But more than adultery is at issue: Ann's age and conquest of a younger lover, her ability to seduce or put the "comether" on him, seem equally central to Stephen's interpretation of Shakespeare.

The older woman's sexual power is central both to Molly's reveries of seducing Stephen and to the world of art into which Joyce desired access. In his autobiographical *Confessions of a Young Man*, Moore, not merely as author but as the eighteen-year-old narrator of the novel (he insisted he *was* the narrator), undertakes the study of painting in Paris. In one chapter, predictably, he inveighs against marriage as destructive of the mystery of intimate relationships. In another chapter, consistent with his attack on marriage, his effusion about the charms of the "woman of thirty" parallels the unconventional, socially disruptive allure of Magda, Molly, and Fanny LeGrand. "It is clear that, by the very essence of her being, the young girl may evoke no ideal but that of home; and home is in his eyes the antithesis of freedom, desire, aspiration. He longs for mystery, deep and endless. . . . He dreams of Pleasure, and he is offered duty. . . . But the woman of thirty presents from the outset all that is necessary to ensnare the heart of a young man."[33] The young artist's attraction to the older woman, therefore, might both enslave and inspire him, finalizing his break from home and leading him to artistic accomplishment. Accordingly, the older woman becomes an overdetermined symbol of various revolts – sexual, social, and artistic – both in popular drama and fiction and in *Ulysses*. Ann Hathaway (for Stephen, one instance of the alluring *femme de trente ans*) puts the "comether" on the teenaged Shakespeare, who transforms his personal dilemma into the adultery in *Hamlet;* the woman of thirty captivates the young artist in *Confessions of a Young Man,* eighteen years old as Shakespeare was when he succumbed to his "boldfaced Stratford wench"; Fanny LeGrand in her late thirties enthralls Jean Gaussin. And Molly would make Stephen "feel all over him till he half faints under me" (18:1364), then Stephen would transpose the experience into art: "they all write about some woman in their poetry well I suppose he wont find many like me" (18:1333–34).

One observation recurs in commentary on Olga Nethersole's portrayal of Fanny and similar characters: her extremely "realistic," provocative acting style designed to elicit a strong reaction from the audience. If Joyce interpreted *Magda* as a statement about "genius breaking out in the home," some critics feared that Nethersole's acting might lead to prurient interest breaking out in the theater. Even those who praised her acting expressed concern about the frankness of her impersonations. In late March 1900, the *Irish Playgoer,* for example, criticized the legal obstruction of productions of *Sapho* in New York, arguing that "there is nothing in the piece to warrant the very severe measure which has been dealt out to *Sapho.*" On the contrary, according to the *Playgoer,* much of the offensive dialogue and incidents had been expunged from Fitch's adaptation, leaving "nothing but the good and the artistic" and teaching "young men," better "than any sermon could," of the "folly of leading a dissolute life."[34] Nonetheless, as the *Playgoer* averred in an earlier retrospective of Nethersole's "memorable engagement" at the Gaiety in 1897 as Marguerite Gauthier, some members of the audience were bothered by the "amount of osculation indulged in by the lovers," which was "enormously large and varied in execution" in the early scenes with Duval: "Passion was *never so unreservedly enacted on the stage* in my presence before. It made one feel queer in witnessing so unearnest and unreserved a display; the art of it, however, was perfect and saved it from ridicule" (emphasis added).[35] Many less generous New York and London critics, however, could not detect the "art" of Nethersole's performances, only the unreserved display. One critical target, as Joy Reilly mentions, was the "Nethersole kiss," of which the *New York Dramatic Mirror* complained in regard to Nethersole's impersonation of Marguerite Gauthier:

> If the too-famous Nethersole kiss could be done off the stage—if we could be allowed to imagine it instead of having it made the feature of the play—we ought to get one of the stage's most interesting heroines.
> But when you see Matinee Boys . . . timing a kiss with their watches, as

though it were some record-breaking feat in athletics, it gets you away from the thread of the plot.[36]

Like Molly, who confesses "theres nothing like a kiss long and hot down to your soul almost paralyses you" (18:105–6), Nethersole was not timid about exhibiting the pleasure of passionate kissing, and apparently young males in the audience, like Moore before them, found this *femme de trente ans* very enticing.

The support Nethersole received from the *Irish Playgoer* and the almost playful admonition of the *New York Dramatic Mirror* were accompanied, as could be expected, by far more pointed indictments. Never exhausting his storehouse of cynicisms, Winter compared Fitch's *Sapho* to a "reeking compost of filth and folly" that shows in a "carnal way" how a "harlot and a fool" consorted with each other; the play involved "contemptible proceedings, impure pictures, and, through all, a purulent stream of mawkish cant."[37] Deprecated as a "languorous, insinuating siren" by one critic, Nethersole's Fanny was viewed by another as "coarse, vulgar, and violent," especially vulgar in the "immodest moment" when Jean carries Fanny offstage and does not return.[38] Such an outburst, given the profound distaste for Ibsen and "New Womanhood" of critics like Winter in New York and Clement Scott in London, seems predictable enough. But so too does the allegation of a "too naturalistic" or excessive performance. One might argue, as Shaw did when he saw Nethersole portray Agnes Ebbsmith some five years before the Sapho controversy, that even substantial roles were often attenuated by lesser actresses' uncontrolled, highly emotive histrionics. This weak conventionality, for Shaw, was glaringly obvious in Nethersole's impassioned speech as Agnes against her aristocratic antagonist in Pinero's play: "Miss Nethersole made the speech an emotional outburst, flying out at the Duke exactly as, in a melodrama, she would have flown out at the villain who had betrayed her. My inference is that Miss Nethersole has force and emotion without sense of character" (*Theatres* 1:128). No matter. For young Joyce the emotion would seem to have been enough–or, more fairly, the revolt from home combined with an emotionally vivid representation of sexual passion would have been enough–to draw him to the Gaiety when Olga Nethersole arrived to play a fallen woman like Magda or Fanny.

Through such contextualization of Molly, I believe, not only is her character illuminated, but so too is one function of "Penelope" which pertains to the novel's "comic" reconciliation of husband and wife: namely, a collapsing of the oppositions underlying the late Victorian problem play and a revised conception of home as a place for authority and freedom, repression and desire, male and female rule. Such a contextualization, therefore, makes even more unthinkable what Fredric Jameson disparages as "ethical" readings of *Ulysses* in which Bloom is seen "reasserting his authority" at the novel's conclusion. "In this day and age . . . is it really appropriate to recast 'Ulysses' along the lines of marriage counselling and anxiously to interrogate its characters and their destinies with a view towards saving this marriage and restoring this family? Has our whole experience of Mr Bloom's Dublin reduced itself to this, the quest for a 'happy ending' in which the hapless protagonist is to virilise himself and become a more successful realisation of the dominant, patriarchal, authoritarian male?"[39] The answers are clear: such a recasting of characters and dogged "quest" for comic reconciliation are not "appropriate," but not necessarily for the otherwise politically desirable reasons Jameson gives. For the limited terms of the questions he frames, particularly those ascribing dominance to Bloom, are as oversimplified as the categories into which many male critics once tended to place Molly: Gea Tellus or "thirty-shilling whore."[40]

Given the context of popular dramas I have adumbrated above, Bloom's request for breakfast and Molly's refrain of "yes" are hardly consonant with patriarchal authority as it was represented in Joyce's and the Blooms' Dublin. That Molly's affair with Boylan is conducted *inside* the home–and that she contemplates continuing to seek sexual gratification *outside* of marriage, whether with Boylan or Stephen, whom Bloom has brought home in "Ithaca"–hardly imply a restoration of male authority in the Bloom household. The depiction of home as a trap from which characters like Magda must escape, or as a social abyss into which women like Paula Tanqueray must inevitably sink, is completely overturned by "Penelope." On the contrary, the Blooms' comic reunion–and comic *does* seem the most appropriate modifier here–signals a rupture in the representation of marriage and phallocentric domination of the home (and social status quo) that Joyce had experienced in the theater. In this regard, "Penelope" draws *Ulysses* closer to the Edwardian problem play and its implicit critique of the patriarchy Jameson, today's feminists, and yesterday's fallen women quite justifiably deplore.

In the posing of such questions, Jameson also fails to account for Joyce's radicalized and evolving conception of home. In 1898, after seeing *Magda,* home for Joyce signified that entity against which "genius" revolts;

in August 1904, as he wrote to Nora, home symbolizes "the whole present social order and Christianity" he summarily rejected. Joyce's development of the oppositions home/sexual freedom and home/artistic freedom continues in *Dubliners,* perhaps nowhere so painfully as in "Eveline." Here home is the force that locks an attractive nineteen-year-old girl in the positions of breadwinner for and scullion to an abusive father, preventing her from starting a new life together in Argentina with a man who seems to promise her love and freedom. The motif of home as the enslaving force in Eveline's life recurs throughout the story:

> Now she was going to go away like the others, to leave her *home.*
> *Home!* She looked round the room, reviewing all its familiar objects . . . from which had never dreamed being divided. . . .
> She had consented to go away, to leave her *home.* Was that wise? . . .
> In her *home* anyway she had shelter and food; she had those whom she had known all her life about her. (*D* 37; emphasis added)

But, of course, Eveline is deluding herself, as the narrative confirms. Home provides no refuge from her father's abuse; her money goes to buy the family's food, the supply of which is often low because of his drinking; most of her family and former friends have either died or moved away so those "she had known all her life" are really no longer "about her," save for two small siblings. Frank, her lover from an exotic place with the tumbling hair and face of bronze, embodies the foreign influence that triggers Eveline's contemplation of leaving Dublin. Fearing that her essential self will be drowned, she elects to remain at home, and Frank returns to the sea and romantic beyond.

This characterization of home as a force of containment insofar as sexuality is concerned expands in the later stories of *Dubliners* to include the home's devastation of artistic development. This, I think, is significant, as Joyce implies that not just nineteen-year-old girls regard home in this way, but so too do men in their thirties. There is, though, a difference: the security of home which so attracts Eveline dismays or repulses several of Joyce's older Dubliners. Little Chandler's reunion with Ignatius Gallaher, the accomplished London journalist and equally accomplished ladies' man in "A Little Cloud," helps make this connection for the pathetic, would-be writer, Chandler, When Chandler returns home, he recalls Gallaher's conquests of exotic women: "He thought of what Gallaher had said about rich Jewesses.

Those dark oriental eyes, he thought, how full they are of passion, of voluptuous longing" (*D* 83). But there is no passion in Little Chandler's marriage, nor is there within its conventionality any possibility of artistic development. Passion and creativity do not grow at home, which does not admit of a foreign or exotic influence. As a result, Farrington in "Counterparts" prefers the public house, where he brushes against a beautiful woman with a London (foreign) accent, and "loathed returning to his home" (*D* 97). This opposition also underlies Gabriel Conroy's deflating discovery of Gretta's former lover, Michael Furey, in "The Dead." Gretta's home in Galway and the west of Ireland in general, as we learn earlier in Miss Ivors's censure of Gabriel, are to Gabriel more foreign and less interesting than continental Europe. The revelation of Gretta's past relationship with Furey—whom, not coincidentally, she had "implored" to go home and cease his display of shivering passion one night not long before his death–quickly dissipates Gabriel's feelings of cultural superiority and sexual mastery. Conroy sees himself as a "ludicrous figure" and "pitiable fatuous fellow" of "clownish lusts" (*D* 220): the time had come for him to leave home and "to set out on his journey westward" (*D* 223).

These oppositions, so central to *Dubliners* and to the plays I have been discussing, are undone in *Ulysses*. Interested in the "dialectic of home" in *Ulysses*, Jules David Law considers the "priority of language and home" in Joyce, starting with Stephen's professed sense of alienation from the English language in *Portrait*. "Home" is one of the words that sounds "different" on an Englishman's lips and on Stephen's, and from this point Law extrapolates one of the projects of characters in *Ulysses* (and of readers of the novel as well): "trying to work out satisfactory definitions of a culture (national or otherwise) they can feel at home in."[41] Law regards the "Nestor" chapter as crucial to Stephen's project, differentiating his sense of Ireland from that of Deasy, the chauvinistic and anti-Semitic schoolmaster at Stephen's school. For Deasy, history is structured by the repetitive betrayals of women–Eve, Helen of Troy, the wife of the medieval Irish lord MacMurrough, and Kitty O'Shea, Parnell's lover–and these transgressions allow strangers to enter Cathleen Ni Houlihan's home. Stephen, conversely, presents an "ideal of cosmopolitanism over and against Deasy's paranoid isolationism." Employing J. Hillis Miller's deconstruction of the host/parasite binarism, Law distinguishes Stephen's view of home: "In Stephen's mind, then, the integrity of home is preserved not by the expulsion of parasites and traitors but by a participation in the foreign or the strange–by a venture outside the home.

The external thus supplements, and is perhaps superior to, the internal."[42] This venture into the foreign or external is crucial to Stephen's sense of self in *Ulysses,* as he clarifies in "The Wandering Rocks": "Throb always without you and the throb always within. Your heart you sing of. I between them. Where? Between two roaring worlds where they swirl, I. Shatter them, one and both. But stun myself too in the blow. Shatter me you who can" (10:822–26). Stephen sees himself between worlds and feels the pressure of the position, but there is little question that this discomfiture is preferable to Deasy's parochialism – or to Eveline's fear of the world outside her home and Dublin.

Molly, too, is between worlds. In the first images of her in "Calypso," she is literally between two worlds of popular culture: *The Bath of the Nymph,* "splendid masterpiece in art colours," above the bed; and the pornographic *Ruby: The Pride of the Ring* below the bed, "sprawled" inelegantly against the chamberpot like the woman in the novel at whose picture Bloom glances. The Blooms' bed exists, literally, between the celestial realm of masterpieces and nymphs (idealizations even if the artwork is reproduced in a popular periodical) and the more earthly realm of chamberpots. Like Deasy's roster of female transgressors, Molly has admitted a foreign influence into her orbit – into the Bloom house – but the family home still exists, maybe even in a state superior to the one that obtained the day before. On the one hand, Molly is the antithesis of Maria, the "old maid" in "Clay," who, being an "unmarried, childless, and virginal woman endows her with a negative prestige."[43] Molly's vital sexuality places her in a similarly negative category in her social world for precisely the opposite reason – too great an appetite rather than too little – suggesting the impossible social predicament of Irish women, whose sexuality is constantly measured and discussed by men. On the other hand, numerous popular plays in Joyce's Dublin manipulate audiences in such a way as to gather sympathy for the "fallen" or New Woman.[44] Much like Bloom, who gains our admiration by bringing the influence of the foreign (Stephen) home – here Bloom emulates the heroine of Augustin Daly's play *Leah* by wandering in an often hostile anti-Semitic environment, saving a child, and returning the child home – Molly gains our sympathy and understanding in "Penelope." She has bridled against a sterile marriage and challenged the repressive institutions which in the theater Dubliners (and we) despise. In the process, she has transformed the home, a locus of patriarchal authority and repressive ideology, into a foreign enough place where Stephen might very well feel at home.

ARTISTRY AND SPIRITUALITY:
Ibsen's Artist and Eleonora Duse's Art

Besides portraying Molly's entrapment between worlds, her positioning in "Calypso" and throughout much of the novel is a result of Joyce's careful staging of the problematic central both to *Ulysses* and to his own theater-going experience. That is, Molly occupies some middle ground between *The Bath of the Nymph* above and the smudged pages of *Ruby: the Pride of the Ring* below, literally between art and a crudely melodramatic variety of soft-core pornography. This same scene replicates, borrowing Joyce's own terminology in "Ibsen's New Drama," the "naked drama" of the action I shall consider here: either the "perception of a great truth, or the opening up of a great question, or great conflict which is almost independent of the conflicting actors" (*CW* 63). The "great conflict" in which I am interested is waged between the artist and sexuality, sexuality construed here not simply as a synonym for sexual activity but also as a socially constructed category within which one's identity is defined. For all the sympathy Molly elicits situated in the context of New Women like Magda Schwartze and Fanny Legrand, and for all this recontextualization implies about Joyce's attentiveness to representations of female sexuality, another side exists both in the novel and in Joyce's coming to terms with his aspiration to become an artist: namely, the coextensive notion of artistry as transcending the very physical needs Molly expresses. In moments like that at the end of "Lestrygonians" in which, with Handel's *Messiah* resonating in his mind, Bloom clumsily inspects the Greek "goddesses" at the National Library, the polarities spirit/body, art/life are represented comically, even farcically. Nevertheless, reconciling the needs of the body with the spiritual dimensions of artistry posed a more serious dilemma for the young Joyce—and formed the major conflict in many dramas he saw or read. Indeed, the relationship between artistry and sexuality informs the Richard-Bertha-Robert triangle in *Exiles* and illuminates Joyce's reaction to plays like Ibsen's *When We Dead Awaken*. I turn now to the ways in which artistry and spirituality were braided on the late Victorian stage and then adduce ways in which "Nausicaa" was influenced both by romantic notions of the "spirituality" of artists and by the theatrical conventions that realized "spirituality" on stage.

Another aspect of Molly's positioning in "Calypso"—and in "Penelope," too, since the latter chapter takes place in the Blooms' bedroom—is related to this topic as well: the commodification and privatization of forms of culture, processes of which Joyce was acutely aware. This critical awareness, for example, informs Bloom's response to the "art" that adorns his walls: "*The Bath of the Nymph* over the bed. Given away with the Easter number of *Photo Bits:* splendid masterpiece in art colours. . . . Not unlike her with her hair down: slimmer. Three and six I gave for the frame. She said it would look nice over the bed. Naked nymphs" (4:369–73). Though obviously not to so great an extent as today's television viewers, videotape collectors, and tourists armed with instamatic cameras, Joyce's Dubliners resided in a modern culture in which art could be reproduced, possessed, and consumed at an ever-accelerating rate. It could even be employed in a promotion with a popular magazine and, like television today, could be viewed in the privacy of one's own home—or from one's bed. In this process of marketing artistic texts or objects as commodities, such artifacts can no longer be said to possess any "qualitative value" in themselves, but only insofar as they can be "used."[45]

In this regard, John Brenkman's critique of today's mass culture finds a parallel in the effect of culture on Joyce and his characters. "Through its dominant *cultural* forms and practices, late capitalism strives to sever social experience from the formation of counter-ideologies, to break collective experience into the monadic isolation of the private experience of individuals and to pre-empt the effects of association by subsuming the discourses and images that regulate social life." Brenkman maintains that mass culture's effectivity resides in its organization of "symbolic mediations and symbolic interactions in relation to the body and subjectivity," because under capitalism the body is turned into an instrument of production.[46] *Ulysses,* and much of Joyce, registers the effects of these processes as most experiences of popular cultural forms are inflected by the consciousnesses of characters in their relative isolation. The pantomime structure of "Circe," Bloom's psychodrama, remains perhaps the most vivid example of this. So even though Joyce's fiction is replete with allusions to popular culture, we rarely obtain access to the theater or music hall; and with the notable exception of the music in "Sirens," we seldom witness the social or interactive dimension of popular culture in *Ulysses*. Like the "splendid masterpiece" over the Blooms' bed, which we know only through Bloom's response to it, cultural texts in *Ulysses* are relegated to the more private domain of human consciousness—or to the commercial arena of advertising. As I shall discuss momentarily, these texts are refashioned within consciousness into consumable objects or statements with an extremely personal meaning, statements formed in part by the promotion of cultural texts as commodities.

This discussion, therefore, will be premised on a very different position from the one I advocated earlier: Joyce's Dublin as a culturally specific representation, as opposed to Moretti's emphases of privatization in the novel, of "Joyce and *Ulysses* as expressions of English society and culture," and of Dublin as the "literary image *par excellence* of the modern city." Like Cheryl Herr, I still reject the reductiveness of treating Joyce as an English writer, thereby ignoring the referentiality of Joyce's representation of Dublin; yet there is no denying the privatization of cultural forms in *Ulysses* or the influence of European culture on Joyce and Dublin. Richard Ellmann concedes this by stressing the importance of Ibsen's letter to the eighteen-year-old Joyce in April 1900, after the aged playwright had read the young Irishman's essay on *When We Dead Awaken* in the *Fortnightly Review:* "Before Ibsen's letter Joyce was an Irishman; after it he was a European" (*JJ* 75). And this "Europeanness" resulted in, among other things, Joyce's re-doubled consumption of the plays of Gabriele D'Annunzio, Sudermann, Maurice Maeterlinck, Björnstjerne Björnson, and, of course, Ibsen and Hauptmann.

Consequently, here I shall place his early consideration of the artist's spirituality and his "stage design" of various moments in *Ulysses* within his experience of Continental drama. My about-face at this point is necessitated, in part, by the more global influence of the texts and performers which informed Joyce's vision of artistry. Mrs. Campbell and Olga Nethersole, to be sure, played Pinero's and other fallen women in England, Ireland, Canada, and the United States; and several less distinguished plays revived frequently in Dublin like W. S. Gilbert's *Pygmalion and Galatea* and Bulwer-Lytton's *Lady of Lyons* treat the issue of artistry and sexuality. In their treatment of heroic selflessness and idealized love, these plays are more or less typical of several "Dublin favorites" like Wills's *Royal Divorce* and *The Only Way* with Martin Harvey that Gerty MacDowell, Molly, and Milly have all seen. But the influence of these dramas cannot compare with that of *When We Dead Awaken* and the D'Annunzio plays starring Eleonora Duse that Joyce and his father saw in London, which attained a more privileged status among intellectuals and playgoers alike than Wills's drama of Josephine's self-sacrifice to help consolidate Napoleon's political power or Bulwer's poetic drama of a young artist's devotion to an idealized and socially superior beloved.

Though Stanislaus Joyce reiterates that by his middle college days Joyce pursued a "promiscuous sexual life" that was "open and deliberate" (*MBK* 153) – Joyce reviled sentimentality and manifested an "instinctive aversion to what he regarded as a clownish idealization of lust" (*MBK* 154) – Stanislaus also implies that "remnants" of earlier ideas at times insinuate themselves into his brother's writing. These remnants, particularly those communicated by the stage, are the subject of what follows.

As an inaugural example of the way popular drama communicates romantic idealizations and affects representations of such in Joyce, consider the episode in *Portrait* after Stephen invests some of his thirty-three-pound essay and exhibition prizes in theater tickets for his family. One ticket was to *The Lady of Lyons,* which, by 1897, when the Joyce family viewed it, had enhanced star actors' repertories for some sixty years, beginning with William Charles Macready's production in 1838. After the "season of pleasure" came to an end, a season of special treats and avid playgoing for the Dedalus family, the "household returned to its usual way of life," and Stephen found himself burning to "appease the fierce longings of his heart" (*P* 98). He mollifies these longings, initially, through sordid dreams, awakening in the morning to a "keen and humiliating sense of transgression" occasioned by the "dim memory of dark orgiastic riot" (99). Then Stephen begins nightly "wanderings" of "dirty streets" and "foul laneways," burning with "the wasting fires of lust" as he surveys "obscene" scrawls on the "oozing wall of a urinal" (100). Interrupting, momentarily, his trek toward "sin with another of his kind" are images of Dumas's Mercedes (Stephen had earlier been reading *The Count of Monte Cristo*) and the "small white house and the garden of rosebushes on the road that led to the mountains" (99), with Stephen assuming the role of the wronged Edmund Dantes.

In addition to the flowers and perfumed air of Dumas's romance, Dantes shares Stephen's imagination with Bulwer's heroic and eloquent artist from *The Lady of Lyons:* "At those moments the soft speeches of Claude Melnotte rose to his lips and eased his unrest" (*P* 99). In Bulwer's drama, Melnotte, the inherently noble son of a common gardener, impersonates a prince to court his beloved Pauline. He wins her love, then loses it after confessing his duplicity (though in his absence she is overwhelmed by genuine affection for him), then regains it after demonstrating his true quality as a soldier. Though Joyce never specifies which speeches intruded upon Stephen's consciousness, Melnotte's several professions of adoration of Pauline would seem likely candidates. Their utopian imagery and amatory excess contrast sharply with the urban filth and moral decay in which Stephen wallows, and several of Melnotte's more florid speeches concern the relationship between ideal love and artistry. For example:

> I saw thee and the passionate heart of man
> Enter'd the breast of the wild-dreaming boy;
> And from that hour I grew—what to the last
> I shall be—thine adorer! . . .
>   I thought of thee,
> And passion taught me poesy—of thee,
> And on the painter's canvas grew the life
> Of beauty!—Art became the shadow
> Of the dear starlight of thine haunting eyes![47]

In *Portrait,* this residual moment of romantic ideology is finally ineffectual in extinguishing Stephen's emerging desire, as he falls into the embrace of a prostitute. More important, Stephen's moral compunctions are articulated through reference to a play that equates idealized love with artistic accomplishment; and the syntax of Joyce's sentence implies that Stephen is not an active or empowered agent consciously deploying memories from Bulwer's play as an antidote to desire. Rather, Melnotte's speeches constitute the agent of action here: they "rose" to Stephen's lips, just as desire has exploded into lust, while Stephen himself merely receives them in an almost passive fashion.

This episode in *Portrait* not only intimates the power of culture in young Joyce's life but foreshadows ways in which references to the popular theater operate within his later work. The oppositions between romantic (sacred) love/profane lust, natural beauty of the garden/excremental ugliness of the city, high (Mercedes's mountain)/low (swooning into a prostitute's arms) are co-present and maintained throughout the scene. Romantic drama, moreover, tends to reproduce components of the dominant ideology: reiterating the importance of institutions and institutional morality, for instance, and encouraging the reestablishment of absolute values and binarisms. Stephen's naïve adherence to these idealizations recalls Eveline Hill's blind devotion to her family, or the infatuation of the young narrator of "Araby," who carries the "chalice" of his devotion to Mangan's sister "even in places the most hostile to romance" (*D* 31). His infatuation with Mangan's sister evolves during his meditations in the back drawing room of his home, one formerly occupied by a priest. Here the young boy prays to his new god–the "image" of Mangan's sister–as the sacred and the secular, the high and the low become articulated through the same lexicon of Catholicism.

In *Ulysses*, however, the polar oppositions of romantic drama are collapsed: Molly fantasizes about seducing Stephen, then becoming the motivation for his art; Bloom inspects Greek statues for their anuses as he thinks about the "sacred" music of Handel's *Messiah;* Stephen attributes *Hamlet* to Ann Hathaway's adultery. Indeed, it is arguable that one aspect crucial to Joyce's parodic-travestying irony or modernity in *Ulysses* is his implosion of the oppositions that constituted late Victorian romantic drama: the "Scylla" of spirituality, one might say, and the "Charybdis" of sensuality. Conversely, one symptom of his entrapment in the "old" value system from which he sought relief–and of many Dubliners' inability to extricate themselves from the same values–is the instauration of polarities found in the passage taken from *Portrait*. Joyce's ability to collapse these oppositions, to locate himself outside of the world of late Victorian romantic drama, is what separates him from Molly, Bloom, Gerty, the young Stephen of the middle chapters of *Portrait*, and other characters (especially the failed artists of *Dubliners*). It is precisely for this reason that references to romantic dramas like *Leah, The Only Way*, and *A Royal Divorce*–or to operas popularly viewed in Dublin like *The Bohemian Girl* or *Maritana*–surface in Joyce's fiction: because they are meaningful to, part of, the everyday life of Dubliners. This interchange between the romantic and the quotidian is also central to the passage from *Portrait*. Stephen has returned to his "usual" existence and brought with him vivid images from the theater; the residue of this cultural transaction, its long-lasting and incorporative effect, remains with him, manipulating his interactions as it contributes to his sense of identity.

There is little question that, like young Dedalus, Joyce was attracted to the more spiritual representations of love and artistry not only in popular dramas like *The Lady of Lyons* but in Ibsen's dramas as well. Critics like Elliott Simon and Bonnie Kime Scott agree that, in Scott's words, Joyce "clearly prefers the mystical, spiritual Irene to Rubek's alienated wife, Maja" in *When We Dead Awaken*. In other instances, Joyce's alternative constructions of a female typology originate in other Ibsen plays and in Hauptmann's. Scott points to Stephen's meditation in *Portrait* on "the girls and women in the plays of Gerhart Hauptmann; and the memory of their pale sorrows and the fragrance falling from the wet branches mingled in a mood of quiet joy" (P 176); and to Joyce's rejection of the self-sacrificing "womanly woman" and questioning of the "ideal of 'purity' in human relationships."[48] This is as much to say that Stephen's conception of women changes significantly as he grows further from his adolescent "soul-crisis" that night on the streets of Dublin. Joyce's does as well. For as strong as his attraction was to the spirituality of characters like Irene in *When We Dead Awaken*–and to the acting of Duse–Ibsen's and D'Annunzio's plays, unlike the romantic drama so popular on the Dublin stage of his youth, work to deconstruct the oppositions spirit/body, artistry/sexuality on which popular drama is founded. The question remains, however, of how Joyce appropriates the conventions of romantic drama *and* endorses their ideological dismantling by Ibsen's and others plays–how artistry can, at the same time, be both spiritual and admissive of the sexual.

In discussing the latter topic–the deconstruction of the spirit/body duality in Ibsen and playwrights like D'Annunzio–I shall turn first to *When We Dead Awaken,* which moves toward both a "spiritualized" conception of art and a clear skepticism of romantic idealism. As the play begins, Arnold Rubek and his young wife, Maja, discuss their return, after a long absence and much travel, to Rubek's home, a return that makes him happy, but not totally so. Similar to the metaphors of opposing worlds in *Magda,* Rubek advises Maja that their return might require her psychological adjustment, because since she married him and traveled so extensively, she has "been living a generally grander and more spacious life . . . than you were used to at home" (8:241). The artist's home, like Joyce's development of the Bloom home in *Ulysses,* requires both the security of familiarity and the exotic influence of travel. Still, Rubek, the aging artist, desires more. As Maja is distracted and amused by Ulfheim, the great bear hunter, Irene, Rubek's former model for his masterpiece, arrives on the scene, prompting much of the discussion of art and sexuality in the play. As Joyce quotes in "Ibsen's New Drama," Rubek confides to Irene that, in their past collaboration on his sculpture, he was unable to touch her because "for me you became a sacred thing, untouchable, a thing to worship in thought alone." And though he still believes some of this, he has clearly experienced second thoughts: "I was still young then, Irene. I was obsessed with the idea that if I touched you, if I desired you sensually, my mind would be profaned and I would be unable to achieve what I was striving to create. And I still think there is some truth in that" (8:259). Irene counters scornfully, "The work of art first . . . the human being second!" (8:259), a rejoinder of obvious importance to Ibsen's delineation of Rubek's career as an artist. Though he desired Irene, he suppressed his desire and so created a masterpiece—but no more after this, only "trivial modellings." By contrast, since their collaboration Irene abandoned such artistic enterprises, selling herself as a commodity, or so she claims. "I have posed on a revolving pedestal in variety halls. Posed as a naked statue in peep shows. Made a lot of money. I wasn't used to that with you, Arnold—you never had any. And I've also been with men—men I could drive quite mad. I wasn't used to that with you, either" (8:255). The first act of *When We Dead Awaken,* therefore, moves toward a toppling of romantic oppositions: art must go beyond commodification, ascending to the heights Ibsen heroes always seem to envision just beyond their reach; but the human needs of the artist cannot forever be deferred.

Rubek recognizes this and tells Maja in act 2 that "all this business about the artist's mission and the artist's vocation was all so much empty, hollow, meaningless talk" (8:270). When Maja asks him what he prefers instead, Rubek's answer is "Life."[49] Later in the second act, after Maja and Rubek have effected a kind of separation and Maja returns to Ulfheim, Irene reappears and they talk of their past together. Here she alleges what she had only implied earlier, and Rubek begins to acknowledge the truth of her allegation: that he was an artist but not a man. As they recall their "child," Rubek's statue, a reversal begins to take place; as Rubek is renouncing his idealized conception of artistry, Irene begins to enunciate her idealizations, which pertain both to their collaboration and to Rubek as "holy" love object. By act 3, minutes before their burial in an avalanche, the language of spirituality and that of desire merge, as Irene and Rubek struggle to "awaken" from their pasts and its "death" and to ascend to the heights of life:

> IRENE: What has become of that burning desire you battled against when
>   I stood naked before you as the woman risen from the dead?
> RUBEK: Our love is not dead, Irene.
> IRENE: That love which is of our earthly life—the glorious, marvellous,
>   mysterious life on earth—that love is dead in us both. (8:295)

Rubek insists that this love still burns "strongly and passionately" so that their subsequent and fatal ascent to the heights signifies a symbolic joining of sexual desire and spirituality. In this iconography, unlike that of the scene from *Portrait* or the image of Molly between art and pornography, desire is neither located "down" or "below," nor is it the polarized opposite of idealized artistry. On Ibsen's symbolic landscape, the artist's spirituality must coexist with his physicality, a union of great importance to Joyce.

As James Hurt explains, *When We Dead Awaken,* even in its setting, moves steadily toward this resolution of opposites and Rubek's victorious ascent to the heights. The play's dramatic action begins at a coastal spa, shifts in act 2 to a mountain resort situated on a plateau, and ends on the mountaintop where Irene and Rubek can both glory in their nearness to the sun and find an end to their internal torment. Hurt sees the play, as I do and believe Joyce did, not as a "rejection of art" but as a repudiation of Rubek's "false art . . . based upon an untenable rejection of the whole self."[50] A similar rejection accounts in part for the failures of such would-be artists in *Dubliners* as Mr. James Duffy in "A Painful Case" or Little Chandler in "A Little Cloud." Duffy, for example, aspires through his relationship with Mrs. Sinico to ascend, in her eyes, "to an angelical stature"; however, in doing so, much as with Rubek's inability to touch Irene, a "strange impersonal voice" within Duffy mandated "the soul's incurable loneliness. We cannot give ourselves, it said: we are our own" (*D* 111). In "A Painful Case," artistry and sexual intimacy with the love object are immiscible, forever polarized and opposed.

Ibsen's plays work to undo this fatal construction. The last scene of *When We Dead Awaken* resembles the paradoxical victories in death in such other plays as *Hedda Gabler* and *The Master Builder.* Also, in its emphasis of the reconciliation of the spiritual and the human, *When We Dead Awaken* marks the culmination of a long-standing tension in Ibsen's realistic drama between artistry and sexuality (consider the young Joyce's hailing of Eilert Lövborg in *Hedda Gabler,* epitome of this tension, as an Ibsenite "genius"). For example, much of the dialogue in act 4 of *The Lady from the Sea* (1888), another frequently performed play at the end of the century, especially so in Duse's repertory, concerns artistry and marriage:

BOLETTE: Do you think it's right that an artist should get married?
LYNGSTRAND: Yes, I think so. If he can find somebody he really loves. . . .
BOLETTE: Even so, I think he ought rather to live for his art alone.
LYNGSTRAND: Of course he should. But he can do that just as well even though he does marry. (7:87)

When asked what the woman should live for in this arrangement, Lyng-strand replies, "His art." Here the romantic conception of the long-suffering artist–Claude Melnotte devoted to Pauline from afar, or Arnold Rubek and Irene forgoing a lifetime of happiness together for the sake of their sculpted "child"–is countered by another extremely pervasive representation at the turn of the century of this problem: the artist's wife as sacrificial victim to her man's art.

This alternative view finds its most eloquent theatrical expression in the partnership of Eleonora Duse and Gabriele D'Annunzio in plays such as *La Città Morta* (1896) and *La Gioconda* (1899). Joyce's strong reaction to Duse's art and D'Annunzio's plays is, for the most part, ably chronicled by his brother and by Ellmann, though both err slightly in recounting the plays Joyce saw on his trip to London in May 1900. Because I believe Joyce's attraction to Duse to be significant to this exposition and to his conception of "staging" in *Ulysses,* and because Ellmann appropriates so heavily from *My Brother's Keeper* to delineate Joyce's fascination with Duse, Stanislaus's recollection of his brother's viewing the internationally heralded actress merits careful consideration:

> There had been a further visit to London to see Duse in D'Annunzio's *La Gioconda* and *La Città Morta.* On this trip he met William Archer, who invited him to lunch. . . . Archer in comparing Duse with Bernhardt in Suder-mann's *Magda* (I think) gave it as his opinion that 'Duse could act Sarah off the stage', though for Archer Italian was a stumbling-block. My brother, who had not seen Duse act in any of Ibsen's plays, thought that she would be an ideal actress for Ibsen parts. . . .
>
> Before returning to Dublin, Jim procured a photograph of Duse which for a long time stood on his desk. . . . He also addressed some adulatory verses to her. . . . He never received any acknowledgment of the poem. Duse already had one poet on her hands [D'Annunzio], and that was more than enough. The poem was among those my brother burnt. (*MBK* 186–87)

In my view, this passage is significant in several ways. So too, unfortunately, are the confusing chronology and inaccuracy of "Ripening," the chapter in which the younger Joyce recounts his brother's admiration for the celebrated Italian actress. Most of "Ripening" concerns the year 1902, as the context of Stanislaus's remarks about his brother's viewing of Duse and meeting with Archer strongly suggest. Immediately before this, Stanislaus refers to Frank Fay's production of Yeats's *Cathleen Ni Houlihan,* starring Maud Gonne in the title role, at the Molesworth Hall in April 1902. (Here, his memory is slightly inaccurate: *Cathleen Ni Houlihan* and George Russell's *Deirdre* were produced by the Fay brothers on 2 April 1902 at Saint Teresa's Hall.) Just after the passage, Stanislaus mentions his brother's graduation from college on 31 October 1902. One might assume, therefore, that Joyce's "further visit" to London took place in 1902. But Ellmann does not make such an inference, placing the London trip two years earlier, in May 1900, when, according to Stanislaus's diary, Joyce in 1908 saw Duse perform in Ibsen's *Rosmersholm* and compared it to her earlier performance in *La Città Morta* in 1900 (*JJ* 266). In fact, again based on Stanislaus's recollections, Ellmann earlier in *James Joyce* identifies *La Gioconda* and *La Città Morta* as plays Joyce attended in London and also mentions Joyce's luncheon meeting with Archer (77).

The London theatrical calendar for 1900, however, suggests another possibility. As several of Duse's biographers emphasize, *La Città Morta* triggered considerable rancor between Duse and D'Annunzio, then her lover. After D'Annunzio wrote the play in 1896, he gave it to Sarah Bernhardt, who in 1898 performed it in Paris with unspectacular results. Duse first appeared in the play in the spring of 1901 and subsequently took it to North America for her 1902–3 tour.[51] When Duse appeared in May 1900 at London's Lyceum Theatre, her repertory opened on the tenth with *Magda*, then moved to an Italian version of *The Second Mrs. Tanqueray*, and concluded with *La Gioconda*. She did not appear in London at all in 1902. Even in her long season at the Adelphi Theatre in the fall of 1903, one featuring among others *Hedda Gabler*, *La Gioconda*, and D'Annunzio's *Francesca da Rimini* (1901), Duse did not perform *La Città Morta*. Thus Stanislaus Joyce not only misremembered the plays his brother saw but for some inexplicable reason transported an episode that occurred in 1900 to a time two years later. All of this would seem to justify his tentativeness in this passage: his claim to "remember little or nothing" about his brother's conversation with Archer and his parenthetical "I think" regarding Archer's supposed comparison of Duse and Bernhardt.

But if his memory fails him in these ways, Stanislaus Joyce's account seems accurate enough in other respects. Archer, in all likelihood, *did* compare Duse's Magda favorably to Bernhardt's, as his friend Bernard Shaw had done a few years previously. Sudermann's drama grew so successful after its inauspicious premiere, and served so conspicuously as one of those big roles in which actresses earned their status, that in turn-of-the-century London it was not uncommon for as many as three or four different productions of the play to appear during the same year, frequently offered in four languages: Duse's in Italian, Bernhardt's in French, Mrs. Campbell's (or others') in English, and several in German. From the time Shaw saw Duse in Dumas *fils*'s *La Femme de Claude* in 1895, he began singing her praises. "Without qualification," Shaw exclaims, Duse's is "the best modern acting I have ever seen" (*Theatres* 1:144). And, like Archer, Shaw compared Duse favorably to Bernhardt in June 1895 in her portrayals of both Marguerite Gauthier and Magda, with which the two actors competed against each other: Bernhardt at Daly's Theatre and Duse at Drury Lane. Shaw's verdict in the *Saturday Review* is clear and unequivocal: "I doubt whether any of us realized, after Madame Bernhardt's very clever performance as Magda on Monday night, that there was room in the nature of things for its annihilation within forty-eight hours by so comparatively quiet a talent as Duse's. And yet annihilation is the only word for it" (*Theatres* 1:152). How did this middle-aged actress (by May 1900 she was approaching her forty-second birthday) similarly "annihilate" emotionally the young Dubliner in her audience to such an extent that he requested her picture and addressed poetry to her? And how is this related to the way spirituality was represented on the stage and in *Ulysses?*

To begin, *La Gioconda* and, for that matter, *La Città Morta* concern issues very similar to those in *Exiles, When We Dead Awaken, Pygmalion and Galatea,* Hauptmann's *Michael Kramer,* and others: namely, artistry, spirituality and sexuality, and marriage. When Bonnie Kime Scott and Elliott Simon underscore Joyce's preference for the "mystical, spiritual" Irene in Ibsen's plays, their judgment is validated by his fascination with Duse, particularly in roles in D'Annunzio's plays. If we trust contemporary accounts of her acting style, even when playing roles like Magda or Paula Tanqueray—parts an Olga Nethersole might sensationalize—Duse achieved a rare spirituality onstage. Shaw praised her supple and "ambidextrous" movement, her ability to create the "illusion of being infinite in variety of beautiful pose and motion," her distinctive capacity to convince audiences that "behind ever stroke of it [her acting] is a distinctively human idea" (*Theatres* 1:151). In 1900, A. B. Walkley hailed her performance as Silvia Settala in *La Gioconda* as "entirely beautiful"; and, in a backhanded compliment of her 1905 production of *La Seconda Moglie (The Second Mrs. Tanqueray),* a play of which he was not overly fond, Walkley remarked that Duse "inevitably poetises the prose of the play, and so warps it from its real nature," making it more "glorious" but less "true."[52] Some years later, Eva Le Gallienne praised Duse's ability to bring the aura of the spiritual or mystical to every role she assumed. "It might be objected that the plays in which she appeared during the years of her greatest triumphs were in no way 'sublime'; that such works as *La Femme de Claude, La Dame aux Camélias, Denise, Magda, The Second Mrs. Tanqueray* . . . were merely theatre pieces designed to entertain the public with vicarious thrills and decidedly worldly passions. But she succeeded by the peculiar quality of her genius in raising them to a high spiritual level."[53] Le Gallienne stresses that Duse brought sacrificial, self-immolating qualities to roles like Magda and Paul Tanqueray, New Women who, from the orthodox perspective of a William Winter, embodied "modern" selfishness or unhealthy enslavement to the appetites. In *La Gioconda,* Duse found a corollary to her acting style—a role in which a selfless wife sacrifices her most beautiful physical assets, her hands, to save her husband's artwork.

The struggle between an artist's feelings of gratitude to his wife and a frenzied passion for his model, a passion also inspirational of his greatest art, dominates the action of *La Gioconda.* At the beginning of the play, Lucio Settala is convalescing under the care of his devoted wife after his professional and sexually intimate involvement with Gioconda Dianti has left him physically and emotionally debilitated. Silvia Settala, played by Duse, is beatified by other characters as living in a "state of grace" and approaching "martyrdom" for her suffering occasioned by her husband's infidelity. Despite his betrayals, her husband is described as "belonging to the noblest race of mankind"; his art, as being a "continual exaltation of life."[54] As he recovers, Settala praises Silvia's strength: "All that is deep, all that is sweet and heroic in you, I know it all, I feel it all, dear soul." Silvia responds that she is now filled with joy; she, who had "longed for one word from you, only one, no more," enjoys now, because of his renewed ardor, "happiness beyond all expectation" (582). Act 1 concludes with the implication that their marriage will survive and Silvia's tireless devotion will be rewarded.

This expectation is quickly dispelled in act 2 by Settala's admission that though his wife possesses a "soul of inestimable price," he is "not a sculptor of souls." Much like Rubek, and in some senses like Joyce in "Penelope," his art involves the female body. And producing one statue in tribute to this corporeal perfection is not nearly enough to satisfy his immense artistic ambition: "A thousand statues, not one! . . . Every motion of her body destroys one harmony and creates another yet more beautiful. You implore her to stay, to remain motionless; and across all her immobility there passes a torrent of obscure forces, as thoughts pass in the eyes. . . . Imagine that mystery over all her body" (585–86). To his wife's dismay, Settala contemplates returning to his studio in act 2; and, in the most spectacular scene in the play, at the beginning of act 3 she precedes his arrival there to confront Gioconda, who has been watching over Settala's sculpture and tending to his clay. Gioconda's proprietorship of Settala's studio during his illness enables him to counter allegations of his ingratitutde toward Silvia with "The other [Gioconda] preserved my art. Which of the two is worth more?" (587). The issue, though, is more complicated; it concerns the artist's "whole self" that characters like Mr. Duffy in "A Painful Case" never quite recognize (or, rather, recognize too late): namely, the reconciliation of "high" artistic aspiration and "low" physical desire. This erosion of polar opposition is reflected in D'Annunzio's very specific directions about the decoration of Settala's studio: "Here the choice and analogy of every form reveals an aspiration towards a carnal, victorious, and creative life" (592). Physicality and artistic creation are hence inseparable: Gioconda represents both; Silvia, tragically, neither. Lying initially to save her marriage, Silvia informs Gioconda that her husband will have no more to do with her. Furious, Gioconda moves frantically upstage behind a curtain so as to seize his last remaining sculpture and hurl it to the ground. As the act ends, Silvia heroically rescues the artwork at the cost of mangling her hands. Now she, too, has "preserved" his art–but still has inspired neither it nor his passion.

The poignant last act reveals Silvia alone awaiting for her young daughter to return. Her husband has abandoned her, returning to his art and to Gioconda. Duse's hands are tucked neatly away in her sleeves, a constant reminder of her selfless devotion to her husband. In a decidedly maudlin concluding scene, her young daughter begs her mother to pick her up and hold her, but Silvia's sacrifice has rendered her incapable of even this simple act. In the curtain-lowering tableau, Silvia falls to her knees, bursts into a current of tears, and her child "throws herself upon her mother's breast." Like Wills's Josephine in *A Royal Divorce* or Sydney Carton in *The Only Way*, D'Annunzio's martyr to her husband's art pays a heavy price for her heroism.

There is no particular reason to believe that Joyce concurred with the many London critics who found the play deeply tragic. It seems as likely that he would have questioned Silvia's romantic self-sacrifice and the play's several levels of idealization. Still, the notion that physicality and artistry are inseparable—and that, if necessary, this inseparability must be sought outside of marriage or the home if artistic inspiration is endangered—might very well explain Joyce's abiding interest in D'Annunzio. And if Joyce *had* attended a production of *La Città Morta*, which deals with similar themes and also with incest, he would not only have experienced another drama structured by oppositions like art/marriage and spirituality/sexuality but also seen Duse as Anna, the blind and selfless wife of a poet who, like Settala, discovers inspiration and sexual fulfillment outside of marriage. It was not, therefore, the subject positions for which Duse's characters implicitly stood —selfless wives and thus supporters of the institution of marriage—that elicited Joyce's fascination with the actress. On the contrary, both *La Gioconda* and *La Città Morta* locate artistry and sexual passion as co-present, interdependent, and outside of marriage. In these respects, D'Annunzio's artist figures as a precursor of Joyce himself. Brenda Maddox, for example, argues that when Joyce met Nora in June 1904, he "did not know where his instincts, unrestrained might lead him [referring here to fantasies of homosexuality cultivated by four months in Paris]," but he "did know they imperilled his art."[55] Nora's unconventionally aggressive behavior on their first date, according to Maddox, was instrumental in shaping Joyce's conception of her as a rescuer from both convention and unchecked passion. With Nora, he could be simultaneously inside and outside of conventional sexuality: he would be involved in an animated heterosexual relationship, thus his desire would in some ways be constrained and in others gratified, but this relationship would thrive outside of marriage. Together, they could ascend to Ibsenite heights in an avalanche of both desire and artistic inspiration; together, they could found a "home" outside of marriage and outside of Ireland.

But what of Duse's portrait on Joyce's desk and his adulatory verses to her? From all of the above, the most logical explanation of these phenomena has little to do with D'Annunzio's representation of artistry: Joyce had little interest in wives, self-sacrifice, or homes absent of artistic stimulation, all of which Duse represents. One answer must reside in Duse herself, in an acting style that captivated such tough-minded critics as Shaw, Archer, and Walkley. Susan Bassnett has defined this unique acting style. "Duse offered audiences an alternative representation of womanhood and of femininity, and perhaps some of the strangeness of the language of some critics who seem to have been obsessed by a notion of 'spirituality' when discussing her performances derives from their attempts to adequately describe something entirely different in terms of the representation of women."[56] If Bassnett and Eva Le Gallienne are correct, if Duse's style signified a radically different representation of womanhood than that offered by such actresses as Olga Nethersole, we shall find the sources of Joyce's enamorment in the components of this "other" style of acting. We can also detect traces of Duse's celebrated style and impact on Joyce in *Ulysses*.

Nearly every commentator on Duse noticed, as Shaw did, the quiet thoughtfulness of her protrayals and the subtle positioning of her body, methods exactly opposite the high emotions and grand gestures which Shaw found so vulgar in Netherole's Mrs. Ebbsmith. Instead, Duse cultivated smaller, more delicate movements, as Bassnett outlines. "Duse seems to have conspicuously avoided the grand gesture, with its heightened arm movements and dramatic poses, in favour of more contained gestures. She frequently used draped garments, shawls, and cloaks that drew attention to her hands. . . . Her particular type of realistic acting, therefore, derived from a technique that placed emphasis on separate parts of the body rather than on a notion of wholeness embodied in the grand gesture style of acting."[57] Adelaide Ristori recalled that in roles like Marguerite and Paula Tanqueray, Duse appeared "extraordinarily pale"–Shaw termed it a shade of gray as opposed to Bernhardt's thickly cosmetic "crimson"–and very thin ("possibly a *fausse maigré*, as the French would say"). With her "subtle" voice and gestural eccentricities, she in many ways embodied the "*fin-de-siècle* woman" or "abnormal woman with all her weaknesses, quirks, unevenness," and so on.[58] Clearly, Duse played such women in a manner very different from, say, Nethersole's sexually inflamed style so that, in contrast to the visceral effect of Nethersole's long kisses, Duse's spectator responded more dispassionately, more thoughtfully.

When impersonating D'Annunzio's characters rather than Pinero's or Sudermann's, however, Duse modified her style. For both D'Annunzio and Duse the visual elements of production needed to reflect and supplement the poetry of the dialogue; so, not unlike W. B. Yeats's turn to Gordon Craig's New Stagecraft for his plays, Duse and D'Annunzio sought different conventions of staging and design for their collaborations. In these parts, for example, Duse was not at all "languourous, her movements were not pliable and voluptuous"; rather, she became skillful "at the statuesque rendering of intense inner pain when she played D'Annunzio's heroines."[59] Walkley clearly agreed: he remarked that in the "great scene" in *La Gioconda*–Silvia's confrontation with Gioconda at Settala's studio–Duse "stands, silent, posed as nobly as any of the statues around her, while the other woman opens the studio door."[60] In addition to this quality, Duse also expanded her gestural repertory and in some respects discarded the props and the "millions" of subtle positions Shaw had praised so lavishly in her portrayal of Magda. This particular change was necessitated in part by directorial blocking which tended to position Duse far upstage, at considerable distance from the audience. This was the case, as Bassnett explains, for most of her roles in D'Annunzio's nonrealistic dramas. "In *La Città Morta*, for example, Duse [attired in gold while the rest of the stage was apparently dimly lit] was played a long way from the front of the stage, and the photographs show her right at the back, distanced from the audience by a great expanse of space. . . . In terms of gesture, she was constrained to open out into larger patterns of movements, to occupy space differently, more coherently and with greater weight. The photographs of *La Città Morta*, *Francesca da Rimini*, and *La Gioconda* all testify to this."[61] From these accounts, we might reconstruct what Joyce saw on his trip to the theater to see Duse, a trip he presumably relived every time he sat at his desk and gazed at Duse's picture: a distant, pale statue frozen in intense pain, who, at the same time, blazed as the brightest point on the horizon.

It is this distant, beautiful, and pained figure, I believe, that competed successfully with Mrs. Campbell's Magda and Nethersole's Fanny to provide another representation of women by which the young Joyce was enormously intrigued. Insofar as this representation tends to reassert the values of marriage, of wifely self-sacrifice, and of monogamous loyalty as fundamental to the institution's preservation, one might wonder how Joyce's attraction to Duse was possible: after all, by 1900 he had intellectually dismissed these values as destructive of the personal freedom artists required. Interestingly enough, as Nina Auerbach points out, Shaw in 1895 hailed Duse as the quintessence of the New Woman, an analogue to Janet Achurch as Nora, Ibsen's rebellious and independent housewife in *A Doll's House*.[62] But Joyce never saw this woman, as there is little of the New Woman in Duse's roles in *La Gioconda* and *La Città Morta*, only the more romantic and self-sacrificing "womanly woman" whom Joyce grew to despise. The immensely talented actress herself, it would seem, neutralized the young playgoer's growing ideological objections to the very roles she assumed. And when it came time for him to characterize similar fascinations in his Dubliners, he remembered the stage pictures and visual qualities that so brilliantly defined Eleonora Duse's art.

THEATRICAL SPECTATORSHIP, COMMODIFICATION, AND NARRATIVE RECONSTRUCTION IN "NAUSICAA"

> She could see at once by his dark eyes and his pale
> intellectual face that he was a foreigner, the image of the
> photo she had of Martin Harvey, the matinée idol, only
> for the moustache which she preferred because she
> wasn't stagestruck, like Winny Rippingham. (13:415–18)

In a recent lecture on cinematic reception and mass culture, Barbara Klinger considered the ways in which Hollywood films are given a "consumable identity" by the promotional discourses or epiphenomena—"trailers," print and media advertisements, interviews with star actors, T-shirts and other souvenirs from the film, and so on—that accompany them. Klinger rejects the notion that commercial discourses, which generally operate by setting particular elements of a film's narrative in the foreground of a consumer's attention, merely "accompany" a film; on the contrary, they create viable intertexts that allow filmgoers to "re-narrativize" the movie, placing fragments of the text within other narratives of their own assimilation. Such commercial epiphenomena coerce an internalization of certain aspects of the text—a reading by way of the intertexts created for it—and the production of alternative fictions based on a film's promotional discourses.[63] Ostensibly a collector of the pictures and postcards that advertised major actors at the turn of the century, Gerty MacDowell is the predecessor of this sort of spectator. And so is Bloom. And so, to a certain extent, is Joyce. "Nausicaa" contains one of the most elaborate instances in all of Joyce of theatricalized spectation, primarily because there exists a mirroring mechanism whereby at various moments the chapter's two principals—Gerty and Bloom—play both viewer and viewed, spectator and object. In what follows, I shall try to identify the dramatic and theatrical conventions underlying both viewers' spectatorship, beginning with Gerty's, in the process delineating the ways in which Bloom and Gerty refashion each other into theatrical commodities.

From the inaugural paragraph of "Nausicaa," Joyce establishes the setting, lighting, and proxemic relations of figures in the dramatic space in a manner similar to the staging of romantic dramas he had seen. For example, the relationship between distance/proximity and foreground/background in Duse's art—recall that in D'Annunzio's plays she was often prominently situated far upstage, at a great distance from the audience – is very much evident in "Nausicaa." Equally derivative of theatrical convention is the faint lighting of the episode. As the chapter opens, the sun "far away" is sinking, and the lighting of the shore, like that of Duse's *La Città Morta,* seems "mysterious" in its "last glow." While the "paly light of evening" falls upon Gerty's "infinitely sad and wistful" face (13:193–94), Joyce's narrator wryly remarks about "how moving the scene there in the gathering twilight" (13:624). Like the gaze of the bird-girl Stephen encounters in *Portrait,* Gerty's vision is directed outward to sea: though seated "near her companions," Gerty was "lost in thought, gazing far away into the distance" (13:79–80). She "gazed out towards the distant sea" (13:406) when she first spotted Bloom, likening him to one of Dublin's favorite touring stars from the London stage, Martin Harvey. Although the Caffrey twins and Gerty's friends also occupy the fictive space, the narrative proceeds to isolate Gerty, to place her and her reflections at some distance from the others. Thus, though separating the fractious twins or engaging in idle conversation with friends constitute the foregrounded "everyday" realities of Gerty's life, actors like Martin Harvey – or figures like the bird-girl – reside in the romantic distance, somewhere beyond the nearness of the everyday.

The equation of distance with romantic idealization – and proximity with both the everyday and the sensual – appears in much of Joyce's writing, especially in the representation of love and youthful illusion. Compare, for instance, the horizontal expansiveness of "Nausicaa" with vertical distantiation in *Chamber Music* or *Giacomo Joyce.* Of the several poems in the former which separate the female love object from her devoted spectator, one – Poem V, "Lean out of the window" – seems especially replicative of the staging practice discussed above. In the poem, the studious narrator, lured by his beloved's song, has left his reading and his room, journeyed to her window, and once there requests a more intimate view of the singer:

> Lean out of the window,
> Goldenhair,
> I heard you singing
> A merry air. (*CM* 117)

As Archie K. Loss argues, the singer's beautiful hair in the "Goldenhair" poems of *Chamber Music* owes much to both Art Nouveau and Pre-Raphaelite representations of female beauty. And Loss's relation of Polly

Mooney in "The Boarding House" to the Symbolist *femme-enfant*, a sort
of rival representation to the *femme de trente ans*, is very persuasive.[64] Still,
regardless of the prominent eyes and flowing hair of so many of Dante Gabriel Rossetti's paintings and Joyce's women, the perspective and spatial relations of romantic drama are rather different from those of Rossetti's *Astarte
Syriaca* or *La Pia de' Tolomei*. Joyce's appropriations from various iconographic
conventions, therefore, cannot alone account for the carefully articulated
setting of episodes like "Nausicaa."

Nor can the supposedly voyeuristic origins of Joyce's meeting with one
model for Gerty, Marthe Fleischmann, whom he first observed from a distance pulling a toilet chain, fully explain the setting of "Nausicaa."[65] In
Ellmann's emphasis of the spectatorial dimension of Joyce's attraction to Marthe, he notes that Joyce spent much of his time in December 1918 "watching for" Marthe, who grew to possess the same "talismanic significance" as
the girl he had seen wading in the Irish Sea in 1898. Marthe became a "vision of secular beauty" for Joyce, a "pagan Mary beckoning him to the life
of art which knows no division between body and soul" (*JJ* 448). In a telling note, Ellmann develops an analogy between Joyce's view of Marthe and
Earwicker's crime in Phoenix Park in *Finnegans Wake*, which involves
voyeurism of young girls' micturation. But here, as in Joyce's view of Marthe in the toilet, distance and proximity merge; youthful romance gives way
to the harsher reality of the middle-aged spectator, or so Joyce apparently
wrote to Marthe. Though this more jaded scopophilia partially describes
Bloom's view of Gerty, it fails to reveal the theatricality of Gerty's spectation
of Bloom.

As an example, like the "Nausicaa" chapter *Chamber Music* V owes
much to the staging practices of romantic drama, replicating similar figures
in Maeterlinck's *Pelléas and Mélisande* (1896), which Joyce read and had opportunities to see in Dublin and on the Continent. In one of the most lavishly produced scenes of the play, act 3, scene 2 begins with Mélisande at
a window in her castle combing her long hair and singing "like a bird that
is not native here." An admiring Pelléas enters below. Like the "foreign-
ness" of Bloom's face in Gerty's construction, Mélisande's air sounds exoti-
cally strange to her admirer; like the dim light of Sandymount shore, shadows
obscure Pelléas's view of Mélisande's face, so he makes the same request Joyce's
student makes in *Chamber Music:* "Do not stay in the shadow, Mélisande;
lean forward a little till I see your unbounded hair."[66] Several conventions
are in evidence here. The young woman's loosening of her hair in *Chamber*

Music XI – "And softly to undo the snood / That is the sign of maidenhood" (*CM* 129) – connotes budding sexuality, hence this activity and leaning forward to the spectator combine to suggest to the poem's speaker the acquiescence of a figure of purity and remoteness (spirituality, virginity).

In his introduction to *Giacomo Joyce*, Ellmann refers to the "Nausicaa" episode as a parodic counter to Giacomo's bragging about "possession by long distance," and certainly his point is well taken.[67] "Distance," as conventionally deployed in the staging of romantic drama, signifies just the opposite: the impossibility of possessing the other. Joyce knows this, and he frequently uses nearness or proximity not only to signify the everyday or mundane, but also to denote possession or its possibility. Marthe Fleischmann, as Ellmann points out, soon became "accessible" to Joyce, whose habit of viewing her from his room, regardless of the dubious nature of its origin, seemed to gratify her as well. This dynamic is suggested in *Portrait*, when the bird-girl turns "her eyes toward" Stephen in "quiet sufferance of his gaze" (*P* 171), and earlier as well when Stephen waits at the tram station: "He on the upper step and she on the lower. She came up to his step many times and went down to hers again between their phrases and once or twice stood close beside him for some moments on the upper step, forgetting to go down, and then went down" (*P* 69). Given this "blocking," Stephen reaches the logical conclusion: "She too wants me to catch hold of her. . . . I could hold her and kiss her" (*P* 70). Joyce's stage design does its semiotic work.

In addition to Joyce's emphasis of the dim lighting and idealizing distance of the episode, Gerty's contextualization of Bloom within the conventions of romantic drama is revealed in her musings on his appearance: his "dark eyes" and "pale intellectual face" convinced Gerty that Bloom was a "foreigner." He had an "aquiline nose," or one "slightly *retroussé*," and was dressed in dark clothing. Most important, from Gerty's perspective, "He was in deep mourning, she could see that, and the story of a haunting sorrow was written on his face" (13:421–22). The metaphorical relation of spectating with reading is suggestive here: if sorrow is "written" on Bloom's face, the acts of watching and reading are, equally, interpretive acts. As part of the metaphor, the body is objectified, transformed into a thing: in this case, a text to be deciphered. Because of her experience in the theater, Gerty totally misreads Bloom, constructing him by way of the conventions that typically operate in the staging of romantic drama. One result of her misreadings is Gerty's eagerness to play Duse's devoted wives: she "would make the great sacrifice" for this distant figure, and then "dearer than the whole world would she be to him and gild his days with happiness" (13:653–54). Bloom becomes, in this depiction, the romantic complement of Gerty's own cosmetic reconstruction of herself as a romantic heroine: her face possesses a "waxen pallor" that was "almost spiritual in its ivorylike purity" (13:87–88) to match Bloom's spirituality or haunting sorrow; she has a "languid queenly *hauteur,*" with "dark expressive brows" and "rather sad downcast eyes" (13:97, 108, 123) to match his mournful countenance. To be sure, much of this reconstruction stems from Gerty's reading of the *Lady's Pictorial* and her "instinctive taste of a votary of Dame Fashion." Much, too, is attributable to Gerty's longing to "write herself into a work of romantic fiction," as Suzette Henke comments, and to the "competitive sexual market" of 1904 from which her physical deformity has isolated her.[68] Throughout the chapter, Joyce's narrator implies the impossibility of Gerty's project and the ideality of such representations: her "almost spiritual face" is counterbalanced by her "rosebud mouth," which is a "genuine Cupid's bow" (13:87–88); her "dark expressive brows" are "silkily seductive" (13:108–9). Her desire undermines her self-construction; her spectator's desire induces misreading of the representation.

Gerty's perception of Bloom is also as typical as it is exceptional or eccentric, the product of a self-construction closely akin to that of other Dubliners. In particular, Gerty's "reading" of Bloom is inflected by her devotion to Martin Harvey and the romantic roles he played so successfully in Dublin from 1899 to the end of World War I. As Molly's comments about her daughter's response to Harvey in "Penelope" suggest—"she clapped when the curtain came down because he looked so handsome then we had Martin Harvey for breakfast dinner and supper" (18:1054–55)—Harvey was by 1904 one of Dublin's favorite actors, especially in his portrayal of Sydney Carton in *The Only Way,* Freeman Wills's and Frederick Langbridge's adaptation of Dickens's *Tale of Two Cities.* But neither Molly's reaction nor the narrator's description in "Nausicaa" of Harvey as a "matinée idol" should obscure the fact that he was widely popular to all classes of Dubliners for any number of reasons. Here, again, a distinction between "high" art and popular culture in turn-of-the-century Dublin is extremely difficult to enforce. Harvey's visits to Dublin often occasioned trips to the theater by the Lord Governor and his wife, and Harvey describes in his autobiography the many social functions he attended with Dublin's leading political and artistic figures. He was, for instance, invited to lecture at Trinity College on the art of acting and in 1906 attended a luncheon with Dublin's most famous literati, including Yeats, Synge, and Lady Gregory; before this, he had met Maud Gonne and the Countess Markievicz as well.[69]

To less aristocratic theatergoers, Harvey was not a college lecturer or a cultural ornament to dress up a social occasion. He was *the* romantic actor: attractive, foreign, exotic, and deeply passionate. Even within this general category, however, Harvey as a widely circulated cultural object could be apprehended in widely varying ways. Molly recalls seeing *The Only Way* at the Theatre Royal and describes her reaction to it, which differs from Gerty's view of the actor: "I thought to myself afterwards it must be real love if a man gives up his life for her that way for nothing I suppose there are a few men like that left its hard to believe in it though . . . to find two people like that nowadays full up of each other that would feel the same way as you do theyre usually a bit foolish in the head" (18:1055–58, 1059–61). The temporal dimension of Molly's recollection–"then we had Martin Harvey" as opposed to the more modern, less idealized "nowadays"–might suggest that a long history separates June 1904 from Harvey's first appearance in *The Only Way*. Such is not the case: the play was licensed as *The Jackal* in 1898 and not performed in Dublin until October 1899. Its success was clear and decisive, as a review in the *Freeman's Journal* confirms: "A great actor in a great play. . . . The consummating sacrifice of his [Sydney Carton's] life for the life of his successful rival is an episode as dramatic, as heart-moving, as any in all of literature, outside the magic pages of Shakespeare himself" (10 October 1899). The same reviewer remarked that, for Harvey's appearance, there was not "a single vacant seat," and "last night the theatre was crowded in all parts, as it has not been since its opening." As played by Harvey, Dickens's novel of the French Revolution could be read in the pale face and haunting sorrow of the great actor. The difference between Gerty's and Molly's readings of that face, however, is profound: for Gerty, the actor and his role are entirely separable or consumable apart from the narrative in which they are situated, whereas for Molly they are not.

In subsequent trips to Dublin, Harvey enhanced his popularity with a repertory of romantic plays like Boucicault's *Corsican Brothers* and an adaptation of Bulwer's *Eugene Aram,* more recent works like the Napoleonic drama *The Exile,* and in the autumn of 1904 *Hamlet,* which he first played at Dublin's Theatre Royal. His success was again complete: "Let us say at once that Mr. Harvey has justified his ambition by a brilliant success. . . . No single seat vacant. . . . By last night's performance Mr. Martin Harvey takes rank at once as one of the great Hamlets – the Hamlets that men talk about, and write about, and read about, and set up as standards for future comparison" (*Freeman's Journal*, 22 November 1904). Harvey's face, the same reviewer opined, was that of "an ideal Hamlet," which "at one suggests the melancholy Dane." In its "delicate features," Harvey's mournful visage reminded the *Freeman's Journal* reviewer of John Philip Kemble, "the very finest Hamlet the stage has ever seen," and along with his voice was his strongest asset in playing Shakespeare that night in Dublin when many felt a distinguished chapter in theater history had been written.

Harvey's face, then, not only contributed to his portrayal of Hamlet but also adorned Gerty's imagination and provided the means through which she re-narrativized Bloom's appearance on Sandymount shore. Virtually all photographs or souvenir postcards of this time captured romantic actors in their most celebrated impersonations, inducing audiences to regard dramatic narrative or thematic complexity as subordinate to the oscillations of a star's emotional register. In his most famous role as Sydney Carton – by 1921 he had played the part two thousand times – the darkly attired, spectrally pale Harvey is "discovered" in an act 1 tableau with his head lowered to the top of his cluttered desk, his posture and unkempt flow of dark hair the result of inebriation, which is itself the result of his selfless love for the golden-haired Lucie Manette. The act ends with a duplication of this same stage picture in which Carton's profound sorrow and dissolution are attributable to his excessive and unrequited love. At the same time, through the fond suggestion of his loyal servant, the audience recognizes that Carton, if reformed, would strongly resemble his handsome rival, Charles Darnay.[70] Like several other widely performed Victorian romantic plays which Irving and later Harvey revived – Boucicault's *Corsican Brothers* and Charles Reade's adaptation from the French, *The Courier of Lyons* (1851), for instance, to which Joyce alludes in "Circe" – the dramatic action of *The Only Way* finally centers around mistaken identity, as Carton is able to substitute himself for Darnay at the guillotine so Lucie might be restored to her true love. The opposite of the dissipated Carton, then, is the handsome Darnay; and, when shaken from his dissolution to save Lucie's beloved, Carton himself is transformed into the sort of "real man" who would "love" Gerty, "his ownest girlie, for herself alone" (13:439–41).

As Joyce's narration clarifies, "No prince charming is her beau ideal to lay a rare and wondrous love" at Gerty's feet, but a "manly man . . . perhaps his hair slightly flecked with grey," that in his "deep passionate nature" would "comfort her with a long long kiss" (13:209–11, 213–14). In this reverie, Gerty's prince is not so much Harvey in the role of Dickens's hero, but rather in the part of Louis dei Franchi in Boucicault's *Corsican Brothers,* who dies for the honor of a woman he loved but could not have. One reviewer describes the effect: "He [Harvey] never raises his voice in the play. He indulges in no violent gesture. . . . The supernatural broods over the play, deepening the tragedy. . . . He is specially powerful when his passion of love breaks out in fervour, more intense from long repression, for the wife of his friend, whose honour he guards at the cost of his life" (4 November 1906). These were the performances that brought Dubliners to the theater. They even motivated one resident of Maynooth to request that a special train be assigned to leave Dublin at 11:30 P.M. so that playgoers living in outlying suburbs could see Harvey when he visited Dublin and still manage to find their way home that night.[71]

Of course, Harvey's persona predisposed other Dubliners to read him and the plays in which he appeared in very different ways. For Molly, although Harvey was indeed handsome, *The Only Way* seemed sadly outdated; "nowadays," as Molly reflects, one might like to imagine that such men as Carton exist, but reality renders such a belief untenable. For the *Freeman's Journal* reviewer, Harvey's face and the passion it was capable of expressing were central to a *Hamlet* of theatrically memorable proportions. Still other Dubliners received or "read" Harvey in widely divergent ways, as he bemusedly recalls in his autobiography. When he and his company stayed at the Gresham Hotel, "exuberant and somewhat hysterical little crowds used to wait at the hotel doors to watch our departure for our work o' nights at the theatre" and later "assemble outside the stage door to cheer us home." Harvey recalls sympathetic Dubliners in particular wondering if he was dying of consumption, "the doom to which the public loves to imagine the actors of Romance will succumb," or if he "lifts the little finger pretty often" in attempts to assuage his "unquenchable thirst." Apparently many Irish theatergoers believed Harvey required drink before he could act. Harvey further remembers that emotionally intense actors like Irving and Fred Terry were thought by some to have "thrashed their wives periodically."[72] In these depictions as hard drinkers or abusive spouses, one might speculate, working-class theatergoers (Harvey clearly identifies the holders of these views as such) reconstructed Harvey and some of his impersonations into mirrors of their own conditions and proclivities. He was, in sum, a figure of romantic idealization to Gerty, an aristocrat to Dublin's upper class, and, at base, just another bloke to many of the poorer classes. Such actors could be commodified and consumed in a wide variety of ways.

To shift the focus to the object of Gerty's spectation, the narration of "Nausicaa" also reveals the theatrical mediation of Bloom's viewing of Gerty and lays bare the ideological implications of the male gaze. Bloom's commentary about Gerty, in particular, evokes comparison with descriptions of the perfection of artists' models in plays like *When We Dead Awaken, La Gioconda,* and *Pygmalion and Galatea;* with Duse's assumption of statuesque poses in D'Annunzio's plays; and with the directorial instruction such late Victorian actresses as Ellen Terry received.

In her biography of Terry, Nina Auerbach underscores the important stage convention of womanly motionlessness in the art of actresses of Terry's stature. Such was the advice Terry received from the beginning of her career. As Auerbach recalls, the "formidable Leonora Wigan took her [Ellen Terry] in hand to cure her of her fidgeting and fooling: *'Stand still!'* she would shout from the stalls. 'Now you're of value! Motionless! Just as you are *That's* right!'"[73] From directions such as these, Auerbach extrapolates Irving's rationale for refusing Terry the opportunity to play some of Shakespeare's most "mobile" comedic parts, Rosalind in *As You Like It,* for instance.[74] Hence in Auerbach's reading, a stage convention can be understood synecdochically as a figure for other instances of Victorian subjugation of women. In Terry's case, this meant limited opportunities to assume roles other than the loyal wives and daughters she played or to appear in plays subversive of the dominant ideology to which Irving catered at the Lyceum. For Michael Booth, also speaking of Terry, the "pictorialization of both acting and production reached its peak in the middle and late Victorian period"; as a result, the actor at "this unique juncture in the history of the theatre, became a statue and a painting, or a subject in a painting as well as a player."[75]

Not surprisingly, given his theatergoing past and his often-expressed fascination with womens' bodies, erotic photographs, and statuary in such chapters as "The Lotus Eaters" and, obviously, "Lestrygonians," Bloom in "Nausicaa" regards the motionless woman, the theatricalized body, as both symbolic of female perfection and necessary for the male viewer's satisfactory arousal: "See her as she is spoil all. Must have the stage setting, the rouge, costume, position, music. The name too. *Amours* of actresses. Nell Gwynne, Mrs. Bracegirdle, Maud Branscombe. Curtain up. Moonlight silver effulgence. Maiden discovered with pensive bosom. Little sweetheart come and kiss me" (13:855–59). This postonanistic revelation is prompted by Gerty's moving from the rock upon which she was seated, exposing her lameness. Bloom thinks, "A defect is ten times worse in a woman" (13:774–75), and continues to consider women, spectation, and Molly as he composes himself. What is striking about his meditation, especially juxtaposed to Gerty's, is its decidedly unromantic quality: its endorsement of a different order of viewing and its implicit commodification of women. In "Nausicaa," then, to state the matter in terms more consistent with those employed above, Gerty's romantic idealism or higher "spiritualized" love coexists with its opposite, an instinctual, crassly physical conception of love and the love object.

As Mary C. King has observed, Bloom is an "archetypal representative of the commodity world of capitalism, which, as an advertising man, he is employed to serve." For King, as "Ithaca" demonstrates, Bloom is "obsessed by things as commodities;" he "loves to estimate their market value" and "takes an enthusiastic delight in reading, composing, and improving upon advertisements."[76] King thus regards the activation of objects in the Nighttown episode not only as replicating the "magical" manipulations of pantomimes but also as signaling commodity fetishism within *Ulysses*; moreover, the urban poverty of "Circe" serves as Joyce's "evocation of the lumpenproletariat of a colonized city in Britain's backyard, in which typhus and cholera were endemic and infant mortality exceeded that of the disease- and famine-ridden Asiatic cities of her far-flung empires."[77] But one need not read this far into *Ulysses* to confront the discouraging signs of Irish colonialism and impoverishment; they are coextensive with Gerty's gaze toward the romantic distance, and they reduce the love object from a symbol of moral perfection to a commodity, pure and simple. In this transformation, the object is emptied of its essence and reduced to its exchange value. The same economy determines Bloom's view of women and theatricality: "See her as she is spoil all." In *Ulysses* and in the theater, women are reduced to images, and images are always marketable as commodities.

Thus, as Gerty moves away from her distant idealization, "Nausicaa" turns sharply from the spiritual to the material. Bloom thinks about the peepshow he had seen and the fakery involved in producing it, landing finally on a cliché-ridden abolition of the real insofar as women are concerned: "Say a woman loses her charm with every pin she takes out. Pinned together" (13:802–3). He ponders the ease with which sexual transactions in the East are managed: there, "No reasonable offer refused"; there, the women are in effect "Out on spec probably" (13:806, 808). The sexual economy follows the workings of the economy at large, with women marketing themselves accordingly. Bloom remembers when they were "on the rocks in Holles street" getting ten bob for Molly's combings and then considers the transaction going on at home between Molly and Boylan: "Suppose he gave her money. Why not? All a prejudice. She's worth ten, fifteen, more, a pound" (13:841–42). These ruminations, taken together, form a side of romance diametrically opposite to Gerty's–or Stephen's in Chapter 2 of *Portrait* for that matter. And, in my view, they are in determinative ways tied to the convention of female immobility on the late Victorian stage, especially as it was communicated by way of price or worth: "Now you're of value," Ellen Terry was reminded, if she could only remain still enough.

Joyce's fiction is replete, however, with instances in which male spectators are confronted with female "objects" who will not stand still and thus be contained by their spectators' view. Such is frequently the case in *Dubliners,* for instance, as petit bourgeois men are frustrated in their rare opportunities of viewing attractive, apparently wealthier women. In "Counterparts," Farrington's eyes "wandered at every moment in the direction" of a young woman who joins his table at a pub in which he is drinking. Dressed in bright colors, the woman moves her "plump" arm "very often and with much grace" and exchanges glances with him. She brushes him slightly as she leaves, which irritates Farrington even further because, had he more money and therefore more opportunity, his gaze of such women might continue. The woman, curiously enough, is associated with the popular theater: a performer at the Tivoli Theatre of Varieties and thus constantly "on the move." Similarly, before his meeting with Gallaher in "A Little Cloud," Chandler watches lavishly attired women arrive at the door of the restaurant. "He had seen cabs drawn up before the door and richly dressed ladies, escorted by cavaliers, alight and enter quickly. They wore noisy dresses and many wraps. Their faces were powdered and they caught up their dresses, when they touched earth, like alarmed Atalantas" (*D* 72). Here, women are, on the one hand, figured in the elevated terms associated with romantic idealization (like Atalantas); on the other hand, this elevation is marked by class and material wealth. Given Chandler's timidity and domestic circumstances, these women are thus as distant as Martin Harvey's or Eleonora Duse's portrayals, but the distance is defined here in material terms.

This pattern of thwarted spectation continues in *Ulysses.* In "Calypso," Bloom hopes the butcher can fetch his kidney quickly so he can "catch up and walk behind her [a neighbor's maid] . . . behind her moving hams.

Pleasant to see first thing in the morning" (4:171–73). Unfortunately for Bloom, by the time he leaves the butcher's shop, the "girl" has headed in the wrong direction so he returns home. In "Lotus Eaters" Bloom's view of a woman boarding a cab outside the Grosvenor Hotel is obstructed by a passing tram, and he recalls another woman he had seen at a polo match some time before. All of this frustrated voyeurism leads to the final moments of "Lestrygonians," where Bloom hatches a scheme to bend down unobserved in front of the statues of Greek goddesses at the National Library so as to obtain a low-angle perspective of their anatomical configuration. He fails somewhat in his scheme, as Buck Mulligan jeeringly reports in "Scylla and Charybdis": "I found him over in the museum where I went to hail the foamborn Aphrodite. . . . His pail Galilean eyes were upon her mesial groove" (9:609–10, 615).

One premise seems to underlie Bloom's voyeuristic project at the National Library: namely, though mortal women are "all for caste till you touch the spot" (5:104) and then can be made one's own, goddesses in their superiority may not possess so many spots to touch and thus in their perfection may not be possessed. When he approaches the statues, Bloom contemplates the perfection of classical feminine beauty by way of reference to the story of Pygmalion and Galatea, which was popularized in Dublin by W. S. Gilbert's play. As Bloom considers the "curves the world admires" (8:921), he implies that a man cannot simply "possess" ideal beauty "once" and "take the starch out of her" (5:106), as he had speculated earlier about most women. On the contrary, the perfection of the female form—of Venus, Juno, or Galatea in Gilbert's play before she becomes animated and intrudes upon her artist's marriage—will "put you in your proper place!" (8:925). Here is precisely where the paradox of late Victorian representations of the female body is most evident: the motionless, ideal woman is, in her likeness to statuary, both glorified as a figure of perfection and contained, made a subaltern by the very gaze that extols her beauty. In Gilbert's play, Pygmalion's creation is "excellent in every attribute of womankind" and "perfect in . . . loveliness," more beautiful than Pygmalion's wife, Cynisca, who served as her husband's model. As Pygmalion explains, Cynisca is imperfectly beautiful, so in creating Galatea he has appropriated his wife's best features and in the marble "made them lovelier still."[78] Yet, after Pygmalion grows to deprecate the lifelessness of his creation, he immediately realizes the distinction between human imperfection and idealization: once the statue moves and Pygmalion breaks faith with his wife by his dalliance with Galatea, he suffers the traditional penalty of blindness. Gilbert's play ends with the restoration of the artist's vision and Galatea's return to immobility on her pedestal, actions which in the process illuminate the representational paradox intrinsic to Bloom's analysis in "Nausicaa" of the stagecraft of desire: perfect beauty is, in part, perfect because it is immobile and can be contained or controlled by the viewer. And, most often, that viewer is male.

Like most forms of popular culture, therefore, the popular theater Joyce frequented presented instances of resistance to the dominant ideology and instances of containment within it. For every Magda Schwartze, Paula Tanqueray, or Fanny LeGrand, there was a Sydney Carton or Galatea. But as is always the case in the theater, the ideological implication or trajectory of a play can be, alternatively, supplemented or subverted by the acting or theatrical conventions that realize it onstage. And, as I have tried to show, by functioning as a commodity within capitalism, the popular theater can be consumed in ways that have very little to do with the text created in the theater. Joyce recognized this, even as he found himself attracted to and fascinated with these commodities.

O'Casey's Negotiations with the Popular

> Intellect can never banish emotion from the theatre, for
> emotion is deep within us and round us everywhere;
> it is . . . in the sound of a Beethoven Symphony and
> the monotonous and insistent beat of the Rock 'n' Roll.
> —Sean O'Casey "An Irishman's Plays" (1960)

ONE MOMENT IN *Drums under the Windows* (1945), the third of Sean O'Casey's
six autobiographical volumes, epitomizes, I believe, an issue continually represented in his plays and almost obsessively reprised in his critical writing.
In "Song of a Shift," O'Casey recounts the turbulent response to Synge's
Playboy of the Western World in January 1907. Finding himself in an agitated
crowd "brimming with zeal for Ireland's holy reputation," O'Casey was
pushed and repeatedly "jostled," not by "real" Dubliners, but by their emis-
saries from popular culture: Mother mo Chree, Willy Reilly and his colleen
bawn, the Lily of Killarney, and so on. Sean rushed past this mob to attend
a meeting of his branch of the Gaelic League, where members angrily lam-
basted the "terrible play" by "a fellow named Singe or Sinje or something,"
who, for all some knew, was a "foreigner paid to say th' things he said"
(*Autobiographies* 1:511). This condemnation of Synge and the Abbey Theatre
ultimately reached a point of bellicose debate between the Lad from Largy-
more, "foaming at the mouth" at the "pagan-minded, anti-Irish ravisher of
decency, Yeats and his crony Synge," and a "young man from Tourmakeady,"

who defended Yeats as "a flame in the sword of light . . . a banner of song in the midst of the people!" (*Autobiographies* 1:516–17). Retreating to a pub across from the Abbey, Sean and Yeats's defender, joined by a thirsty tram conductor, paused for a bottle of stout and more conversation while a crowd threatened "ructions" outside the theater. Here O'Casey contemplated the relationship between a poet and the people, parrying his friend's near beatification of Yeats with aspersions he had heard that Yeats regarded his voice as that of God, "not that of the people." Wandering outside later and reflecting on the matter, O'Casey concludes the chapter with a metaphor attempting to represent the relationship between an artist and the people. "A gleaming star, low down in the sky, seemed to be entangled in its [a leafless tree's] delicate higher branches: like Yeats and Ireland, thought Sean; Ireland, naked and quivering waiting for a spring, and the glittering poet caught in its branches" (*Autobiographies* 1:519–20). The higher branches of a naked, quivering people and a poet-star low in the sky are thus wed ineluctably in an always vexed, at times volatile, relationship. Or, to allude both to Ayamonn Breydon's phrase in *Red Roses for Me* and to the title of Carol Kleiman's study of O'Casey and Expressionism,[1] the "bridge of vision" between O'Casey's early and later work is his ongoing attempt to connect the artist and the people.

O'Casey has endured his share of detractors recently, both Marxist and Irish, who might detect in this passage from *Drums under the Windows* evidence of an elitism that blunts the political edge or diminishes the revolutionary potential of his work. For some of these, elitism is the only unpardonable offense, and writers working in any but a realistic form seem vulnerable to the charge. After all, in the vehicles of O'Casey's metaphor the poet is figured as a descending star and the people as an earthbound Nemesis; moreover, throughout "Song of a Shift," the majority of Dubliners are depicted as a "rabblement" of ignorant nationalists. In other writings, some might point out, O'Casey insists that the author is "answerable only to himself," making clear his own intention of serving art first, the people later.[2] I refer such readers to David Krause's "The Risen O'Casey: Some Marxist and Irish Ironies," a refutation of Anthony Butler's, C. Desmond Greaves's, and others' emphases of O'Casey's "inability to think his way through to clarity" about the relationship between the 1916 Easter rising and the aims of the international labor movement, of O'Casey's often fallible historical memory employed in his autobiographies to distort embarrassing lapses of integrity or courage, and of the putatively determinative psychological effect on O'Casey of not "being out" in 1916.[3] In Greaves's view, "something approaching a cult of O'Casey," one populated mostly by American "literary critics," has "uncritically" accepted as gospel the life story of the autobiographies with the result that this bardolatrous sect is unable to reconcile the nationalist O'Casey with the socialist author-god it has created.[4] Albeit persuasive, Krause's rejoinder finally rests upon an orthodox and, given the work of Roland Barthes and Michel Foucault on the issue of authorship, not unfamiliar supposition that ironically tends to justify Greaves's comparison of literary criticism to religious zeal: namely, Krause's conception of O'Casey as his "own man." For Krause, O'Casey "was never a captive or mouthpiece of any cause," but a "visionary artist who could embrace Christ and Shelley, Marx and Whitman," and who was determined "to live in a world where reactionary as well as radical artists were allowed to work and live in freedom."[5] Fair enough. But what does it mean, as Robert Hogan also claims O'Casey "utterly was," to "be your own man"?[6] And how might we read the earlier, almost surreal moments of "Song of a Shift" in which O'Casey is jostled by figures from Irish popular culture?

While I have no desire to intervene in this disagreement or to situate myself on one side or the other, I believe that the critical privileging of O'Casey as his "own man" has meant dismissal of or, at the very least, a discounting of the union of the glittering star and the earthbound tree. Such a move, for many of the reasons Michael Kinneally advances in his study of O'Casey's autobiographies, might now be reconsidered. As Kinneally stresses, the autobiographical economy would seem to dictate authorial selection of "representative events from the amorphous past" that provide a "clearer rationale for the unique evolution of the author's current sense of identity."[7] That is, when in his autobiography O'Casey develops an extended metaphor to describe his feelings in 1907, there is every likelihood that this poetic figure pertains to a position he holds while writing his chronicle – or, in this instance, reflects O'Casey's sense of self in 1945, not necessarily in 1907. All historical accounts, then, especially those written so long after the period of time they treat, are to be read with a degree of skepticism (whether such skepticism should approach that of Greaves and his compatriots is another matter). Unlike the memoirist, Kinneally explains, whose account of the past generally focuses on external events, the autobiographer "transforms events into images designed to approximate the influences moulding the inner man."[8]

In my view, the episode in "Song of a Shift" contains several such images; Sean's entrapment in an angry crowd of popular cultural characters and the figurative union of the star and the tree are two of these. Based on the evidence of some of O'Casey's last plays and critical essays, it seems clear that he continued to ponder the relationship between the artist and the people, between art and popular culture, throughout his life. If the artist, following Krause and Hogan, must be "his own man" (or her own woman), then how, following O'Casey's metaphors and the tenor of such essays as "Art Is the Song of Life," can he or she also be connected to the people and their culture? Because this popular culture pushes and shoves the artist in directions he may not always wish to go, he cannot always be "his own man"; and because the artist is inextricably connected to the people, he cannot be an "elitist" either.

For O'Casey, drama was irreducibly public, as the opening sentence of his essay "The People and the Theatre" (1946) attests: "The people are the theatre." Unlike Yeats, for example, O'Casey was inexhaustibly attentive to the everyday lives of modern Irishmen, sympathizing here, questioning or overturning there. "Every art is rooted in the life of the people," he insisted in his 1946 essay, "what they see, do, how they hear . . . how they live, love, and go to the grave."[9] This fundamental relationship between art and the masses is one that Donal Davoren, the working-class and would-be poet in *The Shadow of a Gunman,* disparages until he finally apprehends his inherent connectedness to those around him. Early in act 2, Davoren articulates his presumption that the poet lives "on the mountain-top" while the masses reside in an "abyss" of devotion to "creeds" and mindless "customs." Try as he may to distance himself from this abyss, Davoren finally cannot deny its existence: when Minnie Powell dies at the end of the play to protect him and his cowardly roommate, he is implicated in the ideologies he despises. So are other artist figures in O'Casey's plays such as the contentious and comical group of Wycherly McGeera, Leslie Horawn, Bunny Conneen, and Jack McGeelish in *Behind the Green Curtains* (1961) and such bookish, clearly autobiographical working-class heroes as Jack Rocliffe in *The Harvest Festival* and Ayamonn Breydon in *Red Roses for Me.* Nor could O'Casey divorce himself from the people, no matter how much he reviled several of their "creeds" and endeavored to debunk them in his antiheroic Abbey plays.

In certain respects, however, O'Casey's conception of the relationship between art and the people is inherently paradoxical. For instance, although he claimed that the theater belonged to the people, he refused to succumb to the popular will; one result of this refusal was the violent response *The Plough and the Stars* elicited on the fourth night of its inaugural run in February 1926. Even before its premiere, O'Casey rebutted the protests of Abbey actors over his language and characterization and, in responding to their objections, referred to an issue taken up earlier in this book: the relationship between drama and reality. Having already been "modified" by the Abbey's directors, the play itself, he argued, is "a deadly compromise with the actual" and should not suffer further alteration (*Letters* 1:165–66). This same issue of dramatic representation and reality surfaced later both in public outcry over the play and in the Abbey's rejection of *The Silver Tassie* in 1928, a rift between playwright and theater that could never be repaired. In a letter to Lady Gregory, Lennox Robinson detailed his rationale for rejecting *The Silver Tassie* and, in a generous moment, declared that though the "idea" in O'Casey's plays is "always obvious," the "treatment" makes the difference and illuminates O'Casey's "genius" (*Letters* 1:238). *Treatment* functions here as a synonym for representation, and in the case of complaints by audience and cast alike against *The Plough and the Stars,* the realism of his representation of Dublin life formed the locus of disagreement. O'Casey's "idea" in *The Plough and the Stars* did seem "obvious" to much of his audience and has seemed equally transparent to more recent critics as well: Ireland's "household gods" of religion and nationalism, Saint Patrick and Cathleen Ni Houlihan, are ineffectual at relieving people's misery and may indeed exacerbate it.[10] Where, then, in O'Casey's treatment of Dublin life exists the incendiary difference, the "genius" that could incite both the audience's violence and Robinson's admiration? And how in O'Casey is representation related to issues of both populism and elitism, intertextuality and authorial autonomy?

Hanna Sheehy-Skeffington, an ardent nationalist whose husband was murdered during the Easter 1916 uprising, engaged O'Casey in public debate over *The Plough and the Stars,* finding little genius in his representation of this historical moment.[11] The dialogue between Sheehy-Skeffington and O'Casey over *The Plough and the Stars* (much of which was conducted in the press because O'Casey was ill and thus somewhat constrained when the two met in person) centers around the issues of representation and realism, at times contradictorily so. In her letter to the *Irish Independent* of 15 February 1926, she maintained that there is a point beyond which "realism [becomes] not art, but morbid perversity." O'Casey, in her view, had passed this point in his odious portrayal of Irish nationalists and their wives: "It is the realism that would paint not only the wart on Cromwell's nose, but that would add carbuncles and running sores in a reaction against idealisation" (*Letters* 1:168). In a subsequent letter eight days later, reacting to O'Casey's response to her initial salvo, Sheehy-Skeffington again attacked representation in *The Plough and the Stars,* on this occasion contradicting the position she had taken just a week before. This time, she not only indicted the comic perspective of O'Casey's play but also accused it of *not* being realistic: "The Greeks . . . used to require of a tragedy that it evokes feelings in the spectator of 'pity and terror,' and Shakespeare speaks of holding the 'mirror up to nature.' Submitted to either criterion, *The Plough and the Stars* is assuredly defective" (*Letters* 1:172). In the view of O'Casey's nationalist detractors, then, he commits the same transgression some reviewers of *Saint Joan* felt Bernard Shaw had committed – employing comedy to relate a serious historical episode[12] – and fails in his treatment either by holding the mirror up too closely to Irish life, revealing its ideological blemishes, or by dispensing with mimetic reflection altogether.

Not surprisingly, in the scholarship of O'Casey's present defenders and attackers, formalists and Marxists, representation is also a crucial issue, particularly in aesthetic verdicts against plays like *The Harvest Festival* or *The Star Turns Red* (1938). For Krause, Hogan, and Ronald Ayling, such plays fail, in part, because of their resemblance to propaganda. Krause calls *The Star Turns Red* a "piece of straight anti-Fascist propaganda," and Ayling describes the co-presence of "propaganda and art" in *The Harvest Festival,* a pre-Abbey play presumed lost until he discovered a holograph draft of the drama in 1964.[13] Taking a completely opposite view of *The Star Turns Red* and disagreeing with indictments such as Hogan's that it is O'Casey's "poorest" work, Jack Mitchell praises its "positive historical perspective" and O'Casey's ability to produce in the play a "new synthesis of the kind he and the times needed."[14] In what ways are such plays mere "propaganda"? And in labeling them as such are not the same critics who insist upon O'Casey's autonomy inevitably backsliding on one of their most fundamental tenets? Apparently, O'Casey was "his own man" sometimes, when writing *The Plough and the Stars* for instance; sometimes he wasn't. When composing *The Star Turns Red,* a play clearly related to those dramas regarded as O'Casey's most autobiographical such as *The Harvest Festival* and *Red Roses for Me,* was O'Casey somehow not his own man? In these times, as I shall outline, he moved too near the domain of the popular, precisely the move many scholars, like the Abbey directors before them who passed over O'Casey's early submissions, cannot abide.

Underlying much critical disagreement about O'Casey today, therefore, is a very familiar subtext: disdain for the popular and the estimation of aesthetic value based on a text's distance from or proximity to the ideologies and conventions of popular culture. Incorporated into this critical discourse are other issues raised earlier: issues of representation and of the contexts within which Irish writers create their work. These matters inform both more traditional and Marxian readings of O'Casey's drama and properly so, as O'Casey found himself in a constant process of negotiation with popular convention both in his most prized and most problematic plays. If O'Casey's early play *The Harvest Festival* and later *The Star Turns Red* advance unrealistic representations of social reality because they depend too heavily on popular convention, his "Dublin Trilogy" appears more realistic precisely because plays like *The Plough and the Stars* subtly undermine conventions that O'Casey appropriates from the popular theater. That is, as critics of various political persuasions can seemingly agree, in *The Plough and the Stars* O'Casey strikes a formidable blow against the dominant ideologies of Irish society, religion and nationalism. What has not been adequately explained, however, are the formal and allusive means O'Casey employs to achieve his demythologizing work. These means find their provenience, by and large, in Irish popular culture so that as O'Casey assaults the dominant ideology he also overturns the very devices which, on the popular stage, conveyed it. Hence, early in his career and not yet of the stature of a Yeatsian star, O'Casey became entangled in a tree of popular culture in which he could neither rest for too long if he wished his plays performed at the Abbey nor completely extricate himself from if he intended to further the cause of a redistribution of economic and political power. This entanglement persists throughout his writing and forms the focus of this chapter.

"PROPAGANDA" AND MELODRAMA

When "Captain" Jack Boyle tells his "butty" Joxer Daly in *Juno and the Paycock* that "real" Dubliners "know more about Charlie Chaplin an' Tommy Mix than they do about SS. Peter and Paul," we should assume he knows of what he speaks. A similar hypothesis informs *The Drums of Father Ned*, O'Casey's later critique of the bourgeois class's obsession with social status and its obstruction of a younger generation's attempts to escape sexual repression and reclaim such Irish cultural forms as historical melodrama.[15] The Binningtons and McGilligans, targets of O'Caseyean parody in *The Drums of Father Ned*, in fact care very little about anything beyond the social hierarchy of Doonavale, a staid community transformed by Father Ned's Tosthal and its infusion of cultural energy. Boyle's Dubliners know little more than Binnington about Irish culture, though they are more familiar with such popular cultural forms as the emerging cinema. As a denizen of drinking "snugs," Boyle must surely overhear "real" Dubliners exchanging opinions about an array of actors, singers, and popular cultural texts which by the 1920s was wide indeed: a mixture of the new and the old, the innovative and the conventional, the native and the imported. In 1926, for example, when *The Plough and the Stars* opened at the Abbey Theatre, two Chaplin films—*The Gold Rush* and *The Kid*—ran at the Metropole Cinema and La Scala Theatre in January. Against the formidable competition of Chaplin and Abbey dramas, Dublin theaters turned to the still unvanquished popular champion of Christmases past: the pantomime. The Gaiety produced *Humpty Dumpty* and the Queen's mounted *Dick Whittington*, two perennially successful subjects for treatment in the pantomime. J. M. Barrie's *Peter Pan* was revived in January at the Pavilion, and contemporary London comedies were booked at the Theatre Royal and the Olympia. American film, English comedy, old-fashioned pantomime, and a revival of Barrie—such varied fare constituted the Dublin theatrical world before *The Plough and the Stars* intruded so noisily.

If "real" Dubliners of O'Casey's age knew a great deal about Charlie Chaplin and Tom Mix, they knew even more about Irish melodrama and brought this knowledge with them to the theater. Boucicault's Irish dramas and those of other writers had, in fact, enjoyed a resurgence of popularity in the second decade of this century and continued to be revived with great success throughout the 1920s and 1930s as well.[16] And O'Casey was a real Dubliner. In such chapters as "Shakespeare Taps at the Window" and "Touched by the Theatre" in *Pictures in the Hallway* (1942) and "The Temple Entered" (the "Temple" here being the Abbey Theatre) in *Inishfallen, Fare Thee Well* (1949), O'Casey relates his considerable experience of melodrama. This latter chapter is both illuminating and poignant, as it deals with O'Casey's reaction to the controversy surrounding *The Plough and the Stars*, his then being informed by Sean Barlow that he was persona non grata at the Abbey, and finally O'Casey's decision "never after" to "set a foot either on the Abbey stage or in the Abbey Green Room" (*Autobiographies* 2:157).

Here O'Casey ponders the sharp criticism *The Plough and the Stars* had sparked—particularly that which denounced the play as having the structure of the cinema or the music-hall revue—and hints at the influence of melodrama on his play. "He [O'Casey refers to himself in the third person] wondered how he could have built on the revue structure, for he had never seen a revue in his life. He knew nothing about the cinema. If any of them had only mentioned melodrama, he would have cocked an ear, for he had seen many of these, and had enjoyed them all. They saw in Sean that of which they themselves were full—the cinema and the revue" (*Autobiographies* 2:155).[17] Also, when O'Casey considered the implications of his banishment from the Abbey, his first thoughts were of his younger days on the Abbey stage when it was still the Mechanics' Theatre. "Ordered from the stage he had trod so many years ago and he a kidger, ay, mouthed the part of Father Dolan in *The Shaughraun* from its boards, ere ever the Abbey Theatre had entered its beginning; the stage on which his brother, Archie, had played Harvey Duff in the same play, and others in *Peep o'Day Boys, The Unknown, Green Bushes,* and *The Colleen Bawn*" (*Autobiographies* 2:157). Though these reminiscences affirm his intimate acquaintance with melodrama, O'Casey is rather close-mouthed about its specific influence on his writing.

As I have mentioned, the issue of O'Casey's acquaintance with and deep imbuement in the conventions of popular drama and theater underlies the Abbey Theatre's rejection of his earliest plays. This, again, was the principal reason for the failure of *The Harvest Festival,* both in Yeats's judgment and in that of an anonymous reviewer. The reviewer criticized the typicality of O'Casey's characters, their appearing as "unreal as the 'Stage Irishman' of 20 years ago"; and Yeats deplored O'Casey's "old Irish idea of a good play—Queen's melodrama brought up to date"—in a plot constructed to elicit boos and hisses at every turn (*Letters* 1:91, 90). There is doubtless a good deal of accuracy in these evaluations. In 1918, unfortunately, O'Casey had little theatrical experience to draw upon other than that of his youth. And when the Abbey declined to produce *The Frost in the Flower* on the differing grounds that its characters were too much like those in several Abbey plays, Eileen O'Casey recalled her husband's recognition of the error of this judgment: "Sean guessed this comment was wrong, and a little ridiculous, since he had been in the Abbey Theatre but twice. . . . He had seen nothing . . . that he could try to imitate."[18] His wife's recollection is corroborated by O'Casey's entirely believable statement of regret in his "Song of a Shift" that by 1907 he was woefully unfamiliar with Yeats and

the Abbey: "Sean wished he had seen Yeats's *Cathleen ni Houlihan,* so that
he might know more about the man; but a shilling was too much for him
to spare for a play. He wished he could see this play by Singe or Sinje" (*Autobiographies* 1:519). Regrettably, he could not.

His poverty also prevented him from frequenting the theater in the
years immediately preceding the composition of his first plays. As Krause
emphasizes, from 1911 to 1923, when O'Casey "was mainly unemployed
and unemployable due to his union connection, and notoriously too proud
to beg for help, he was on many occasions characterized by those who knew
him as a perpetually hungry and often sick scarecrow of a man."[19] Like
Ayamonn Breydon, from time to time O'Casey scraped together what money
he could to purchase books, as he did for a sixpenny edition of Shaw's *John
Bull's Other Island,* a play that had an enormous impact on him. So did
Shakespeare's plays. But so too, quite obviously, did the popular theater of
his youth, really the only theater he knew intimately before trying his hand
at writing plays.

The Harvest Festival confirms this intimacy, and its "intrinsic features"
resemble those of O'Casey's later plays, even his very last works: its dealing
with issues of exploitation, religious hypocrisy, and class struggle; its "sympathy for the underdog" and creation of a "sense of warmth among the poor";
and so forth.[20] Yet, of course, these ideas alone did not motivate either the
Abbey's negative decision in 1920 or critical arraignment of the play's merits
now. O'Casey's melodramatic "treatment" accounts for most of the items
on Ayling's list of *The Harvest Festival*'s "many artistic shortcomings": characters "really engaged in talking to the audience, making set speeches, striking poses thought appropriate to the context"; the plot's "artificial patterning"
that frequently "splits up" the action into "dialogues between two people";
and the lack of "functional tension between the *dramatis personae*" in a text
that, finally, "too often reads like a series of contrived set pieces." These
defects, added to the conventional characterizations to which the Abbey
reviewer objected, signal both melodrama and propaganda. Ayling implies
as much when he refers to characters on both sides of the class struggle as
"caricatures" painted mostly "in black and white colours," particularly Jack
Rocliffe, the working-class predecessor of Ayamonn Breydon and Jack in
The Star Turns Red, who delivers speeches "blatantly loaded in favour of
the causes which the author favored."[21] My intention here is not to interrogate the accuracy of Ayling's somewhat harsh assessment or of Emile Jean
Dumay's thesis that *The Harvest Festival* anticipates the political and thematic

content of O'Casey's later plays. Rather, I wish to identify the several specific features of *The Harvest Festival* and *The Star Turns Red* that seem especially tied to popular Irish drama and to outline a few ways in which these plays transcend the melodramatic, approaching the materialist theater of Bertolt Brecht and, one of several important contemporary dramatists writing in the Brechtian tradition, Edward Bond. Melodramatic and propagandistic discourse do, in some senses, rely upon similar conventions and, to paraphrase a statement Bond made some years ago, if revolution is necessarily preceded by propaganda, it might also be preceded or accompanied by melodrama.

The so-called "black and white colours" of O'Casey's characterization offer one example both of his proximity to and final transcendence of the melodramatic. To be sure, Jack Rocliffe and his successor in *The Star Turns Red* resemble the Tones, Sarsfields, and McCrackens of Whitbread's Irish historical drama. Eloquent, courageous, and self-sacrificing, O'Casey's characters may be even more laudable than their counterparts in popular drama in that they are poor and largely self-taught, like O'Casey himself, lacking the social advantages of the historical and fictional heroes in the limelight at the Queen's Theatre. By contrast, O'Casey's "organic intellectuals," Antonio Gramsci's term for the intellectual element in a particular social class, are therefore not typical subjects interpellated by formal educational systems so much as they are the results of their own "bookishness." They are, for this reason, less standardized than intellectuals produced "by the system," and in this narrow respect "their own men," occupying a mediative position between a subaltern class and that in power.[22] By comparison, Whitbread's characters certainly do not flaunt their position, and in fact at the beginning of *Wolfe Tone* the title character's indebtedness to the villain causes considerable concern. But Tone *does* have a servant eager to help (and, although rather unlikely, the capital to do so). The first scene of the play is set in front of Trinity College, as Tone, like Charles O'Malley in *The Irish Dragoon*, has had the benefit of a formal education O'Casey's laborers and railwaymen could never afford. Somewhat similarly, O'Casey's heroes also have loyal companions, fellow workers in fact, but these confederates are not able to effect rescues and have even less education than their friends. And all of O'Casey's proletarian heroes, in these plays and in *Red Roses for Me*, are opposed by adversaries as heartless as those who plague Whitbread's aristocratic nationalists. With the notable exception of either cowardly or outright villainous clerics, Protestant and Catholic, the opponents of striking workers in O'Casey's plays in several respects differ very little from the antagonists to Irish patriots in Whitbread's.[23]

Melodramatic villains in popular Irish drama are generally marked by several qualities that apply almost equally as well to clerics and bourgeois figures of economic or political power in *The Harvest Festival*, *The Star Turns Red*, and *Red Roses for Me*. Curiously enough, the two later plays seem even more melodramatic than *The Harvest Festival* in this respect. In O'Casey's first play, Rocliffe's adversaries are an unfeeling and self-indulgent bourgeois family, the Williamsons, supported both by the Protestant parish of Saint Brendan's and by the aristocracy, represented by a "leading man of commerce," Sir Jocelyn Vane. As we learn near the end of act 2, one of Vane's scab laborers has shot Jack, wounding him fatally, as he led a group of strikers in protest. We see little of Vane, however, as O'Casey's sights seem squarely trained upon an overfed middle class preparing to adorn its church with a surplus harvest, while a terribly underfed proletariat is expected to watch as much-needed food is turned into decoration and their jobs are stolen by scab laborers. Those jobs the workers still hold are overseen by employers like Mrs. Williamson, who watches her workers so closely with her "harsh & proud" face that, as one laments, "she won't let you try to straighten your back" (*CP* 5:412, 416). Meanwhile, the Williamson house is a flurry of activity as their festival day, their celebration of a material plenitude denied the workers, approaches.

More sinister are the clerics and figures of legal authority in *The Star Turns Red* and *Red Roses for Me*. In the former play, the communist workers and a priest somewhat sympathetic to their cause are opposed by the priest of the bourgeois class (the "Purple Priest"), the fascists ("Saffron Shirts"), the Christian Front, and the police; in the latter, the working-class hero struggles against an indifferent church and a sharply repressive police, represented by Inspector Tom Finglas. In both dramas, the opponents of the working class evince a malevolence, even a sadism, that far surpasses the callousness and ostentation of the Williamsons in *The Harvest Festival*. Matching the cruelty of British officers like Major Sirr in Boucicault's *Robert Emmet* and Captain Fox in Whitbread's *Ulster Hero*, the Purple Priest in *The Star Turns Red* enters Jack's house in act 1 with O'Casey's foreboding description: "A cowl hides all but the front of his face, which is pale, fixed like a mask in lines of cold severity" (*CP* 2:270). Seeing Julia, Jack's girlfriend, dressed in a provocative costume for a dance and hissing obstinance at the Saffron Shirts who have accompanied him, the Purple Priest supports the recommendation of the fascist leader of the same course of correction for

Julia that Sirr administers to Anne Devlin, Robert Emmet's loyal and courageous confederate. There is even a hint of Inquisitional logic in the priest's
intimation that his recommendation is offered for Julia's spiritual well-being:
"A passing pain will take some glitter out of the dress and dream of seduction. It is good that the little immodest wretch should have the lash laid
on her back, lest worse befall her" (*CP* 2:273). The malevolence of both
the Saffron Shirts and Purple Priest is confirmed moments later when Julia's father, attempting to rescue his daughter from this threatened ill-
treatment, is shot down by Kian, Jack's brother and staunch opponent of
the labor movement.

Inspector Finglas in *Red Roses for Me* becomes a figure of similar cruelty. In act 3, which reveals the influence of Expressionist art on O'Casey,[24]
Finglas loses his temper when a beggar spits on his boot, necessitating the
rector's admonition to Finglas that he should restrain himself because he
wears the king's uniform. Soon after this, Finglas compares Ayamonn to
the sleepy loungers who litter the street by terming him a "neat slab of a
similar slime"; and in act 4, when Sheila, Ayamonn's girl, beseeches Finglas
to do his best to "save us from another sorrow" by not responding violently
to the striking railwaymen, Finglas only promises to do his worst: "Remember, all! When swords are drawn and horses charge, the kindly Law, so fat
with hesitation, swoons away, and sees not, hears not, cares not what may
happen" (*CP* 3:212). Moments later, the news comes that Ayamonn has
been killed, and Finglas returns to the churchyard of St. Burnupus only
to add insult to the injury done. When men praise Ayamonn's sacrifice as
noble, Finglas can see only the small amount of salary increase that prompted
the strike in the first place: "It wasn't a very noble thing to die for a single
shilling" (*CP* 3:225). Near the end of the play, he attempts to befriend
Sheila, and for a moment his kindness and pleas of innocence in Ayamonn's
death seem almost genuine. After Sheila runs away from him, however, the
real Finglas returns as he threatens Brennan, Ayamonn's grieving friend, with
further violence: "My men don't wait to ask the way you worship when
they raise their arms to strike" (*CP* 3:226). This threat of harshly repressive
action and the arrogance of powerful parishioners who earlier demanded
that Ayamonn be expelled from the parish—a direct replication of the situation in the last act of *The Harvest Festival*, when politically powerful members of the congregation prevail upon the rector of Saint Brendan's to refuse
Rocliffe burial from their church—combine to form a major obstacle for
Breydon's vision of greater social equality in *Red Roses for Me*.

Although not so obviously melodramatic in heritage as Inspector

Finglas and the Purple Priest, other bourgeois or clerical opponents of social reform in O'Casey's plays bear affinity with their melodramatic predecessors. In particular, O'Casey replicates a popular dramatic tactic in reversing
stereotypes of Irishmen as effeminate or weak. Thus such characters as the
diminutive and cowardly Lord Mayor in *The Star Turns Red* resemble many
informers in Whitbread's melodramas such as Joey Rafferty, the "imp of inequity" in *Wolfe Tone,* and foils of Wild Irish Boys in Hubert O'Grady's
plays. As act 4 of *The Star Turns Red* opens, workmen preparing for a party
at the mayor's residence refer deprecatingly to him as a "little shower off"
and an "under-sized scut" who is not "fit to become, even with the help
of the saints, a flea in a hidden feather of a mighty angel's wing" (*CP* 2:330).
Like the "unmanly" Irish informants and traitors in popular Irish drama,
the Lord Mayor becomes "frantic with fright" when the sounds of sirens
from the foundry alert him to trouble nearby. Attempting nervously to call
the Saffron Shirts' headquarters for assistance, he comes "very close to a
swoon," according to O'Casey's stage directions (*CP* 2:345–46). Similarly
undersized are Councillor Reiligan, the "biggest money-man in the district"
and "a loyal pillar of the clergy," and his friend Canon Burren, parish priest
of Ballyoonagh, in *The Bishop's Bonfire* (1955). Although neither is called
upon to exert the force that Finglas does in *Red Roses for Me*–or placed in
a predicament designed to exhibit his cowardice as is the Lord Mayor in
The Star Turns Red–both are typical figures of combined bourgeois-clerical
repression in O'Casey's late plays. And as Burren reminds Father Boheroe,
a popular priest of liberal politics, both possess a level of power analogous
to that of the villains of many an Irish drama: "You're very popular with
our people, but remember that the love they may have for you doesn't come
near the fear they have for Reiligan [*he pauses*] or the reverence they must
have for their Parish Priest" (*CP* 5:84). Bishopson in *The Harvest Festival,*
the clerical friend of the Williamsons, is also small, and when such a figure
is matched with the often stout and stern representatives of the bourgeois
class in these plays, the cause of social reform faces a powerful aggregation
of obstacles.

These similarities notwithstanding, O'Casey's characters are *not* identical to their counterparts on the popular stage, especially O'Casey's women
characters. Equally, in his plot construction O'Casey transcends popular convention and approaches the materialist theater of Brecht and Bond. For example, it is difficult to see Mrs. Rocliffe in *The Harvest Festival,* Julie in *The
Star Turns Red,* and Sheila in *Red Roses for Me* as mere replicants of the loyal

wives of historical heroes and chaste colleen bawns of Ireland's peasant villages. In melodramatic emplotment, the testing of such characters' virtue forms the action around which the entire play revolves. It is thus the consistency of the melodramatic heroine in the face of overwhelming trials and temptations—or, alternatively, the patriotism of the historical hero in the face of death—that dominates the popular Irish drama O'Casey knew so well. As Peter Brooks explains, "Melodrama typically not only employs virtue persecuted as a source of its dramaturgy, but also tends to become the dramaturgy of virtue misprized and eventually recognized. It is about virtue made visible and acknowledged, the drama of a recognition." In such plays as Boucicault's *Colleen Bawn,* typical in this respect and accurately described by Brooks's emphasis upon recognition, the play ends "with public recognition of where virtue and evil reside, and the eradication of one as the reward of the other."[25] Eily O'Connor's basic goodness wins over Mrs. Cregan and chastens Hardress, the husband who at one point would have been happy to be rid of her, and Corrigan's villainy is finally exposed for what it is. In more historical Irish drama, similarly, all attempts to discredit the nationalist hero, to convince others of his cowardice or betrayal, are finally undone; and even if a resolution to historical conflicts cannot be effected, by the closing scenes of these plays no doubts remain as to the veracity and courage of Robert Emmet, Henry Joy McCracken, Edward Fitzgerald, and Wolfe Tone. Nor does any doubt remain about the fidelity and courage of their wives or female associates. Resolution in some cases but recognition in all is the rule of popular Irish drama, verifying Brooks's hypothesis that melodrama is constituted of repeated challenges to and affirmations of a character's real identity.

By comparison, the narrative structure of O'Casey's so-called propagandistic plays such as *The Harvest Festival* and *The Star Turns Red* is obviously very different. Yet similarities do exist between the materialist theater of a playwright like Edward Bond—or O'Casey—and Irish melodrama, if for no other reason than that both move toward recognition. The kinds of recognition are, however, very different. As Bond emphasizes in his critical prose, the theater is remarkably well-suited to provide us with a better understanding of the "relation of cause and effect in practical human life." The theater's purpose, for Bond, ought properly to be the creation of an expanded self-consciousness, a "viable knowledge of the self in relation to practical involvement in the world." In addition, this self-consciousness combines with a refined and expanded "interpretation of the world and self that restores moral action to our lives."[26] Both melodrama and the kind of political drama often critically devalued as propaganda, therefore, share a common, deeply vested interest in recognition. The difference concerns what exactly is recognized both by characters in a drama and audiences viewing it. From this perspective, the structure of O'Casey's *Harvest Festival* and *The Star Turns Red* brings them closer to Bond's theater than to Boucicault's.

If O'Casey's sole or even principal interest in either play were to construct melodrama, to develop a dramatic action culminating either in the victory of his hero or in a public recognition of his courage or political commitment, the plots of *The Harvest Festival* and *The Star Turns Red* are decidedly ineffectual at realizing this intention. Rather, both plays evolve to locate other characters' transformed senses of values or newly achieved political consciousnesses in the foreground, their awareness of the social causes of the heroes' deaths. The matter of Jack Rocliffe's heroic sacrifice for his fellow workers is concluded at the end of act 2, and, although moving, his death and last speeches in no way rival the sensation with which such events were portrayed on the popular stage. More significant, the last act of the play concerns Rector Jennings's capitulation to the wealthier members of his congregation over the issue of Jack's burial and emphasizes Mrs. Rocliffe's valorization of her dead son's politics. Earlier in act 2, Mrs. Rocliffe had inveighed against Jack's self-education as the cause of his misguided union activism: "It's the readin' that has ruined him, the readin', the readin'. . . . Whatever he saw in the books I don't know, but they were never out of his hands. An' from bein' gay an' always laughin' he got quiet and thoughtful" (*CP* 5:448). Besides its obvious biographical patina, this speech establishes the importance of Mrs. Rocliffe's changed opinion in act 3 after the rector wavers on his promise to allow Jack burial in the church: "I have eyes to see an' ears to hear, an' a heart to feel, an' I can understand now that there was wisdom in his foolishness. I wouldn't let him into your church now, no; not if you all went down on your bended knees to me" (*CP* 5:468). Before she exits with the workers to bury her dead son, Mrs. Rocliffe specifies what her improved vision has allowed her to see: "My poor, poor Jack was right—the Church is always again' the workin'-class" (*CP* 5:470). Nevertheless, this recognition does not instigate Mrs. Rocliffe's malice against her son's murderer. When Jack's loyal friend Bill tells her the workers have avenged themselves on Vane's scabs, Mrs. Rocliffe's response anticipates those of suffering mothers in later plays: "Maybe he, too, was the only son of some poor, heartbroken mother" (*CP* 5:471). The dramatic action of *The*

Harvest Festival, in sum, leads to a blanket denunciation of class inequities and of the church's participation in perpetuating them, and this may seem propagandistic. Yet we can detect in this, O'Casey's earliest surviving play, one way in which he transcends the melodramatic: by structuring a plot that leads to the political epiphany of his characters and audiences, not to a sensational stage picture.

Melodramatic convention and the creation of an expanded political consciousness reside equally closely in *The Star Turns Red*, especially in Kian's response to his brother's murder in act 4. Some critics have labeled such conclusions as the final scene in *The Star Turns Red* "bathetic," but it is also possible to view them as evidence of O'Casey's undoing of melodramatic formulas. Early in the play Kian plays the villain, opposing Jack's political agenda by serving with the Saffron Shirts and unflinchingly shooting down Julia's father in front of his daughter. Jack's death near the play's end causes Kian to reconsider his actions, and he eventually elects to "pass away" with his brother, if necessary, rather than escape harm's way by further association with the Saffron Shirts. In the play's final tableau, the Red Star, grown larger and promising better times ahead for the workers, is contrasted to Kian's "consolate" and lonely figure guarding his fallen brother's body. As in *The Harvest Festival*, a political recognition marks the end of *The Star Turns Red*, not a sensational execution, unlikely victory, or heroic oration.

Such endings show, I believe, two ways in which O'Casey surpasses melodrama in these plays. The most obvious is the reformation of a character like Kian and the increased awareness of Mrs. Rocliffe, transformed from an opponent of the workers' movement to a supporter of it. In the black-and-white world of melodrama, such transformations seldom occur because characterization typically matches the bipolar and Manichaean qualities of the melodramatic world: the conflict of good and evil in melodrama is absolute, "not subject to compromise," thus "characters represent extremes" not subject to change or even much modulation.[27] O'Casey's characters, especially women like Julia in *The Star Turns Red* and Sheila in *Red Roses for Me*, form compromises, especially when the revolutionary zeal of O'Casey's young heroes interferes with their personal objectives or plans. At the beginning of *The Star Turns Red*, Julia places her own gratification before the revolution by dressing up and attending a local dance with Jack, but she quickly recognizes the greater urgency of Jack's political goal. In *Red Roses for Me*, Sheila at first attempts to persuade Jack to "divide" himself from the "foolish" men and their strike, stick to his job, and become a foreman someday even though to do so means becoming a "blackleg." Of course, he refuses. Later, after his death, she defends his project to Finglas: when he insinuates that dying for a shilling raise hardly seems noble, she retorts: "Maybe he saw the shilling in th' shape of a new world" (*CP* 3:225). Julia and Sheila, like Mrs. Rocliffe, resemble the loyal wives of Queen's Theatre melodrama; but unlike their predecessors, these characters undergo a process of political education that exerts profound changes in their goals and worldviews. Further, neither Julia nor Sheila resembles Anne Devlin or Eily O'Connor—they are more sensual, more skeptical, more modern—even if they eventually assume roles analogous to those of their nineteenth-century antecedents.

The last scene of *The Star Turns Red,* much like the earlier wake of Julia's father, suggests another way in which O'Casey exceeds the melodramatic: namely, in the way he treats onstage violence and creates a stage picture with a dual focus.[28] Though he advocates the use of violence to shock audiences into greater political awareness, Bond is extremely careful to avoid melodramatic renderings of violent action in such plays as *Lear* (1972), *Bingo* (1973), and *The Bundle* (1978). One method of avoiding melodrama is the construction of a double picture or dual image, with cause and effect linking the two presentations. Thus, in scene 3 of *Bingo,* a play about William Shakespeare's business dealings while in retirement in Stratford, a gibbetted young woman, having been beaten and abused earlier, appears upstage while Shakespeare talks to the audience and other characters downstage. The dialogue makes it clear that the young lady is the victim of Shakespeare's earlier actions, thereby connecting the twin visual foci through causality.

Somewhat similarly, though not nearly so dispassionately or causally presented as most of Bond's scenes involving the effects of violence, the corpse of Julia's father (Michael) is displayed in act 3 of *The Star Turns Red.* As Jack's mother and father discuss recent events in front of their dead friend, it seems clear that their passivity and quickly changing sympathies are in part responsible for the victimization of the proletariat that Michael's murder represents. A group of "wretched-looking" mourners—blind and lame men, a withered baby, a hunchback, and the like—enter to pay their respects, and another dual focus is achieved: the same extreme conditions responsible for Michael's death cause the deformities of these mourners. Certainly such pitiful characters also appear frequently in melodrama to represent the extreme conditions of the melodramatic world; but here they are linked in the stage picture to Michael, both victims of a devastating inequity aided by the church. The dual picture of Kian standing over his dead brother's body at the end of the play achieves much the same effect, as Jack's death and Kian's disconsolation are both effects of the same social causes.

These and other aspects of O'Casey's plays resemble several characteristics Brecht describes as essential to his epic theater: spectators confront the social realities of poverty, class inequity, and institutional rationalizations for these conditions; if the playwright is successful, spectators are led to a recognition along with characters; unlike the static depictions of the popular theater, human beings are seen to be alterable, not fixed (though O'Casey's references to the masklike faces of some clergy and bourgeois Irishmen suggest their fixedness); and, most important, O'Casey and Brecht both illuminate the ways in which social being determines thought.[29] Because the materialist theater investigates matters of political power, economy, and institutional authority, its means of representation often appear melodramatic: extreme, unfair, slanted so as to induce sympathy with the powerless. Therefore, though the epic theater attempts to displace the popular or what Brecht terms the "dramatic" theater—replacing its inherent emotionalism with social analysis—it is inevitable that it will replicate melodramatic characterization and emplotment. Brecht's Galileo and Mother Courage are trapped by many of the same institutions as O'Casey's Irishmen. So, yes, *The Harvest Festival* and *The Star Turns Red* contain numerous elements of melodrama, but they are certainly not only melodramatic or propagandistic even if O'Casey's negotiations with the popular in *The Harvest Festival* were, finally, unsuccessful. As he wrote his more famous Abbey dramas, he developed a new strategy in dealing with the popular tradition, a strategy to which I now turn.

MELODRAMA AND THE "DUBLIN TRILOGY":
A Map of Misreading

If O'Casey ventured too near the popular in his early Abbey submissions, he seemed intent upon distancing himself from the conventions of popular drama in *The Shadow of a Gunman, Juno and the Paycock,* and *The Plough and the Stars*. In other words, he deployed popular conventions in a much different way in these plays and for very different ends. Some years ago Harry M. Ritchie scanned the Dublin trilogy for traces of melodrama and in the process discovered that O'Casey was reluctant to admit to much influence from the popular theater he had "enjoyed in his younger days." "Melodrama as such has no influence on me. Bouc. [Boucicault] was familiar because I knew well those who had played them in the old Mechanics' Theatre–now the Abbey–I played myself in *Shaughraun*, the part of Father Dolan. All I got from melodrama was a love for 'tableaux' giving me a device to form pictures in my plays . . . and the 'incidental music' that invariably went with melodrama. Above all, the reading of them–Dick's Standard Plays–gave me a reading love and knowledge of the playform."[30] O'Casey's grudging acknowledgment of the various influences of melodrama on his plays, in Ritchie's view, constitutes a "key" with which one might unlock O'Casey's appropriation of melodramatic techniques in *Juno and the Paycock*, *The Shadow of a Gunman*, and *The Plough and the Stars*. For Ritchie, the "true links" between melodrama and O'Casey are found not in "sentimental philosophies," but in the "mechanical techniques" of Boucicault's stage–in tableaux, incidental music, and "above all" in the playform–that in effect lulled the Abbey audience "into a false sense of security" in a "melodramatic code of values" shattered by the ends of these plays.[31] This observation is particularly useful in opening up an area of inquiry I wish to pursue here. What values make up this code, and what textual features induce O'Casey's audience to misread his plays in this way?

As I discussed earlier in regard to the Queen's Royal Theatre, no single code of values existed in popular nineteenth-century Irish drama–there seem to have been at least two. And O'Casey's Dublin plays, particularly *The Plough and the Stars*, oppose both: the codes of comic reconciliation of which, among others, Boucicault's Irish dramas are composed, and those of historical heroism that inform numerous melodramatic history plays, Irish historical ballads, popular journalism, and other cultural forms. Virtually every aspect of O'Casey's plays, the "mechanical" ones Ritchie identifies and the more significant ideological and historical issues he does not, are not merely informed by but composed of the dialectical opposition of these codes. The conclusions of all three Dublin plays advance a third reading of Irish life and Irish history, particularly in the case of *The Plough and the Stars*, a reading evolving from O'Casey's deconstruction of the two myths he had learned in, among other places, the popular theater. Most important, *The Plough and the Stars* ignited rioting in the Abbey not only because of its desacralizing of the Easter 1916 uprising but also because at every turn O'Casey employs conventions of popular drama to create well-defined generic expectations in his audience and then demolishes them. Such generic "signals" are of enormous importance, especially at the beginning of a narrative, for they help to establish in the reader or audience an "appropriate mental 'set' that allows the work's generic codes to be read."[32] Throughout *The Shadow of a Gunman, Juno and the Paycock,* and especially *The Plough and the Stars,* O'Casey sends his audiences misleading signals, thus inducing them to form provisional misreadings of his plays that must continually be revised and eventually discarded, perhaps angrily after having been so hoodwinked. In O'Casey's plays the textual agents responsible for this deception and creation of false expectations typically come from the conventions of the popular theater.

Described in some detail above, the historical basis and principal conventions of both popular myths might profitably (and briefly) be reviewed here, starting with Boucicault, whom O'Casey clearly respected and enjoyed. Boucicault's plays might appear far removed from the concerns of historical or political drama, but in several respects they are not. Part of the historicism of *Arrah-na-Pogue* and *The Shaughraun,* for instance, is conveyed in ways typical of melodrama. As Louis Althusser observes, melodrama constitutes a "law of the heart" which finally deludes itself (and its audience) as to "the law of the world." Melodrama operates by way of identification with bourgeois morality: with the ownership of private property, with religious institutions and ideologies, and most especially with marriage. This identification, according to Althusser, predisposes the characters of melodrama "to disguise their problems and even their condition" within "the arguments of a religious and moral conscience" rooted in bourgeois values. In sum, for Althusser melodrama acts as a "foreign consciousness" or a "veneer on a real condition," and this foreign consciousness is immanent in Boucicault's plays—and interrogated in O'Casey's as well.[33] The ends of plays like *The Colleen Bawn* supply this veneer by signaling either the obliteration or mediation of the oppositions on which the text is constructed: Englishness/Irishness, upper class/peasant class, and ownership/dispossession. These or similar oppositions underlie all of Boucicault's Irish plays, Edmund Falconer's *Peep o'Day* and *Eileen Oge,* hosts of other melodramas—and O'Casey's plays as well. As is the case in most melodramas, in Boucicault's plays the "law of the heart" overcomes all obstacles and unites all divisions both in Irish society and in history. In Boucicault's myth of reconciliation, therefore, very real historical tension between the two countries is dissipated harmlessly. Irish comic melodrama asserts the power of humanity to topple political, social, and economic barriers.

Another myth also pervaded the Dublin popular theater both before and after the Abbey Theatre achieved its reputation for artistic accomplishment: the myth of the national hero, as developed by J. W. Whitbread and Boucicault in such plays as *Robert Emmet*. Although Whitbread typically intruded romantic interests into a well-defined historical context, as Boucicault does in his melodrama and in *Robert Emmet,* he also privileged historical characters' public actions and subsequent tragic sacrifices, as these historical heroes elect to fight for Ireland regardless of the risks involved. The almost pastoral environment of Boucicault's plays often gives way in Whitbread's to urban settings—Belfast and Dublin—and absent too from many of Whitbread's plays are the blarney, drinking, and singing that enliven Irish comic melodrama. In short, the myth of cohesion—of the bringing together of disparate strands of Irish society or the abolition of social divisions—disappears from the majority of Whitbread's plays.

The conventions of this kind of melodrama are, of course, often related to, or more serious versions of, those of comic melodrama. The Irish stage villains in historical melodrama, for example, become increasingly politicized, more similar to Harvey Duff and Corey Kinchela of *The Shaughraun* than to Michael Feeny of *Arrah-na-Pogue* or Corrigan of *The Colleen Bawn.* Irish villains in plays like *The Ulster Hero* and *Robert Emmet* typically come in two varieties: police informers like Danny Niblock in *The Ulster Hero* and close associates of the hero who eventually betray him, James Hughes in Whitbread's play and Quigley in *Robert Emmet.* And although usually fictive, these characters are modeled after historical traitors. Such informants usually operate under the direction of reprehensible British soldiers that more comic Irish melodrama, for the most part, lacks. In *Robert Emmet* the villain is a historical figure, Major Sirr; in *The Ulster Hero* it is Captain Fox. Both use their positions of power and their well-lined pockets to coerce informants, and both are capable of the most brutal cruelties. Opposing them and reconciling various tensions in Irish society are historical heroes like Robert Emmet and Henry Joy McCracken in Whitbread's *The Ulster Hero.* Like Emmet, McCracken vows to give his life for the liberation of Ireland and continually exhorts his colleagues (and, by extension, the audience) to do the same in a series of eloquent speeches. Given the power of the heroic myth, McCracken himself, a wealthy factory owner, is of course *not* associated in any way with these "aristocrats" or the material advantages of the ruling class. One means of achieving this critical disjunction is through an image pattern in which religious faith and nationalism are linked, typically in the historical hero's discourse, as they are in many of Emmet's and Mc-

Cracken's speeches. The focus throughout *Robert Emmet* and *The Ulster Hero,* as a result, remains sharply on a passionate nationalism analogous to religious fervor. Tensions between England and Ireland intensify, and patriotic Irishmen like McCracken and Emmet die gladly for their country.

O'Casey's plays reiterate these myths in a variety of sometimes extremely subtle ways. O'Casey's use of the stage set, for example, or meticulously designed "tableaux" as he called it—the setting, properties, and sounds of Dublin tenement life—entrenches the plays firmly within a dialectic formed by the nineteenth-century comic and historical myths. That is, the mise-en-scènes of these plays reflect O'Casey's critical opposition of these myths. That he recognized the irony of impoverished, deluded people immersing themselves in historical or religious fictions that merely disguised their powerlessness is exceedingly clear in his autobiographies in which O'Casey frequently employs mise-en-scène to help make precisely this point. In *I Knock at the Door* (1939), for instance, O'Casey re-creates in intimate detail the O'Casside family parlor in which his father's wake was held. On one wall a picture of Admiral Nelson standing on a burning deck and exhorting his men to fight hung conspicuously; the opposite wall was dominated by a portrait of Queen Victoria, "all decked out in her coronation robes, with none of the fun and all of the pomp, power, wealth, and parade of her colonial empire." In between and under these icons of martial heroism and British imperialism—under the "stare from the paper faces of Lord Nelson and Queen Victoria"—a "cold, stiff and quiet thing lay" (*Autobiographies* 1:32). This "thing" was Michael O'Casside of Limerick, O'Casey's father.

O'Casey decorates the sets of *The Plough and the Stars,* particularly those of acts 1 and 2, with equal care, and the sets underline the antithesis between the heroic and comic myths in the context of the 1916 uprising. The paintings bordering the entrance to the front drawing room of the Clitheroes' apartment—Jean-François Millet's *Gleaners* (1857) and *The Angelus* (1855–57)—evoke the pastoral unity of Boucicault's Irish plays and, at the same time, create a sharp contrast with life in a Dublin tenement. The Millet paintings, as Michael Kaufman suggests, "sentimentalize rural life" by depicting peasants "at one with the rhythms of nature" and thus oppose the portrait of Robert Emmet—displayed prominently over the Clitheroes' mantelpiece—that "hangs like a cloud over the play."[34] But the two Millet paintings and the picture of Emmet constitute a battle of opposing views of Irish life (and history) that Kaufman overlooks: the male-dominated myth of Irish patriotism and the "green world" myth that more democratically concerns women like Boucicault's Eily O'Connor and Arrah.

Like O'Casey's plays, especially *The Plough and the Stars*, which O'Casey dedicated to his mother, Millet's paintings stress the importance of women in the family. In the foreground of *The Angelus*, a farmer stands, humbly holding his hat, his hayfork planted in the earth and his face masked by shadows. A woman, presumably his wife, stands by him, her face bathed in light and her hands folded in prayer. In front of her rests a basket, in the near background a cart, and in the distance behind her the spire of the church at Chailly pierces the sky. In their study of Millet, Robert L. Herbert, Roseline Bacou, and Michel Laclotte note a consistent opposition in *The Angelus* between the functions of men and women in rural families; indeed, Millet's painting seems to glorify women in a manner analogous to O'Casey's development of strong women in his plays:

> Ce n'est pas l'homme qui reçoit la lumière dans le tableau de Millet. Elle [la lumière] vient au contraire de derrière lui et tombe par devant sur la femme pour l'isolater et la glorifier. Les autres éléments de la peinture repondent aussi à cette opposition entre le rôle de le femme et celui de l'homme. . . . Millet a accumulé les objects symbolisant la fonction de la femme.[35]

> [It is not the man who receives the light in Millet's picture. The light to the contrary comes behind him and falls in front of the woman to isolate and glorify her. The other elements of the painting also respond to this opposition between the role of the woman and that of the man. . . . Millet has accumulated objects symbolizing the woman's function.]

Like *The Angelus*, *The Gleaners* depicts the life-giving functions of women and their efforts to glean the earth at harvest time. In the painting three women dominate the foreground, bending toward the earth gathering hay. In both paintings, besides the division of labor based on gender and the seeming glorification of the wife in *The Angelus*, Millet represents the peasants' intimate, nonalienated connection with the earth. The full wagons in the background of *The Gleaners* may represent a surplus supply moving away from the field to be transformed into surplus value. Still, there is no denying the relationship between Millet's subjects and the earth: the farmer in *The Angelus* stands by his hayfork, stuck firmly in the earth; the women in *The Gleaners* gaze downward, intent upon their business. The Millet paintings, in this sense, form an opposition to Emmet's portrait, just as Boucicault's peasant comedies in many ways oppose the myth of Irish patriotism that might undermine the relationships between man and family, man and nature.

The Millet/Emmet paintings also suggest another manner in which *The Plough and the Stars* in effect criticizes the myth of the historical hero, a critique grounded in the hegemony of the Irish upper class. Historical melodrama typically fails to consider patriots' positions in the aristocratic superstructure of Irish society. Because patriotism is tantamount to Christian martyrdom in plays like *The Ulster Hero,* McCracken's factory management is conspicuously innocent with the clear implication that Irish servants (or workers) and their masters are made equal by their affection for each other and for Ireland. The historical melodramatist thus projects evil upon stage villains and in the process obscures the effects social class or economic advantage might have exerted on this history. But of paramount import for O'Casey are the plight of workers and the power structure in which they are entrapped, as Mary Boyle and Jerry Devine discuss in *Juno and the Paycock.* Millet's *Angelus* and especially *The Gleaners* echo these concerns in taking as their subjects the labors of a peasant class. From this perspective, O'Casey's appropriation of Millet's paintings originates in his empathy for a working class that labors to glean the world for what detritus remains after a harvest. The handful of sheaves for which the women in *The Gleaners* stoop amounts to their meager share of the earth's plenitude, a plenitude that weights down an owner's wagon in the distance. The steeple, far removed from the fields of *The Angelus* yet exerting control over the laboring peasants by pealing its noontime message, serves as another icon of containment (ideological, not material like the wagon and the lone rider surveying fields in *The Gleaners*). In short, O'Casey's pairing of the Millet paintings with the Emmet portrait not only juxtaposes Boucicault's world with the historical hero's but also demythologizes the utopian resolutions of Irish green world comedies as it challenges the innocence of Irish nationalism.

The most volatilely received convergence of the two Irish myths in the play quite clearly occurs in act 2. While Rosie Redmond, Fluther Good, the Covey, and others cavort and argue in a public house, the speech of an "anonymous" leader of the Irish Citizen Army filters into the pub through open windows. The leader's speech, which O'Casey adapted primarily from pieces of Padraic Pearse's 1914 speech "The Coming Revolution" and his 1915 "Peace and the Gael," posits dogmatically the myth of heroic sacrifice for Irish independence. O'Casey's leader most resembles Pearse by asserting that blood given by patriots is "comparable to the blood of Christ the Redeemer,"[36] and this kind of polemic was conventional in the popular melodrama O'Casey knew so well. And Pearse's actual discourse *does* portray nationalistic revolt through the same religious metaphors one expected to hear at the Queen's Theatre, both during Whitbread's tenure until 1907 and after: Irish nationalistic revolt against the English amounted to "an august homage to God," a "cleansing and sanctifying thing," a "sign that heroism has come back to earth." O'Casey's appropriation of such passages establishes the Emmet ideal in the play. As a call to heroic action and Irish independence, the leader's speech echoes similar oratory in the nineteenth-century historical drama and, indeed, in Irish history itself. The most famous of these remains Emmet's oration at the dock before his execution.

O'Casey could have selected no more incongruous setting for patriotic discourse than a public house, for if patriotic discourse was associated on the Dublin popular stage with historical plays and martyred sons of Cathleen Ni Houlihan, public houses were frequently connected in the public imagination with the worst variety of Stage Irishmen. Boucicault's Stage Irishman, to be sure, "put his lips to the jug" with some regularity, but not nearly so predictably nor with such deleterious effects as the Stage Irishman on the London and American stages. And by the turn of the century, even Dublin critics who generally regarded both Boucicault and Whitbread highly began to speak out against scenes in public houses. Not surprisingly, O'Casey's critics expressed deep resentment over such a representation being in any way related to the events of Easter 1916. Hanna Sheehy-Skeffington objected especially to O'Casey's claiming the "right" to display the tricolor flag in a public house. O'Casey responded that though Sheehy-Skeffington "apparently wanted to bring everyone out of the public-house," he was "anxious to bring everyone into the public-house to make them proper places of amusement and refreshment" (*Letters* 1:171–73, 180).

Nevertheless, O'Casey's theatrical wedding of the objectionable haunt of the Stage Irishman to the historical context of Easter Week only further provoked his audience's anger. Besides connecting Pearse's speeches to public-house activities, act 2 includes Jack Clitheroe and his comrades' oath of allegiance to Ireland set in the tavern, a scene jarringly inconsistent with the curtain-lowering *tableaux vivants* of historical melodrama. Act 3 of Boucicault's *Robert Emmet*, as I have mentioned, ends with Andy Devlin's heroic death for Ireland (and an appropriately mournful stage setting); the ends of *Robert Emmet* and *The Ulster Hero* bring with them spectacular tableaux. In addition, the middle acts of Irish historical melodramas often highlighted grandiloquent oaths of allegiance similar to Clitheroe's. Act 1 of *The Ulster Hero*, to cite one such example, concludes with six United Irishmen (including Wolfe Tone and McCracken) pledging their last efforts against England and kissing their swords while proclaiming "We swear" in a curtain-lowering stage picture. Bussing swords to signify patriotic allegiance is one thing; drinking in a pub to seal such a pledge is quite another, and this is exactly how O'Casey contrasts Clitheroe and his friends' drastically undercut heroic ritual with that of their predecessors in popular melodrama:

> CAPT. BRENNAN [*catching up The Plough and the Stars*]. Imprisonment for th' Independence of Ireland!
> LIEUT. LANGON [*catching up the Tri-colour*]. Wounds for th' Independence of Ireland!
> CLITHEROE. Death for th' Independence of Ireland! (*CP* 1:213–14)

They drink, while Rosie Redmond and Fluther carry on indecorously, effectively travestying the elevated conventions of Whitbread's and Boucicault's historical melodramas.

In sum, the mise-en-scène of *The Plough and the Stars* becomes the site of the collision of two myths of Irish life and history developed by the popular Irish melodrama. And this same opposition emerges in another direct borrowing from melodrama in O'Casey's plays: Irish ballads steeped in nationalist politics and the glorifying historical views they embody. Ballads, references to well-known songs, and the host of historical allusions they generate in O'Casey's plays constitute more than what O'Casey himself termed a "mechanical borrowing" of so-called "incidental music" from nineteenth-century melodrama. On the contrary, music plays an intertextual function in O'Casey's drama, one that signals the existence of a text "lurking inside another, shaping meanings, whether the author is conscious of this or not."[37] Inherent in the historical and romantic ballads O'Casey appropriates—and in much Irish popular music of the nineteenth and early twentieth centuries—are views of Irish life and history corresponding to the comic and heroic myths of Dublin popular drama. Since these songs either originate in a sentimental pastoralism closely akin to that of Boucicault's plays or focus on the same historical episodes that gave rise to patriotic historical drama, songs in O'Casey's plays and, more broadly, references to music in them frequently mirror the opposition of romantic and historical myths in his "Dublin Trilogy."

It is demonstrable, I think, that more than any other national literary or aesthetic corpus, Irish songs form an almost hagiographic historical record: the "master narrative" of Irish history is, it seems, both melodramatic and reverential. That O'Casey appropriates this narrative for his plays is hardly surprising. After all, songs of revolution or nationalist politics appear in toto or through allusion in Irish literature of varied reputation: "The Wearing of the Green" in Boucicault's *Arrah-na-Pogue* and a ballad about the Fenian O'Donovan Rossa echoing through the streets of "Araby" in Joyce's *Dubliners*, for instance. At the same time, Irish ballads and folksongs also addressed subjects more typical of popular music in most epochs, especially love and the beauty of nature. The pastoral settings of Boucicault's plays were enlivened by songs of this variety: "Oh, Limerick Is Beautiful" and "Pretty Girl Milking Her Cow" in *The Colleen Bawn* and "My Pretty Maid" in *The Shaughraun*, to name but three. But like the augmented historical and political scope of Boucicault's Irish plays from *The Colleen Bawn* through *The Shaughraun* and *Robert Emmet*, ballads of love also became vehicles for the expression of Irish nationalism and historical heroism. One of the most famous of these is James Clarence Mangan's "Dark Rosaleen," the title of which like "Inishfallen" and "Cathleen Ni Houlihan" serves as a synonym for Ireland, both Mother Ireland and Ireland as a lover. In his allusion to "Dark Rosaleen" in *The Shadow of a Gunman*, Seumas Shields conjures up memories of the nationalist love ballad of the same title.

> O the Erne shall run red
>   With redundance of blood
> The earth shall rock beneath our tread
>   And flames wrap hill and wood, . . .
> Ere you shall fade, ere you shall die,
>   My dark Rosaleen!
>   My dark Rosaleen![38] (*Resistance* 81)

These historical and nationalist ballads in O'Casey's Dublin plays aid in clarifying the opposing myths to which these plays respond, and the songs in *The Shadow of a Gunman* and *Juno and the Paycock* anticipate both the ballads and the conflicts in *The Plough and the Stars*.

   The Shadow of a Gunman most explicitly of the three plays delineates through songs the opposing myths of Irish history that underlie the Dublin trilogy. At the same time, through Donal Davoren and Minnie Powell, O'Casey poses two extreme views of art's relationship to history and heroism. The play opens with Davoren's song evoking the green world myth of innocent, simple life:

> Or when sweet Summer's ardent arms outspread,
> Entwined with flowers,
> Enfold us, like two lovers newly wed,
> Thro' ravish'd hours—
> Then sorrow, woe and pain lose all their powers,
> For each is dead, and life is only ours. (*CP* 1:94)

In all of his pastoral lyrics, Davoren absents himself from the troubled history that songs of the historical hero trace, attempting to justify his claim to Tommy Owens that he has "no connection with politics of the day" and that he wants no such connection. Minnie Powell, by contrast, insists that art be connected to history:

> MINNIE: Poetry is a grand thing, Mr. Davoren, I'd love to be able to write a poem—a lovely poem on Ireland an' the men o' '98.
> DAVOREN: Oh, we've had enough of poems, Minnie, about '98, and of Ireland, too. (*CP* 1:107)

Davoren argues further that a man should "always be drunk" when talking of "politics" and that no man—not even Robert Emmet, whom Minnie idolizes—"willingly dies for anything," his country included. In this exchange O'Casey's stage directions also add a disturbing note of class bias in describing Minnie, who, "like all of her class," is unable "to converse very long on the one subject and her thoughts spring from one thing to another." Popular drama, as we have seen, presented a decidedly different view both of 1798 and of the people who remembered that year with reverence. Here again, one gets the sense of O'Casey endeavoring to distance himself from the view of history conveyed by Irish popular culture.

The first act of *The Shadow of a Gunman* continues its unraveling of the myth of the historical hero. Tommy Owens's worshipful allusions to Sarsfield and Vinegar Hill—and especially his loud singing of T. D. Sullivan's "God Save Ireland," a song also known as "The Prayer of the Manchester Martyrs of 1867"—contribute to the development of the myth in act 1. A song so well-known that it served for fifty years as Ireland's unofficial national anthem, "God Save Ireland" memorializes the three Fenian heroes who on 18 September 1867 rescued Fenian leaders held in a Manchester prison. Tragically, the rescuers themselves were captured and executed by the British two months after their successful rescue of their colleagues. Owens's tearful, ultimately self-deluded claim that he would gladly die for Ireland and his bellowing of this well-known song establish this popular view of history just as concretely as Davoren's opening song, his remarks about poetry, and his recitation of "The Golden Celandine" reveal his ahistorical stance toward poetry. And the last lines of the chorus of "God Save Ireland," as succinctly as any lines in O'Casey, summarize the myth of the historical hero which permeates Irish history and Jack Clitheroe's consciousness in *The Plough and the Stars:* "'God save Ireland!' said the heroes, 'God save Ireland!' said they all. / 'Whether on the scaffold high or the battle-field we die. / O, what matter when for Ireland dear we fall!'" (*Resistance* 83). Life given unreservedly for Cathleen Ni Houlihan is life well spent. *The Plough and the Stars* challenges this recurring theme in Irish ballads and in popular historical melodrama. Thus, as Jack Mitchell hypothesizes, song in *The Shadow of a Gunman* functions in a manner exactly opposite that in Brecht.[39] In Brecht, song alienates the audience from the political content of the play; here, song forms this content, from which the audience is alienated by the laughable characters who endorse its beatification of nationalist martyrs.

By the end of the first act, Davoren accedes to some extent to the myth of the historical hero through which his neighbors have constructed him and allows them to believe he is a republican gunman in hiding. This charade, too, leads to historical ballads in Mrs. Henderson's association of Davoren with the heroes of Ireland's past and the songs that immortalize them. Mrs. Henderson asks God to strengthen and keep "all the men that are fightin' for Ireland's freedom." She also beams with pride—and tells Davoren that his heart would "thrill like an alarm clock"—when recounting the Gallogher children's singing of "Faith of Our Fathers" and "Wrap the Green Flag Around Me." Of course, this latter song is yet another summons for young men to die bravely for Ireland, a sacrifice which by convention is rendered less horrific because of the nationalist project. The chorus of this song glorifies a joyful martyrdom for Ireland's sake: "Then wrap the green flag round me, boys, / To die were far more sweet / With Ireland's noble emblem, boys, / To be my winding sheet" (*Resistance* 76). Although Mrs. Henderson only mentions this well-known ballad, her placing of

Davoren within this context elevates his stature in the tenement from mere lone gunman to the larger-than-life, male-dominated tradition of the Irish martyr.

As all of O'Casey's "paycocks" seem to be, Seumas Shields is both well-versed in Irish popular culture and too selfishly perceptive to be swayed by the ideology of songs like "Wrap the Green Flag Around Me, *Boys*" (Mrs. Henderson omits the last word from the song's title). None of O'Casey's comic Irishmen – Shields, Joxer Daly in *Juno and the Paycock,* and to a lesser extent the more admirable Fluther Good in *The Plough and the Stars* – rises consistently to heroic action like their predecessors in Boucicault's plays, and Shields's overt cowardice (claiming his name is "Jimmie," not Seumas, when questioned by the Black-and-Tans) in part stems from his awareness of the false consciousness promoted by Irish song and its excessive admiration of martyrdom. Nevertheless, Shields, like Owens and Mrs. Henderson, expresses his definition of the heroical consciousness in terms of the excesses of Irish ballads. For Shields, Minnie Powell is little more than a hero worshiper who, after Davoren was shot or hanged for his republican activities, would go about "like a good many more" singing "'I do not mourn me darlin' lost, for he fell in his Jacket Green'" (*CP* 1:130).

Songs like "The Jackets Green" interestingly combined a tradition of love ballads, chauvinistic ones at that, with concrete historical events and contexts. Beginning with allusions to Sarsfield, the song fatuously suggests that women love only Irish nationalists and martyrs: "O love had you come in those colours dressed and wooed with a soldier's mien / I'd have laid my head on your throbbing breast for the sake of your Jacket Green" (*Resistance* 97). Through this adversion to a well-known ballad, Shields betrays not only what Bernard Benstock has labeled the "supreme weakness" of O'Casey's paycocks – underestimating the strength of women, in this case Minnie Powell's potential to take courageous and decisive action – but also isolates a male-generated myth about women that attended numerous transmissions of Irish popular history.[40]

The last line of "The Jackets Green" – "So Irish maids love none but those who wear the Jacket Green" – seems particularly applicable to O'Casey's deflation of the heroic myth in *The Plough and the Stars.* In his myopia to real conditions caused by sentiments similar to those in the last line of this ballad, Captain Brennan unwittingly reveals the absurdity of the heroic consciousness when describing Jack Clitheroe's death to Bessie Burgess:

BRENNAN: His [Clitheroe's] last whisper was to "Tell Nora to be brave; that I'm ready to meet my God, an' that I'm proud to die for Ireland." . . . Mrs. Clitheroe's grief will be a joy when she realizes that she has had a hero for a husband. (*CP* 1:244)

Bessie, like many of O'Casey's female characters, knows better; she knows that the myth of the historical hero will not console Nora. Bessie simply and directly corrects Brennan's assumption about Nora's response: "If you only seen her, you'd know to th' differ." Sadly, characters like Jack Clitheroe and Minnie Powell whose view of history is dominated by the heroic myth do not "know to the differ." This view of history marshals them to their deaths and in O'Casey's plays, unlike popular melodrama, these deaths are not conveyed through speeches at docks or spectacular stage effects. The tableaux are modest, the discourse slight and unpoetic: clichéd slogans off- stage from Minnie ("Up the Republic") and short, painful gasps from Clitheroe.

If ballads concretizing the myth of the historical hero dominate *The Shadow of a Gunman* and anticipate the importance of this myth in *The Plough and the Stars,* songs more clearly originating in the comic myth dominate *Juno and the Paycock.* Given the closeness of both Joxer Daly and Jack Boyle to the shiftless, blarney-talking, hard-drinking Stage Irishman of the London stage, the ascendance of the comic myth in the play seems inevitable. Pastoral love songs in act 1 of *Juno and the Paycock,* much like those in Boucicault's plays, mark the presence of the green world myth in the play. More important, when compared to the songs of the first act of *The Plough and the Stars,* Jack Boyle's song anticipates Clitheroe's characterization of devoted lovers, a characterization more akin to that of romantic comedy and comic Irish drama which opposes the myth of the historical hero:

BOYLE: When the robins nest agen,
And the flowers are in bloom,
When the Springtime's sunny smile seems to banish all sorrow
an' gloom;
Then me bonny blue-ey'd lad, if me heart be true till then –
He's promised he'll come back to me,
When the robins nest agen! (*CP* 1:21)

CLITHEROE: Th' violets were scenting th' woods, Nora,
Displaying their charm to th' bee,
When I first said I lov'd only you, Nora,

> An' you said you lov'd only me!
> Th' chestnut blooms gleam'd through th' glade, Nora,
> A robin sang loud from a tree,
> When I first said I lov'd only you, Nora,
> An' you said you lov'd only me! (*CP* 1:186)

Nora kisses him, implying if only for a moment that romantic comedy might still exist in Dublin tenements. These songs' emphasis of the simple joys of young love and natural beauty, however, clashes sharply with the stark realities of both plays: the Boyle family disintegrates in part because of the civil war (Johnny's execution), but also because of Boyle's intransigent response to Mary's pregnancy by a man who will never return to her even after the robins "nest agen." In an analogous fashion, by the second act of *The Plough and the Stars* Jack Clitheroe has retracted his pledge to love only Nora. He has sworn with his fellow soldiers in the Irish Citizen Army that Ireland "is greater than a wife," even though Nora has "lov'd only" him and never been dissuaded from her amatory commitment by the fatal premises underlying the heroic myth. Both songs, then, stress the importance of mutual trust and promises ("He's promised he'll come back to me" in Boyle's song), just as plays and songs about historical heroes include oaths, pledges, and more sensational demonstrations of fidelity to Cathleen Ni Houlihan. O'Casey's Clitheroes show that these two promises are inherently contradictory, that the two myths advanced both by popular melodrama and song are irremediably opposed.

Much like the mise-en-scènes of these plays, therefore, the ballads and allusions to popular songs originate in the two myths that had not only dominated the late nineteenth- and early twentieth-century Dublin popular theater but also led to melodramatic readings of Irish history. Like Whitbread's and other popular historical drama, nationalist ballads elevated the historical hero to the stature of both martyr and romantic idol. Against this tradition, O'Casey creates ballads of pastoral simplicity that distance both Ireland's historical past and bleak present. And the appearance of both types of songs in his plays signals a more important battle of ideologies. Like Mild Millie in O'Casey's *Drums under the Windows,* Minnie Powell, Tommy Owens, and Jack Clitheroe are "lit up" by the intoxicating influence of Ireland's past; Joxer Daly, conversely, drunkenly finds "darlin'" consolation in sentimentally melodramatic stories like *Willy Reilly and His Colleen Bawn* and in songs of a green world vastly more appealing than his own. Nora's quiet singing of Jack's love song near the end of *The Plough and the Stars* as the sounds of war rage outside her now broken home reasserts the incompatibility of these myths. And, ultimately, these songs—like the myths— are destructive: they blur urban social and economic realities, and they deny the pain of Irish history.

NARRATIVE STRUCTURE, CHARACTERIZATION,
AND DECONSTRUCTION

> Every case of a binary opposition is marginal because the self-identity of each case is defined as a margin between the two poles of the binary.
> —Michael Ryan

The narrative structure of each of O'Casey's Dublin plays evolves into a dismantling of both myths and an undercutting of the characters central to them: the nationalist hero and the Stage Irishman. On the most obvious level, both the narrative resolutions and concluding tableaux of all three plays are wrenchingly incompatible both with those of Boucicault's plays and with the ways in which most plays of Irish historical heroes are closed. *Juno and the Paycock*, for example, the closest of the three plays to the concerns of domestic melodrama, concludes neither with the promise of marriage nor with familial reunion and the reclamation of the family home —prominent concerns in plays like *The Colleen Bawn*, Boucicault's *The Octoroon*, and others—but with the disintegration of the Boyle family and the unsettling results of Charles Bentham's seduction of Mary Boyle. (Here the convention of the joining of lovers of various social classes so frequently celebrated in Irish melodrama is first suggested, then overturned, as it is in *The Shadow of a Gunman* as well.) Because of its lack of historical referentiality, because it appears to make no specific denigration of "real" historical personages, and because of outstanding comic performances by Barry Fitzgerald as Jack Boyle and F. J. McCormick as Joxer, the play attracted crowded houses at the Abbey. Curiously enough, the play elicited sharp responses for more "literary" or aesthetic reasons from Dublin critics, particularly the last scene in which Joxer and the Captain stumble into the ruined Boyle household, drunken and barely coherent, following on the heels of

Juno's tragic lament for her murdered son in the previous scene. This juxtaposition of high tragic sentiment and knockabout comedy seemed to some critics "artistically indefensible."[41] Rather like the controversial Epilogue in Shaw's *Saint Joan,* which "opens" Joan's heretofore closed history and ironically undoes its tragic implications, O'Casey's last scene in *Juno and the Paycock* undercuts both the tragic potential of the play (Johnny Boyle's death and Juno's grief) and its comic promise (Mary Boyle's new child and the founding of a matriarchal society in which such children—and life itself—are nurtured).

This open-endedness or lack of clear generic resolution is, in part, the result of O'Casey's often-discussed repudiation of the heroic consciousness. What has not been sufficiently explained, though, are the ways in which the narrative structures of the Dublin trilogy systematically dismantle or deconstruct the two dominant myths outlined above. I use the term "deconstruct" in a general way here, although J. Hillis Miller's conception of the process is especially germane to my reading of O'Casey: "Deconstruction is not a dismantling of the structure of a text but a demonstration that it has already dismantled itself." Deconstruction, Miller continues, "annihilates the ground on which the building stands by showing that the text has already annihilated that ground knowingly or unknowingly."[42] The text, then, is a self-consuming cultural artifact which moves toward a final indeterminacy. The "ground" in O'Casey's plays is sacred ground, mythic ground, ground cultivated by popular theater, among other cultural forms, and its representation of historical process. Each of O'Casey's Dublin plays systematically topples itself, creating a vast chasm of uncertainty in what was once very solid ideological ground. The "artistically indefensible" admixture of comedy and tragedy, then, performs a deconstructive function in O'Casey's drama that erodes the interpretive ground from under his audience's feet.

Consider, for instance, the progress of *Juno and the Paycock.* As is the case in all three plays, O'Casey thrusts his audience into a world inhabited by familiar characters, analogous to those in several kinds of melodrama: juvenile male and female, male and female leads, old man and woman, and of course the comic Irishmen or paycocks. The conflicts in *Juno and the Paycock* are familiar enough to a Dublin audience with even a limited experience of the popular theater: Will the family home be preserved? Will the comic Irishman ever work at anything but drinking? Will the badly battered young nationalist die in a moment of glory and have the green flag wrapped around him? Will the young lovers wed? The first act closes with strong intimations of a typically comic resolution to these questions. Mary has discovered Bentham, the good-looking, well-educated suitor; the will of Boyle's cousin (the mandatory document upon which so many melodramas depend) will apparently ameliorate the Boyles' acute financial difficulties and allow them to save their home; and Jack Boyle sings of his devotion to Juno. The curtain lowers on Boyle "clasping Juno's hand, and singing emotionally": "O, me darlin' Juno, I will be thrue to thee; / Me own, me darlin' Juno, you're all the world to me" (*CP* 1:35). The exposition of *Juno and the Paycock* develops very typical dramatic situations and, at the lowering of the first-act curtain, hints at the preeminence of what I have termed the comic myth in resolving them.

Act 2 more seriously presents the ramifications of historical conflict and immediately undercuts the end of act 1 in which Boyle promises Juno that he is "done with" Joxer. In the second act, O'Casey more poignantly represents the realities of civil war through Mrs. Madigan's and Mrs. Tancred's reports of fighting and death. Johnny Boyle's fears and religious superstitions dominate the act, which ends with an evocation of the myth of the historical hero. A young man, clearly a former colleague of Johnny's, enters the Boyle home demanding that Johnny honor his oath and follow the precedent established by Emmet and a host of Irish patriots: "Boyle, no man can do enough for Ireland." With this reminder of the "manly" code of sacrifice, a faint prayer in the distance brings down the curtain. The first two acts of the play, then, close with two contradictory narrative possibilities and resultant emotional investments in the spectator: promises of love alternate with oaths of allegiance to martyrdom and thereby create dialectical tension in O'Casey's plays. In which direction will the play head? Which popular myth will be upheld?

But these two foundations of Dublin popular drama and of historical consciousness are crumbled by the end of *Juno and the Paycock*. Not surprisingly, both myths are given consideration in the play's closing moments, only to be dispelled by Jack Boyle's last speech. In their drunken, truncated dialogue, both Joxer and Boyle fall momentarily into the false security of these myths. Boyle recalls Easter Week and yet another version of the historical hero's passing, a version about which Boyle will importantly editorialize in the last sentence of the play: "Commandant Kelly died . . . in them . . . arms . . . Joxer. . . . Tell me Volunteer Butties . . . says he . . . that . . . I died . . . for Irelan'!" (*CP* 1:88). Joxer then recalls a version of the popular ballad "Willy Reilly," juxtaposing one vehicle of the comic myth with Boyle's more heroic story. "Darlin'" stories such as this provided yet another melodramatic consciousness–a secure one that reduced the complexities of Irish life–but neither it nor memories of Easter Week remain at the end of the play. The curtain lowers on a play carefully structured to lead to Boyle's last statement that the whole world is "in a terr . . . ible state o' . . . chassis!" "Chassis" or "chaos," indeterminacy–finally, this is O'Casey's depiction of a Dublin torn by violence and civil turmoil. The endings of the first two acts of the play are thus false centers, traces of two consciousnesses that disguise the realities of life and, finally, of history. And the last word of the play aptly encapsulates what is left after all the ideological "veneer" has been peeled away–"chassis."

More like popular historical drama, *The Shadow of a Gunman* and *The Plough and the Stars* culminate with the deaths of central characters, but in no way do O'Casey's characters, particularly Johnny Boyle, Minnie Powell, and Bessie Burgess, resemble the heroes of popular ballads or history plays– or those of *The Harvest Festival*, *The Star Turns Red*, and *Red Roses for Me*, for that matter. Minnie and Bessie are poor, uneducated women, not eloquent martyrs who march gallantly and polemically to the gallows or firing squad. Nor are they Christ-like (Emmet-like) in their nationalistic perfection: Minnie fantasizes too much and lacks religious conviction, Bessie drinks too much and is vulgarly antagonistic to the nationalist struggle. Also, O'Casey appropriates no extravagant tableaux from nineteenth-century historical drama to heighten his characters' deaths; in fact, we never see Minnie after she leaves Davoren's apartment, and we hear and see all too clearly that Bessie regrets ever having placed herself in harm's way. The final sights and sounds of *The Plough and the Stars* form no tribute to the heroes of the 1916 Easter uprising but instead focus on British soldiers–often the villains of popular Dublin historical drama, especially of the last acts of these plays– singing "Keep the Home Fires Burning." The homesickness or sentiment of British soldiers is perhaps the last thing an Abbey audience expected to encounter at the end of an Irish history play. This last scene smolders with irony as Dublin burns in the background and the British soldiers take over the Clitheroe home because Jack has not kept his home fires burning. Both in the presence of atypical, unconventional scenes and in the absence of more conventional ones, therefore, the closings of these plays obliterate the popular theatrical tradition that preceded them. Here there are no rural marriage celebrations or heroical tableaux, only a bare wasteland of a room once crowded with life and furniture (*Juno and the Paycock*) and intruders in a house no longer a home (*The Plough and the Stars*).

Like the narrative construction of *Juno and the Paycock*, the first two

acts of *The Plough and the Stars,* set in 1915 months before the Easter uprising, juxtapose the promise of the comic myth with the impending tragedy
of the heroic myth. The play opens with strong evidence of the maintenance of both family home and society, the ends to which Boucicault's comedies and the comic myth move: Fluther has repaired the lock on the
Clitheroes' door while men labor outside mending the street; Mrs. Gogan's
censures of Nora's "notions of upperosity" attest more to Nora's laudable
attempts to preserve her marriage than to the shortcomings Mrs. Gogan
cites; Nora's handling of Uncle Peter and the Covey's early arguments assert
the power of the mother to restore domestic order, even if overaged children attempt to disturb it. Nora's home, organized down to the folded linen
Uncle Peter thoughtlessly crumples, represents order and beauty striving
for expression in the poverty of tenement living and the chaos of warring
ideologies and nations. At the same time, the first act develops Nora's love
for Jack, a love upon which the house's survival depends. All of Nora's manifestations of "swank" or "upperosity" originate in her love for Jack; without
him, there is no comic myth, no family or home. Nora knows this, and
we know this is why she pleads with Jack to resign his position in the Irish
Citizen Army, a point he raises toward the end of act 1. For a fleeting moment near the end of the first act, it seems as if Jack has indeed reconsidered: his singing to Nora of love and natural beauty seems to counterbalance
his nationalist, finally dangerous, ambition.

All manifestations of this comic world are collapsed by Brennan's arrival near the end of act 1. The letter from James Connolly summoning
"Commandant" Clitheroe to action exposes Nora's chicanery to keep him
at home and initiates a series of scenes and reports in which her love opposes Jack's heroic aspirations. Indeed, Brennan's arrival, which interrupts
Jack's song and Nora's kiss in act 1, anticipates her desperate embrace of
Jack in act 3, which is likewise interrupted by his resolve to continue his
trek toward martyrdom. Jack's abuse of Nora in act 1 after learning of her
burning of Connolly's earlier letter and her pained responses foreshadow
a similar encounter later in act 3 and, in the process, disqualify Clitheroe
from heroic stature:

> CLITHEROE [*fiercely*]:   You burned it [an earlier letter announcing his promo-
> tion in the Irish Citizen Army], did you? [*He grips her arm*] Well, me
> good lady—
> NORA: Let go—you're hurtin' me!
> CLITHEROE: You deserve to be hurt. . . . (*CP* 1:189–90)

In act 3 this brutal scene is repeated when Nora begs Jack to come home:

CLITHEROE [*struggling to release himself from Nora*]: Damn you, woman, will you let me go! . . .

NORA [*pitifully*]: Please, Jack. . . . You're hurting me, Jack. . . . Honestly. . . . Oh, you're hurting . . . me! . . . I won't, I won't, I won't. . . . Oh, Jack, I gave you everything you asked of me. . . . Don't fling me from you, now! (*CP* 1:236)

As the would-be historical hero struggles to "break" his wife's "hold," then "roughly loosens" her grip and marches toward his destiny, Nora "sinks to the ground and lies there," assuming the pose of many a heroine before her in nineteenth-century domestic melodrama. But in the historical drama preceding O'Casey's, the historical hero is never depicted as so egotistical or callous. As the comic myth inevitably dissipates in *The Plough and the Stars* as a result of the play's historical context, so too do the elevated codes of behavior of which the heroical myth is constituted. Jack Clitheroe, the closest of O'Casey's characters to Whitbread's historical heroes, manages finally to die bravely for Ireland, but in the process tarnishes the tradition of historical figures which dominated the Dublin popular theater.

The highly provocative second act of *The Plough and the Stars* in effect maintains the same tension between the comical and the heroic myths, while it shifts slightly the focus of the comic myth. That is, act 2 replaces an earlier emphasis on one component of the comic myth—marriage, family, and maintenance of the home—with another—the function of the comic Stage Irishman. In Boucicault's Irish plays, characters like Shaun the Post and Conn emerge as more than stereotypical drunken sots to take an active, at times courageous part in the political conflicts of their worlds, conflicts that are overcome at least in part by their bravery and loyalty to the nationalist cause. O'Casey's Stage Irishmen, conversely, are clearly cast from a less heroic and, in some ways, more paradoxical mode. Of particular importance in this regard is Fluther Good, an offspring both of Boucicault's characters and of the Wild Irish Boys in Whitbread's *Nationalist* and Hubert O'Grady's *Gommock* and *Emigration*. The early moments of the second act, like the beginning of the play in which Fluther is testing the door he has just fixed, confirm both his constructive potential and his nationalist courage. He exclaims that the blood was "boilin'" in his veins at seeing the patriotic zeal of his fellow Irishmen and punctures Peter's shallow pretensions by recognizing the laughable hypocrisy of his wearing of a Forester's uniform: "Ah, sure, when you'd look at him, you'd wondher whether th' man was makin' fun o' th' costume, or th' costume was makin' fun o' th' man!" (*CP* 1:200). Later, Fluther proves his courage and humanity by searching battle-scarred Dublin streets for Nora. Rather than saving nationalist heroes from their enemies, as Stage Irishmen nearly always attempt to do in both comic and historical melodrama, Fluther performs an equally conventional rescue: he finds Nora, who by this time has been transformed into the hapless heroine of *The Colleen Bawn* or John Baldwin Buckstone's *Green Bushes*. In these instances, O'Casey would seem to be preserving, rather than travestying, popular convention.

As the second act progresses, however, Fluther's claim to nobility is undermined by the very shortcomings he sees in Peter; by the end of the act, Fluther has become drunk and is ready to fight the Covey, spouting self-aggrandizing epithets in the process. More significant, as the leader's speech and the sounds of the mobilized Irish Citizen Army marching filter through to the public house, Fluther is ushered away by Rosie Redmond, the prostitute who has bolstered his false sense of courage. While men ready to defend Ireland are preparing for their British adversaries, Fluther—and with him the comic myth in which the Stage Irishman figured so largely— has been markedly diminished.

This diminution and the incongruity of the comic Irishman in such a context are made more apparent when Fluther's combativeness and language are compared with the similar traits of the Wild Irish Boy, whom Fluther most resembles in his gladiatorial posture and linguistic vituperation. Wild Irish Boys like Hughey in O'Grady's *Emigration* and Larry in *The Gommock* routinely thrash villains, often because of their impugning of an innocent colleen's virtue or their attempts to enforce their unwanted affection, and enliven their punitive ministrations with extravagant punning and joking at the expense of the vanquished. O'Casey totally inverts these conventions. Fluther's taunts to the Covey that he is "temptin' Providence when you're temptin Fluther," that the Covey might "open th' door to sudden death" if he continues to challenge him and to refer to Rosie Redmond as a prostitute, are the laughable ramblings of a "Wild Irish man" protecting the virtue of a woman who conspicuously lacks any. In the green worlds of Irish comic melodrama, the Wild Irish Boy protects innocence, thwarts villains' malevolence, and possesses both wit and vigor in abundant quantity; in the public house of O'Casey's Dublin, Fluther's actions are conspicuously less heroic, clearly more pathetic. Such an inversion of popular convention is prominent in several of O'Casey's later plays, *The Silver Tassie* for instance, when Simon Norton attempts to intervene on Mrs. Foran's behalf with her abusive husband. "Phuh, I'll keep him off with the left and hook him with the right," the aging pugilist boasts. "Looking prim and careless 'll astonish him" (*CP* 2:22). When Simon is faced with the prospect of showing that his claims are more than bravado, as Mrs. Foran reports moments later, "the boyo only ran the faster out of the house." So, in addition to O'Casey's controversial juxtaposition of Irish nationalist insurgence and public-house antics, a parallel that infuriated large sectors of the Abbey audience, O'Casey also dismantles a much-loved convention and character in Irish comic melodrama.

This undercutting of the Stage Irishman and deconstruction of the comic myth of history continue in act 3; the most damaging instance of these processes occurs immediately after Clitheroe's ill-treatment of Nora described above. Ironically, the act begins with Mrs. Gogan's allusion to Fluther's courage and humanity in searching for Nora, who has left the tenement to find Jack. "An' thinkin' o' that madman, Fluther, runnin' about through th' night lookin' for Nora Clitheroe to bring her back when he heard she'd gone to folly her husband, an' in dhread any minute he might come staggerin' in covered with bandages, splashed all over with th' red of his own blood" (*CP* 1:216). Shortly thereafter, Fluther returns with Nora, who by this time has nearly dropped from exhaustion and emotional strain. As the Covey remarks, Fluther seems to be carrying her when the pair enter, further indication of his strength and loyalty. Yet when a middle-aged woman enters later asking for help through the dangerous streets, Fluther is quick to move away. More damaging, at the end of act 3, he appears at the tenement door drunk and loudly abusive. In a scene mirroring those in which the Stage Irishman was led by the nose—one most Dubliners resented— Fluther is pulled by Bessie Burgess into the house. He has looted a public house, become shamelessly drunk, and left Bessie and Mrs. Gogan to attend to Nora. The act ends with Bessie braving the perilous Dublin streets to find a doctor for Nora.

In a carefully planned scheme, O'Casey systematically destroys the myths of comic reconciliation and heroism in the first three acts of *The Plough and the Stars*. The last act completes this deconstruction. In addition, throughout the play the character types most clearly derivative of nineteenth-century melodrama have also been denigrated. The most significant of these are the Stage Irishman and the historical hero, characters who appear in various guises in all three of O'Casey's Dublin plays. Fluther Good in *The Plough and the Stars* is preceded by Joxer Daly, Jack Boyle, and Seumas Shields; Jack Clitheroe, by Johnny Boyle and Donal Davoren. Of all these characters, Fluther and Jack in *The Plough and the Stars* most directly evolve from nineteenth-century stereotypes. Jack mouths the heroic oaths and nationalist sentiments that on the popular stage were the sole property of the Emmets and McCrackens. Like his historical predecessors, Jack fights bravely for Ireland's freedom and finally gives his life for it. But O'Casey's play refuses to elevate these actions or revere these sacrifices. The historical hero in O'Casey becomes driven by egotism and reduced to pitifully human proportions; his death is not glorified by elegies or coronets of shamrocks but reported by a terrified colleague. Jack Clitheroe passes from his world in an offstage building, alone and uncelebrated. Similarly, though O'Casey's Stage Irishmen become something more than Victorian-born caricatures, they are also something less than Boucicault's comic heroes. Like their predecessors, they drink too much and work too little; unlike them, they fail to affect the world that surrounds them, in part because they lack nobility and in part because O'Casey's Ireland has outgrown them.

As Benstock notes, O'Casey's Dublin plays appear to ratify the primacy of women, especially mothers, in Irish life.[43] But even this elevation, which has evolved into a convention in orthodox scholarship on O'Casey as Jack Mitchell has recently argued, is neither universal nor unproblematic. For Mitchell, women like Juno and Nora hold no revolutionary potential, contain no agency for social change, but merely reiterate the dominant ideologies of church and society without adding to them a nationalistic zeal.[44] Although I do not entirely agree with Mitchell—Juno, it seems to me, inaugurates a conception of a nonpatriarchal, perhaps non-Catholic family that *does* strike a major blow for social reform[45]—his skepticism about any level of idealization in O'Casey seems well founded. Unlike popular history plays, O'Casey's dramas include no Cathleen Ni Houlihans or Anne Devlins—in short, no Mother Irelands leading their sons to historical heroism. No male historical heroes emerge either to challenge the pragmatism of Juno Boyle or Nora Clitheroe. Of all of O'Casey's women, Minnie Powell, the hero-worshiping victim in *The Shadow of a Gunman*, comes the closest in patriotic sentiment to the archetypal Mother Ireland; however, both her age and naïveté disqualify her from playing Dark Rosaleen or Anne Devlin. And in many respects, Nora Clitheroe resembles the hapless heroines of nineteenth-century domestic melodrama; but in her courage and persistence

Nora, like Juno, demonstrates a strength that the nineteenth-century heroine often lacked. So if O'Casey's works only *at times* form a "veneration of mothers," this veneration seems consistent with his annihilation of the heroic myth that advances death for Ireland as preferable to life. O'Casey finally opts for reality—hence the incompatibility of the comic myth with modern Irish life—but he also argues vehemently for life over deluded martyrdom. His stage mothers make the same argument.

CONCLUSION: O'Casey and Popular Culture

> "Are you goin' to pit our palthry penances an' haltin'
> hummin' o' hymns against th' piercin' pipin' of th' rosary be
> Bing Bang Crosby an' other great film stars?" (*CP* 4:157)
> —Sailor Mahan, *Cock-a-Doodle Dandy* (1949)

The absurdity of this allusion to a Hollywood film actor in O'Casey's later play *Cock-a-Doodle Dandy* suggests both the humor with which he treated popular culture in his drama and the continued importance of the people and their culture in his writing, especially in his critical essays. Even on Michael Marthraun's farm in Nyadnanave, a peasant world of bogs and laughable superstitions light years away from the electronic media and culture industry, popular culture exists, intruding upon the consciousness of Irishmen: in this case, the priestly image of Bing Crosby in *Going My Way* (1944) and *The Bells of Saint Mary's* (1945). The existence of parodic or satirical humor in Sailor Mahan's, Joxer Daly's, or Fluther Good's dialogue should not be construed therefore as merely a casual or cynical dismissal of a topic O'Casey took very seriously. On the contrary, in later essays collected in *The Green Crow* (1956) and *Under a Colored Cap* (1963), an aging O'Casey continued to espouse the cause of a people's theater. In essays like "The Arts Among the Multitude," "The People's Theatre," and "Culture, Inc.," O'Casey served as an advocate for a society in which citizens of all classes could gain access to theater and other art forms. And, as late as 1961 in "Culture, Inc.," he mourned the lack of native Irish culture: "Now, on the eve of the New Year of 1962, Éire is going to flood the farms and firesides with rotten sights and sounds salved from the dustbins of England and the garbage cans of America, and call it all Culture!"[46]

In this and other essays, many written well over a half-century after the founding of the Irish Literary Theatre, O'Casey reiterates many of the positions Yeats, Shaw, and other critics of popular theater took in the 1890s. Yet there is one crucial difference between O'Casey and these other cultural critics: he remained adamantly committed to a theater in which playgoers of all social classes could find both edification and pleasure. This commitment necessitated the artist's familiarity with popular culture and respect for its power, but not capitulation at every turn to the will of the majority. The Abbey, in O'Casey's view, failed on both counts. For example, stung from the reception of *The Plough and the Stars* and smarting from the Abbey's response to him after the riot, O'Casey contemplated Dublin's literary "Gods and half-gods"–Yeats and his colleagues–with a searing, skeptical assessment: "Their sneering, lofty conception of what they called culture . . . was but a vain conceit in themselves which they used for their own encouragement in the pitiable welter of a small achievement" (*Autobiographies* 2:157). The "nationalist" opponents of *The Plough and the Stars* who revered Irish history with "tear-dimmed eyes" equally disgusted O'Casey because of their blindness to the culture of the people: "Is the Ireland that is pouring to the picture houses, to the dance halls, to the football matches, remembering with tear-dimmed eyes all that Easter Week stands for?" (*Letters* 1:170–71). Hence the very playwright who so discomfited his audience by undermining its sense of expectation and assailing popular convention also insisted that Dublin literati and nationalists alike recognize the people and their culture.

After the incident over *The Plough and the Stars* and the Abbey's rejection of *The Silver Tassie*, O'Casey's view of Yeats in particular grew even more embittered. Regardless of the heroic image most of us have of Yeats standing tall on the Abbey stage admonishing the rioters after their disruption of the fourth performance of *The Plough and the Stars*, O'Casey remained unconvinced of Yeats's resolve to stage ideologically challenging dramas. In "Out, Damned Spot" from *Under a Colored Cap*, O'Casey recalls Yeats's "vehemently" advising him, "'A playwright has nothing to do with opinions.'"[47] In an earlier letter to Gabriel Fallon concerning the rejection of *The Silver Tassie*, O'Casey accused Yeats of managing a theater on the very principles he abhorred and had spoken publicly against thirty years earlier: "Comical & curious to note in his last letter Mr. Yeats writes of a 'packed house' [for a revival of *The Plough and the Stars* in May 1928]. Mr. Yeats pines for packed houses. Odd that he seems to have forgotten that a great play may empty a house as well as fill one" (*Letters* 1:244). The same Yeats who in 1899 had lectured to "common playgoers" that the Irish Literary Theatre offered them "plays written in a more sincere spirit than plays which are written to please as many people as possible" was now, in O'Casey's judgment, endeavoring to please as many people as possible.[48]

So, in one sense, we have arrived at precisely the point at which this discussion of popular theater began. The difference is, of course, that O'Casey is not describing the Queen's Royal Theatre in the late 1890s but the "Temple" of Irish high culture, the Abbey Theatre, both between the world wars and long after them. Yet the differences between the two, between the popular and the literary, may not be so extreme as one first suspects. Sneering "gods and half-gods" with lofty conceptions of culture can no more establish an important theater than can more cowardly or pecuniary businessmen concerned only with the financial bottom line. The Shavian idea and the O'Caseyean socioeconomic agenda require a forum; communicated by way of theatrical vehicles sensitive to and invigorated by popular convention, they can succeed, commercially and intellectually. Perhaps that is what the plays of John Arden and Margaretta D'Arcy, Brian Friel, and Anne Devlin are achieving today; perhaps this is what such lovely experiments as the combination of Van Morrison's blues and the Chieftains' traditional music in their recent collaboration *Irish Heartbeat* (1988) portend for the 1990s and beyond. This is, I believe, what O'Casey advocates in his critical prose and drama alike, with one eye cast toward Shakespeare, whom he respected and read voraciously, and one toward Dion Boucicault, whom he enjoyed tremendously. The star and the tree, the poet and the people—this union must be preserved, this problem must continually be negotiated.

Traces of the Popular Theater Today

—Who guided or misguided them [Ulster youth]?
—Ireland. A long history. England. Empire. King William. The Pope. Ian Paisley. Myself. I was a teacher of history.
　　　　　　　　　—Benedict Kiely, *Proxopera* (1977)

People were dying every day, men and women were being crippled and turned into vegetables in the name of Ireland. An Ireland which never was and never would be. It was the people of Ulster who were heroic, caught between the jaws of two opposing ideals trying to grind each other out of existence.
　　　　　　　　　—Bernard MacLaverty, *Cal* (1983)

IN BRIAN FRIEL'S FARCE *The Communication Cord* (1982), set in an "authentic" reproduction of a "traditional" cottage in County Donegal, two young men conspire to impress the father of one of their girlfriends. The authentic reproduction of the cottage plays a major part in their scheme, and at one moment Jack McNeilis, the young man who owns the cottage, parodically expounds upon the power of the peasant tradition for his poor graduate student friend Tim Gallagher, who needs to make a good impression: "This is where we all come from. This is our first cathedral. This shaped our souls. This determined our first pieties."[1] Dr. Donovan, the father about to be
188

duped, is later totally convinced by the deception and waxes nostalgically about a tradition very much alive in his imagination, a tradition of cottages, simple peasant life, and pretty maids milking cows: "A magical scene, isn't it? It's a little scene that's somehow central to my psyche."[2] The image of a bucolic Ireland conveyed by so many nineteenth-century Irish dramas is very much alive in 1982 for Friel's Irishmen, weary of strife and the pressures of modern living. Even if such a cultural memory is transmitted in *The Communication Cord* only to be comically overturned along with other romanticizations of Ireland, the power of the Boucicauldian reverie is still potent; indeed, McNeilis and Gallagher count on it when devising their deception.[3] It's a "magical scene" so central to the psyches of Irishmen that, for Friel's young schemers, it can always be counted on.

This same cottage and comic myth become an all too temporary retreat for a Catholic boy ensnarled in violence in Northern Ireland in Bernard MacLaverty's novel *Cal*. And while it seems self-evident that the harsh material conditions of life in Ulster and the precedent of history, a precedent about which Mr. Binchey in Benedict Kiely's novella *Proxopera* complains bitterly, contribute substantially to the tragic circumstances of Cal's life, a very familiar, essentially comic mythology also plays an appreciable part in the drama. Reluctant to participate further in IRA operations – before the action of the novel begins he served as a driver for his associate, Crilly, who assassinated a Protestant policeman, Robert Morton – Cal must endure Crilly's intimidation and the highly charged ideological arguments of Finbar Skeffington, an IRA leader, before he can defect. In his efforts to induce Cal to stay in the fold, Skeffington, a dilettantish teacher and historian, criticizes history as at the very least indifferent to the everyday lives of common people when he recalls seeing an old man killed in Derry: "There was an old man lying in the open. . . . There was a big hole in the heel of his sock. . . . Will that be recorded in the history books?"[4] The answer is quite obviously no. Yet for MacLaverty's young protagonist, tortured by guilt over his participation in Morton's murder and inflamed by his affection for Morton's widow, Marcella, Skeffington's appeals to Padraic Pearse and the events of 1916 – appeals to history – cannot justify the suffering endured by such families as the Mortons. "It is not like 1916," Cal insists. Consequently, Pearse's poetry (which Skeffington reads to him) and oratory fail to speak to Cal in the way that American rhythm and blues does. Seeing himself in the mirror as a black, he listens to Muddy Waters in the novel and plays his guitar to the Booker T. Jones–William Bell classic "Born Under a Bad Sign" in Pat O'Connor's 1984 film adaptation of the novel (for which MacLaverty wrote the screenplay).[5]

History and a dismal economy, therefore, are neither the only determinants of action in *Cal* nor of our responses to both novel and film, though some materialist readings of MacLaverty are quite persuasive. One such reading is Margaret Scanlan's, which underscores the effects of Northern Ireland's economy and high unemployment rate among Catholics on MacLaverty's characters and stresses Cal's invigoration after finding employment, ironically, on the Morton farm after too many months of living on the dole. As MacLaverty's narrator remarks and Scanlan emphasizes, "For three days, although he ended up each day physically filthy, work had a cleansing effect on him. It was as if idleness had allowed dirt to accumulate on his soul" (61).[6] Clearly, Cal is happy on the farm, working close to Marcella on land with which heretofore he had enjoyed too little contact. No longer must he remain on his guard when walking the streets of the Protestant estate in which he and his father reside, "watching gardens [and] moving slightly out into the roadway when there was a blind wall at a corner" (49).[7] But the romantic mythology arises just when Cal most needs it: after his house is burned down by a gang of Protestant toughs. Forced to move temporarily to a relative's bungalow too small to accommodate both of them, Cal's father asks him where he intends to live. Cal had noticed earlier a "derelict" cottage behind the main house on the Morton farm and answers his father in what appears to be a perfectly logical, almost perfunctory, fashion: "Suddenly Cal thought of a place. If he stayed there it might solve a lot of problems" (87).

In his film, Pat O'Connor offers a deeper ideological explanation of this moment by having Cal silently answer his father through a gaze at a conventional picture displayed on his relative's wall of a peasant cottage nestled serenely in the hills of rural Ireland. This visual cue is by no means accidental, nor does it merely supply O'Connor with a means of transposing MacLaverty's prose into iconic form. Earlier in the film in Skeffington's living room, when Skeffington delivers his homily on Irish history in an attempt to convince Cal of his obligation to the republican project, a similar drawing in the best O'Caseyean fashion competes for our attention with conspicuously placed historical portraiture of Pearse and other leaders of the 1916 rising. In this way history competes with mythology; if they choose to do so, Ulster men and women can simply close their windows to the violent world outside and turn inward to their walls and imaginations for a badly needed dose of romantic Ireland. Throughout the film, the refurbished derelict cottage, which later becomes the site of Marcella Morton's and Cal's sexual fulfillment, represents everything that the urban North has lost. To support this opposition between contemporary history and the pastoral dream, O'Connor cleverly parallels segments of Cal and his father cutting firewood, Cal and others "pulling spuds" or stacking hay, with the petrol bombs and imminent death of city streets. The Morton family estate becomes a microcosm of Northern Ireland, and there on the periphery of the Protestant land and nightmarish city stands a humble cottage, fertile soil, and a last sanctuary. But MacLaverty and Cal, like Friel and the Field Day Theatre Company, are careful not to endorse the pastoral as an answer to contemporary "troubles": as Cal realizes not long after taking up residence in the cottage, people were dying everyday for an Ireland "which never was and never would be."

Opposite this vision of rural Ireland in *Cal* lies modern, urban Ireland, the site of contemporary violence in the North: Friel's Londonderry in *The Freedom of the City* (1973) and Anne Devlin's Belfast in *Ourselves Alone* (1985) for instance. In Devlin's play, Frieda, one of the central characters, is a club singer "fed up with songs where the women are doormats";[8] nevertheless, she sings popular republican songs to her audience with portraits of ten dead hunger strikers pictured prominently behind her. Frieda wants to sing "her own songs," one of which, sadly, is a redaction of "The Volunteer." Devlin's point, it would seem, is that the parts to which women are relegated in contemporary Northern Ireland make it extremely difficult to locate an authentic voice, to sing a song in one's own voice, because the context of violence and tradition is always there, always oppressively shaping identity. As Frieda asks, "When did I ever have a chance to be myself"?[9] This context, I believe, is informed by many of the popular conventions O'Casey and Joyce inherited: conventions of historical heroism, sacrifice, and idealized love. And it is, in part, Devlin's project to reveal these conventions for what they are, following in O'Casey's footsteps in one sense, and in part to embark upon her own long march "alone," not only illuminating the ways in which women's identities and sexuality are constructed by popular convention but also attempting to locate and formulate authentic voices.

I should like here to review briefly two theoretical points about popular Irish drama, specifically about melodrama, and then to consider these in relation not to the contemporary stage or the Northern Irish novel, but to two films that originate in the recent violence in the North, Devlin's *Naming the Names* (BBC, 1986) and Mike Hodges's more commercial offering, *A Prayer for the Dying* (Goldwyn, 1987).[10] All of this will lead, finally, to the following dual thesis: first, that in several respects the narrative and scenic conventions of representations of Anglo-Irish conflict in popular film parallel those employed on the popular nineteenth-century stage of Dion Boucicault and J. W. Whitbread; and second, that Devlin's plays and film scripts transcend the melodramatic in part because of the playful, ironic traces of popular convention she braids into them. In the specific case of *Naming the Names,* such conventions include matters both of a generic nature and of cinematic style. It is to a great extent our recognition of the intertextual relationship between Devlin's work and melodramatic representations of Irish conflict that illuminates her wry sense of humor and a sense of the horrible psychological cost of violence in the North. And, of course, all of this suggests the ways in which the popular theaters of James Joyce and Sean O'Casey are still very much alive today, transported onto our most popular media, movie screens and television sets.

The first truism is heard so often that it seems as fixed a concept in the literary critical lexicon as metaphor or motif: that the terms "history" and "melodrama" refer to diametrically opposite narrative impulses—the first tied directly to the real, indeed to a specific extratextual reality, the second linked to escape from this real. Pronounced as inherently dreamlike or unreal by theater historians such as Michael Booth, melodrama has most recently been assailed on similar grounds by J. L. Wisenthal in *Shaw's Sense of History.* Here Wisenthal explains that the subtitles of Shavian drama function as a measure by which we might gauge a play's relationship to "factual history"; hence the subtitle of *The Devil's Disciple—A Melodrama—*indicates that Shaw's drama of the American revolutionary war is only "superficially a history play."[11] This generalization emanates from arguments like Booth's and from earlier ones by Shaw, Yeats, George Moore, and other modernists that melodrama transports its audiences from their everyday realities: three hours in a land of wish-fulfillment and excitement, then back to the stark existence of the working class. As I mentioned in my opening chapter, however, scholars such as Bernard Sharratt question this notion, arguing among other points that the near drownings, mutilations, and other unspeakable villainies of melodrama hardly constitute a universe into which one craves access. How does one account for the melodramatic text's nearly universal production of fear or, in more everyday terms, precisely why is it that Hollywood producers can become wealthy making films like *Friday the Thirteenth, Part Seven* or *A Nightmare on Elm Street, Part Two Thousand?* For those with teenage children who frequent the cinema, perhaps it would be too unsettling to consider this question too deeply, but at least allow me to register the point in regard to history and melodrama: although the two might be figured as incompatible, totally contradictory, one might pause before arguing that melodrama inherently skirts reality to effect an escape from it.

Sharratt's point is connected to the second truism I have mentioned: that popular culture of various forms furthers a conservative project to deflect the working classes from social activism. We can see that melodrama viewed either in Booth's or Sharratt's terms—as an escape from history or a trip into a fearful, hostile environment from which we are happy to return—results inevitably in a conservative deferral of political action: in the first case, the popular audience slumbers in never-never land; in the second it is damned grateful to receive its meager share of the material pie allotted to it by the ruling class. But Irish melodrama, it seems to me, has *never* abetted only a conservative project. Admittedly, the highly stereotypical, denigrative variety both on the Victorian stage and in Hollywood films during the studio era fosters notions that might serve as justification for an imperialist patriarchy: that the Irish are backward, superstitious, and ill-educated, thus requiring a benevolent domination if they are to survive. Shaw's Broadbent in *John Bull's Other Island* epitomizes framers of this hypothesis as he purchases large sections of Irish land, planning to turn the countryside into resort hotels and in the process raise the standard of living for poor tenant farmers. But most Irish melodrama, theatrical or filmic, seems to follow a paradoxically conservative and radical trajectory at the same time, and here we might recall Stuart Hall's observation about the "double movement of containment and resistance" inherent in popular cultural forms. In my brief readings of *A Prayer for the Dying* and *Naming the Names,* I should like to explore this contradictory quality.

It is important to notice, I think, that *A Prayer for the Dying,* based on the Jack Higgins novel, is merely the most recent of a long line of American and British films grounded in the historical struggle between England and Ireland: John Ford's *Informer* (1935) and his less than successful adaptation of *The Plough and the Stars* (1936), Sir Carol Reed's haunting *Odd Man Out* (1946), and David Lean's *Ryan's Daughter* (1970), to mention only the most celebrated instances. These films are important to remember because by the time contemporary directors or writers like Anne Devlin turn to this material, they must confront the precedents not only of long-established melodramatic conventions born of the nineteenth-century stage but also of a familiar cinematic language refined in earlier films. Both familiar melodramatic strategies and cinematic styles obtain in *A Prayer for the Dying* and *Naming the Names,* but in a self-consciously parodic manner in Devlin's film missing from Hodges's more predictable treatment of a gunman on the run both from British police and from former colleagues whom he has deserted.

In *A Prayer for the Dying,* Mickey Rourke plays Martin Fallon, a gunman with a newfound conscience because of his participation in a bombing that accidentally leads to the deaths of a bus full of schoolchildren; Alan Bates is Jack Meehan, a powerful and sexually perverted London criminal who runs a funeral service on the side more to satisfy his desire to costume older women than to make money; Bob Hoskins portrays a Catholic priest who sees Fallon commit his last murder and befriends him in hopes of reforming him; and Liam Neeson is an old colleague called upon to go to London and either return Fallon to the fold or assassinate him, thereby eliminating any risk he poses to the organization's security. The narrative of the film is relatively uncomplicated. After the schoolbus is destroyed, Fallon escapes to London where a contact is to arrange safe passage and a passport if he will do one last contract job for Meehan: kill the leader of a rival criminal gang. Fallon resists, but in part because of the pressure of being pursued by British police and his desperate need to break the circle of violence in which he has for so long resided, he accedes and murders the man in a cemetery, where Father DeCosta (Hoskins) witnesses the crime. Fallon goes to DeCosta's church to confront him and meets Anna, the priest's blind niece (Sammie Davis) who eventually falls in love with him, and grows fond of both the girl and her uncle, who persists in his efforts to save Martin's soul. Meanwhile, he hides from police in a brothel owned by Meehan and his equally perverted brother, Billy, who upon first seeing Anna notes that he has "never had a blind girl" and is eager to do so. Meehan wants Fallon to kill the priest, who has heard part of Fallon's confession and thus will not divulge information to the police, but Fallon adamantly refuses, emphasizing that "no one touches the priest." The Meehan brothers, however, will rival any sadistic villains from the nineteenth-century stage and ignore Fallon's warning: Billy Meehan tries to rape the blind girl, who finally stabs him with knitting shears, and Jack Meehan obtains explosives with the idea of leveling the church while the priest and Anna are tied on top of it. In the film's spectacular climax, Fallon rescues Anna and the priest and traps Meehan with his satchel of ticking dynamite, but is himself hurled from the top of the church down upon a huge crucifix that hangs from the ceiling. The explosion sends the cross and Fallon plummeting to the church floor, where he lies dying under the cross and other heavy debris. The priest comes in and finally convinces him to complete his confession and thus save himself. This he does, as he gasps his last breath.

A Prayer for the Dying, as this brief exposition indicates, is so strongly melodramatic that readers of Peter Brooks's *Melodramatic Imagination* might wonder if Higgins and Hodges read Brooks before making the film. But important differences distinguish the film from Brooks's influential analysis. For example, Fallon, who never killed for money or pleasure but only for the cause, and who now claims there is nothing left worth killing or living for, plays both hero and, to a certain extent, heroine in this film. That is, Brooks's reading of melodrama stresses the importance of the heroine's identity in shaping dramatic action—one reason why birth certificates, mortgages, and other documents relating to family and identity surface so frequently in melodramatic plots—and defines such action as constituted of the heroine's repetitive displays of virtue that corroborate her identity. Hodges similarly places questions about Fallon's identity in the dramatic foreground. We learn that Fallon is merely one of several names the character uses, and we watch as the narrative thrusts him between Meehan and the priest, both of whom claim affinity with him. Meehan yells to Fallon, "We're two of a kind, you and me," early in the film; and Anna asks her uncle, "Don't you see how alike [you and Martin] are?" which indeed turns out to be the case. Like melodramas on the stages of Dublin's Queen's Theatre, the film becomes a drama of recognition, ours and the priest's, of Fallon's "real identity." True to his word, Fallon never kills again, even though he is presented with numerous opportunities to do so. And like that of his melodramatic predecessors, Fallon's virtue is tested by the prostitute with whom he is hiding and is validated by his polite refusal of her advances. He *does* make love with the blind girl, only at her insistence, in her apartment near the sacristy, a space of innocence so essential to much melodrama and suggestive of the sacred nature of his feeling for her. When the Meehan brothers attempt to despoil the church and the girl, Fallon and the priest are both quick to act. Fallon's rescue is equated with the priest's righteous anger, and his moral identity is confirmed when he rescues the trapped clergyman and girl, is overwhelmed by the giant cross under which he is buried, and makes a final act of contrition. There is, to be sure, tremendous irony in the shot of the gunman clutching a giant crucifix, then being buried under it—an irony O'Casey would enjoy, I think, because here the content of the shot works against the trajectory of the narrative. In the narrative, Martin works toward spiritual salvation; in the shot, the chief symbol of Christianity crushes him, just as it is implicated in the misery of O'Casey's characters. Still, the film contains too strong a connection with the conventions of Irish popular drama to ignore.

The spectacular climax of *A Prayer for the Dying*, with its religious iconography and implication of Messianic sacrifice, is merely one of several visual parallels between this recent film and the earlier classics like Ford's *Informer* and Reed's *Odd Man Out*. Recall the final church scene of Ford's film or the scene in Reed's in which a suffering and nearly dead Johnny Macqueen, the organization gunman on the run played by James Mason, rises from a chair incoherently quoting lines from the New Testament. Both filmmakers employ extreme low- and high-angle shots in a vertical representation of the initial lowness of central characters' real stature—Gypo Nolan's for informing on his friend and Macqueen's for planning a robbery in which he kills a man and is wounded seriously himself—and their final apotheosis achieved through suffering and repentance. Though clearly not mere replications of Robert Emmet or Wolfe Tone—or of Ayamonn Breydon and Jack Rocliffe in O'Casey's plays for that matter—these filmic Irish heroes might most fruitfully be read against a background of melodramatic convention. Anne Devlin calls upon both this history of cinematic iconography and popular convention in *Naming the Names*, based on her short story of the same title.

Devlin's film opens at the Falls Road Bookshop in Belfast, where the police question Finn McQuillen (Sylvestra la Touzel), a young book clerk and republican operative. The interrogation occurs on the store's first floor with Finn's back to the camera, and the first shot tracks the store manager looking down from the staircase on the scene. The manager has descended from the second floor on which is housed the country's largest collection of books on Irish history, so as she exits the collection and oversees the scene below, the symbolic landscape of Devlin's mise-en-scène is clear: the narrative moves from the record of Ireland's history into the lower reality of contemporary conflict. This high-angle view of Finn is repeated throughout the film. Unlike her melodramatic predecessors, she never ascends gloriously to any heights, and the narrative explains why such popular, hagiographic conceptions of republican activities are incompatible with and distortive of the violent realities of the North.

All our experience of melodrama induces us to misread the first half of Devlin's film, which asks conventional questions of its heroine but delivers unconventional answers. Everyone wants to know Finn better, but the fact is, as we eventually learn, she scarcely knows herself. After she is hurried off to the police station, the narrative slowly begins to unfold. In her capacity as a book clerk, Finn has met Henry Kirk (Michael Maloney), a handsome postgraduate student who is conducting research for his doctoral dissertation at Oxford on the topic of Gladstone and the Home Rule movement. She helps him acquire books, expensive ones at that, and appears to fall in love with him. Our own "melodramatic imagination," the pressure of the intertext, we might say, alerts us to the precariousness of her situation: she is a poor Catholic girl living alone (her parents and grandmother have died); he is a wealthy Protestant home from Oxford with a girlfriend back at school. Her loneliness leads her to the bedroom, we fear too quickly. Henry announces several times that he wants to get to know her better, and he certainly appears to fulfill this desire. What no one knows is that Finn, after receiving the first call from Henry about the books he needs, mistook his name for that of his father, an influential Protestant judge, delivered the information to her military superior, and has been instructed to set young Kirk up for murder. In the last scene of the film, one of numerous flashbacks that make up the narrative, she does precisely this: she tells Henry, "I think I've fallen in love with you," and then walks away as his murderers await nearby. The camera watches her from a high angle behind a spider's web in a tree, freezing the frame as she walks away from her victim, framed in the exact middle of the web. She is thus both the deadly queen—earlier for their first liaison she enticed Kirk into her bedroom, a detail that now seems more significant than it once did—and the entrapped victim, caught up in an inglorious web of deceit, violence, and finally destruction as she is apprehended by the police. No spectacular apotheosis, no religious iconography, no suggestion of moral redemption.

By subtle clues Devlin has prepared us for this conclusion. Recalling Stuart Hall's point, does this narrative of what is, after all, a television drama beamed electronically into homes throughout the United Kingdom and America, support a conservative project of containment or a more radical one of emancipation or resistance? I believe it is the latter. In a moment earlier in the film, as Finn plots quietly in the bookstore with her commandant to deliver Kirk to his executioners, a boy walks in looking for detective and mystery stories. He heads for what appears to be a promising title and goes to another clerk, Chrissie, with his find: T. S. Eliot's *Murder in the*

Cathedral. Chrissie tells the lad that this is not a mystery and wonders aloud: "It's a play about martyrdom. Do they always have to be about murders?"[12] In the case of Irish popular convention, the answer is clear: yes. But in Devlin? No, someday—but yes at present, which is part of what Devlin, like O'Casey before her, has to expose before showing us that the differences between martyrs and spiders and spiders and victims are very slight indeed.

APPENDIX
NOTES
WORKS CITED
INDEX

APPENDIX:
Dublin Theatrical Calendar, 1898–1904
Compiled with NONA K. WATT

THEATER ABBREVIATIONS
    G=Gaiety Theatre
        QR=Queen's Royal Theatre
            TR=Theatre Royal

Dates		Plays	Notes of Interest
1898			
Jan. 3–8	G	*Aladdin*	Pantomime
	QR	*In Old Kentucky*	
	TR	Arthur Rousbey Opera Co.	
Jan. 10–15	G	*Aladdin*	Pantomime
	QR	*In Old Kentucky*	
	TR	Arthur Rousbey Opera Co.	
Jan. 17–22	G	*Aladdin*	Pantomime
	QR	*Flying from Justice*	
	TR	Arthur Rousbey Opera Co.	
Jan. 24–29	G	*Aladdin*	Pantomime
	QR	*A Sailor's Knot*	
	TR	Arthur Rousbey Opera Co.	

Dates		Plays	Notes of Interest
Jan. 31– Feb. 3	G	*Aladdin*	Pantomime
	QR	*The Sorrows of Satan*	
	TR	*Dick Whittington*	Pantomime
Feb. 7–13	G	*Aladdin*	Pantomime
	QR	*Lost in New York*	
	TR	*Dick Whittington*	Pantomime
Feb. 14–20	G	*Aladdin*	Pantomime
	QR	*Cissy*	
	TR	*Dick Whittington*	Pantomime
Feb. 21–27	G	*Forget-Me-Not*	
		Moths	
	QR	*Cissy*	
	TR	*Dick Whittington*	Pantomime
Feb. 28– Mar. 6	G	*The Circus Girl*	Geo. Edwardes Co.
	QR	Closed for Lent	
	TR	*The Shop Girl*	
Mar. 7–13	G	*Aunt Jack*	
	QR	Closed for Lent	
	TR	*My Friend the Prince*	
Mar. 14–20	G	*The New Boy*	
	QR	Closed for Lent	
	TR	*The Ballet Girl*	
Mar. 21–26	G	*Miss Francis of Yale*	
	QR	Closed for Lent	
	TR	*The Taming of the Shrew*	Frank Benson Co.
Mar. 28– Apr. 2	G	*A.B.C., or Flossie the Frivolous*	Marie Lloyd
	QR	Closed for Lent	
	TR	*Julius Caesar*	Frank Benson
Apr. 4–9	All theaters closed for Holy Week		
Apr. 11–16	G	D'Oyly Carte Opera Co.	
	QR	*Lord Edward, or '98*	Kennedy Miller Co.
	TR	*The Transit of Venus*	
Apr. 18–23	G	*The Second Mrs. Tanqueray*	Forbes Robertson and
		Hamlet	Mrs. Patrick Campbell
		Macbeth	

Dates		Plays	Notes of Interest
	QR	*Peep o'Day*	
	TR	*The Prince and the Pauper*	Mouillot Co.
Apr. 25–30	G	*Pink Dominos*	Emma Hutchinson Co.
	QR	*The Streets of London*	E. Montefiore Co.
	TR	*The Broken Melody*	
May 2–7	G	*Davy Garrick*	Edward Compton
		The Rivals	
		Henry Esmond	
		She Stoops to Conquer	
		School for Scandal	
	QR	*Current Cash*	
	TR	*My Girl*	
May 9–14	G	*The Sign of the Cross*	
	QR	*Trilby*	Constance Bellamy Co.
	TR	*Madame Sans Géne*	
May 16–21	G	*The Squire of Dames*	
	QR	*Between the Lights*	
	TR	*The Private Secretary*	
May 23–28	G	*The King's Sweetheart*	
	QR	*A Dark Secret*	
	TR	*Sweet Nancy*	
May 30– June 4	G	*Masks and Faces*	
	QR	*The Green Bushes*	Kennedy Miller Co.
	TR	*Charlotte Corday*	Mrs. Brown Potter and Kyle Bellew
June 6–11	G	*Morocco Bound*	
	QR	*My Jack*	
	TR	*Camille*	Mrs. Brown Potter and
		Lady of Lyons	Kyle Bellew
		Forget-Me-Not	
June 13–18	G	*One Summer's Day*	
	QR	*The Penalty of Crime*	
	TR	*Julia*	
June 20	G	Closed for alterations	
	QR	*A City Outcast*	
	TR	*The Old Guard*	

Dates		Plays	Notes of Interest
June 27– July 2	QR TR	*The Sins of the Fathers* *Pepita*	
July 4–10	QR TR	*The Stolen Birthright* *Olivette*	
July 11–17	QR TR	*The Belle of the West* *Madame Favart*	
July 18–24	G QR TR	Reopened: *The Lady Slavey* *Caitheamh an Ghlais* *Tommy Dodd*	Chalmers Mackey Co.
July 25–30	G QR TR	*A Royal Divorce* *A Fight for Life* *An Irish Gentleman*	A. McNeil and F. Victor
Aug. 1–7	G QR TR	*A Modern Don Quixote* *The Terror of Paris* *The Prodigal Daughter*	
Aug. 8–14	G QR TR	*Sweet Briar* *Secrets of the Harem* *The Prodigal Daughter*	
Aug. 15–21	G QR TR	*The Circus Girl* *Under the Czar* *The White Heather*	Geo. Edwardes Co. Fred Jarman Co.
Aug. 22–27	G QR TR	Carl Rosa Opera Co. *A Trip to Chicago* *The Belle of New York*	
Aug. 28– Sept. 3	G QR TR	Carl Rosa Opera Co. *The Colleen Bawn* *The Belle of New York*	Kennedy Miller Co.
Sept. 5–10	G QR TR	*Julius Caesar* *Arrah-na-Pogue* *A Musician's Romance*	H. Beerbohm Tree Kennedy Miller Co.
Sept. 12–17	G QR TR	*A Runaway Girl* *On the Frontier* *The French Maid*	Geo. Edwardes Co.
Sept. 19–24	G	*Oh! Susannah!* *The Cat and the Cherub*	

Dates		Plays	Notes of Interest
	QR	*A Woman's Revenge*	
	TR	*The Transit of Venus*	
Sept. 26– Oct. 1	G	*A Brace of Partridges*	
	QR	*Paul Kauvar*	
	TR	*Young Mr. Yarde*	
Oct. 3–8	G	*The Three Musketeers*	Lewis Waller
	QR	*One of the Bravest*	
	TR	*The White Blackbird*	
Oct. 10–15	G	*A Bachelor's Romance*	John Hare Co.
		Caste	
		Ours	
		A Pair of Spectacles	
	QR	*Saved from the Sea*	
	TR	*Sweet Lavender*	Edward Terry
		Love in Idleness	
		Weak Woman and *Paul Pry*	
Oct. 17–22	G	*Gentleman Joe*	
	QR	*The New World*	
	TR	*A Trip to Chinatown*	
Oct. 24–29	G	*The New East Lynne*	
	QR	*The World's Verdict*	
	TR	*The J. P.*	Lionel Rignold
Oct. 31– Nov. 5	G	*A Greek Slave*	Geo. Edwardes Co.
	QR	*Humanity*	
	TR	*Trelawny of the Wells*	
Nov. 7–12	G	*The Gay Grisette*	
	QR	*The Iron Maiden*	
	TR	*Lord and Lady Algy*	
Nov. 14–19	G	*The Liars*	Emma Hutchinson Co.
	QR	*The Grip of Iron*	
	TR	Grand English Opera Co.	
Nov. 21–26	G	*The Man in the Street*	
		The Dove Cote	
	QR	*How London Lives*	
	TR	*Too Much Johnson*	

Dates		Plays	Notes of Interest
Nov. 28–	G	*A Ray of Sunshine*	
Dec. 3	QR	*From Scotland Yard*	
	TR	*The Ambassador*	George Alexander and
		The Masqueraders	the St. James Co.
		The Man of Forty	
Dec. 5–10	G	D'Oyly Carte Opera Co.	
	QR	*The Magistrate*	Dublin University
	TR	*The Geisha*	Amateur Dramatic Club
Dec. 12–17	G	*My Lady Help*	
		The Private Secretary	
	QR	*The Girl of My Heart*	
	TR	*She Stoops to Conquer*	Frank Benson
		Antony and Cleopatra	
		School for Scandal	
Dec. 19–23	G	*A Royal Divorce*	W. W. Kelly Co.
	QR	*Held in Terror*	
	TR	Closed for preparation of pantomime	
Dec. 24	TR	*Cinderella*	Pantomime
Dec. 26	G	D'Oyly Carte Opera Co.	
	QR	*Wolfe Tone*	Kennedy Miller Co.
	TR	*Cinderella*	Pantomime

1899

Jan. 2–7	G	*The Vicar of Bray*	
	QR	*Wolfe Tone*	
	TR	*Cinderella*	Pantomime
Jan. 9–14	G	Opera	
	QR	*Wolfe Tone*	
	TR	*Cinderella*	Pantomime
Jan. 16–21	G	Opera	
	QR	*Wolfe Tone*	
	TR	*Cinderella*	Pantomime
Jan. 23–28	G	Opera	
	QR	*East Lynne*	
	TR	*Cinderella*	Pantomime

Dates		Plays	Notes of Interest
Jan. 30– Feb. 4	G QR TR	*The Belle of New York* *Babes in the Wood* *Cinderella*	 Pantomime Pantomime
Feb. 6–11	G QR TR	*The Lucky Star* *Babes in the Wood* *Cinderella*	 Pantomime Pantomime
Feb. 13–18	G QR TR	*The Lucky Star* *The God of War* *Cinderella*	 Pantomime
Feb. 20–25	G QR TR	*The Greek Slave* *No Cross, No Crown* *My Friend the Prince*	
Feb. 27– Mar. 4	G QR TR	*Our Cousins* *Muldoon's Picnic* *The Adventures of Lady Ursula*	
Mar. 6–11	G QR TR	*Charley's Aunt* *The Sins of the Fathers* *Magda* *The Notorious Mrs. Ebbsmith* *The Second Mrs. Tanqueray*	 Mrs. Patrick Campbell
Mar. 13–18	G QR TR	*La Tosca* *Romeo and Juliet* *Pygmalion and Galatea* *The Penalty of Crime* *Brother Officers*	
Mar. 20–25	G QR TR	*The Liars* *The Luck of Life* *Jane*	
Mar. 27– Apr. 1	G QR TR	*The Red Lamp* *The Luck of Life* Closed	
Apr. 3–8	G QR TR	*The Runaway Girl* *Lord Edward, or '98* Closed	
Apr. 10–15	G	*The Manoeuvres of Jane*	

Dates	Plays		Notes of Interest
	QR	*In Old Kentucky*	
	TR	Opera	
Apr. 17–22	G	*Our Irish Cousins*	
	QR	*Black-Eyed Susan*	
	TR	*The Topsy Turvey Hotel*	
Apr. 24–29	G	*My Soldier Boy*	
	QR	*The Face at the Window*	
	TR	*Little Miss Nobody*	
May 1–6	G	*The Merchant of Venice* *Masks and Faces*	
	QR	*The Three Musketeers*	
	TR	*The New Mephisto*	

Special Attraction

First performance of W. B. Yeats's *Countess Cathleen* at Antient Concert Rooms, May 8, and Edward Martyn's *Heather Field,* May 9

May 8–13	G	*What Happened to Jones*	
	QR	*The Man in the Iron Mask*	
	TR	*The Pantomime Rehearsal* *The Highwayman* *Faithful James*	
May 15–20	G	*The Brixton Burglary*	
	QR	*Cissy*	
	TR	*The Merry-Go-Round*	
May 22–27	G	*The King's Outcast*	
	QR	*A Fast Life*	Hubert O'Grady Co.
	TR	*The Three Musketeers*	
May 29– June 3	G	*His Excellency the Governor*	
	QR	*For Life and Liberty*	
	TR	*The Skirt Dancer*	
June 5–10	G	*Dandy Dick* *The Schoolmistress* *The Magistrate* *The Amazons* *The Hobby Horse*	
	QR	*The Trail of the Serpent*	
	TR	*Jim the Penman*	

Dates		Plays	Notes of Interest
June 12–17	G	*Dandy Dick*	
		The Schoolmistress	
		The Magistrate	
		The Amazons	
		The Hobby Horse	
	QR	*Our Sailor Lad*	
	TR	*Falka*	
June 19–24	G	*Niobe*	
		Cyrano de Bergerac	
		Tartuffe	
		Les Précieuses Ridicules	
	QR	*In Fear of the Law*	
	TR	*The Broken Melody*	
June 26– July 1	G	*Tom, Dick, and Harry*	
	QR	*The Slave Girl*	
	TR	*Our Boys*	
July 3–8	G	*Nerves*	
	QR	*The Shaughraun*	Kennedy Miller Co.
	TR	*Arrah-na-Pogue*	
		The Colleen Bawn	
July 10–15	G	Closed	
	QR	*London Streets*	
	TR	*The Case of Rebellious Susan*	
July 17–22	G	Closed	
	QR	F. S. Gilbert's Opera Co.	
	TR	Closed	
July 24–29	G	Closed	
	QR	F. S. Gilbert's Opera Co.	
	TR	Closed	
July 31– Aug. 5	G	Closed	
	QR	*The Poisoner of Milan*	
	TR	*The Shop Girl*	
		The Circus Girl	
		The Gaiety Girl	
Aug. 7–12	G	*The New East Lynne*	
	QR	*Secrets of the Harem*	
	TR	Closed	

Dates		Plays	Notes of Interest
Aug. 14–19	G	*The Lady Slavey*	
	QR	*The Diver's Luck*	
	TR	*Lord and Lady Algy*	
Aug. 21–26	G	*Ma Mie Rosette*	
	QR	*Wolfe Tone*	Kennedy Miller Co.
	TR	*The Geisha*	Geo. Edwardes Co.
Aug. 28– Sept. 2	G	*The Gay Grisette*	
	QR	Closed	
	TR	*The Geisha*	
Sept. 4–9	G	*The Plight of Uncle Cyrus* *Niobe* *Dutch Metal*	
	QR	*The Irishman*	Kennedy Miller Co.
	TR	*Orlando Dando*	
Sept. 11–16	G	*The Telephone Girl*	
	QR	*The Green Bushes*	Kennedy Miller Co.
	TR	*The Cuckoo*	
Sept. 18–23	G	*A Greek Slave*	Geo. Edwardes Co.
	QR	*Death or Glory, Boys*	
	TR	*Great Caesar*	
Sept. 25–30	G	*Paul Jones*	
	QR	*The Gamester of Metz*	
	TR	*The Great Ruby*	
Oct. 2–7	G	*The Three Musketeers* *The Rebels*	
	QR	*Alone in London*	
	TR	*The Little Minister*	
Oct. 9–14	G	*Sweet Lavender* *Love in Idleness* *The Rocket*	Edward Terry
	QR	*The Famine*	Hubert O'Grady Co.
	TR	*The Only Way*	Martin Harvey
Oct. 16–21	G	*The Tyranny of Tears*	
	QR	*The Greed of Gold*	
	TR	*The French Maid*	

Dates		Plays	Notes of Interest
Oct. 23–28	G	*The Runaway Girl*	
	QR	*The Rose of Rathboy*	
	TR	*Little Miss Nobody*	
Oct. 30– Nov. 4	G	*The American Heiress*	
	QR	*The Grip of Iron*	
	TR	Moody-Manners Opera Co.	
Nov. 6–11	G	*Ma Mie Rosette*	
	QR	*The Silver King*	
	TR	Moody-Manners Opera Co.	
Nov. 13–18	G	*On and Off*	
	QR	*Man's Enemy*	
	TR	*An American Citizen*	
Nov. 20–25	G	D'Oyly Carte Opera Co.	
	QR	*Dangers of London*	
	TR	*On the Move*	
Nov. 27– Dec. 2	G	*The Sorrows of Satan*	
	QR	*Caitheamh an Ghlais*	Chalmers Mackey Co.
	TR	*The Prisoner of Zenda*	Geo. Alexander Co.
		Rupert of Hentzau	
		In Days of Old	
		The Ambassador	
Dec. 4–9	G	*Davy Garrick*	Compton Comedy Co.
		The Rivals	
		School for Scandal	
		She Stoops to Conquer	
		The Scarlet Coat	
	QR	*The Father's Oath*	Chalmers Mackey Co.
	TR	*The Prisoner of Zenda*	Geo. Alexander Co.
		Rupert of Hentzau	
		In Days of Old	
		The Ambassador	
Dec. 11–16	G	*The Belle of New York*	
	QR	*The 10:30 Down Express*	
	TR	*The Colleen Bawn*	E. C. Matthews Co.
		Rogue Riley	
		Arrah-na-Pogue	
		The Shaughraun	

Dates		Plays	Notes of Interest
Dec. 18–23	G	*New Men and Old Acres*	
	QR	*In the Shadow of Night*	
	TR	*The Colleen Bawn*	E. C. Matthews Co.
		Rogue Riley	
		Arrah-na-Pogue	
		The Shaughraun	
Dec. 26–30	G	*Red Riding Hood*	Pantomime
	QR	*Arrah-na-Pogue*	Kennedy Miller Co.
	TR	*Robinson Crusoe*	Pantomime

1900

Jan. 1–6	G	*Red Riding Hood*	Pantomime
	QR	*The Colleen Bawn*	Kennedy Miller Co.
	TR	*Robinson Crusoe*	Pantomime
Jan. 8–13	G	*Red Riding Hood*	Pantomime
	QR	*A True Son of Erin*	
	TR	*Robinson Crusoe*	Pantomime
Jan. 15–20	G	*Red Riding Hood*	Pantomime
	QR	*East Lynne*	
	TR	*Robinson Crusoe*	Pantomime
Jan. 22–27	G	*Red Riding Hood*	Pantomime
	QR	*The Life We Live*	
	TR	*Robinson Crusoe*	Pantomime
Jan. 29–Feb. 3	G	*Red Riding Hood*	Pantomime
	QR	*Blue Beard*	Pantomime
	TR	*Robinson Crusoe*	Pantomime
Feb. 5–10	G	*Red Riding Hood*	Pantomime
	QR	*Blue Beard*	Pantomime
	TR	*The Merchant of Venice*	Frank Benson
		The Rivals	
		Hamlet	
		The Tempest	
Feb. 12–17	G	*Red Riding Hood*	Pantomime
	QR	*Blue Beard*	Pantomime
	TR	*A Royal Divorce*	

Dates		Plays	Notes of Interest
Feb. 19–24	G	*Maeve*	Irish Literary Theatre
		The Bending of the Bough	
		The Last Feast of the Fianna	
	QR	*Blue Beard*	Pantomime
	TR	*La Poupée*	Comic opera
Feb. 26– Mar. 3	G	*The Lady of Ostend*	
	QR	*The Patriot's Wife*	Melodrama
	TR	*A Trip to Chinatown*	
Mar. 5–10	G	*The Manoeuvres of Jane*	
	QR	*Great Temptations*	
	TR	*The Private Secretary*	
Mar. 12–17	G	*East Lynne*	
	QR	*The Two Mothers*	
	TR	*Cyrano de Bergerac*	Charles Wyndham Co.
Mar. 19–24	G	*The Gay Lord Quex*	John Hare Co.
	QR	*Known to the Police*	Sensational drama
	TR	*A Greek Slave*	"New" Roman Opera
Mar. 26–31	G	*Trilby* preceded by *A Canker in the Rose*	
	QR	Closed (Nearly always closed for all or part of Lent and Easter Week)	
	TR	*Dorothy*	
Apr. 2–7	G	*The Gay Grisette*	
	QR	Closed	
	TR	*La Poupée*	
Apr. 9–14	G	Closed	
	QR	Closed	
	TR	Moody-Manners Opera Co.: *Faust, Il Trovatore,* *The Lily of Killarney,* *The Bohemian Girl,* etc.	
Apr. 16–21	G	D'Oyly Carte Opera Co.: *The Gondoliers, The Mikado,* *The Yeoman of the Guard,* *Iolanthe, Patience*	
	QR	*Rory O'More*	Kennedy Miller Co.

Dates		Plays	Notes of Interest
	TR	Moody-Manners Opera Co.: *Carmen, The Bohemian Girl, Maritana, Tannhauser, Faust, Il Trovatore,* etc.	
Apr. 23–28	G	*The Lost Legion*	
		Charley's Aunt	
	QR	*The Slave Girl*	
	TR	Moody-Manners Opera Co.	
Apr. 30– May 5	G	*San Toy*	
	QR	*The Streets of London*	
	TR	*Why Smith Left Home*	
May 7–12	G	*Jim the Penman*	Mr. and Mrs. Charles Sugden
	QR	*The Shaughraun*	
	TR	*My Girl*	
May 14–19	G	*The Merchant of Venice*	Special Shakespeare week under the direction of Michael Gunn
		She Stoops to Conquer	
		King René's Daughter	
		The Taming of the Shrew	
		Hamlet	
		The Lady of Lyons	
		The Merchant of Venice	
	QR	*Shadows of a Great City*	
	TR	*The Broken Melody*	
May 21–26	G	*The Merchant of Venice*	
		She Stoops to Conquer	
		King René's Daughter	
		The Taming of the Shrew	
		Hamlet	
		The Lady of Lyons	
		The Merchant of Venice	
	QR	*Denounced*	
	TR	*The Adventures of Lady Ursula*	Ida Molesworth
May 28– June 2	G	*A Runaway Girl*	
	QR	*Gipsy Jack*	
	TR	*The Case of Rebellious Susan*	
June 4–9	G	D'Oyly Carte Opera Co.: *The Rose of Persia*	

Dates		Plays	Notes of Interest
	QR	*A Fast Life*	Mrs. Hubert O'Grady
	TR	*The Squire*	Kate Rorke
June 11–16	G	*Ingomar*	Cowpert Calvert Co.
		Black-Eyed Susan	
		Mary, Queen of Scots	
		A Wife's Secret	
		Life and Honour	
	QR	*The Stowaway*	Winifred Maude Co.
	TR	*As You Like It*	Julia Neilson
June 18–23	G	*The New Magdalen*	Mabel Manisty Co.
	QR	*The Prodigal Parson*	
	TR	*A Pair of Spectacles*	
June 25–30	G	*Bootles' Baby*	
	QR	*The Stolen Birthright*	
	TR	*The Squatter's Daughter*	
July 2–7	G	*The Varsity Girl*	
	QR	*Rip Van Winkle*	Lionel Ellis Co.
	TR	*Caste*	Mrs. Mouillot
July 9–14	G	Closed	
	QR	*Shoulder to Shoulder*	
	TR	*Our Flat*	
July 16–21	G	Closed	
	QR	*Emigration*	Frank O'Grady
	TR	*A Royal Divorce*	Miss Sidney Crowe and Frederick Moyes
July 23–28	G	Closed	
	QR	*The Hand of Iron*	
	TR	*Our Boys*	
		The Guv'nor	
July 30– Aug. 4	G	Closed	
	QR	*1000 Reward*	
	TR	*A Gaiety Girl*	Morrell/Mouillot Co.
Aug. 6–11	G	*The Cruise of the HMS Irresponsible*	
	QR	*On the Frontier*	
	TR	*The Shop Girl*	Morrell/Mouillot Co.

Dates		Plays	Notes of Interest
Aug. 13–18	G	*A Merry Madcap*	
	QR	*The God of War*	
	TR	*The Belle of New York*	
Aug. 20–25	G	*The Lady Slavey*	
	QR	*The Marvellous Steens*	
	TR	*Magda*	Mrs. Patrick Campbell
		The Canary	
Aug. 27– Sept. 1	G	*The Messenger Boy*	Geo. Edwardes Co.
	QR	*Two Little Vagabonds*	
	TR	*The Second Mrs. Tanqueray*	Mrs. Patrick Campbell and
		Pelléas and Mélisande	Gerald du Maurier
Sept. 3–8	G	*Lady Huntworth's Experiment*	
	QR	*Lord Edward, or '98*	Kennedy Miller Co.
	TR	*A Message from Mars*	
Sept. 10–15	G	*The Telephone Girl*	
	QR	*Wolfe Tone*	Kennedy Miller Co.
	TR	*The Geisha*	
Sept. 17–22	G	*School for Scandal*	Cyril Maude
		The Little Minister	
		She Stoops to Conquer	
		The Rivals	
	QR	*The Green Bushes*	Kennedy Miller Co.
	TR	*My Friend the Prince*	
Sept. 24–29	G	Carl Rosa Opera Co.	
	QR	*Arrah-na-Pogue*	Kennedy Miller Co.
	TR	*Much Ado About Nothing*	Frank Benson Co.
		Romeo and Juliet	
		Hamlet	
		The Taming of the Shrew	
Oct. 1–6	G	*The Elder Miss Blossom*	
	QR	*Under the Czar*	Fred Jarman Co.
	TR	*The Merry Wives of Windsor*	Frank Benson Co.
		Richard II	
		Romeo and Juliet	
		Macbeth	
Oct. 8–13	G	*Not Wisely But Too Well*	Mr. and Mrs. Kendal
	QR	*Jack O'Hearts*	

Dates		Plays	Notes of Interest
	TR	*The Degenerates*	Mrs. Langtry Co.
Oct. 15–20	G	*The Messenger Boy*	Geo. Edwardes Co.
	QR	*The Famine*	Mrs. O'Grady; Frank O'Grady as Sadler
	TR	*Hamlet*	Forbes Robertson Co.
		The Devil's Disciple	
		Othello	
Oct. 22–27	G	D'Oyly Carte Opera Co.	
	QR	*The Fenian*	Frank O'Grady
	TR	*Sweet Nell of Old Drury Lane*	Julia Neilson and Fred Terry
Oct. 29–Nov. 3	G	*The Toy*	Geo. Edwardes Co.
	QR	*Dangers of London*	
	TR	*Zaza*	Lewis Waller Co.
Nov. 5–10	G	*A Model Wife*	Lionel Ringold
	QR	*A London Arab*	
	TR	*A Royal Family*	
Nov. 12–17	G	*Kitty Grey*	Geo. Edwardes Co.
	QR	*The Face at the Window*	
	TR	*Florodora*	
Nov. 19–24	G	*The Passport*	Edward Terry
		Sweet Lavender	
		Love in Idleness	
		The Churchwarden	
		Kerry	
	QR	*Two Little Drummer Boys*	
	TR	Moody-Manners Opera Co.	
Nov. 26–Dec. 1	G	D'Oyly Carte Opera Co.	
	QR	*Caitheamh an Ghlais*	
	TR	*Hearts Are Trumps*	
Dec. 3–8	G	*Facing the Music*	
	QR	*The Patriot's Wife, A Tale of 1798*	
	TR	*Hearts Are Trumps*	
Dec. 10–15	G	*The Lady of Ostend*	
	QR	*London's Curse*	
	TR	*Her Majesty's Guests*	

Dates		Plays	Notes of Interest
Dec. 17–22	G	Closed	
	QR	Closed	
	TR	Closed	
Dec. 24–29	G	*Sinbad the Sailor*	Pantomime
	QR	*Rory O'More*	Kennedy Miller Co.
	TR	*Aladdin*	Pantomime

1901

Jan. 1–5	G	*Sinbad the Sailor*	
	QR	*The Irishman*	
	TR	*Aladdin*	
Jan. 7–12	G	*Sinbad the Sailor*	
	QR	*Honour Thy Father*	
	TR	*Aladdin*	
Jan. 14–19	G	*Sinbad the Sailor*	Pantomime
	QR	*East Lynne*	Melodrama
	TR	*Aladdin*	Pantomime
Jan. 21–26	G	*Sinbad the Sailor*	Pantomime
	QR	*The House That Jack Built*	
	TR	*Aladdin*	Pantomime
Jan. 28–	G	*Sinbad the Sailor*	Pantomime
Feb. 2	QR	*The House That Jack Built*	
	TR	*Aladdin*	Pantomime
Feb. 4–9	G	*Sinbad the Sailor*	Pantomime
	QR	*The House That Jack Built*	
	TR	*Aladdin*	Pantomime
Feb. 11–16	G	*Sinbad the Sailor*	Pantomime
	QR	*The House That Jack Built*	
	TR	*Merchant of Venice*	Henry Irving, Ellen Terry, and Lyceum Co.
		Robespierre	
		Nance Oldfield and *The Bells*	
		Merchant of Venice	
		Waterloo and *The Bells*	
Feb. 18–23	G	*The School for Scandal*	
		She Stoops to Conquer	

Dates		Plays	Notes of Interest
		The Rivals	
		An Emperor's Romance	
		and *Davy Garrick*	
	QR	*The Colleen Bawn*	Kennedy Miller Co.
		My Neighbour's Wife	
	TR	Opera	
Feb. 25– Mar. 2	G	*The Tyranny of Tears*	
	QR	Closed for Lent	
	TR	*Madame Butterfly*	
Mar. 4–9	G	*Lady Huntsworth's Experiment*	
	QR	Closed for Lent	
	TR	*Mrs. Dane's Defence*	
Mar. 11–16	G	*The Muddle Up*	
	QR	Closed for Lent	
	TR	*Lady Windermere's Fan* and	
		The School for Scandal	
Mar. 18–23	G	*The Messenger Boy*	
	QR	Closed for Lent	
	TR	*A Message from Mars*	
Mar. 25–30	G	*In the Soup*	
	QR	Closed for Lent	
	TR	Various French plays	
Apr. 1–6		All Theaters Closed for Holy Week	
Apr. 8–13	G	*Les Cloches de Corneville*	
	QR	*The Shaughraun*	Kennedy Miller Co.
	TR	*Bo Peep*	
Apr. 15–20	G	*The Prisoner of Zenda*	
		Rupert of Hentzau	
	QR	*The Stowaway*	
	TR	*Bo Peep*	
Apr. 22–27	G	*The Private Secretary*	
	QR	*The Rebel's Wife*	
	TR	*Bo Peep*	
Apr. 29– May 4	G	*The Lost Legion* and	
		Charley's Aunt	

Dates		Plays	Notes of Interest
	QR	*A Marked Man*	
	TR	*The Geisha*	
May 6–11	G	*Quo Vadis?*	
	QR	*The Stolen Birthright*	
	TR	*What Happened to Jones*	
May 13–18	G	*Why Smith Left Home*	
	QR	*The Red Coat*	
		A Bid for Fortune	
	TR	*A Runaway Girl*	
May 20–25	G	*The Varsity Belle*	
	QR	*Brave Hearts*	
	TR	*A Greek Slave*	
May 27–	G	D'Oyly Carte Opera Co.	
June 1	QR	*On the Frontier*	
	TR	*A Royal Divorce*	
June 3–8	G	*Our Flat*	
	QR	*The Guilty Man*	
	TR	Closed	
June 10–15	G	*The Little Intruder*	
	QR	*Denounced*	
	TR	Various entertainments	
June 17–22	G	*The Shaughraun*	E. C. Matthews Co.
		The Colleen Bawn	
	QR	*A Life's Revenge*	
	TR	*The Shop Girl*	
June 24–29	G	*Sowing the Wind*	
	QR	*Peep o'Day*	
	TR	*The Circus Girl*	
July 1–6	G	*Niobe*	
	QR	*A Fight for Life*	
	TR	*Magda*	Changed by request
		Mariana	Mrs. Patrick Campbell
July 8–13	G	*Those Terrible Twins*	
	QR	*Jack O'Hearts*	
	TR	*The New East Lynne*	

Dates		Plays	Notes of Interest
July 15–20	G	*Those Terrible Twins*	
	QR	*The Seal of Silence*	
	TR	*The Boys of Wexford*	
July 22–27	G	Closed	
	QR	*Such Is Life*	
	TR	*Rogue Riley*	
July 29– Aug. 3	G	Closed	
	QR	*The Penalty of Crime*	
	TR	*A Message from Mars*	
Aug. 5–10	G	*La Cigale*	
	QR	*Maritana*	English Opera Co.
	TR	*The Girl from Up There*	
Aug. 12–17	G	*The Adventure of Lady Ursula* *Count Max, the Swashbuckler*	
	QR	*Caitheamh an Ghlais*	Chalmers Mackey Co.
	TR	*The Man from Blankleys*	
Aug. 19–24	G	*The Belle of New York*	
	QR	*The Law and the Man*	
	TR	*A Daughter of Erin*	
Aug. 26–31	G	*San Toy*	Geo. Edwardes Co.
	QR	*Lord Edward, or '98*	
	TR	*Twelfth Night* *Herod*	H. Beerbohm Tree
Sept. 2–7	G	*San Toy*	
	QR	*Arrah-na-Pogue*	Kennedy Miller Co.
	TR	*The Broken Melody*	
Sept. 9–14	G	*The Second in Command*	Cyril Maude
	QR	*Wolfe Tone*	Kennedy Miller Co.
	TR	*A Royal Necklace*	Lily Langtry
Sept. 16–21	G	*The Thirty Thieves*	
	QR	*Shoulder to Shoulder*	
	TR	*The Casino Girl*	
Sept. 23–28	G	*A Royal Rival*	Lewis Waller
	QR	*Two Little Sailor Boys*	
	TR	*A Lady from Texas*	

Dates		Plays	Notes of Interest
Sept. 30– Oct. 5	G QR TR	*The Lady Slavey* *The Bank of England* *The Only Way* *The Cigarette Maker's Romance*	 Martin Harvey
Oct. 7–12	G QR TR	*The Gay Parisienne* *The Klondyke Nugget* *After All*	 Martin Harvey
Oct. 14–19	G QR TR	D'Oyly Carte Opera Co. *The Still Alarm* *Sweet Lavender*	 Edward Terry
Oct. 21–26	G QR TR	*Diarmuid and Grania* *Casadh an tSúgáin* *(Twisting of the Rope)* *King Lear* *A Fast Life* *For the Crown* *Hamlet* *Othello*	Frank Benson Mrs. Hubert O'Grady Co.
Oct. 28– Nov. 2	G QR TR	*The Wedding Guest* *The Face at the Window* *The Silver Slipper*	
Nov. 4–9	G QR TR	*The Emerald Isle* *Sentenced for Life* *A Night Out*	
Nov. 11–16	G QR TR	*The Messenger Boy* *Two Little Vagabonds* *Sweet Nell of Old Drury Lane*	 Julia Neilson and Fred Terry
Nov. 18–23	G QR TR	*The Fisher Girl* *The Power of Gold* *The Wilderness* *The Importance of Being Earnest* *The Idler* *The Awakening*	 George Alexander
Nov. 25–30	G QR TR	Carl Rosa Opera Co. *The Fenian* *When We Were Twenty-One*	 Mrs. Hubert O'Grady Co.

Dates		Plays	Notes of Interest
Dec. 2–7	G	Carl Rosa Opera Co.	
	QR	*The Diver's Luck*	
	TR	*Florodora*	
Dec. 9–14	G	*Why Smith Left Home*	
	QR	*Mysteries of the Thames*	
	TR	*A Royal Divorce*	W. W. Kelly Co.
Dec. 16–21	G	*Cinderella*	Pantomime
	QR	*The Colleen Bawn*	
	TR	*The Geisha*	Geo. Edwardes Co.
Dec. 23–28	G	*Cinderella*	Pantomime
	QR	*The Outlaws*	Kennedy Miller Co.
	TR	Moody-Manners Opera Co.:	
		The Bohemian Girl,	
		The Lily of Killarney,	
		Carmen, etc.	
Dec. 30–	G	*Cinderella*	Pantomime
Jan. 4	QR	*The Outlaws*	Kennedy Miller Co.
	TR	Moody-Manners Opera Co.	

1902

Jan. 6–11	G	*Cinderella*	Pantomime
	QR	*The Irishman*	
	TR	Moody-Manners Opera Co.	

Special Attraction Throughout December and January

Edison's Electric Animated Pictures: 70,000 Dubliners in December alone view Edison's films at the Round Room Rotunda

Jan. 13–18	G	*Cinderella*	Pantomime
	QR	*The Greed of Gold*	
	TR	Moody-Manners Opera Co.	
Jan. 20–25	G	*Cinderella*	Pantomime
	QR	*The Red Lamp*	
	TR	*Sleeping Beauty*	Pantomime

Dates		Plays	Notes of Interest
Jan. 27–	G	*Cinderella*	Pantomime
Feb. 1	QR	*Emigration*	Mrs. Hubert O'Grady Co.
	TR	*Sleeping Beauty*	Pantomime
Feb. 3–8	G	*Cinderella*	Pantomime
	QR	*East Lynne*	
	TR	*Sleeping Beauty*	Pantomime
Feb. 10–15	G	*Cinderella*	Pantomime
	QR	Closed	
	TR	*Sleeping Beauty*	Pantomime
Feb. 17–22	G	*Othello*	Edmund Tearle
		The Three Musketeers	
		Julius Caesar	
		Macbeth	
		Richard III	
	QR	Closed	
	TR	*The Silver Slipper*	
Feb. 24–	G	*Why Smith Left Home*	
Mar. 1		*A Smart Set*	
	QR	Closed for Lent	
	TR	*The Christian*	
Mar. 3–8	G	*The Gay Grisette*	
	QR	Closed for Lent	
	TR	*Morocco Bound*	
Mar. 10–15	G	*Under Two Flags*	Ida Molesworth
	QR	Closed for Lent	
	TR	*The Man from Blankley's*	
Mar. 17–22	G	*Lady of Ostend*	
	QR	Closed for Lent	
	TR	*La Poupée*	
Mar. 24–29	G	D'Oyly Carte Opera Co.	
	QR	Closed for Lent	
	TR	Opera	
Mar. 31	QR	*The Insurgent Chief*	Kennedy Miller Co.
Mar. 31–	All Theaters Closed for Holy Week		
Apr. 5			
Apr. 7–12	G	*The Toreador*	Geo. Edwardes Co.

Dates		Plays	Notes of Interest
Apr. 14–19	G	*Tom Noddy's Secret*	Edw. Compton Co.
		Davy Garrick	
		School for Scandal	
		The Rivals	
	QR	*Secrets*	
	TR	*The Dandy Fifth*	
Apr. 21–26	G	*The Belle of New York*	
	QR	*A Little Outcast*	
	TR	*Mrs. Dane's Defence*	Emma Hutchinson Co.
Apr. 28– May 3	G	*Charley's Aunt*	
	QR	*A Beautiful Fiend*	
	TR	*English Nell*	
May 5–10	G	*San Toy*	Geo. Edwardes Co.
	QR	*The Day of Reckoning*	
	TR	*The Colleen Bawn*	
		The Shaughraun	
May 12–17	G	*Judged by Appearances*	
		The New Clown	
	QR	*Lost in Paris*	
	TR	*The Wrong Mr. Wright*	
May 19–24	G	*Are You a Mason?*	Geo. Edwardes and
	QR	*On the Frontier*	Charles Frohman
	TR	*Sherlock Holmes*	William Gillette
May 26–31	G	*A Smart Set*	
	QR	*The Anarchist's Terror*	
	TR	*Becky Sharp*	
June 2–7	G	*On Change*	
	QR	*A Triple Vengeance*	
	TR	*The Twin Sister*	H. B. Irving
June 9–14	G	*Uncle Tom's Cabin*	"with *real* Negroes"
	QR	*The Hand of Iron*	
	TR	*The Shop Girl*	
June 16–21	G	*Betsy*	
	QR	*Uncle Tom's Cabin*	
	TR	*The Circus Girl*	

Dates		Plays	Notes of Interest
June 23–28	G	*The Red Lamp*	H. Beerbohm Tree
	QR	*The Octoroon*	
	TR	*A Runaway Girl*	
June 30– July 5	G	*La Dame aux Camélias* *Frou Frou*	Sarah Bernhardt – two performances only
	QR	*Two Men and a Woman*	
	TR	*The Three Musketeers*	
July 7–12	G	Closed	
	QR	*The Shaughraun*	
	TR	*Caste*	
July 14–19	G	Closed	
	QR	*By the Hand of a Woman*	
	TR	*School* *Ours*	
July 21–26	G	Closed	
	QR	*The Wild Irish Boy*	Mrs. Hubert O'Grady Co.
	TR	Closed	
July 28– Aug. 2	G	Closed	
	QR	*The Penalty of Crime*	
	TR	Closed	
Aug. 4–9	G	*The Private Secretary*	
	QR	*Shadows of a Great City*	
	TR	Closed	
Aug. 11–16	G	*The Marriage Market*	
	QR	*The King of Crime*	
	TR	*The Geisha*	
Aug. 18–23	G	*H.M.S. Irresponsible*	
	QR	*The Face at the Window*	
	TR	*The Belle of New York*	
Aug. 25–30	G	*A Country Girl*	Geo. Edwardes Co.
	QR	*The Insurgent Chief*	Kennedy Miller Co.
	TR	*The Only Way* *A Cigarette Maker's Romance*	Martin Harvey Co.
Sept. 1–6	G	*The Children of Kings*	
	QR	*Lord Edward, or '98*	Kennedy Miller Co.
	TR	*The Only Way*	Martin Harvey Co.

Dates		Plays	Notes of Interest
Sept. 8–13	G	*There and Back*	
	QR	*Arrah-na-Pogue*	Kennedy Miller Co.
	TR	*The Night of the Party*	
Sept. 15–20	G	*Are You a Mason?*	Edwardes and Frohman
	QR	*Wolfe Tone*	Kennedy Miller Co.
	TR	Albert Chevalier Recitals	
Sept. 22–27	G	Carl Rosa Opera Co.	
	QR	*Queen of the Night*	
	TR	*A Greek Slave*	
Sept. 29– Oct. 4	G	*San Toy*	Geo. Edwardes Co.
	QR	*Rich and Poor of London*	
	TR	*A Message from Mars*	
Oct. 6–11	G	*Mice and Men*	Forbes Robertson Co.
	QR	*The Famine*	Mrs. Hubert O'Grady Co.
	TR	*A Chinese Honeymoon*	
Oct. 13–18	G	*Sapho*	Olga Nethersole
	QR	*Shamus*	
	TR	*The Broken Melody*	
Oct. 20–25	G	*The Toreador*	Geo. Edwardes Co.
	QR	*The Heart of a Woman*	
	TR	*The Mummy and the Hummingbird*	
Oct. 27– Nov. 1	G	*Holly Tree Inn* *My Pretty Maid*	Edward Terry
	QR	*The Guilty Man*	James Hare
	TR	*Sweet and Twenty* *David Garrick*	Charles Wyndham and Mary Moore
Nov. 3–8	G	*Paolo and Francesca* *King René's Daughter* *The Merchant of Venice*	Frank Benson Co.
	QR	*Driven from Home*	
	TR	*Florodora*	
Nov. 10–15	G	*Three Little Maids*	
	QR	*Sentenced for Life*	
	TR	*The Little French Milliner*	Emma Hutchinson
Nov. 17–22	G	*My Lady Molly*	
	QR	*The Fenian*	

Dates		Plays	Notes of Interest
	TR	*The Merchant of Venice*	Henry Irving and
		Faust	Ellen Terry
Nov. 24–29	G	*A Lost Memory*	
	QR	*The 10:30 Down Express*	
	TR	*The Eternal City*	H. Beerbohm Tree
Dec. 1–6	G	D'Oyly Carte Opera Co.	
	QR	*Denounced*	
	TR	*The Casino Girl*	
Dec. 8–13	G	*A Woman of No Importance*	
	QR	*The Seal of Silence*	
	TR	*My Awful Dad*	
		What Happened to Jones	
Dec. 15–20	G	Closed	
	QR	*The Dawn of Freedom*	
	TR	*Honours Divided*	
Dec. 22–27	G	Closed	
	QR	*The Insurgent Chief*	Kennedy Miller Co.
		The Green Bushes	
	TR	Closed	
Dec. 29–	G	*Aladdin*	Pantomime
Jan. 3	QR	*The Irishman*	Kennedy Miller Co.
	TR	*The Silver Slipper*	

1903

Jan. 5–10	G	*Aladdin*	Pantomime
	QR	*The Colleen Bawn*	Kennedy Miller Co.
	TR	*The Silver Slipper*	Tom Davis Co.
Jan. 12–17	G	*Aladdin*	Pantomime
	QR	*The Ulster Hero*	Kennedy Miller Co.
	TR	Moody-Manners Opera Co.	
Jan. 19–24	G	*Aladdin*	Pantomime
	QR	*The Stolen Birthright*	
	TR	*Jack and the Beanstalk*	Pantomime
Jan. 26–31	G	*Aladdin*	Pantomime
	QR	*The Greed of Gold*	
	TR	*Jack and the Beanstalk*	Pantomime

Dates		Plays	Notes of Interest
Feb. 2–7	G	*Aladdin*	Pantomime
	QR	*Mysteries of London*	
	TR	*Jack and the Beanstalk*	Pantomime
Feb. 9–14	G	*Aladdin*	Pantomime
	QR	*The Klondyke Nugget*	
	TR	*Jack and the Beanstalk*	Pantomime
Feb. 16–21	G	*Aladdin*	Pantomime
	QR	*East Lynne*	
	TR	*Sherlock Holmes*	Charles Frohman Co.
Feb. 23–28	G	*The Three Musketeers*	Edmund Tearle and
		Richard III	Kate Clinton
		Othello	
		Macbeth	
		Hamlet	
	QR	*Born to Good Luck*	Benefit of Kennedy Miller
	TR	*Our Boys*	
Mar. 2–7	G	*Arizona*	
	QR	Closed for Lent	
	TR	*Blue-Bell in Fairyland*	
Mar. 9–14	G	D'Oyly Carte Opera Co.	
	QR	Military Amateur Theatricals	
	TR	*The Fatal Wedding*	
Mar. 16–21	G	*Brown at Brighton*	
	QR	Closed for Lent	
	TR	*The Eternal City*	H. Beerbohm Tree Co.
Mar. 23–28	G	*Caste*	with Maud Jeffries
		Confusion	
	QR	Closed for Lent	
	TR	*Mrs. Willoughby's Kiss*	
Mar. 30– Apr. 4	G	*Tom, Dick, and Harry*	
	QR	Closed for Lent	
	TR	*A Country Mouse*	Emma Hutchinson Co.
Apr. 6–11	G	*The Night of the Party*	
	QR	Closed for Holy Week	
	TR	Closed for Holy Week	

Dates		Plays	Notes of Interest
Apr. 13–18	G	*The Night of the Party*	
	QR	*The Old Land*	By Robt. Johnston: Irish drama; winner of 100-pound prize offered by
	TR	Opera	J. W. Whitbread
Apr. 20–25	G	*A Country Girl*	Geo. Edwardes Co.
	QR	*The Shaughraun*	Kennedy Miller Co.
	TR	Opera	
Apr. 27– May 2	G	*Three Little Maids*	Edwardes and Frohman Co.
	QR	*From Scotland Yard*	
	TR	*There's Many a Slip*	
May 4–9	G	*Charley's Aunt*	
	QR	*A Fast Life*	Mrs. Hubert O'Grady Co.
	TR	*Resurrection*	H. Beerbohm Tree Co.
May 11–16	G	*The Toreador*	Geo. Edwardes Co.
	QR	*The Dark Egyptian*	
	TR	*The Liars* *Mrs. Dane's Defence*	
May 18–23	G	*The Importance of Being Earnest*	Arthur Hare Co.
	QR	*Fair Play*	
	TR	*Uncle Ned*	
May 25–30	G	*The New Clown*	
	QR	*For Life and Liberty*	
	TR	*My Friend the Prince*	
June 1–6	G	*Mice and Men*	Forbes Robertson Co.
	QR	*On the Frontier*	
	TR	*A Royal Divorce*	W. W. Kelly Co.
June 8–13	G	*Much Ado About Nothing* *Romeo and Juliet* *Pygmalion and Galatea* *King René's Daughter* *Twelfth Night*	
	QR	*A Little Outcast*	
	TR	*A Doll's House* *The Marriage of Kitty*	Madame Réjane
June 15–20	G	*Mary, Queen of Scots* *East Lynne*	Mrs. Bandmann-Palmer

Dates		Plays	Notes of Interest
		Hamlet	
		Nell Gwynne	
		Jane Shore	
	QR	*The Insurgent Chief*	Kennedy Miller Co.
	TR	Madame Réjane's Repertory Continues	
June 22–27	G	*His Fatal Beauty*	
	QR	*The Heather Field*	
	TR	*Our Flat*	
June 29– July 4	G	*The Sorrows of Satan*	
	QR	*A Little Vagrant*	
	TR	Great Motor Carnival Program	
July 6–11	G	*The Idler*	
	QR	*For the Woman He Loves*	
	TR	*The New Boy*	
July 13–18	G	Closed	
	QR	Opera	
	TR	*Too Many Cooks*	
July 20–25	G	*The Toreador*	Geo. Edwardes Co.
		The Linkman	
	QR	Opera	
	TR	*Just Like Callaghan*	
July 27– Aug. 1	G	*Aubrey's Sister*	
	QR	*A Woman's Error*	
	TR	*The Arabian Nights*	
Aug. 3–8	G	*Richard Lovelace*	Laurence Irving
	QR	*Driven from Home*	
	TR	*The Sign of the Cross*	
Aug. 10–15	G	Opera	
	QR	*Two Little Heroes*	
	TR	*My Lady Molly*	
Aug. 17–22	G	*Peril*	
	QR	*Her One Great Sin*	
	TR	*A Chinese Honeymoon*	
Aug. 24–29	G	*The School Girl*	Edwardes and Frohman Co.
	QR	*Lord Edward, or '98*	Kennedy Miller Co.
	TR	*Monsieur Beaucaire*	Lewis Waller Co.

Dates		Plays	Notes of Interest
Aug. 31–	G	*The School Girl*	
Sept. 5	QR	*Arrah-na-Pogue*	Kennedy Miller Co.
	TR	*The Admirable Crichton*	Charles Frohman Co.
Sept. 7–12	G	*The Light That Failed*	Forbes Robertson Co.
	QR	*The Ulster Hero*	Kennedy Miller Co.
	TR	*The Geisha*	Mouillot Co.
Sept. 14–19	G	Carl Rosa Opera Co.	
	QR	*The Old Land*	100-pound prize drama
	TR	*Kitty Grey*	
Sept. 21–26	G	*Mrs. Gorringe's Necklace*	Charles Wyndham Co.
	QR	*Alone in London*	
	TR	*Gentleman Joe*	
Sept. 28–	G	*A Country Girl*	Geo. Edwardes Co.
Oct. 3	QR	*A Face at the Window*	
	TR	*Sweet Lavender*	Edward Terry Co.
		A Motor Marriage	
		Kerry	
		Burnside & Co.	
		The Passport	
Oct. 5–10	G	*Magda*	Olga Nethersole
		Sapho	
	QR	*The Famine*	Mrs. Hubert O'Grady Co.
	TR	*Quality Street*	
Oct. 12–17	G	*The Elder Miss Blossom*	Kendal Company
		Afterglow	
		Still Waters Run Deep	
	QR	*The Wild Irish Boy*	Mrs. Hubert O'Grady Co.
	TR	*The Joy of Living*	Mrs. Patrick Campbell
		The Second Mrs. Tanqueray	
		A Dream and *Undine*	
Oct. 19–24	G	*San Toy*	Geo. Edwardes Co.
	QR	*Over Niagara Falls*	
	TR	*The Exile*	Martin Harvey Co.
		The Only Way	
Oct. 26–31	G	*Mice and Men*	
	QR	*Paul Kauvar*	
	TR	*The Breed of the Treshams*	Martin Harvey
		The Only Way	

Dates	Plays	Notes of Interest
Nov. 2–7	G *Whitewashing Julia*	
	QR *A Trip to Chicago*	
	TR *The Best of Friends*	

Special Attraction

Advertised as the first time in Ireland, color photography was on display at the Tivoli Theatre during the week of Nov. 2–7

Dates	Plays	Notes of Interest
Nov. 9–14	G *The Lady Slavey*	H. Cecil Beryl Co.
	QR *Life's Handicap*	
	TR *The Belle of New York*	
Nov. 16–21	G *Are You a Mason?*	Edwardes and Frohman Co.
	QR *Uncle Tom's Cabin*	
	TR *If I Were King*	
Nov. 23–28	G *Three Little Maids*	
	QR *The Crimson Club*	
	TR *Sweet Nell of Old Drury Lane*	Julia Neilson and Fred Terry
	The Scarlet Pimpernel	
Nov. 30–	G *The Private Secretary*	
Dec. 5	QR *A Woman's Redemption*	James Hare Co.
	TR *A Message from Mars*	
Dec. 7–12	G *The Liars*	Emma Hutchinson Co.
	Mrs. Dane's Defence	with Henry Neville
	QR *The World's Desire*	
	TR Irish opera	
Dec. 14–19	G Closed	
	QR *Shamus*	
	TR *The Marriage of Kitty*	
Dec. 21–26	G Closed for preparation of pantomime	
	QR *The Sham Squire*	Kennedy Miller Co.
	TR Closed	
Dec. 28–	G *Babes in the Wood*	Pantomime
Jan. 2	QR *The Sham Squire*	Kennedy Miller Co.
	TR Moody-Manners Opera Co.	

1904

Dates	Plays	Notes of Interest
Jan. 4–9	G *Babes in the Wood*	Pantomime
	QR *Wolfe Tone*	Kennedy Miller Co.
	TR Moody-Manners Opera Co.	

Dates		Plays	Notes of Interest
Jan. 11–16	G	*Babes in the Wood*	Pantomime
	QR	*When the Lights Are Low*	
	TR	Moody-Manners Opera Co.	
Jan. 18–23	G	*Babes in the Wood*	Pantomime
	QR	*Honour Thy Father*	
	TR	Moody-Manners Opera Co.	
Jan. 25–30	G	*Babes in the Wood*	Pantomime
	QR	*The Green Bushes*	
	TR	Closed	
Feb. 1–6	G	*Babes in the Wood*	Pantomime
	QR	*The Little Sailor Boys*	
	TR	*Dick Whittington*	Pantomime
Feb. 8–13	G	*Amorelle*	
	QR	*East Lynne*	
	TR	*Dick Whittington*	Pantomime
Feb. 15–20	G	*When We Were Twenty-One*	
	QR	Benefit for Kennedy Miller	
	TR	*Dick Whittington*	Pantomime
Feb. 22–27	G	*Mrs. Gorringe's Necklace*	
	QR	Closed	
	TR	*Dick Whittington*	Pantomime
Feb. 29– Mar. 5	G	*The Prisoner of Zenda*	
	QR	Closed	
	TR	*Sherlock Holmes*	
Mar. 7–12	G	*The Orchid*	Geo. Edwardes Co.
	QR	Amateur theatricals and *The Manoeuvres of Jane*	Benefit of Soldiers and Sailors' Help Society
	TR	*The Marriage of Kitty*	
Mar. 14–19	G	*The Three Musketeers*	Edmund Tearle
	QR	Closed	
	TR	*A Country Mouse*	
Mar. 21–26	G	*Billy's Love Affair*	
	QR	Closed	
	TR	*The Gay Parisienne*	
Mar. 28– Apr. 2	G	*The Girl from Kay's*	
	QR	Closed	
	TR	Closed	

Dates		Plays	Notes of Interest
Apr. 4–9	G	*The Girl from Kay's*	
	QR	*The Irishman*	
	TR	*The Medal and the Maid*	
Apr. 11–16	G	*The School Girl*	Geo. Edwardes Co.
	QR	*The Victoria Cross*	
	TR	*The Darling of the Gods*	H. Beerbohm Tree Co.
Apr. 18–23	G	*The Mikado*	Geo. Edwardes Co.
		HMS Pinafore	
	QR	*From Scotland Yard*	
	TR	*Twelfth Night*	H. Beerbohm Tree Co.
		The Merry Wives of Windsor	
		Julius Caesar	
Apr. 25–30	G	*The Belle of New York*	Geo. Edwardes Co.
		A Country Girl	
	QR	*Queen of the Night*	
	TR	*Twelfth Night*	H. Beerbohm Tree Co.
		The Merry Wives of Windsor	
		Julius Caesar	
May 2–7	G	*A Country Girl*	Geo. Edwardes Co.
	QR	*Shield of David*	
		Sally in Our Alley	
		Humanity	
	TR	*Winnie Brooke Widow*	
May 9–14	G	*The Never-Never Land*	
	QR	*The Anarchist's Terror*	
	TR	*La Poupée*	
May 16–21	G	*A Hot Night*	
	QR	*Sentenced for Life*	
	TR	*Becket*	Henry Irving Co.
		Waterloo	
		The Bells	
		The Merchant of Venice	
		Louis XI	
May 23–28	G	*Davy Garrick*	Edw. Compton Co.
		She Stoops to Conquer	
		School for Scandal	
		Tomorrow	

Dates		Plays	Notes of Interest
	QR	*The Female Swindler*	
	TR	*The Broken Melody*	
May 30– June 4	G	*Uncle Tom's Cabin*	
	QR	*The Shaughraun*	
	TR	*Our Boys*	
June 6–11	G	*Charley's Aunt*	
	QR	*On Shannon's Shore*	Fred Cooke Co. musical
	TR	*A Pair of Spectacles*	
June 13–18	G	*Mary, Queen of Scots*	Mrs. Bandmann-Palmer
		East Lynne	
		Hamlet	
		Leah	
		Jane Shore	
	QR	Elster-Grimes Opera Co.	
	TR	Eugene Stratton ("The Greatest Coon Delineator of the Age") plus *Fun on the Bristol*	
June 20–25	G	*What Became of Mrs. Rackett?*	
	QR	Elster-Grimes Opera Co.	
	TR	Closed	
June 27– July 2	G	*The Houp-La Girl*	Sarah Bernhardt
	QR	*Who Is the Woman?*	
	TR	Closed	
July 4–9	G	*La Dame aux Camélias*	Sarah Bernhardt
		La Sorcière	
		Trooper Hunt's Widow	
	QR	*The Colleen Bawn*	
	TR	Closed	
July 11–16	G	Closed	
	QR	*Rory O'More*	
	TR	*Dandy Dick*	
July 18–23	G	Closed	
	QR	*On Circumstantial Evidence*	
	TR	*Betsy*	
July 25–30	G	Closed	
	QR	*A Rogue's Daughter*	
	TR	*Liberty Hall*	

Dates		Plays	Notes of Interest
Aug. 1–6	G	*The Happy Life*	
	QR	*The Web of Fate*	
	TR	*A Royal Divorce*	"Return visit of the old
Aug. 8–13	G	*Thoroughbred*	Dublin favourite"
	QR	*Her One Great Sin*	
	TR	*The New Barmaid*	
Aug. 15–20	G	*The New Clown*	
	QR	*The Penalty of Crime*	
	TR	*Little Mary*	
Aug. 22–27	G	*The Cingalée*	Geo. Edwardes Co.
	QR	*Arrah-na-Pogue*	Kennedy Miller Co.
	TR	*My Lady Molly*	
Aug. 29–	G	*The Cingalée*	Geo. Edwardes Co.
Sept. 3	QR	*Lord Edward, or '98*	
	TR	*Boy Bob*	
Sept. 5–10	G	*Saturday to Monday*	
	QR	*The Insurgent Chief*	
	TR	*A Chinese Honeymoon*	
Sept. 12–17	G	*Madame Sherry*	
	QR	*What a Woman Did*	
	TR	*The Earl and the Girl*	
Sept. 19–24	G	*Sunday*	
	QR	*The Temptress*	
	TR	*A Man and His Wife*	Nina Boucicault
Sept. 26–	G	*Sunday*	
Oct. 1	QR	*Napoleon the Great*	Frank Thorne Co.
	TR	*The Darling of the Gods*	H. Beerbohm Tree Co.
Oct. 3–8	G	*The Orchid*	Geo. Edwardes Co.
	QR	*The Grip of Iron*	
	TR	*The Cardinal*	
Oct. 10–15	G	*Joseph Entangled*	
	QR	*The Mysteries of the Thames*	
	TR	*A Country Girl*	
Oct. 17–22	G	*Quality Street*	
	QR	*The Indian Mutiny*	
	TR	*Old Heidelberg*	

Dates		Plays	Notes of Interest
Oct. 24–29	G	*Mice and Men*	Forbes Robertson Co.
		The Light That Failed	
	QR	*The Face at the Window*	
	TR	*In Dahomey*	
Oct. 31– Nov. 5	G	*The Fairy's Dilemma*	
	QR	*The Famine*	Mrs. Hubert O'Grady Co.
	TR	*Marguerite*	Lena Ashwell in her
		Mrs. Dane's Defence	original part
Nov. 7–12	G	*Othello*	Frank Benson Co.
		As You Like It	
		The Taming of the Shrew	
		Macbeth	
		She Stoops to Conquer	
		Richard II	
		Hamlet	
	QR	*The Fenian*	
	TR	*Letty*	Irene VanBrugh
Nov. 14–19	G	*Elizabeth's Prisoner*	Lewis Waller Co.
	QR	*Under the Russian Flag*	
	TR	*The Breed of the Treshams*	Martin Harvey
Nov. 21–26	G	*The House of Burnside*	Edward Terry
		The Passport	
		Sweet Lavender	
	QR	*The Two Vagabonds*	
	TR	*Hamlet*	Harvey's first appearance
Nov. 28– Dec. 3	G	*The Duke of Killicrankie*	as Hamlet
	QR	*The Manxman*	
	TR	*Florodora*	
Dec. 5–10	G	*The Private Secretary*	
	QR	*The Biggest Scamp on Earth*	
	TR	*The Geisha*	
		A Greek Slave	
Dec. 12–17	G	Carl Rosa Opera Co.	
	QR	*The Plucky Nipper*	
	TR	*Kitty Grey*	

Dates		Plays	Notes of Interest
Dec. 19–24	G	Closed for preparation of pantomime	
	QR	*The Shaughraun*	
		The Colleen Bawn	
	TR	Closed	
Dec. 26–31	G	*Sleeping Beauty*	Pantomime
	QR	*Sarsfield*	Kennedy Miller Co.
	TR	Moody-Manners Opera Co.	

NOTES

PREFACE

1. C. Desmond Greaves, *Sean O'Casey: Politics and Art* (London: Lawrence and Wishart, 1979), p. 27.

2. John Wilson Foster, *Fictions of the Irish Literary Revival: A Changeling Art* (Syracuse: Syracuse Univ. Press, 1987), p. 145.

3. David Cairns and Shaun Richards, *Writing Ireland: Colonialism, nationalism and culture* (Manchester: Manchester Univ. Press, 1988), p. 84.

1. A POPULAR THEATER FORGOTTEN AND REMEMBERED

1. Two recent biographies of Ellen Terry are Nina Auerbach, *Ellen Terry: Player in Her Time* (New York: Norton, 1987); and Joy Melville, *Ellen and Edy: A Biography of Ellen Terry and Her Daughter, Edith Craig, 1847–1947* (London: Pandora Press, 1987).

2. Michael R. Booth, *Prefaces to English Nineteenth-Century Theatre* (Manchester: Manchester Univ. Press, 1980), p. 1. This book is a collection of the prefaces Booth wrote for the five-volume edition, *English Plays of the Nineteenth Century* (Oxford: Oxford Univ. Press, 1969–76).

3. See Hugh Hunt, *The Abbey: Ireland's National Theatre, 1904–1979* (Dublin: Gill and Macmillan, 1979). See also Christopher Fitz-simon, *The Irish Theatre* (London: Thames and Hudson, 1983); D. E. S. Maxwell, *A Critical History of Modern Irish Drama, 1891–1980* (Cambridge: Cambridge Univ. Press, 1984); and Andrew E. Malone, *The Irish Drama* (London: Constable, 1929). Malone is remarkably inconsistent in his characterization of popular drama in Ireland before the rise of the Abbey Theatre. At one point he proclaims, "It may be said boldly as a fact that all drama in Ireland until the beginning of the twentieth century was English drama" (p. 12), an obvious overstatement; at another point, he expresses mild admiration for Irish melodrama at the Queen's which followed in Boucicault's footsteps: "These

plays were Irish in theme and mood . . . and almost for the first time gave to Ireland a drama which had some connection with the life and thought of the people" (p. 17).

4. For my purposes, the most valuable of Robert Hogan's editions on Irish drama and theater are Frank Fay's *Towards a National Theatre* (Dublin: Dolmen Press, 1970), which collects the best of Fay's theater reviews from the *United Irishman* from 1899 to 1902; and *Joseph Holloway's Irish Theatre*, 3 vols., ed. Hogan and Michael J. O'Neill (Newark, Del.: Proscenium Press, 1968–70).

5. See Cheryl Herr, *For the Land They Loved: Irish Political Melodramas, 1890–1925* (Syracuse: Syracuse Univ. Press, 1991). Herr's introduction is especially good on popular theater in these years. See also James Hurt, "The Canon of Irish Drama," *Éire-Ireland* 24 (Fall 1989): 135–38.

6. Booth estimates that between 1851 and 1900 the number of playhouses in London grew from twenty to sixty-one. In Dublin, after the rebuilding and reopening of the new Theatre Royal in 1897, there were three theaters in operation before the 1899 program of the Irish Literary Theatre. Also, several variety houses did a brisk business at this time: the Tivoli, the Empire Palace Theatre (formerly the Star of Erin Theatre, opened by Dan Lowrey in 1879), and the Round Room Rotunda.

7. Peter Kavanagh, *The Irish Theatre* (Tralee: Kerryman Limited, 1946), p. 401.

8. For a list of London stars on tour in Dublin at the end of the century, see the Appendix. See also Séamus de Búrca, *The Queen's Royal Theatre, Dublin: 1829–1969* (Dublin: de Búrca, 1983). Here de Búrca notes that the "Eighties and Nineties saw the touring policy firmly established"–and with it the dissolution of stock companies (p. 3). A similar chronology that emphasizes the "extinction" of the provincial tragedian by 1880 is offered by Kathleen Barker, "Charles Dillon: A Provincial Tragedian," in *Shakespeare and the Victorian Stage,* ed. Richard Foulkes (Cambridge: Cambridge Univ. Press, 1986), pp. 283–94.

9. The notion that a state's "ideological apparatus" hails or "interpellates" individuals into subjects comes from Louis Althusser's much-cited essay "Ideology and Ideological State Apparatuses" in *Lenin and Philosophy and Other Essays,* trans. Ben Brewster (London: Monthly Review Press, 1971), esp. pp. 170–86.

10. One of the clearest explications of deconstruction's undoing of structural oppositions and the implications of this undoing is in Michael Ryan, *Marxism and Deconstruction: A Critical Articulation* (Baltimore: Johns Hopkins Univ. Press, 1982), pp. 9–42.

11. Leo Lowenthal, *Literature, Popular Culture, and Society* (Englewood Cliffs, N.J.: Prentice-Hall, 1961), pp. 10–11.

12. Fitz-simon, *Irish Theatre,* p. 94.

13. Homi K. Bhabha discusses the ambivalence and repeatability of the colonial stereotype in "The Other Question–The Stereotype and Colonial Discourse," *Screen* 24 (Nov.–Dec. 1983): 18–36. For a response to Bhabha and the theory of colonialist discourse as furthering a refusal of the "possibility" of a rapprochement between self (colonizer) and other (colonized), see Abdul R. JanMohamed, "The Economy of Manichean Allegory: The Function of Racial Difference in Colonialist Literature," *Critical Inquiry* 12 (Autumn 1985): 59–87.

14. Maxwell, *Critical History,* p. 3.

15. I emphasize that Irish melodrama served as a model for *some* Irish drama because O'Casey and, more recently, John Arden and Margaretta D'Arcy were strongly influenced by popular melodrama. The subtitles of D'Arcy's and Arden's *Hero Rises Up* (1969; "A Romantic Melodrama"), *Vandaleur's Folly* (1981; "An Anglo-Irish Melodrama"), *A Little Grey Home in the West* (1982; "An Anglo-Irish Melodrama"), and others suggest this indebtedness.

16. Fredric Jameson, "Postmodernism and Consumer Society," in *The Anti-Aesthetic: Essays on Postmodern Culture,* ed. Hal Foster (Port Townsend, Wash.: Bay Press, 1983), p. 112.

17. William Butler Yeats, "The Theatre," in *Essays and Introductions* (New York: Macmillan, 1961), p. 166. For further discussion of Yeats's intricate, variegated politics insofar as theater is concerned, see Adrian Frazier, *Behind the Scenes: Yeats, Horniman and the Struggle for the Abbey Theatre* (Berkeley: Univ. of California Press, 1990), esp. pp. 24–63.

18. Ibid., p. 166.

19. *The Letters of W. B. Yeats,* ed. Allan Wade (London: Rupert Hart-Davis, 1954), pp. 308–9.

20. Ibid., p. 286.

21. William Archer, "The Real Ibsen," in *William Archer on Ibsen,* ed. Thomas Postlewait (Westport, Conn.: Greenwood Press, 1984), p. 66. Edward Martyn agreed with Archer that "master-poet" best described Ibsen's genius. See Sister Marie-Thérèse Courtney, *Edward Martyn and the Irish Theatre* (New York: Vantage Press, 1956), pp. 65–71.

22. John Eglinton, W. B. Yeats, A.E., and William Larminie, *Literary Ideals in Ireland* (London/Dublin: T. Fisher Unwin/*Daily Express,* 1899), p. 27.

23. Yeats, ibid., p. 36.

24. A.E., ibid., p. 54.

25. Cairns and Richards, *Writing Ireland,* pp. 66, 120.

26. Fredric Jameson, "Reification and Utopia in Mass Culture," *Social Text* 1 (Winter 1979): 137.

27. David Mamet, *Speed-the-Plow* (New York: Grove Press, 1985), pp. 74, 71.

28. George Moore, *The Bending of the Bough* (Chicago: Herbert F. Stone, 1900), p. xiv.

29. Ibid., p. xvi; Lowenthal, p. 11.

30. Hugh Cunningham, "Class and Leisure in Mid-Victorian England," in *Popular Culture: Past and Present,* ed. Bernard Waites, Tony Bennett, and Graham Martin (London: Croom Helm, 1982), p. 68. A. E. Green explains his uneasiness with one common definition of popular culture as describing a work "generally sympathetic to working class life and experience" in "Popular Drama and the Mummers' Play," in *Performance and Politics in Popular Drama,* ed. David Bradby, Louis James, and Bernard Sharratt (Cambridge: Cambridge Univ. Press, 1980), pp. 139–41. The popular theater Shaw and Yeats disparage may be "commercial," but it is not necessarily working class.

31. Althusser, *Lenin and Philosophy,* pp. 148–58.

32. See Austin E. Quigley, *The Modern Stage and Other Worlds* (New York: Methuen, 1986), pp. 69–90. Here Quigley responds to Hamilton Clayton, editor of *The Social Plays of Arthur Wing Pinero,* 4 vols. (New York: Dutton, 1918), who pronounces in his "General Introduction" that the "modern English drama was ushered into being on the night of May 27th, 1893, when *The Second Mrs. Tanqueray,* by Arthur Wing Pinero, was acted for the first time on the stage of the St. James's Theatre in London" (1:3). For Shaw's and O'Casey's decidedly different view of the matter, see, for example, Shaw, *Our Theatres in the Nineties,* 3 vols. (London: Constable, 1932), 1:59–66; and O'Casey, *The Green Crow* (New York: George Braziller, 1956), pp. 57–72.

33. "An Unwholesome Play," *Irish Playgoer,* 29 Mar. 1900, p. 13. R. B. Kershner in *Joyce, Bakhtin, and Popular Culture: Chronicles of Disorder* (Chapel Hill: Univ. of North Carolina Press, 1989) similarly discusses the manner in which the "queer old josser" in Joyce's "An Encounter" combines sexual perversity with an "assumed context of social superiority," a superior-

ity adverted to by his reading of Victorian literature as opposed to the boys' consumption of (and lower-class) interest in popular boys' periodicals (p. 43). Here Holloway's connection of prurience with upper-class theatergoers finds an analogue in Joyce's story.

34. *The Collected Letters of John Millington Synge*, 2 vols., ed. Ann Saddlemyer (Oxford: Clarendon Press, 1983), 1:74–75.

35. Bernard Sharratt, "The Politics of the Popular?–From Melodrama to Television," in *Performance and Politics in Popular Drama*, ed. Bradby, James, and Sharratt, pp. 278, 279.

36. Jeremy Crump, "The Popular Audience for Shakespeare in Nineteenth-Century Leicester," in *Shakespeare and the Victorian Stage*, ed. Foulkes, pp. 276–77.

37. Lawrence W. Levine, *Highbrow/Lowbrow* (Cambridge, Mass.: Harvard Univ. Press, 1988), pp. 21, 34.

38. Nelson Goodman, *Ways of Worldmaking* (Indianapolis: Hackett Publishing, 1978), p. 20.

39. The excerpts here and in the following paragraph from Joseph Holloway's address to the National Literary Society of Ireland come from "Irish Drama in Modern Dublin," *Irish Playgoer*, 12 and 19 Apr. 1900, pp. 13, 15–16. Despite his attacks on the "literary" and his enthusiasm for the Queen's Theatre, Holloway became a strong supporter of the Abbey Theatre.

40. In Aug. 1899 Frank Fay reviewed *Wolfe Tone* in a mildly positive way, although he disagreed that it could be accurately termed "A Romantic Irish Drama." For Fay, Whitbread's play was "really neither more nor less than a well-constructed melodrama with some of the leading incidents in Wolfe Tone's career utilised to produce those dramatic situations to which its success is due." See Fay, *Towards a National Theatre*, pp. 24–26.

41. Kershner, *Joyce, Bakhtin, and Popular Literature*, p. 124.

42. Ibid., pp. 126–27. As Kershner advises, for further discussion of narration in "A Mother," see David Hayman, "A Mother," in *James Joyce's "Dubliners": Critical Essays*, ed. Clive Hart (New York: Viking, 1969), pp. 122–33.

43. For more information about Daly's adaptations of German drama, see Marvin Felheim, *The Theatre of Augustin Daly* (Cambridge, Mass.: Harvard Univ. Press, 1956), pp. 157–75.

44. For a summary of these and other reviews, see Donald Mullin, *Victorian Actors and Actresses in Review* (Westport, Conn.: Greenwood Press, 1983), pp. 54–57.

45. Tom Stoppard, *Rosencrantz and Guildenstern Are Dead* (New York: Grove Press, 1967), p. 83.

46. Peter Brooks, *The Melodramatic Imagination* (1976; rpt. New York: Columbia Univ. Press, 1984), pp. 24–28, argues convincingly that melodrama "typically . . . is about virtue made visible and acknowledged, the drama of recognition" (p. 27). This point is certainly true of Daly's melodrama *Leah*.

47. Patrick Brantlinger, *Bread and Circuses: Theories of Mass Culture as Social Decay* (Ithaca: Cornell Univ. Press, 1983), pp. 20, 21.

48. Patrick Parrinder, *James Joyce* (Cambridge: Cambridge Univ. Press, 1984), p. 4.

49. Stuart Hall, "Notes on Deconstructing 'The Popular,'" in *People's History and Socialist Theory*, ed. Raphael Samuel (London: Routledge & Kegan Paul, 1981), p. 232.

50. See Suzette Henke and Elaine Unkeless, eds., *Women in Joyce* (Urbana: Univ. of Illinois Press, 1982), pp. xviii, 135. See also Bonnie Kime Scott, *Joyce and Feminism* (Bloomington: Indiana Univ. Press, 1984). Women writers share this cultural constriction with Joyce's female characters, as Christine Froula has recently emphasized in "Gender and the Law of Genre:

Joyce, Woolf, and the Autobiographical Artist-Novel," in *New Alliances in Joyce Studies*, ed. Bonnie Kime Scott (Newark: Univ. of Delaware Press, 1988), pp. 155–64.

51. Cheryl Herr, *Joyce's Anatomy of Culture* (Urbana: Univ. of Illinois Press, 1986), p. 15.

52. For Shaw's recollection of the Theatre Royal, see the first paragraph of the following chapter.

53. See Herr, *For The Land They Loved*, pp. 12–15.

54. Robert Hogan, "O'Casey, Influence and Impact," *Irish University Review* 10 (Spring 1980): 147.

55. The only two productions of Ibsen in Dublin between 1897 and 1904 were Madame Réjane's *A Doll's House* (Theatre Royal, 8–13 June 1903) and the Players' Club production of *Hedda Gabler* (Antient Concert Rooms, 18–21 Apr. 1904).

56. For a brief discussion of the "Victorian Shakespeare," see Maurice Willson Disher, *The Last Romantic: The Authorised Biography of Sir John Martin-Harvey* (London: Hutchinson, 1944), pp. 60–65.

57. For a discussion of Joyce's use of the stage, especially of pantomime, see Herr, *Joyce's Anatomy of Culture*, pp. 96–221. See also James S. Atherton, *The Books at the Wake* (New York: Viking, 1960), pp. 149–65; and Henry Ward Swinson, "Joyce and the Theater" (Ph.D. diss., Univ. of Illinois, 1969).

58. J. F. Byrne, *Silent Years* (New York: Farrar, Straus and Young, 1953), p. 49.

59. Stanislaus Joyce, *The Complete Dublin Diary of Stanislaus Joyce*, ed. George H. Healey (Ithaca: Cornell Univ. Press, 1962), p. 38.

60. In its idealized depiction of Josephine, Wills's *A Royal Divorce* counters in some ways the "modern" issues of divorce and sexuality so prominent in "problem plays" of the 1890s— and also counters the motif of betrayal in Joyce. This idealization is underscored by the verse that serves as prologue to Wills's play:

> A tale of one who loved her lord so well,
> That on the topmost stormy heights of fame,
> She holds her glory but an empty wand—
> . . . .
> *Now*, when they would see heaven as in a glass,
> When they would utter in a single word
> *FAITH, LOVE, DEVOTION*—men say—*Josephine!*
> (P. 1, Wills's capitalization and punctuation)

The manuscript of Wills's play is in the Lord Chamberlain's Collection, Manuscript Division, British Library, Add. MS 53474D (112).

61. See Herr, *Joyce's Anatomy of Culture*, p. 38.

62. Franco Moretti, *Signs Taken for Wonders* (London: Verso, 1983), p. 15.

63. Cairns and Richards, *Writing Ireland*, p. 8.

64. Louis A. Montrose, "Professing the Renaissance: The Poetics and Politics of Culture," in *The New Historicism*, ed. H. Aram Veeser (New York: Routledge, 1989), p. 17.

65. Jonathan Dollimore, "Introduction–Shakespeare, Cultural Materialism and the New Historicism," in *Political Shakespeare: New Essays in Cultural Materialism*, ed. Dollimore and Alan Sinfield (Manchester: Manchester Univ. Press, 1985), pp. 2, 4.

66. Jameson, "Reification and Utopia in Mass Culture," p. 133.

67. Swinson, "Joyce and the Theater," p. 1.

68. Richard Brown, *James Joyce and Sexuality* (Cambridge: Cambridge Univ. Press, 1985), pp. 6–7.

69. Montrose, "Professing the Renaissance," p. 21. For a fuller discussion of the issues of agency and the subject, see Paul Smith, *Discerning the Subject* (Minneapolis: Univ. of Minnesota Press, 1988), pp. 56–69. Smith argues that resistance "takes place only within a social context which has already construed subject-positions for the human agent. The place of that resistance has, then, to be glimpsed somewhere in the interstices of the subject-positions which are offered in any social formation. More precisely, resistance must be regarded as the by-product of contradictions in and among subject-positions" (p. 25).

70. Michel Foucault, "What Is an Author?" in *Language, Counter-Memory, and Practice,* ed. Donald F. Bouchard (Ithaca: Cornell Univ. Press, 1977), p. 115. See also Roland Barthes, "The Death of the Author," in *Image–Music–Text,* trans. Stephen Heath (New York: Hill & Wang, 1977), pp. 142–48.

71. Frank Budgen, *James Joyce and the Making of Ulysses* (1934; rpt. Bloomington: Indiana Univ. Press, 1960), p. 48.

72. See chap. 4 below for a discussion of O'Casey as "his own man" and the critical presuppositions that attend this view.

73. See Brown, *Joyce and Sexuality,* pp. 2–11. See also Alick West, "James Joyce: *Ulysses,*" in *Crisis and Criticism: 7 Literary Essays* (London: Lawrence and Wishart, 1975), pp. 109–16.

74. Jean Kimball, "Freud, Leonardo, and Joyce: The Dimensions of a Childhood Memory," in *The Seventh of Joyce,* ed. Bernard Benstock (Bloomington: Indiana Univ. Press, 1982), p. 58.

75. Foucault, "What Is an Author?" pp. 124, 137.

76. Barthes, "Death of the Author," p. 146.

77. Jennifer Schiffer Levine, "Originality and Repetition in *Finnegans Wake* and *Ulysses,*" *PMLA* 94 (Jan. 1979): 113, 109.

78. Cairns and Richards, *Writing Ireland,* p. 1.

79. For a discussion of colonialism and contemporary drama, see William E. Holladay and Stephen Watt, "Viewing the Elephant Man," *PMLA* 104 (Oct. 1989): 868–81.

80. Franco Moretti, *Signs Taken for Wonders: Essays in the Sociology of Literary Forms* (London: Verso, 1983), pp. 189–90.

81. Franco Moretti, "The Spell of Indecision," in *Marxism and the Interpretation of Culture,* ed. Cary Nelson and Lawrence Grossberg (Urbana: Univ. of Illinois Press, 1988), p. 343.

82. Colin MacCabe, Discussion following Moretti's paper, ibid., p. 345.

83. Cheryl Herr, "Subworlds, Props, and Settings in Joyce's *Exiles,*" *Theatre Journal* 39 (May 1987): 188.

84. Timothy J. Wiles, *The Theater Event: Modern Theories of Performance* (Chicago: Univ. of Chicago Press, 1980), p. 3.

85. For a brief discussion of the end of stock companies in Dublin, see Martin Meisel, *Shaw and the Nineteenth-Century Theater* (Princeton: Princeton Univ. Press, 1963), pp. 11–37.

86. Disher, *Last Romantic,* p. 23.

87. See Lady Constance Benson, *Mainly Players: Bensonian Memories* (London: Thornton Butterworth, 1926), pp. 107–18. See also J. C. Trewin, *Benson and the Bensonians* (London:

Barrie and Rockliff, 1960), pp. 125–31, which describes Benson's popularity in Ireland and his performance in *Diarmuid and Grania* at the Gaiety Theatre in October 1901.

88. Raymond Williams, *Writing in Society* (London: Verso, 1983), p. 18.

2. THE QUEEN'S ROYAL THEATRE AND THE POLITICS OF IRISH MELODRAMA

1. Hunt, *The Abbey,* p. 4.

2. Barry Sullivan's repertory prominently included *Richard III, Hamlet, Macbeth*, and *Richelieu*, all of which, for example, he performed in an eighteen-day stay at Dublin's Theatre Royal in the fall of 1872. MS 14,995(5) at the National Library of Ireland provides a playlist for the Theatre Royal, 1872–75.

3. Bernard Shaw, "Preface: Fragments of an Autobiography," in *The Matter with Ireland*, eds. David H. Greene and Dan H. Laurence (London: Rupert Hart-Davis, 1962), pp. 11–12.

4. Fay, *Towards a National Theatre*, p. 27. All other quotations from Fay's reviews for the *United Irishman* come from the newspapers themselves.

5. There has been some disagreement on the exact dates of Whitbread's tenure as manager of the Queen's. In *The Irish Theatre* Peter Kavanagh maintains that Whitbread assumed management in 1887; more recently Séamus de Búrca, in *The Queen's Royal Theatre*, places the date at 1882. The *Freeman's Journal*, however, reported in July 1884 that after a repertory of Boucicault's *Arrah-na-Pogue, The Shaughraun*, and *The Colleen Bawn*, Falconer's *Eileen Oge*, and Samuel Lover's *The Happy Man*, the Queen's Royal Theatre would reopen under Whitbread's management on 4 Aug. 1884 with Thomas Sennett's Company playing in *Redemption*. Further evidence of 1884 as the year Whitbread began his management can be found in various announcements of his annual benefits. For instance, on 26 Feb. 1895 the *Freeman's Journal*, p. 4, col. 8, announced that Whitbread was taking his eleventh annual benefit before the theater closed for Lent.

6. This quotation comes from MS 14,995(2), Manuscript Division, National Library of Ireland, Dublin.

7. For more information on Kennedy Miller and his tenure at the Queen's, see the *Irish Playgoer,* 22 Mar. 1900, pp. 5–6.

8. de Búrca, *Queen's Royal Theatre*, p. 1.

9. Martin Meisel discusses Shaw's appropriations from the popular Victorian theater throughout *Shaw and the Nineteenth-Century Theater,* as I do in "Shaw's *Saint Joan* and the Modern History Play," *Comparative Drama* 19 (Spring 1985): 58–86.

10. For a brief discussion of Boucicault and Whitbread, see Malone, *The Irish Drama*, esp. pp. 15–18. Malone characterizes Whitbread's (which he spells Whitebread's) plays as "mainly melodramas of the most vivid kind," poor ones at that, which "made history real for many thousands of people" (p. 17). For a discussion, again brief, of Whitbread's productions at the Queen's Royal Theatre, see Kavanagh, *Irish Theatre*, pp. 387–91; and Fay, *Towards a National Theatre*, esp. pp. 24–29, 34–36, 38, and 43.

11. Hall, "Notes on Deconstructing 'The Popular,'" p. 228.

12. For a discussion of Boucicault's staging techniques in, among others, *The Colleen Bawn*, see A. Nicholas Vardac, *Stage to Screen: Theatrical Method from Garrick to Griffith* (Cambridge, Mass.: Harvard Univ. Press, 1949), esp. pp. 41–56, who suggests that *The Colleen Bawn* was "little short" of being the "first of the sensation dramas" (p. 41). Other "Irish" plays such as Falconer's *Peep o'Day* (1861) were, as Vardac explains, similarly "sensational."

13. For Boucicault's views of Irish history, see Richard Fawkes, *Dion Boucicault: A Biography* (London: Quartet Books, 1979), pp. 112–32.

14. For Boucicault's comments on the Stage Irishman, see Robert Hogan, *Dion Boucicault* (New York: Twayne, 1969), pp. 79–96.

15. R. B. Graves, "The Stage Irishman Among the Irish," *Theatre History Studies* 1 (1981): 35. See also James Malcolm Nelson, "From Rory and Paddy to Boucicault's Myles, Shaun, and Conn: The Irishman on the London Stage, 1830–1860," *Éire-Ireland* 13 (1977): 79–105.

16. Maxwell, *Critical History*, p. 3.

17. Hall, "Notes on Deconstructing 'The Popular,'" pp. 233–34.

18. See Cairns and Richards, *Writing Ireland*, pp. 42–57. This chapter, appropriately, is entitled after Arnold's comment, "Essentially a Feminine Race."

19. L. Perry Curtis, Jr., *Apes and Angels: The Irishman in Victorian Caricature* (Washington, D.C.: Smithsonian Institution Press, 1971), p. 35.

20. Karl Marx and Frederick Engels, *Ireland and the Irish Question*, ed. L. I. Golman and V. E. Kunina (Moscow: Progress Publishers, 1971), pp. 43–44.

21. Ibid., p. 159. For a discussion of the opposition between civilization and barbarism as it applies to Ireland, see Seamus Deane, *Civilians and Barbarians*, Field Day Pamphlet No. 3 (Derry: Field Day Theatre Company Limited, 1983).

22. See Sander L. Gilman, "Black Bodies, White Bodies: Toward an Iconography of Female Sexuality in Late Nineteenth Century Art, Medicine, and Literature," *Critical Inquiry* 12 (1985): 204–42; see also JanMohamed, "The Economy of Manichean Allegory."

23. Dion Boucicault, *A Fireside Story of Ireland* (London: Bradbury, Agnew and Company Printers, 1881), p. 2. This pamphlet was also published in Dublin and in Boston by James R. Osgood in 1881 under the title *The Story of Ireland*. I am grateful to Sven Eric Molin and Robin Goodefellowe, "Nationalism on the Dublin Stage," *Éire-Ireland* 21 (Spring 1986): 135–38, for emphasizing the significance of Boucicault's essay.

24. Kavanagh, *Irish Theatre*, p. 401.

25. There remains some degree of imprecision in fixing the dates of composition and even the total number of plays in O'Grady's canon. Allardyce Nicoll in *A History of English Drama, 1660–1900*, 6 vols. (Cambridge: Cambridge Univ. Press, 1952–59), cites eight titles by O'Grady in his "Handlist of Plays" (vol. 6), but misses at least two dramas popularly attributed to O'Grady: *The Outlaws*, played by Mrs. O'Grady at the Queen's in 1901, and *The Wild Irish Boy*. It is possible that O'Grady's *Gommock* (1877), cited by Nicoll, was known as *The Wild Irish Boy* at the end of the century. In any case, this play bears no relationship to the Charles Maturin novel of the same title written much earlier in the century (1808). The manuscripts of most of O'Grady's plays are located in the Lord Chamberlain's Collection, Manuscript Division, British Library, London. All quotations from O'Grady's plays are from these manuscripts, which, when cited below, are accompanied by their catalog numbers and, when possible, page numbers.

26. "Hubert O'Grady's Death," *Irish Playgoer*, 28 December 1899, pp. 4–5.

27. Hubert O'Grady, *The Fenian*, Add. MS 53416G (296), n.p.

28. Like most of O'Grady's plays, many of Whitbread's plays are located in the Manuscript Division, British Library, London; all the citations below except those to *Wolfe Tone* refer to manuscripts in the Lord Chamberlain's Collection and will be accompanied by catalogue numbers. Two of Whitbread's plays were printed by W. J. Alley and Company, Dublin: *Miss Maritana*, an "operatic burlesque," in 1890, and *The Nationalist*, a "New Irish Drama

in Four Acts," in 1892. All quotations from *The Nationalist* refer to this edition. In addition, a prose version of *Shoulder to Shoulder,* upon which the play of the same title was based, was printed by W. J. Alley in 1888. These three W. J. Alley printings are in the Raymond Mander and Joe Mitchenson Theatre Collection, Beckenham, Kent, England. Also, an informative series of obituaries was run in the *Scarborough Daily Post* on 10 June 1916, 13 June 1916, and 17 June 1916. The last notice announces the demise of Whitbread's forty-one-year-old daughter Nellie, who died the day her father was buried. Nellie was the author of at least one melodrama herself, *The Blackmailer,* produced at the Queen's in 1905.

29. Before Whitbread's version of Willy Reilly, this character was the hero of a popular ballad and of William Carleton's novel *Willy Reilly and the Colleen Bawn* (1855).

30. One indication of the enduring popularity of Whitbread's drama in Ireland was pointed out to me recently by Séamus de Búrca, who showed me a request from the Kilteely Dramatic Society in Limerick in 1912 for various costumes to mount a production of *Wolfe Tone.* He also remembers seeing a revival of *Wolfe Tone* at the Queen's Theatre in 1923.

31. Robert Donovan, "A Heroine of 1803," *Weekly Freeman,* 14 Mar. 1903, p. 29, col. 5.

32. Calma, "Napoleon and Ireland," *United Irishman,* 17 Nov. 1900, p. 6, col. 4. Irish reverence for Napoleon is aptly related in a review of *A Royal Divorce* in the *Weekly Freeman,* 6 June 1903, p. 9, col. 3. The reviewer notes that the play introduces "one of the greatest, if not the greatest, personage of modern history" and stirs "the sympathies of the audience" through "the expression of noble sentiments."

33. *Irish Orators and Oratory* (London, Dublin, and Belfast: Gresham Publishing Company, n.d.), p. 422.

34. For the entire text of this advertisement, see, for example, *United Irishman,* 6 Jan. 1900, p. 8, col. 2.

35. See "Methuen Murders Irish Prisoners of War," *United Irishman,* 13 Jan. 1900, p. 5, col. 2. See also F. Hugh O'Donnell, "The Slaughter of Irish Regiments," *United Irishman,* 17 Feb. 1900, p. 5, cols. 1–3.

36. Robert Bechtold Heilman, *The Iceman, The Arsonist, and the Troubled Agent* (Seattle: Univ. of Washington Press, 1973), p. 53.

37. Fredric Jameson, "Metacommentary," *PMLA* 86 (Jan. 1971): 12.

38. Scholars have begun to notice the political dimensions of Boucicauldian melodrama. In his introduction to *Selected Plays of Dion Boucicault* (Gerrards Cross/Washington, D.C.: Colin Smythe/Catholic Univ. Press of America, 1987), Andrew Parkin refers to the "theme of a subject race or nation" in Boucicault's Irish plays (p. 19) but does not undertake much analysis of Boucicault's development of this theme. For a more thorough investigation of the political dimensions of one of Boucicault's melodramas, see Gary A. Richardson, "Boucicault's *The Octoroon* and American Law," *Educational Theatre Journal* 34 (1982): 155–64. Richardson argues that *The Octoroon,* a sensational melodrama, conveys Boucicault's condemnation of slavery and his clear message that it should be abolished.

39. "The Land Question," *Freeman's Journal,* 17 Apr. 1903, p. 6, col. 6.

40. Hubert O'Grady, *The Gommock,* Add. MS 53185H, p. 13; Whitbread, *The Nationalist,* pp. 5–6.

41. All quotations from Whitbread's *Wolfe Tone* come from Herr's edition in *For the Land They Loved,* pp. 171–257.

42. *Times,* 16 Dec. 1867, as quoted in Norman McCord, "The Fenians and Public Opinion in Great Britain," in *Fenians and Fenianism,* ed. Maurice Harmon (Seattle: Univ. of Washington Press, 1970), p. 47.

43. "The Truth About Ireland," *Quarterly Review* 127 (1869): 281.

44. Curtis, *Apes and Angels,* p. 29.

45. For Boucicault's comments about Fenianism, see Fawkes, *Boucicault,* pp. 195–97.

46. Herbert Lindenberger, *Historical Drama: The Relation of Literature and Reality* (Chicago: Univ. of Chicago Press, 1975), p. 72.

47. For a discussion of the chief secretary's role in the colonial government, see Leon Ó Broin, *The Prime Informer* (London: Sidgwick and Jackson, 1971), pp. 16–18.

48. For further discussion of the Catholic church's response to Fenianism, see Donal McCartney, "The Church and Fenianism," in *Fenians and Fenianism,* ed. Harmon, pp. 13–27. McCartney generously directs readers to E. R. Norman, *The Catholic Church and Ireland in the Age of Rebellion* (Ithaca: Cornell Univ. Press, 1965), esp. chap. 3. McCartney's advice in this matter is well worth taking.

49. Hubert O'Grady, *The Fenian,* Add. MS 53416G.

50. Lindenberger, *Historical Drama,* p. 72.

51. J. W. Whitbread, *Sarsfield,* Add. MS 1905/18 (305). Because the manuscript is paginated consecutively by act, I have not placed page numbers after quotations.

52. All quotations from Boucicault's *Robert Emmet* come from *Forbidden Fruit and Other Plays,* ed. Allardyce Nicoll and F. Theodore Cloak (Princeton: Princeton Univ. Press, 1940). Page numbers will follow quotations in the text. Boucicault's play was one of three written during this period on the martyrdom of Robert Emmet: the others are Joseph I. C. Clarke's *Robert Emmet, A Tragedy of Irish History* (1888) and James D. Pilgrim's *Robert Emmet, The Martyr of Irish Liberty,* published in 1903 but written several years earlier. Willie Fay directed Pilgrim's play in Dublin for the Saint Teresa's Total Abstinence and Temperance Association, 24 and 25 Oct. 1900.

53. J. W. Whitbread, *The Irish Dragoon,* Add. MS 1906/10 (172).

54. J. W. Whitbread, *The Ulster Hero,* Add. MS 1905/19 (320). Because the manuscript of *The Ulster Hero* is not paginated, I have not placed page citations after quotations from the play.

55. These allegations are discussed briefly in Ó Broin, *Prime Informer,* pp. 26–27.

56. One indication of the conventional use of last-act gallows or other sensational means of execution in late Victorian historical drama is provided by one weary commentator writing for the *Saturday Review.* After viewing one of a number of sensational dramas about Joan of Arc in 1871, he wrote, "It is probably by way of penance for a long course of burlesque that the British public is now going in generally for a scaffold hung with black for the last scene of a play" (22 Apr. 1871, p. 450). Irish plays at the Queen's concluded in a variety of ways, but this particular ending, when the victim was a historical hero like Emmet or McCracken, evoked especially indignant responses from Irish audiences.

57. For a discussion of the carnivalesque and of transgression, see Peter Stallybrass and Allon White, *The Politics and Poetics of Transgression* (Ithaca: Cornell Univ. Press, 1986), esp. pp. 1–26, 171–90. Irish melodrama contains a number of the characteristics of and functions similarly to the carnivalesque; a closer comparison of Irish melodrama of this period and aspects of carnivalization might prove extremely valuable.

3. JOYCE: SEXUALITY, ARTISTRY, AND THE POPULAR THEATER

1. Henrik Ibsen, *When We Dead Awaken*, as quoted by Joyce in "Ibsen's New Drama," *CW*, p. 54. All further quotations from Ibsen's plays come from *The Oxford Ibsen*, 8 vols., ed. James Walter McFarlane (Oxford: Oxford Univ. Press, 1960–77). Quotations will be followed by volume and page numbers in the text.

2. Sometimes a return to denotations of a theoretical term can prove useful, as is the case here. In *The Critical Twilight: Explorations in the Ideology of Anglo-American Literary Theory from Eliot to McLuhan* (London: Routledge & Kegan Paul, 1977), John Fekete defines "problematic" in precisely the way I employ it here: a "social, ideological, or theoretical framework within which complexes of problems are structured and single problems acquire density, meaning and significance" (pp. 217–18).

3. In *The Last Romantic,* Disher emphasizes the romantic actor's ability to evoke "the forces of mysterious subconscious" (p. 11) and combine it with "strangeness," the "quality" of romance (p. 26).

4. See Brown, *Joyce and Sexuality,* pp. 50–88.

5. In addition to Kershner, *Joyce, Bakhtin, and Popular Literature,* for Joyce's use of popular fiction see Michael Seidel, *Exile and the Narrative Imagination* (New Haven: Yale Univ. Press, 1986), chap. 3.

6. Dominic Manganiello, *Joyce's Politics* (London: Routledge & Kegan Paul, 1980), pp. 1–2.

7. I am thinking here particularly of Florence Walzl's and Suzette Henke's efforts to locate Joyce's representation of women within the specific context of turn-of-the-century Dublin. See Walzl's "*Dubliners:* Women in Irish Society" in *Women in Joyce,* ed. Henke and Unkeless, pp. 31–56, which addresses questions about "Joyce's accuracy in depiction of the social milieu of his women characters and of the realism of his portraits of women as social entities" (p. 33). Concerned with similar matters, in this case the construction of sexuality in popular women's periodicals and in advertisements, see in the same volume Henke's "Gerty MacDowell: Joyce's Sentimental Heroine," pp. 132–48.

8. For a discussion of the accumulation of inconsequential details in realistic representation, see Menachem Brinker, "Verisimilitude, Conventions, and Beliefs," *New Literary History* 14 (Winter 1983): 253–67.

9. Alick West, "James Joyce: *Ulysses,*" in *Crisis and Criticism,* p. 118.

10. Ibid., p. 104.

11. Wolfgang Iser, *The Implied Reader* (Baltimore: Johns Hopkins Univ. Press, 1974), pp. 197, 225.

12. See Wilfried Passow, "The Analysis of Theatrical Performance: The State of the Art," *Poetics Today* 2 (1981): 237–54. Here Passow defines the "theatrical contract" as continually requiring "confirmation." Theater, for Passow, is "to be understood as the constant process of the conventionalization of signs, which may apply often for a mere instant or for a whole evening" (p. 242). Reading *Ulysses* demands a similar process.

13. Iser, *Implied Reader,* p. 226.

14. For a discussion of *Exiles* and the Edwardian "problem play," see Elliott M. Simon, "James Joyce's *Exiles* and the Tradition of the Edwardian Problem-Play," *Modern Drama* 20 (Mar. 1977): 21–35. This term refers to most of the plays I examine here.

15. Judith L. Fisher takes this observation one step further in a Lacanian direction by asserting that in Pinero's and Jones's plays women's "sexual behavior is not the issue"; "individuality," construed as the fallen woman's striving "for independence from a linguistically limited role which carries automatic behavioral limits," is. See "The 'Law of the Father': Sexual Politics in the Plays of Henry Arthur Jones and Arthur Wing Pinero," *Essays in Literature* 16 (Fall 1989): 203–23; quotation on p. 203.

16. All quotations from Jones's *The Case of Rebellious Susan* and *The Liars* come from *Plays by Henry Arthur Jones,* ed. Russell Jackson (Cambridge: Cambridge Univ. Press, 1982). All quotations from Jones's *Mrs. Dane's Defence* come from the Samuel French edition (New York, 1905). Page numbers will follow quotations in the text.

17. *Selected Letters of James Joyce,* ed. Richard Ellmann (New York: Viking Press, 1975), p. 25.

18. *Freeman's Journal,* 19 Apr. 1898, p. 6, col. 3.

19. All quotations from Hermann Sudermann's *Magda* come from *Contemporary Drama: European Plays II,* ed. E. Bradlee Watson and Benfield Pressey (New York: Charles Scribner's Sons, 1952), pp. 187–278. All further quotations from this translation will be followed in the text by page numbers.

20. Quigley, *Modern Stage,* p. 89.

21. The critical and popular failure of Louis N. Parker's translation of *Magda* in London – it closed after only fifteen performances in June 1896 – greatly disappointed Stella Campbell, though A. B. Walkley, a number of her friends, and some audiences were very generous in their support of her performance. Mrs. Campbell discusses this in her *My Life and Some Letters* (London: Hutchinson, 1922), pp. 112–16.

22. William Winter, *The Wallet of Time,* 2 vols. (New York: Moffat, Yard and Company, 1913), 2:339.

23. Grant Allen, *The Woman Who Did* (London: John Lane, 1895). Page numbers follow quotations in the text.

24. For various sources Joyce read on the subject of marriage, see Brown, *Joyce and Sexuality,* pp. 12–49. See also Scott, *Joyce and Feminism,* pp. 29–53, who cites Hauptmann, Ibsen, and George Moore as sources influential on Joyce of a sympathetic view of women caught in conventional traps.

25. For London reviews of *Rosmersholm,* especially negative ones which emphasize the mixing of gender in Ibsen's characters, see Archer, *William Archer on Ibsen,* ed. Postlewait, pp. 38–39.

26. Margot Peters, *Mrs. Pat: The Life of Mrs. Patrick Campbell* (New York: Alfred A. Knopf, 1984), p. 129.

27. "Crazes Die Young. 'Trilby's' Reign Is Over," *Irish Playgoer,* 5 Apr. 1900, p. 17. Here the *Playgoer* reports that the crowds the play once drew are now, five years after its premiere, no longer nearly so interested in it.

28. Arthur Wing Pinero, *Sweet Lavender* (Boston: Walter H. Baker, 1893).

29. For a brief analysis of *Sweet Lavender* and Edward Terry's acting style, see Clement Scott, *The Drama of Yesterday and To-day,* 2 vols. (London: Macmillan, 1899), 2:400–401. For a brief history of Edward Terry's great success in London with *Sweet Lavender,* see H. G. Hibbert, *A Playgoer's Memories* (London: Grant Richards, 1920), pp. 87–98.

30. See David Krause, *The Profane Book of Irish Comedy* (Ithaca: Cornell Univ. Press, 1982), esp. pp. 18–57.

31. Alphonse Daudet, *Sapho* (New York: Book League of America, 1932), p. 33.

32. See Joy Harriman Reilly, "From Wicked Woman of the Stage to New Woman: The Career of Olga Nethersole (1870–1951); Actress-Manager, Suffragist, Health Pioneer" (Ph.D. diss., Ohio State Univ., 1984), pp. 210–13, for a plot synopsis of Fitch's adaptation and a discussion of differences between it and Daudet's novel. An informative distillation of Reilly's work on Nethersole, "A Forgotten 'Fallen Woman': Olga Nethersole's *Sapho*," appears in *When They Weren't Doing Shakespeare: Essays on Nineteenth-Century British and American Theatre*, ed. Judith L. Fisher and Stephen Watt (Athens: Univ. of Georgia Press, 1989), pp. 200–21.

33. George Moore, *Confessions of a Young Man*, ed. Susan Dick (Montreal: McGill-Queen's Univ. Press, 1972), pp. 89–90.

34. "Miss Nethersole's 'Sapho,'" *Irish Playgoer*, 22 Mar. 1900, p. 14.

35. "Nights at the Play in Dublin: Peeps into the Past," *Irish Playgoer*, 10 May 1900, p. 11.

36. Reilly, "Wicked Woman," p. 135.

37. Winter, *Wallet of Time*, 2:313.

38. Reilly, "Wicked Woman," pp. 205–26.

39. Fredric Jameson, "'Ulysses' in History," in *James Joyce and Modern Literature*, ed. W. J. McCormack and Alistair Stead (London: Routledge & Kegan Paul, 1982), p. 127.

40. See Scott, *Joyce and Feminism*, p. 157, who elaborates on Mark Shechner's comment that male critics of *Ulysses* tend to view Molly either as "earth mother" or "thirty-shilling whore."

41. Jules David Law, "Joyce's 'Delicate Siamese' Equation: The Dialectic of Home in *Ulysses*," *PMLA* 102 (Mar. 1987): 203.

42. Ibid., p. 202.

43. Margot Norris, "Narration Under a Blindfold: Reading Joyce's 'Clay,'" *PMLA* 102 (Mar. 1987): 207.

44. See Simon, "Joyce's *Exiles*," pp. 26–27. Here Simon argues that the "real dramatic interest" of plays like *The Second Mrs. Tanqueray*—and also greater dramas like Ibsen's *Hedda Gabler*—lies "in the crisis created by the audience's sympathy for Paula and their recognition of their own unjust social laws which created the double standard which has become an inescapable influence on her tragic life" (p. 26). From this perspective, Molly Bloom is also a recipient of our sympathy.

45. Fredric Jameson, "Reification and Utopia in Mass Culture," *Social Text* 1 (Winter 1979): 131.

46. John Brenkman, "Mass Media: From Collective Experience to the Culture of Privatization," *Social Text* 1 (Winter 1979): 98, 94.

47. Sir Edward Bulwer-Lytton, *The Lady of Lyons*, in *Nineteenth-Century British Drama*, ed. Leonard R. N. Ashley (Glenview, Ill.: Scott, Foresman, 1967), p. 171.

48. Scott, *Joyce and Feminism*, pp. 49–50.

49. There is a strong parallel between Rubek's newly found lust for life and Joyce's. In *The Complete Dublin Diary*, Stanislaus Joyce declared, "Jim wants to live. Life is his creed" (p. 51).

50. James Hurt, *Catiline's Dream: An Essay on Ibsen's Plays* (Urbana: Univ. of Illinois Press, 1972), p. 198.

51. For brief accounts of early difficulties with *La Città Morta*, see Bertita Harding, *Age Cannot Wither: The Story of Duse and D'Annunzio* (Philadelphia: J. B. Lippincott, 1947), pp. 130–40; and the introductory essay to *Duse on Tour: Guido Noccioli's Diaries, 1906–07*, ed. Giovanni Pontiero (Manchester: Manchester Univ. Press, 1982), pp. 13–20.

52. A. B. Walkley, *Drama and Life* (London: Methuen, 1907), pp. 254, 261.

53. Eva Le Gallienne, *The Mystic in the Theatre: Eleonora Duse* (Carbondale: Southern Illinois Univ. Press, 1965), p. 18.

54. All quotations from *La Gioconda* come from *Chief Contemporary Dramatists*, 2d ser., ed. Thomas H. Dickinson (Boston: Houghton Mifflin, 1921). Page citations will follow quotations in the text.

55. Brenda Maddox, *Nora: The Real Life of Molly Bloom* (Boston: Houghton Mifflin, 1988), p. 32.

56. Susan Bassnett in John Stokes, Michael R. Booth, and Susan Bassnett, *Bernhardt, Terry, Duse: The Actress in Her Time* (Cambridge: Cambridge Univ. Press, 1988), p. 134.

57. Ibid., 143–45.

58. Ibid., p. 137.

59. Ibid., p. 149.

60. Walkley, *Drama and Life*, pp. 252–53.

61. Bassnett, *Bernhardt, Terry, Duse*, pp. 158, 160.

62. Nina Auerbach, *Ellen Terry: Player in Her Time* (New York: Norton, 1987), p. 296.

63. Barbara Klinger, "Digressions at the Cinema: Reception and Mass Culture," lecture delivered in the Mass Culture lecture series, Indiana University, Dec. 1988.

64. Archie K. Loss, "The Pre-Raphaelite Woman, the Symbolist *Femme-Enfant*, and the Girl with Long Flowing Hair in the Earlier Work of Joyce," *Journal of Modern Literature* 3 (Feb. 1973): 3–23.

65. Maddox doubts that Joyce first observed Marthe Fleischmann in the manner he related to Frank Budgen: "If Joyce did glimpse Marthe in her bathroom, he must have strained his eyes very hard" (*Nora*, pp. 159–60).

66. Maurice Maeterlinck, *Pelléas and Mélisande*, in *Representative Modern Dramas*, ed. Charles Huntington Whitman (New York: Macmillan, 1936), p. 420.

67. Richard Ellmann, "Introduction" to James Joyce, *Giacomo Joyce* (London: Faber and Faber, 1968), p. xxv.

68. Henke, *Women in Joyce*, p. 134.

69. See Sir John Martin-Harvey, *The Autobiography of Sir John Martin-Harvey* (London: Sampson Low, Marston & Company, 1933), pp. 347–61.

70. See Freeman Wills, *The Only Way* (London: Frederick Muller, 1942).

71. In Nov. 1906, M. and J. Dawson wrote a letter to the editor of the *Freeman's Journal* requesting that the Midland G & W Railway run a late train going as far as Mullingar so that "us country folk" could see actors like Harvey when they toured Dublin (4 Nov. 1906, p. 7).

72. See Martin-Harvey, *Autobiography*, pp. 347–61.

73. Auerbach, p. 133.

74. Auerbach discusses the effect of "female immobility" throughout her biography of Terry, extending this notion to explain Irving's refusal to allow Terry to assume several famous comedic parts in Shakespeare. See *Ellen Terry*, esp. pp. 223–37.

75. Michael R. Booth on Terry in *Bernhardt, Terry, Duse,* pp. 79, 81.

76. Mary C. King, "*Ulysses:* The Dissolution of Identity and the Appropriation of the Human World," in *James Joyce: The Augmented Ninth,* ed. Bernard Benstock (Syracuse: Syracuse Univ. Press, 1988), pp. 343, 338.

77. Ibid., p. 340.

78. All quotations from *Pygmalion and Galatea* come from W. S. Gilbert, *Original Plays* (London: Chatto and Windus, 1905), pp. 47–86.

4. O'CASEY'S NEGOTIATIONS WITH THE POPULAR

1. Carol Kleiman, *Sean O'Casey's Bridge of Vision: Four Essays on Structure and Perspective* (Toronto: Univ. of Toronto Press, 1982), builds a "bridge" between influence and impact, between Expressionism and Absurdism, in an effort to gain a "new perspective on O'Casey's place in the development of the modern drama" (p. xiii).

2. David Krause discusses this statement, found in *Letters* 1:538–39, in "The Risen O'Casey: Some Marxist and Irish Ironies," *O'Casey Annual No. 3,* ed. Robert G. Lowery (London: Macmillan, 1984), pp. 143–49.

3. For a discussion critical of O'Casey's suspect memory and his putatively inadequate understanding of the relationship between Irish nationalism and labor issues—his limited capacity to "hold no more than one idea in his head at a time"—see Greaves, *Sean O'Casey,* esp. pp. 35–81, quotation on p. 69.

4. Greaves casts these aspersions against American scholars in his Preface to ibid., pp. 7–11.

5. Krause, "The Risen O'Casey," p. 145.

6. Robert Hogan, "O'Casey, Influence and Impact," *Irish University Review* 10 (Spring 1980): 158.

7. Michael Kinneally, *Portraying the Self: Sean O'Casey and the Art of Autobiography* (Gerrards Cross/Totowa, N.J.: Colin Smythe/Barnes and Noble, 1988), pp. 15–16.

8. Ibid., p. 16.

9. Sean O'Casey, *Under a Colored Cap* (London: Macmillan, 1963), p. 213.

10. For a discussion of O'Casey's comic "desecration" of Ireland's "household gods," see Krause, *Profane Book of Irish Comedy,* pp. 105–70.

11. One of the most interesting accounts of O'Casey's debate with Hanna Sheehy-Skeffington is still that of his friend and Abbey actor Gabriel Fallon. See Fallon's *Sean O'Casey: The Man I Knew* (Boston: Little, Brown, 1965), pp. 85–100.

12. For an attack on the use of comedy in historical representation, specifically of Shaw's use of comedy in *Saint Joan,* see Johan Huizinga, "Bernard Shaw's Saint," in *Saint Joan: Fifty Years After,* ed. Stanley Weintraub (Baton Rouge: Louisiana State Univ. Press, 1973), p. 59.

13. Ronald Ayling discusses the discovery of the manuscript of *The Harvest Festival* in his introduction to Volume 5 of *The Complete Plays of Sean O'Casey,* pp. ix–xi; and in "Seeds for Future Harvest: Propaganda and Art in O'Casey's Earliest Play," *Irish University Review* 10 (Spring 1980): 25–40.

14. Jack Mitchell, *The Essential O'Casey: A Study of the Twelve Major Plays of Sean O'Casey* (New York: International Publishers, 1980), p. 154.

15. O'Casey's linking of cultural repression and sexual repression in this Irish village, one found in other plays such as *The Bishop's Bonfire*, finds numerous analogues on the contemporary stage. In her introduction to the revised edition of *Cloud 9* (New York: Methuen, 1984), Caryl Churchill alludes to the "idea of colonialism as a parallel to sexual oppression" (p. viii). A similar figure appears in Bernard Pomerance's *The Elephant Man* (New York: Grove Press, 1979), when Merrick, playing Treves in a dream, refers to Treves's hand "covering the genitals which were treated as a sullen colony in constant need of restriction, governance, punishment. For their own good" (p. 62).

16. For discussion of revivals of Boucicault in Dublin of the 1920s and 1930s, see *Joseph Holloway's Irish Theatre,* ed. Robert Hogan and Michael J. O'Neill, 3 vols. (Newark, Del.: Proscenium Press, 1968–70). Holloway reports, for example, attending the Torch Theatre in Capel Street on 27 May 1935 to see a revival of *The Shaughraun* (2:43).

17. Greaves and Krause, interestingly, both agree on the significance of O'Casey's early experience of Boucicault and the theater. See Greaves, *O'Casey,* pp. 26–28, 36; see also Krause, *Sean O'Casey: The Man and His Work,* enlarged ed. (New York: Macmillan, 1975), pp. 18–22. For an informative review of O'Casey's early dramatic efforts, see Robert Hogan, "O'Casey's Dramatic Apprenticeship," *Modern Drama* 4 (Dec. 1961): 243–53.

18. Eileen O'Casey, "Foreword," in Sean O'Casey, *The Harvest Festival* (New York: New York Public Library; Astor, Lenox and Tilden Foundations and Readex Books, 1979), p. ix.

19. Krause, "The Risen O'Casey," p. 160.

20. Emile Jean Dumay, "Enter O'Cathasaigh," *Études Irlandaises* 1 (Dec. 1976): 93.

21. Ayling, "Seeds for Future Harvest," pp. 32, 35.

22. See Antonio Gramsci, *Selections from the Prison Notebooks of Antonio Gramsci,* ed. and trans. Quintin Hoare and Geoffrey Nowell-Smith (New York: International Publishers, 1971), pp. 3–23.

23. The major exception to this rule, however, concerns the lack of paid informants or Irish traitors in O'Casey's plays.

24. For a discussion of Expressionism and especially act 3 of *Red Roses for Me,* see Kleiman, *O'Casey's Bridge of Vision,* pp. 49–83.

25. Peter Brooks, *The Melodramatic Imagination* (1976; rpt. New York: Columbia University Press, 1984), pp. 27, 32.

26. Edward Bond, "A Note on Dramatic Method," in *The Bundle* (London: Eyre Methuen, 1978), p. x.

27. Brooks, *Melodramatic Imagination,* p. 36.

28. For a brief discussion of the notion of a "dual-centre" stage picture, see Malcolm Hay and Philip Roberts, *Bond: A Study of His Plays* (London: Eyre Methuen, 1980), pp. 190–91.

29. Bertolt Brecht, "The Modern Theatre Is the Epic Theatre," in *Brecht on Theatre,* trans. John Willett (New York: Hill & Wang, 1964), p. 37.

30. Harry M. Ritchie, "The Influence of Melodrama on the Early Plays of Sean O'Casey," *Modern Drama* 5 (Sept. 1962): 167.

31. Ibid., p. 173.

32. Alastair Fowler, *Kinds of Literature: An Introduction to the Theory of Genres and Modes* (Cambridge, Mass.: Harvard Univ. Press, 1982), p. 88.

33. Louis Althusser compares melodrama to the "materialist theatre" in *For Marx,* trans. Ben Brewster (London: New Left Books, 1977), pp. 131–51.

34. Michael W. Kaufman, "The Position of *The Plough and the Stars* in O'Casey's Dublin Trilogy," *James Joyce Studies* 8 (Fall 1970): 52.

35. Robert L. Herbert, Roseline Bacou, and Michel Laclotte, *Jean-François Millet* (Paris: Editions des Musées Nationaux, 1975), p. 104.

36. W. A. Armstrong, "The Sources and Themes of *The Plough and the Stars*," *Modern Drama* 4 (Dec. 1961): 235.

37. Robert Scholes, *Semiotics and Interpretation* (New Haven: Yale Univ. Press, 1982), p. 145.

38. Patrick Galvin, *Irish Songs of Resistance* (London: Oak Publications, 1962), p. 1. All songs quoted in the text which are not sung in O'Casey's plays but merely alluded to are taken from Galvin's book; page numbers following such songs refer then to Galvin's text. For songs actually sung in O'Casey's plays, I have quoted from the plays themselves.

39. Mitchell, *Essential O'Casey*, p. 23.

40. Bernard Benstock, *Paycocks and Others: Sean O'Casey's World* (Dublin: Gill and Macmillan, 1976), p. 25.

41. Fallon discusses these reviews, *Sean O'Casey*, pp. 23–26.

42. J. Hillis Miller, "Stevens' Rock and Criticism as Cure, II," *Georgia Review* 30 (Summer 1976): 341.

43. See Benstock, *Paycocks and Others*, pp. 66–93.

44. See Mitchell, *Essential O'Casey*, pp. 54–61, 81–84.

45. I mention this potential in Juno merely to point out her project of founding a very nontraditional kind of Irish family. In *Women in Ireland: Voices of Change* (Bloomington: Indiana Univ. Press, 1987), Jenny Beale emphasizes the manner in which Irish conceptions of the family are dominated by the Catholic church and patriarchy, two sources of domination Juno may very well be attempting to escape. See esp. pp. 1–19.

46. O'Casey, *Under a Colored Cap*, pp. 231–32.

47. Ibid., p. 254.

48. See chapter 1, above, for a brief discussion of Yeats's views of popular theater.

5. TRACES OF THE POPULAR THEATER TODAY

1. Brian Friel, *The Communication Cord* (London: Faber and Faber, 1983), p. 15.

2. Ibid., p. 55.

3. For discussion of Friel's and Field Day Theatre Company's demythologizing of understandings of the "troubles" in Northern Ireland, see F. C. McGrath, "Introducing Ireland's Field Day," *Éire-Ireland* 23 (Winter 1988): 145–55.

4. Bernard MacLaverty, *Cal* (London: Jonathan Cape, 1983), p. 74. All other quotations from *Cal* will be followed by page numbers in the text.

5. In *Writing Ireland*, Cairns and Richards are surely right when discussing a process of negricization inherent to colonialist representations of Irishness. Cal's seeing himself in the mirror as a black confirms MacLaverty's understanding of such colonialist discourse; one significant difference, though, is that in *Cal* the subject sees himself as a subaltern rather than his being depicted as such by way of stereotyping. See also MacLaverty's earlier story "Between Two Shores" from *Secrets and Other Stories* (1977; rpt. New York: Penguin, 1984), in which

the central character, attending a party in London, is called a "noble savage." Later his girl-friend argues to him that "All your values belong to somebody else" (p. 55).

6. See Margaret Scanlan, *Traces of Another Time: History and Politics in Postwar British Fiction* (Princeton: Princeton Univ. Press, 1990), pp. 66–71. As persuasive as Scanlan's emphasis on Northern Irish economy is, she misses a crucial point about class consciousness in *Cal* (and, by extension, in much of MacLaverty's writing). She refers to Skeffington as an "IRA gunman" who "quotes Pearse's 'Mother'" to Cal (p. 71), but of course Skeffington is *not* a gunman nor is he working class; rather, he is a pretentious middle-class intellectual who manipulates working-class toughs like Crilly into doing his dirty work for him. MacLaverty makes a similar point about social class and the "troubles" in one of his finest short stories, "My Dear Palestrina," in *A Time to Dance and Other Stories* (New York: George Braziller, 1982). Here a politically active blacksmith tells the central character, "Dukes and bloody linen lords squeezing us for everything we've got, setting one side against the other. Divide and conquer. It's an old ploy and the Fenians and Orangemen of this godforsaken country have fallen for it again" (p. 51). For MacLaverty, mythologies about romantic Ireland thus conceal a pernicious social hegemony.

7. Michel de Certeau's point about walking urban streets seems especially relevant to representations of city life in novels like *Cal.* For de Certeau, the "act of walking is to the urban system what the speech act is to language or to the statements uttered" (p. 97). For de Certeau, walking in the city is accomplished in an enunciatory space that reveals the very organization that would repress any pollution or chaos that might compromise the urban structure. Walking in much Northern Irish fiction reveals this daily repression – assaults, searches, and the necessity of ever-vigilant surveys for potential dangers lurking ahead – inscribed within what would seem the simplest act. See de Certeau, *The Practice of Everyday Life,* trans. Steven Rendall (Berkeley: Univ. of California Press, 1984), pp. 91–110.

8. Anne Devlin, *Ourselves Alone,* in *Ourselves Alone and Other Plays* (London: Faber and Faber, 1986), p. 13.

9. Ibid., p. 21.

10. The short story upon which Devlin's television film was based, published previously in Devlin's short story collection *The Way-Paver* (London, 1986), has recently been reprinted in *Territories of the Voice: Contemporary Stories by Irish Women Writers,* eds. Louise DeSalvo, Kathleen Walsh D'Arcy, and Katherine Hogan (Boston: Beacon Press, 1989), pp. 93–113. I am quoting from the film, directed by Stuart Burge for the BBC in 1986; and from *A Prayer for the Dying,* directed by Mike Hodges for Samuel Goldwyn Productions in 1987.

11. J. L. Wisenthal, *Shaw's Sense of History* (Oxford: Clarendon Press, 1988), pp. 54–55.

12. There is a slight difference in dialogue between the film version and the short story. See DeSalvo, D'Arcy, and Hogan, p. 96.

WORKS CITED

LISTED BELOW are all primary and secondary sources referred to in the text except for theatrical reviews and other items taken from newspapers or popular periodicals at the turn of the century. These are cited within the text.

Allen, Grant. *The Woman Who Did*. London: John Lane, 1895.

Althusser, Louis. *For Marx*. Translated by Ben Brewster. London: New Left Books, 1979.

———. *Lenin and Philosophy and Other Essays*. Translated by Ben Brewster. London: Monthly Review Press, 1971.

Archer, William. *William Archer on Ibsen*. Edited by Thomas Postlewait. Westport, Conn.: Greenwood Press, 1984.

Armstrong, W. A. "The Sources and Themes of *The Plough and the Stars*." *Modern Drama* 4 (Dec. 1961): 234–42.

Ashley, Leonard R. N., ed. *Nineteenth-Century British Drama*. Glenview, Ill.: Scott, Foresman, 1967.

Atherton, James S. *The Books at the Wake*. New York: Viking, 1960.

Auerbach, Nina. *Ellen Terry: Player in Her Time*. New York: Norton, 1987.

Ayling, Ronald. "Introduction." In *The Complete Plays of Sean O'Casey*. Vol. 5. (London: Macmillan, 1984), pp. vii–xxviii.

———. "Seeds for Future Harvest: Propaganda and Art in O'Casey's Earliest Play." *Irish University Review* 10 (Spring 1980): 25–40.

Barker, Kathleen. "Charles Dillon: A Provincial Tragedian." In *Shakespeare and the Victorian Stage,* edited by Richard Foulkes, pp. 283–94. Cambridge: Cambridge Univ. Press, 1986.

Barthes, Roland. "The Death of the Author." In *Image—Music—Text,* translated by Stephen Heath, pp. 142–48. New York: Hill & Wang, 1977.

Beale, Jenny. *Women in Ireland: Voices of Change.* Bloomington: Indiana Univ. Press, 1987.

Benson, Lady Constance. *Mainly Players: Bensonian Memories.* London: Thornton Butterworth, 1926.

Benstock, Bernard. *Paycocks and Others: Sean O'Casey's World.* Dublin: Gill and Macmillan, 1976.

———, ed. *James Joyce: The Augmented Ninth.* Syracuse: Syracuse Univ. Press, 1988.

———. *The Seventh of Joyce.* Bloomington: Indiana Univ. Press, 1982.

Bhabha, Homi K. "The Other Question." *Screen* 24 (Nov.–Dec. 1983): 18–36.

Bond, Edward. *The Bundle.* London: Eyre Methuen, 1978.

Booth, Michael R. *Prefaces to English Nineteenth-Century Theatre.* Manchester: Manchester Univ. Press, 1980.

Boucicault, Dion. *The Dolmen Boucicault.* Edited by David Krause. Dublin: Dufour Editions, 1963.

———. *A Fireside Story of Ireland.* London: Bradbury, Agnew and Company Printers, 1881.

———. *Forbidden Fruit and Other Plays.* Edited by Allardyce Nicoll and F. Theodore Cloak. Princeton: Princeton Univ. Press, 1940.

———. *Selected Plays of Dion Boucicault.* Edited by Andrew Parkin. Gerrards Cross/ Washington, D.C.: Colin Smythe/Catholic Univ. Press of America, 1987.

Bradby, David, Louis James, and Bernard Sharratt, eds. *Performance and Politics in Popular Drama.* Cambridge: Cambridge Univ. Press, 1980.

Brantlinger, Patrick. *Bread and Circuses: Theories of Mass Culture as Social Decay.* Ithaca: Cornell Univ. Press, 1983.

Brecht, Bertolt. *Brecht on Theatre.* Translated by John Willett. New York: Hill & Wang, 1964.

Brenkman, John. "Mass Media: From Collective Experience to the Culture of Privatization." *Social Text* 1 (Winter 1979): 94–109.

Brinker, Menachem. "Verisimilitude, Conventions, and Beliefs." *New Literary History* 14 (Winter 1983): 253–67.

Brooks, Peter. *The Melodramatic Imagination.* 1976. Reprint. New York: Columbia Univ. Press, 1984.

Brown, Richard. *James Joyce and Sexuality.* Cambridge: Cambridge Univ. Press, 1985.

Budgen, Frank. *James Joyce and the Making of "Ulysses."* 1934. Reprint. Bloomington: Indiana Univ. Press, 1960.

Bulwer-Lytton, Sir Edward. *The Lady of Lyons.* In *Nineteenth-Century British Drama,* edited by Leonard R. N. Ashley, pp. 138–92. Glenview, Ill.: Scott, Foresman, 1967.

Byrne, J. F. *Silent Years.* New York: Farrar, Straus, and Young, 1953.

Cairns, David, and Shaun Richards. *Writing Ireland: Colonialism, Nationalism and Culture.* Manchester: Manchester Univ. Press, 1988.

Campbell, Mrs. Patrick. *My Life and Some Letters.* London: Hutchinson, 1922.

Churchill, Caryl. *Cloud 9.* Rev. ed. New York: Methuen, 1984.

Courtney, Sister Marie-Thérèse. *Edward Martyn and the Irish Theatre.* New York: Vantage Press, 1956.

Crump, Jeremy. "The Popular Audience for Shakespeare in Nineteenth-Century Leicester." In *Shakespeare and the Victorian Stage,* edited by Richard Foulkes, pp. 271–82. Cambridge: Cambridge Univ. Press, 1986.

Cunningham, Hugh. "Class and Leisure in Mid-Victorian England." In *Popular Culture: Past and Present,* edited by Bernard Waites, Tony Bennett, and Graham Martin, pp. 66–91. London: Croom Helm, 1982.

Curtis, L. Perry, Jr. *Apes and Angels: The Irishman in Victorian Caricature.* Washington, D.C.: Smithsonian Institution Press, 1971.

D'Annunzio, Gabriele. *La Gioconda.* Translated by Arthur Symons. In *Chief Contemporary Dramatists,* 2d ser., edited by Thomas H. Dickinson, pp. 571–605. Boston: Houghton Mifflin, 1921.

Daudet, Alphonse. *Sapho.* New York: Book League of America, 1932.

Deane, Seamus. *Civilians and Barbarians.* Field Day Pamphlet No. 3. Derry: Field Day Theatre Company Limited, 1983.

de Búrca, Séamus. *The Queen's Royal Theatre, Dublin, 1829–1969.* Dublin: de Búrca, 1983.

de Certeau, Michel. *The Practice of Everyday Life,* translated by Steven Rendall. Berkeley: Univ. of California Press, 1984.

DeSalvo, Louise, Kathleen Walsh D'Arcy, and Katherine Hogan, eds. *Territories of the Voice: Contemporary Stories by Irish Women Writers.* Boston: Beacon Press, 1989.

Devlin, Anne. *Naming the Names.* Directed by Stuart Burge. BBC Television, 1986.

———. "Naming the Names." In *Territories of the Voice: Contemporary Stories by Irish Women Writers,* edited by Louis DeSalvo, Kathleen Walsh D'Arcy, and Katherine Hogan, pp. 93–113. Boston: Beacon Press, 1989.

———. *Ourselves Alone: with The Long March and A Woman Calling.* London: Faber and Faber, 1986.

Disher, Maurice Willson. *The Last Romantic: The Authorised Biography of Sir John Martin-Harvey.* London: Hutchinson, 1944.

Dollimore, Jonathan, and Alan Sinfield, eds. *Political Shakespeare: New Essays in Cultural Materialism*. Manchester: Manchester Univ. Press, 1985.

Dumay, Emile Jean. "Enter O'Cathasaigh." *Études Irlandaises* 1 (Dec. 1976): 85–98.

Eglinton, John, W. B. Yeats, AE, and William Larminie. *Literary Ideals in Ireland*. London/Dublin: T. Fisher Unwin/*Daily Express* Office, 1899.

1871–1971: One Hundred Years of Gaiety. Gaiety Theatre Souvenir Program. Dublin, 1971.

Ellmann, Richard. *The Consciousness of Joyce*. New York: Oxford Univ. Press, 1977.

———. *James Joyce*. Rev. ed. New York: Oxford Univ. Press, 1982.

Engels, Frederick. *The Condition of the Working-Class in England*. Moscow: Progress Publishers, 1973.

Fallon, Gabriel. *Sean O'Casey: The Man I Knew*. Boston: Little, Brown, 1965.

Fawkes, Richard. *Dion Boucicault: A Biography*. London: Quartet Books, 1979.

Fay, Frank J. *Towards a National Theatre*. Edited by Robert Hogan. Dublin: Dolmen Press, 1970.

Fekete, John. *The Critical Twilight: Explorations in the Ideology of Anglo-American Literary Theory from Eliot to McLuhan*. London: Routledge & Kegan Paul, 1977.

Felheim, Marvin. *The Theatre of Augustin Daly*. Cambridge, Mass.: Harvard Univ. Press, 1956.

Fisher, Judith L. "The 'Law of the Father': Sexual Politics in the Plays of Henry Arthur Jones and Arthur Wing Pinero." *Essays in Literature* 16 (Fall 1989): 203–23.

Fisher, Judith L., and Stephen Watt, eds. *When They Weren't Doing Shakespeare: Essays on Nineteenth-Century British and American Theatre*. Athens: Univ. of Georgia Press, 1989.

Fitz-simon, Christopher. *The Irish Theatre*. London: Thames and Hudson, 1983.

Foster, John Wilson. *Fictions of the Irish Literary Revival: A Changeling Art*. Syracuse: Syracuse Univ. Press, 1987.

Foucault, Michel. *Language, Counter-Memory, and Practice*. Edited by Donald F. Bouchard. Ithaca: Cornell Univ. Press, 1977.

Foulkes, Richard, ed. *Shakespeare and the Victorian Stage*. Cambridge: Cambridge Univ. Press, 1986.

Fowler, Alastair. *Kinds of Literature: An Introduction to the Theory of Genres and Modes*. Cambridge, Mass.: Harvard Univ. Press, 1982.

Frazier, Adrian. *Behind the Scenes: Yeats, Horniman, and the Struggle for the Abbey Theatre*. Berkeley: Univ. of California Press, 1990.

Friel, Brian. *The Communication Cord*. London: Faber and Faber, 1983.

———. *Translations*. London: Faber and Faber, 1981.

Froula, Christine. "Gender and the Law of Genre: Joyce, Woolf, and the Autobiographical Artist-Novel." In *New Alliances in Joyce Studies,* edited by Bonnie Kime Scott, pp. 155–64. Newark: Univ. of Delaware Press, 1988.

Galvin, Patrick. *Irish Songs of Resistance.* London: Oak Publications, 1962.

Gilbert, W. S. *Original Plays.* London: Chatto and Windus, 1905.

Gilman, Sander L. "Black Bodies, White Bodies: Toward an Iconography of Female Sexuality in Late Nineteenth-Century Art, Medicine, and Literature." *Critical Inquiry* 12 (1985): 204–42.

Goodman, Nelson. *Ways of Worldmaking.* Indianapolis: Hackett Publishing, 1978.

Gramsci, Antonio. *Selections from the Prison Notebooks of Antonio Gramsci.* Edited and translated by Quintin Hoare and Geoffrey Nowell-Smith. New York: International Publishers, 1971.

Graves, R. B. "The Stage Irishman Among the Irish." *Theatre History Studies* 1 (1981): 29–38.

Greaves, C. Desmond. *Sean O'Casey: Politics and Art.* London: Lawrence and Wishart, 1979.

Green, A. E. "Popular Drama and the Mummers' Play." In *Performance and Politics in Popular Drama,* edited by David Bradby, Louis James, and Bernard Sharratt, pp. 139–66. Cambridge: Cambridge Univ. Press, 1980.

Hall, Stuart. "Notes on Deconstructing 'The Popular.'" In *People's History and Socialist Theory,* edited by Raphael Samuel, pp. 227–40. London: Routledge and Kegan Paul, 1981.

Harding, Bertita. *Age Cannot Wither: The Story of Duse and D'Annunzio.* Philadelphia: J. B. Lippincott, 1947.

Harmon, Maurice, ed. *Fenians and Fenianism.* Seattle: Univ. of Washington Press, 1970.

Hay, Malcolm, and Philip Roberts. *Bond: A Study of His Plays.* London: Eyre Methuen, 1980.

Hayman, David. "A Mother." In *James Joyce's "Dubliners": Critical Essays,* edited by Clive Hart, pp. 122–33. New York: Viking, 1969.

Heilman, Robert Bechtold. *The Iceman, The Arsonist, and the Troubled Agent.* Seattle: Univ. of Washington Press, 1973.

Henke, Suzette, and Elaine Unkeless, eds. *Women in Joyce.* Urbana: Univ. of Illinois Press, 1982.

Herbert, Robert L., Roseline Bacou, and Michel Laclotte. *Jean-François Millet.* Paris: Editions des Musées Nationaux, 1975.

Herr, Cheryl. *Joyce's Anatomy of Culture.* Urbana: Univ. of Illinois Press, 1986.

———. "Subworlds, Props, and Settings in Joyce's *Exiles.*" *Theatre Journal* 39 (May 1987): 185–203.

————, ed. *For the Land They Loved: Irish Political Melodramas, 1890–1925*. Syracuse: Syracuse Univ. Press, 1991.

Hibbert, H. G. *A Playgoer's Memories*. London: Grant Richards, 1920.

Hodges, Mike, director. *A Prayer for the Dying*. Samuel Goldwyn Productions, 1987.

Hogan, Robert. *Dion Boucicault*. New York: Twayne, 1969.

————. "O'Casey, Influence and Impact." *Irish University Review* 10 (Spring 1980): 146–58.

————. "O'Casey's Dramatic Apprenticeship." *Modern Drama* 4 (Dec. 1961): 243–53.

Hogan, Robert, and Michael J. O'Neill, eds. *Joseph Holloway's Irish Theatre*. 3 vols. Newark, Del.: Proscenium Press, 1968–70.

Holladay, William E., and Stephen Watt. "Viewing the Elephant Man." *PMLA* 104 (Oct. 1989): 868–81.

Holloway, Joseph. Playlist of the Queen's Royal Theatre for 1899, MS 14,995 (2); and Playlist of the Theatre Royal, 1872–75, MS 14,995 (5). Manuscript Division, National Library of Ireland, Dublin.

Huizinga, Johan. "Bernard Shaw's Saint." In *Saint Joan: Fifty Years After*, edited by Stanley Weintraub, pp. 54–85. Baton Rouge: Louisiana State Univ. Press, 1973.

Hunt, Hugh. *The Abbey: Ireland's National Theatre, 1904–1979*. Dublin: Gill and Macmillan, 1979.

Hurt, James. "The Canon of Irish Drama." *Éire-Ireland* 24 (Fall 1989): 135–38.

————. *Catiline's Dream: An Essay on Ibsen's Plays*. Urbana: Univ. of Illinois Press, 1972.

Ibsen, Henrik. *The Oxford Ibsen*. 8 vols. Edited by James Walter McFarlane. Oxford: Oxford Univ. Press, 1960–77.

Irish Orators and Oratory. Introduction by T. M. Kettle. London: Gresham Publishing Co., n.d.

Iser, Wolfgang. *The Implied Reader*. Baltimore: Johns Hopkins Univ. Press, 1974.

Jameson, Fredric. "Metacommentary." *PMLA* 86 (Jan. 1971): 9–18.

————. "Postmodernism and Consumer Society." In *The Anti-Aesthetic: Essays on Postmodern Culture*, edited by Hal Foster, pp. 111–25. Port Townsend, Wash.: Bay Press, 1983.

————. "Reification and Utopia in Mass Culture." *Social Text* 1 (Winter 1979): 130–48.

————. "'Ulysses' in History." In *James Joyce and Modern Literature*, edited by W. J. McCormack and Alistair Stead, pp. 126–41. London: Routledge & Kegan Paul, 1982.

JanMohamed, Abdul R. "The Economy of Manichean Allegory: The Function of Racial Difference in Colonialist Literature." *Critical Inquiry* 12 (Autumn 1985): 59–87.

Jones, Henry Arthur. *Mrs. Dane's Defence*. New York: Samuel French, 1905.

————. *Plays by Henry Arthur Jones*. Edited by Russell Jackson. Cambridge: Cambridge Univ. Press, 1982.

Jordan, John. "The Passionate Autodidact: The Importance of *Litera Scripta* for O'Casey." *Irish University Review* 10 (Spring 1980): 59–76.

Joyce, James. *Chamber Music*. Edited by William York Tindall. New York: Columbia Univ. Press, 1954.

————. *The Critical Writings of James Joyce*. Edited by Ellsworth Mason and Richard Ellmann. New York: Viking Press, 1959.

————. *Dubliners*. Edited by Robert Scholes. New York: Viking Press, 1967.

————. *Finnegans Wake*. New York: Viking Press, 1939.

————. *Giacomo Joyce*. London: Faber and Faber, 1968.

————. *"A Portrait of the Artist as a Young Man": Text, Criticism, and Notes*. Edited by Chester G. Anderson. New York: Viking Press, 1968.

————. *Selected Letters of James Joyce*. Edited by Richard Ellmann. New York: Viking Press, 1975.

————. *Stephen Hero*. Edited by John J. Slocum and Herbert Cahoon. New York: New Directions, 1944.

————. *Ulysses: The Corrected Text*. Edited by Hans Walter Gabler with Wolfhard Steppe and Claus Melchior. New York: Vintage Books, 1986.

Joyce, Stanislaus. *The Complete Dublin Diary of Stanislaus Joyce*. Edited by George H. Healey. Ithaca: Cornell Univ. Press, 1962.

————. *My Brother's Keeper: James Joyce's Early Years*. Edited by Richard Ellmann. New York: Viking Press, 1958.

Kaufman, Michael W. "The Position of *The Plough and the Stars* in O'Casey's Dublin Trilogy." *James Joyce Studies* 8 (Fall 1970): 48–63.

Kavanagh, Peter. *The Irish Theatre*. Tralee: Kerryman Limited, 1946.

Kermode, Frank. *The Sense of an Ending: Studies in the Theory of Fiction*. New York: Oxford Univ. Press, 1967.

Kershner, R. B. *Joyce, Bakhtin, and Popular Literature: Chronicles of Disorder*. Chapel Hill: Univ. of North Carolina Press, 1989.

Kiely, Benedict. *Proxopera*. London: Victor Gollancz, 1977.

Kimball, Jean. "Freud, Leonardo, and Joyce: The Dimensions of a Childhood Memory." In *The Seventh of Joyce*, edited by Bernard Benstock, pp. 57–73. Bloomington: Indiana Univ. Press, 1982.

King, Mary C. "*Ulysses*: The Dissolution of Identity and the Appropriation of the Human World." In *James Joyce: The Augmented Ninth*, edited by Bernard Benstock, pp. 337–45. Syracuse: Syracuse Univ. Press, 1988.

Kinneally, Michael. *Portraying the Self: Sean O'Casey and the Art of Autobiography*. Gerrards Cross/Totowa, N.J.: Colin Smythe/Barnes and Noble, 1988.

Kleiman, Carol. *Sean O'Casey's Bridge of Vision: Four Essays on Structure and Perspective.* Toronto: Univ. of Toronto Press, 1982.

Klinger, Barbara. "Digressions at the Cinema: Reception and Mass Culture." Lecture presented in the Mass Culture series, Indiana University, Dec. 1988.

Krause, David. *The Profane Book of Irish Comedy.* Ithaca: Cornell Univ. Press, 1982.

————. "The Risen O'Casey: Some Marxist and Irish Ironies." In *O'Casey Annual No. 3,* edited by Robert G. Lowery, pp. 134–68. London: Macmillan, 1984.

————. *Sean O'Casey: The Man and His Work.* Enlarged ed. New York: Macmillan, 1975.

————, ed. *The Letters of Sean O'Casey, 1910–41.* New York: Macmillan, 1975.

Law, Jules David. "Joyce's 'Delicate Siamese' Equation: The Dialectic of Home in *Ulysses.*" *PMLA* 102 (Mar. 1987): 197–205.

Le Gallienne, Eva. *The Mystic in the Theatre: Eleonora Duse.* Carbondale: Southern Illinois Univ. Press, 1965.

Levine, Jennifer Schiffer. "Originality and Repetition in *Finnegans Wake* and *Ulysses.*" *PMLA* 94 (Jan. 1979): 106–20.

Levine, Lawrence W. *Highbrow/Lowbrow.* Cambridge, Mass.: Harvard Univ. Press, 1988.

Lindenberger, Herbert. *Historical Drama: The Relation of Literature and Reality.* Chicago: Univ. of Chicago Press, 1975.

Loss, Archie K. "The Pre-Raphaelite Woman, the Symbolist *Femme-Enfant,* and the Girl with the Long Flowing Hair in the Earlier Work of Joyce." *Journal of Modern Literature* 3 (Feb. 1973): 3–23.

Lowenthal, Leo. *Literature, Popular Culture, and Society.* Englewood Cliffs, N.J.: Prentice-Hall, 1961.

MacCabe, Colin. Response in discussion following Franco Moretti's paper. In *Marxism and the Interpretation of Culture,* edited by Cary Nelson and Lawrence Grossberg, pp. 345–46. Urbana: Univ. of Illinois Press, 1988.

McCartney, Donal. "The Church and Fenianism." In *Fenians and Fenianism,* edited by Maurice Harmon, pp. 13–27. Seattle: Univ. of Washington Press, 1970.

McCord, Norman. "The Fenians and Public Opinion in Great Britain." In *Fenians and Fenianism,* edited by Maurice Harmon, pp. 35–48. Seattle: Univ. of Washington Press, 1970.

McGrath, F. C. "Introducing Ireland's Field Day." *Éire-Ireland* 23 (Winter 1988): 145–55.

MacLaverty, Bernard. *Cal.* London: Jonathan Cape, 1983.

————. *Secrets and Other Stories.* 1977. New York: Penguin Books, 1985.

————. *A Time to Dance and Other Stories.* New York: George Braziller, 1982.

Maddox, Brenda. *Nora: The Real Life of Molly Bloom.* Boston: Houghton Mifflin, 1988.

Maeterlinck, Maurice. *Pelléas and Mélisande*. In *Representative Modern Dramas*, edited by Charles Huntington Whitman, pp. 409–33. New York: Macmillan, 1936.

Malone, Andrew E. *The Irish Drama*. London: Constable, 1929.

Mamet, David. *Speed-the-Plow*. New York: Grove Press, 1985.

Manganiello, Dominic. *Joyce's Politics*. London: Routledge & Kegan Paul, 1980.

Martin-Harvey, Sir John. *The Autobiography of Sir John Martin-Harvey*. London: Sampson Low, Marston & Company, 1933.

Marx, Karl, and Frederick Engels. *Ireland and the Irish Question*. Edited by L. I. Golman and V. E. Kunina. Moscow: Progress Publishers, 1971.

Maxwell, D. E. S. *A Critical History of Modern Irish Drama, 1891–1980*. Cambridge: Cambridge Univ. Press, 1984.

Meisel, Martin. *Shaw and the Nineteenth-Century Theater*. Princeton: Princeton Univ. Press, 1963.

Melville, Joy. *Ellen and Edy: A Biography of Ellen Terry and Her Daughter, Edith Craig, 1847–1947*. London: Pandora Press, 1987.

Miller, J. Hillis. "Stevens' Rock and Criticism as Cure, II." *Georgia Review* 30 (Summer 1976): 330–48.

Mitchell, Jack. *The Essential O'Casey: A Study of the Twelve Major Plays of Sean O'Casey*. New York: International Publishers, 1980.

Molin, Sven Eric, and Robin Goodefellowe. "Nationalism on the Dublin Stage." *Éire-Ireland* 21 (Spring 1986): 135–38.

Montrose, Louis A. "Professing the Renaissance: The Poetics and Politics of Culture." In *The New Historicism*, edited by H. Aram Veeser, pp. 15–36. New York: Routledge, 1989.

Moore, George. *The Bending of the Bough*. Chicago: Herbert F. Stone, 1900.

———. *Confessions of a Young Man*. Edited by Susan Dick. Montreal: McGill-Queen's Univ. Press, 1972.

Moretti, Franco. *Signs Taken for Wonders: Essays in the Sociology of Literary Forms*. London: Verso, 1983.

———. "The Spell of Indecision." In *Marxism and the Interpretation of Culture*, edited by Cary Nelson and Lawrence Grossberg, pp. 339–44. Urbana: Univ. of Illinois Press, 1988.

Mullin, Donald. *Victorian Actors and Actresses in Review*. Westport, Conn.: Greenwood Press, 1983.

Nelson, James Malcolm. "From Rory and Paddy to Boucicault's Myles, Shaun, and Conn: The Irishman on the London Stage, 1830–1860." *Éire-Ireland* 13 (Fall 1978): 79–105.

Nicoll, Allardyce. *A History of English Drama*. 6 vols. Cambridge: Cambridge Univ. Press, 1952–59.

Norris, Margot. "Narration Under a Blindfold: Reading Joyce's 'Clay.'" *PMLA* 102 (Mar. 1987): 206–15.

Ó Broin, Leon. *The Prime Informer.* London: Sidgwick and Jackson, 1971.

O'Casey, Eileen. "Foreword." In Sean O'Casey, *The Harvest Festival,* pp. ix–x. New York: New York Public Library; Astor, Lenox and Tilden Foundations and Readex Books, 1979.

O'Casey, Sean. *Autobiographies.* 2 vols. London: Pan Books, 1980.

———. *Blasts and Benedictions.* Selections and introduction by Ronald Ayling. London: Macmillan, 1967.

———. *The Complete Plays of Sean O'Casey.* 5 vols. London: Macmillan, 1984.

———. *The Green Crow.* New York: George Braziller, 1956.

———. *The Harvest Festival.* New York: New York Public Library; Astor, Lenox and Tilden Foundations and Readex Books, 1979.

———. *Under a Colored Cap.* London: Macmillan, 1963.

O'Grady, Hubert. *Emigration.* Edited by Stephen Watt. *Journal of Irish Literature* 14 (Jan. 1985): 14–25.

———. *The Eviction, or the Mountain Home.* Add. MS 53226D (213). Lord Chamberlain's Collection, Manuscript Division, British Library, London.

———. *The Famine.* Edited by Stephen Watt. *Journal of Irish Literature* 14 (Jan. 1985): 25–49.

———. *The Fenian.* Add. MS 53416G (296). Lord Chamberlain's Collection, Manuscript Division, British Library, London.

———. *The Gommock.* Add. MS 53185H (87). Lord Chamberlain's Collection, Manuscript Division, British Library, London.

Parrinder, Patrick. *James Joyce.* Cambridge: Cambridge Univ. Press, 1984.

Passow, Wilfried. "The Analysis of Theatrical Performance: The State of the Art." *Poetics Today* 2 (1981): 237–54.

Peters, Margot. *Mrs. Pat: The Life of Mrs. Patrick Campbell.* New York: Knopf, 1984.

Pinero, Arthur Wing. *The Social Plays of Arthur Wing Pinero.* 4 vols. Edited by Hamilton Clayton. New York: Dutton, 1918.

———. *Sweet Lavender.* Boston: Walter H. Baker, 1893.

Pomerance, Bernard. *The Elephant Man.* New York: Grove Press, 1979.

Pontiero, Giovanni, ed. *Duse on Tour: Guido Noccioli's Diaries, 1906–07.* Manchester: Manchester Univ. Press, 1982.

Quigley, Austin. *The Modern Stage and Other Worlds.* New York: Methuen, 1986.

Reilly, Joy Harriman. "From Wicked Woman of the Stage to New Woman: The Career of Olga Nethersole (1870–1951); Actress-Manager, Suffragist, Health Pioneer." Ph.D. diss., Ohio State Univ., 1984.

Richardson, Gary A. "Boucicault's *The Octoroon* and American Law." *Educational Theatre Journal* 34 (1982): 155–64.

Ritchie, Harry M. "The Influence of Melodrama on the Early Plays of Sean O'Casey." *Modern Drama* 5 (Sept. 1962): 164–73.

Ryan, Michael. *Marxism and Deconstruction: A Critical Articulation.* Baltimore: Johns Hopkins Univ. Press, 1982.

Saddlemyer, Ann, ed. *The Collected Letters of John Millington Synge.* 2 vols. Oxford: Clarendon Press, 1983.

Scanlan, Margaret. *Traces of Another Time: History and Politics in Postwar British Fiction.* Princeton: Princeton Univ. Press, 1990.

Scholes, Robert. *Semiotics and Interpretation.* New Haven: Yale Univ. Press, 1982.

Scott, Bonnie Kime. *Joyce and Feminism.* Bloomington: Indiana Univ. Press, 1984.

———, ed. *New Alliances in Joyce Studies.* Newark: Univ. of Delaware Press, 1988.

Scott, Clement. *The Drama of Yesterday and To-Day.* 2 vols. London: Macmillan, 1899.

Seidel, Michael. *Exile and the Narrative Imagination.* New Haven: Yale Univ. Press, 1986.

Sharratt, Bernard. "The Politics of the Popular? – From Melodrama to Television." In *Performance and Politics in Popular Drama,* edited by David Bradby, Louis James, and Bernard Sharratt, pp. 275–95. Cambridge: Cambridge Univ. Press, 1980.

Shaw, Bernard. *Complete Plays with Their Prefaces.* 7 vols. Edited by Dan H. Laurence. New York: Dodd Mead, 1971.

———. *The Matter with Ireland.* Edited by David H. Greene and Dan H. Laurence. London: Rupert Hart-Davis, 1962.

———. *Our Theatres in the Nineties.* 3 vols. London: Constable, 1932.

Simon, Elliott M. "James Joyce's *Exiles* and the Tradition of the Edwardian Problem-Play." *Modern Drama* 20 (Mar. 1977): 21–35.

Smith, Paul. *Discerning the Subject.* Minneapolis: Univ. of Minnesota Press, 1988.

Stallybrass, Peter, and Allon White. *The Politics and Poetics of Transgression.* Ithaca: Cornell Univ. Press, 1986.

Stokes, John, Michael R. Booth, and Susan Bassnett. *Bernhardt, Terry, Duse: The Actress in Her Time.* Cambridge: Cambridge Univ. Press, 1988.

Stoppard, Tom. *Rosencrantz and Guildenstern Are Dead.* New York: Grove Press, 1967.

Sudermann, Hermann. *Magda.* In *Contemporary Drama: European Plays II,* edited by E. Bradlee Watson and Benfield Pressey, pp. 187–278. New York: Charles Scribner's Sons, 1952.

Swinson, Henry Ward. "Joyce and the Theater." Ph.D. diss., Univ. of Illinois, 1969.

Trewin, J. C. *Benson and the Bensonians.* London: Barrie and Rockliff, 1960.

Vardac, A. Nicholas. *Stage to Screen: Theatrical Method from Garrick to Griffith.* Cambridge, Mass.: Harvard Univ. Press, 1949.

Veeser, H. Aram, ed. *The New Historicism.* New York: Routledge, 1989.

Walkley, A. B. *Drama and Life*. London: Methuen, 1907.

Walzl, Florence L. *"Dubliners:* Women in Irish Society." In *Women in Joyce,* edited by Suzette Henke and Elaine Unkeless, pp. 31–56. Urbana: Univ. of Illinois Press, 1982.

Watt, Stephen. "Boucicault and Whitbread: The Dublin Stage at the End of the Nineteenth Century." *Éire-Ireland* 18 (Fall 1983): 23–53.

———. "Shaw's *Saint Joan* and the Modern History Play." *Comparative Drama* 19 (Spring 1985): 58–86.

West, Alick. *Crisis and Criticism: 7 Literary Essays*. London: Lawrence and Wishart, 1975.

Whitbread, J. W. *The Irish Dragoon*. Add. MS 1906/10 (172). Lord Chamberlain's Collection, Manuscript Division, British Library, London.

———. *The Nationalist*. Dublin: W. J. Alley and Company, 1892.

———. *Sarsfield*. Add. MS 1905/18 (305). Lord Chamberlain's Collection, Manuscript Division, British Library, London.

———. *The Ulster Hero*. Add. MS 1905/19 (320). Lord Chamberlain's Collection, Manuscript Division, British Library, London.

———. *Wolfe Tone*. In *For The Land They Loved: Irish Political Melodramas, 1890–1925,* edited by Cheryl Herr, pp. 171–257. Syracuse: Syracuse Univ. Press, 1991.

Wiles, Timothy J. *The Theater Event: Modern Theories of Performance*. Chicago: Univ. of Chicago Press, 1980.

Williams, Raymond. *Writing in Society*. London: Verso, 1985.

Wills, Freeman. *The Only Way*. London: Frederick Muller, 1942.

Wills, W. G. *A Royal Divorce*. Add. MS 53474D. Lord Chamberlain's Collection, Manuscript Division, British Library, London.

Winter, William. *The Wallet of Time*. 2 vols. New York: Moffat, Yard, and Company, 1913.

Wisenthal, J. L. *Shaw's Sense of History*. Oxford: Clarendon Press, 1988.

Yeats, William Butler. *Essays and Introductions*. New York: Macmillan, 1961.

———. *The Letters of W. B. Yeats*. Edited by Allan Wade. London: Rupert Hart-Davis, 1954.

———. *Uncollected Prose*. 2 vols. Edited by John P. Frayne and Colton Johnson. New York: Columbia Univ. Press, 1970–76.

INDEX

271

Joyce, O'Casey, and the Irish Popular Theater
was composed in 10 on 13 Galliard on Digital Compugraphic equipment
by Metricomp;
designed by Sara L. Eddy;
printed by sheet-fed offset on 50-pound, acid-free Glatfelter Natural Hi Bulk,
Smyth-sewn and bound over binder's boards in Holliston Roxite B,
with dust jackets designed by Mary Peterson Moore and Victoria M. Lane
and printed in 2 colors
by Braun-Brumfield, Inc.;
and published by

SYRACUSE UNIVERSITY PRESS
SYRACUSE, NEW YORK 13244-5160

RICHARD FALLIS, Series Editor

IRISH STUDIES presents a wide range of books interpreting important aspects of Irish life and culture to scholarly and general audiences. The richness and complexity of the Irish experience, past and present, deserves broad understanding and careful analysis. For this reason an important purpose of the series is to offer a forum to scholars interested in Ireland, its history, and culture. Irish literature is a special concern in the series, but works from the perspectives of the fine arts, history, and the social sciences are also welcome, as are studies which take multidisciplinary approaches.

SELECTED TITLES IN THE SERIES ARE:

BEVERLY BRANCH
2121 W. 95th STREET
CHICAGO, ILLINOIS 60643

BEVERLY BRANCH
2121 W. 95th STREET
CHICAGO, ILLINOIS 60643

BEVERLY BRANCH
2121 W. 95th STREET
CHICAGO, ILLINOIS 60643

BEVERLY BRANCH
2121 W. 95th STREET
CHICAGO, ILLINOIS 60643